Rod Machado's
Instrument Pilot's Survival Manual

Written by Rod Machado

Published by the Aviation Speakers Bureau

Foreword by Dave Gwinn
Airline Pilot, Radar Expert and Aviation Journalist

First Printing - November 1991
Second Printing - June 1993
Third Printing - July 1994. All material updated with new airspace, FAR and chart information as of this date.

Published by:
The Aviation Speakers Bureau, P.O. Box 6030, San Clemente, California 92674-6030

Don't even think about using any chart in this book for navigation!

ISBN 0-9631229-0-8 $29.95 Softcover
Library of Congress Catalog Card Number 91-076750

Cover Design by Diane Titterington
Cover Drawing by Rod Machado
Cover Graphic Art Work by Keith Milne
Text Illustrations: Designed and Drawn by Rod Machado

DEDICATION

This book is dedicated to five of the most important people in my life: my mother, my father, my brother, my sister and my darling wife.

This book is also dedicated to the memory of my friend Barry Zielinski who was the most incredible teacher I have ever known.

ACKNOWLEDGMENTS

The author wishes to thank the following organizations who have been instrumental in helping make this book a reality: Jeppesen Sanderson Inc., the Federal Aviation Administration, National Ocean Service, the Aviation Safety Reporting System, Airline Ground Schools, Aviation Business Services, Aviation Media and Azure Soft. Additionally, special thanks are also in order for the following individuals:

Sarah Cochrane, Ralph Butcher, Tim Peterson, Rich Coffin, Pam Hengsteler, Steve Kahn, Danny Mortensen, Sally Weed, Captain John Dill, Skip Forster, James P. Johnson, Ron Wiener, Bob Crystal, and Henry G. (Hank) Smith.

I would like to offer my special thanks to my editor, Kathy Carey for her help and to my two technical editors, Diane Titterington and David Gwinn for their deep insights into the workings of aviation and human nature.

FOREWORD

The day that education becomes fluid intake, Rod Machado might be reincarnated as a happy sponge. He's an educational blotter now, assembling any academia proximate to his person and depleting himself in giving it to others. Fortunately for all of us, his field is aviation.

People are so typically enchanted with his communication skills that they rarely appraise the nucleus of all this talent: Machado loves people. He studies them as a psychologist. He teaches them as an instructor. The more plentiful his immediate population the better and that's why he's electric and alive in front of large audiences. His idea of a refreshing retreat is Oshkosh in August.

In his classic, masterful aviator/author Richard Bach described <u>Jonathan Livingston Seagull</u> (and in my biased view, he concurrently mentions Machado): "...he was born to be an instructor, and his own way of demonstrating love was to give something of the truth that he had seen to (one) who asked only to see the truth for himself." From coast to coast, internationally, to thousands of attentive people, he has fervently shared his experience, perspective, practical thinking and his endless attitude of gratitude.

It has been my enjoyable task to both read and chuckle as Rod's Technical Editior. Should an error or omission have crept by, I'll plead associated guilt with the rationale that I was laughing too often to recognize some minor flaw. However, nothing diminishes the intense affection by which Rod Machado shares with you "some of the truth" that he has learned for himself, and by which you can become a more competent, confident, happier and safe IFR pilot.

Therefore, I invite you to learn from a genuine professional, one of the most creative, intelligent and kind persons in my world. As an instructor, Rod has summoned from his students, levels of superior performance that they themselves had failed to inventory as their potential. Bach's <u>Jonathan</u> also knew the technique: "You have to practice and see the...good in every one of them and to help them see it in themselves."

Dave Gwinn
Kansas City
August 14th, 1991

CONTENTS

Foreword v

About the Author.. vii

Introduction.. ix

Chapter 1. Thinking Like the Professionals............................ 1

Chapter 2. The Art of The Instrument Scan......................... 9

Chapter 3. Self-Talk Dialogues... 23

Chapter 4. Managing Cockpit Resources............................. 35

Chapter 5. ADF Navigation Made Simple............................ 43

Chapter 6. The Truth About Holding Patterns.................... 51

Chapter 7. How The IFR System Works.............................. 63

Chapter 8. The Art of The Approach................................... 77

Chapter 9. Thunderstorm Avoidance.................................... 93

Chapter 10. Avoiding Structural Icing................................... 111

Chapter 11. Understanding IFR Charts................................. 125

Chapter 12. Equipment For The Approach............................ 135

Chapter 13. Secrets of The Front Side................................. 149

Chapter 14. Procedure Turn Secrets..................................... 169

Chapter 15. Approach Segments... 181

Chapter 16. Decision Altitude and MDA's............................ 195

Chapter 17. Instrument Departures....................................... 207

Chapter 18. Enroute Chart Secrets....................................... 217

Editor and Technical Editors... 234

The Publisher.. 235

Products and Presentations.. 236

Suggested Reading.. 241

Index... 242

ABOUT THE AUTHOR

Rod Machado began his career in aviation at the age of two when his parents heard him say, "Airrrrpwaaaane." Since then, his enthusiasm for aviation has grown almost unchecked. In fact, he is one of the few airline transport rated pilots that still gets excited by a Cessna 172 fly-by. Although Rod does live in Southern California, he doesn't live in the Seal Beach VOR, contrary to popular misconception.

Rod is a professional speaker who travels across the fifty United States and Europe delighting his listeners with upbeat and lively presentations. Machado truly loves mixing it up with the audience. His unusual talent for simplifying the difficult and adding humor to make the lessons stick has made him a popular lecturer both in and out of aviation. Rod's presentations include topics as diverse as: Cockpit Resource Management, Risk Assessment, IFR charts and Aviation Weather. His non-aviation topics include: Persuasion Skills, Dealing With Difficult People, Humor as a Management Tool and Safety Awareness. Additionally, he is well known for his rapid fire, humorous banquet presentations.

He is a National Accident Prevention Counselor with twenty-two years in aviation and over 8,000 hours of flight time earned the hard way, one CFI hour at a time. Named the 1991 Western Region Flight Instructor of the Year, in the last 15 years Rod has taught hundreds of Flight Instructor Revalidation Clinics and Safety Seminars. He can be seen on *Wonderful World of Flying* and heard on *Pilot's Audio Update*.

Rod's eclectic interests are reflected in his equally varied academic credentials. He holds a degree in Aviation Science and degrees in Psychology from California State University at Long Beach. Rod believes you must take time to exercise or you'll have to take time to be sick. Holding black belts in the Korean disciplines of Tae Kwon Do and Hapkido, he gets his exercise from practicing and teaching martial arts. Rod never has trouble collecting money from any of his students.

Don't even think about using this book for navigation!

INTRODUCTION

This book was born of the motivation to *provide IFR pilots with answers to questions they most frequently ask*. These are questions no single IFR publication has ever attempted to address. Typical of those that remain unanswered in the minds of many IFR pilots are:

How do I know whether those clouds have thunderstorms in them?
What do I have to do to avoid icing conditions?
How can I tell if there is icing present?
What is the most efficient way to scan my instruments?
Is there a precise way to determine inflight visibility from the cockpit?
What is the best way to acquire confidence when flying instruments?
How are instrument approaches built to accommodate pilot performance?

These questions and many, many more are what this book is all about. And that is why this book is called "Rod Machado's Instrument Pilot's Survival Manual."

With so many wonderful books available on instrument flying, my strategy has been to avoid duplicating what has been adequately covered in other publications. Therefore, the reader will not find anything about VOR navigation, basic IFR regulations, or information on how to pass a written test. Questions on these topics, generally, do not rob pilots of sleep, and deprive them of peace of mind, as they attempt to ponder the apparent imponderables of the IFR world.

This is a book to be used in learning how to think differently in the cockpit, a book to be used in acquiring the IFR decision making skills of a professional pilot. This book attempts to establish connections and relationships that often take many, many years, and thousands of hours of flight experience, to identify. These relationships offer a pilot greater cockpit confidence and more effective decision making ability. *It's a text for both students and professionals*. This book is a supplement to all the other excellent IFR texts available.

The reader will quickly identify my affection for Jeppesen IFR charts. However, I've used both NOS and Jeppesen charts in this book. I have made it a point to compare and contrast differences and similarities between the two brands where appropriate. The principles applied to these charts apply to instrument charts throughout the United States.

This book is designed to be practical and fun to read. The most precious legacy each of us can leave to the other is our experience. Many years of inflight experience has been gathered in the form of Aviation Safety Reporting System (ASRS) excerpts. These are the stories of pilots who have made mistakes, some humorous, some quite serious. These experiences convey important ideas that mere moralizing could hardly hope to duplicate.

I love to laugh! I hope the reader does also. Anyone who has ever attended any of my programs knows my humor is used to create portals of receptiveness in the minds of my audience. I first realized the awesome power of humor when I asked my first instrument instructor how my ILS's were looking. Being kind, and gifted with a great sense of humor, he stated that he really couldn't tell because the needles were moving faster than money dropped at a kleptomaniac convention. I hope, this book makes you laugh and learn. This is what learning should be, a fun and enjoyable experience.

Laugh and Learn!

Rod Machado

1. THINKING LIKE THE PROS

Aviators who can consistently land without popping the needle off the seismograph, or having all three wheels disappear in a puff of smoke, are often given the accolade of being "Good Pilots." But skill at landing smoothly is of little importance when critical decisions are made aloft concerning the safety of flight. Genuine mastery of an airplane is acquired on a much higher level than the physical. The primary factor in the safe operation of an aircraft is a function of mind, not body.

An Airline Transport Pilot's license requires 1500 hours of flight experience. This is certainly more flight time than is necessary to competently pilot an airplane. New private pilots have probably acquired about 90% of the physical skills they will need throughout their piloting career. They are physically skilled enough to fly safely. Yet, physical proficiency was not the intent when 1500 hours of tenure aloft was envisioned. Founding fathers of the regulations were hoping for higher, more ethereal knowledge to be absorbed by the aviator beyond technical skill. This higher knowledge is a professional way of thinking, developed after hundreds of hours of "cause and effect" exposure to inflight decision making. This professional thinking style is of primal value in an aircraft, yet it is the one area of a pilot's development that has been left to chance by aviation educators.

FLYING A 747 ON FLOATS OR A CESSNA 150 STRETCHED — HEAVY, THE SEASONED IFR PROFESSIONAL HAS LEARNED TO THINK IN A VERY SPECIFIC WAY WHILE IN THE COCKPIT.

Several years ago, I became enchanted by magic. Wanting to learn quickly, I followed the counsel of a wise teacher who said, "Learn to think like the person possessing the skill desired and that skill will quickly evolve." I set about learning to think like a magician, instead of just reproducing the mechanical manipulations of magicdom. My own progress accelerated dramatically when I learned to think of creating distractions, which is how most professional magicians think.

With the same "learning priorities" in aviation as in magic, my learning curve would have been steeply sloped. Unfortunately, aviation teaching methods are antiquated. Students are often taught to mimic the physical behaviors of an instrument pilot, instead of being caused to think like an experienced pilot. The assumption is that with enough exposure to instrument flying, pilots will eventually acquire the appropriate thinking skills through osmosis. While this may be true, it seems educationally primitive to rely on luck, with all the precision of a crap shoot, rather than goal-minded teaching, to guarantee that pilots will acquire the proper mental skills. After all, the final objective of instrument training is not physical skill as much as it is mental development.

Over the years, instrument students have exhibited reflexes that were so slow, they could get run over by two guys pushing a car with a flat tire. Despite their demonstrated physical inertia, they compensated for weaknesses by developing strengths in complementary areas. While their instrument flying wasn't of the precise caliber expected in a professional airline pilot, they nevertheless were safe, competent pilots because they had learned to think. Physical skills are necessary for safe instrument flight, but they have a priority value right behind having a big fancy watch. The only time instrument students' physical skills concern me is if they regularly manage to stumble out of an airplane and choke themselves to unconsciousness on a seat belt. This would make them highly suspect of success at instrument flying.

Pilots can accelerate their cognitive maturation by more specifically and intentionally learning to think like experienced aviation professionals. Remember, what is happening in the mind of the seasoned pro is more important than how they manipulate the controls of their aircraft. This professional instrument mentality consists of many components, five of which can be easily acquired.

THINKING AHEAD

First, instrument pilots should learn to think ahead of their airplane. This is the most obvious quality separating the neophyte from the experienced professional. Experienced pilots never seem to be surprised by events in flight. They have an uncanny ability to anticipate problems before they arise. What appears to be a mystical talent is nothing other than suspicion, anticipation and predetermined action, born out of asking the right question at the proper time.

GOOD ATTITUDE INDICATOR

Many years ago, when taking an instrument flying lesson, my instructor tapped me on the shoulder and asked, "Machado, what are the two most important things in aviation?" I replied, "Well, ahhhh, never eat at the airport restaurant and always reconnect the hobbs meter when you're done flying?" He shook his head and said, "The two most important things in aviation are THE NEXT TWO THINGS." From then on, when he would tap me on the shoulder, I was to salivate like Pavlov's dog and tell him the next two steps or tasks to accomplish for this IFR flight. This subtle process of conditioning would thereby develop my ability to think ahead of the airplane. After five hours of this behavior modification scheme, I was responding automatically, asking myself, "What are the next two things I'm supposed to do to successfully fly this airplane?"

AUTHOR

Acquiring the skill of thinking ahead can be accelerated by taping a small business card on the panel with the words, "Next two things" written on it. A casual glance will provide a peripheral reminder to think ahead of the airplane. In a few hours a pilot will be perceiving events several steps in advance. Simply place the paper over a non-critical instrument, like the hobbs meter, where it can be easily viewed. The last thing an instrument pilot needs to do is to include the hobbs meter in his scan. It's very easy to start thinking in terms of dollars and cents, especially during instrument training. One of my instrument students once determined that each circuit in a holding pattern should cost him approximately $3.50 in a Cessna 172, without errors. For him, however, it was 10 to 12 dollars per circuit in a calm wind environment.

DEVELOPING ALTERNATIVES

Second, instrument pilots should learn to think about choices. Competent pilots are always thinking of having choices or alternatives, never letting themselves get trapped in blind canyons or in holding patterns without sufficient fuel. For instance, Captain Robert Buck, in his book, <u>Weather Flying</u>, suggests learning to fly in weather by obtaining some practical weather experience. He recommends getting experience flying in actual weather, but, with a warning of always having "an out." In other words, have alternate choices of action if the first plan doesn't work.

Professional thinking demands alternatives be considered in every situation. What would happen if a zero visibility takeoff was made? Would there be anyplace to go if the engine failed -- other than down? What about flying over a fog shrouded area? An engine failure above fog is like having the Grim Reaper for a copilot. Flying VFR over fog is a sure sign that pilots have been getting too much aluminum in their diet. Wise pilots never fly where they can't make a successful emergency landing. The most elite of the cautious may never fly anywhere but over mattress factories.

Most pilots say they would rather do a fire walk while gargling gasoline than fly over a mountainous area at night in a single engine airplane. However, skilled charter pilots, who are masters at contemplating alternatives, suggest it is possible to do this with a greater degree of safety by following major highways. When civil engineers build roads, they do so over the most accessible and easily navigated topography. If pilots are following a highway and experience an engine failure, they can land on the road. Essentially, the airplane becomes a car. An added benefit is the little mobile runway lights, moving along the road, to help light it up as pilots prepare to land. This is known as the BLS, or Buick Lighting System.

HUMULONIMBUS

I was flying VFR and Approach assigned me a squawk code. Several minutes later, the controller asked me my altitude, and I responded 7,500. He told me to squawk my altitude. I replied, "Squawking 7500," and the controller confirmed my code. When the controller cleared me to the Tower frequency, he asked me to continue my current squawk. After landing, Ground directed me to a specific parking area, and I was immediately surrounded by three police cars with a number of officers pointing their weapons at me. It was about 20 minutes before the helicopter circling overhead said something...and an officer motioned me out of my plane. They instructed me to lie face down, spread-eagle, with my forehead on the 100-plus degree tarmac. They frisked me and handcuffed me!

I would suggest that controllers never use the terminology "Squawk your altitude." Had the controller at any time indicated that he was not receiving my altitude, I could have recycled my transponder. He also asked me at one point, "What is your beacon number?" I had to respond I didn't know what he meant..

The reporter, an experienced pilot with several ratings was evidently unfamiliar with Paragraph 170(h) of the AIM, which explains radar beacon (transponder) phraseology in full including "squawk altitude" (meaning "activate Mode C"). Even so, he might have escaped this ordeal had he not been at an altitude the controller interpreted (on hearing "Squawking 7500") as the hijack code. — **ASRS REPORT**

While approaching to land, experienced pilots will scout the departure end of the runway, ferreting out emergency landing sites for use in the event of an engine failure on the subsequent takeoff. They also may check the ATIS when many miles from the destination to check for deteriorating weather. These pilots are playing the "What if?" game. Asking "What if?" is the essence of generating choices and having options. Simply asking, "What would I do if the engine quit here?" or " What would I do if I were running low on fuel here and the visibility was deteriorating?" is provocation enough to generate several life saving options. Asking questions like these is a habitual part of the professional thinking mentality.

CAUGHT WITH WHEEL PANTS DOWN

A faithful CALLBACK customer reports an interesting conversation he overheard on the party line and suggests a need for continuing education. Try AIM if you don't understand this:

Approach Control: "We have the REIL lights up all the way; do you have the runway in sight?"

Pilot (after some hesitation): "How do you tell the difference between real lights and imitation lights?"

TAKE COMMAND

Third, instrument pilots should be assertive and willing to command the aircraft. Professionals realize they are responsible for the operation of the aircraft, and they must be willing to do what is necessary to fly safely. The ability to make quick decisions, to refuse to act on an inappropriate ATC clearance or be influenced by the psychological pressures of "Get-Home-itis" are all representative of a pilot's ability to act assertively. Unfortunately, pilots are seldom taught this valuable command quality necessary for safe flight.

PROPERLY DONE

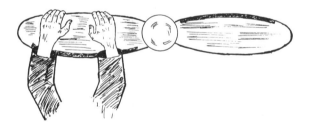

On a left turn into final approach, prior to the flaps being lowered, a pilot accelerated rapidly to avoid a single engine propeller aircraft. Visibility was marginal. I was sitting on the right side and saw the prop aircraft almost directly overhead. I was able to see the other aircraft because we were turning left. Our pilot had to take evasive action in order to avoid a mid-air. I would estimate distance to be between 150-400 feet. I was 38 years old upon entering the plane. I felt like 80 years old upon departure.

Few general aviation pilots realize there is a federal aviation regulation giving them as much power and authority in a Cessna 150 as the captain of a Boeing 747. The only real difference between the two is that there are fewer restrooms on board. Federal Aviation Regulation 91.3(a) states, "The pilot in command of an aircraft is directly responsible for, and is the final authority as to, the operation of the aircraft." This regulation is quite explicit as to the authority of the pilot in command. Nevertheless, few pilots fly as if they are in command. Professionals know they are totally responsible and accountable for the operation of their aircraft. They operate with pragmatic assertiveness, whether they are flying a J-3 Cub or an SST. Old salts have learned it is better to ask for clarification, when in doubt about a particular clearance, than to let themselves be talked into an undesired course of action. They are willing to do what is necessary to be safe.

One area in which the instrument pilot is sure to suffer difficulty is understanding ATC clearances. Perhaps this is because controllers speak at 60 with peak gusts to 90. Pilots of all skill levels may be nonplussed by talking to controllers. One instrument student, raised in a non-control tower environment and having little or no experience with controllers, asked his instructor for guidance during a callup. The instructor said, "Just tell him who you are and where you want to go." The student picked up the microphone, stuttered and said, "Tower, who am I and where do I want to go?" The tower controller replied, "Well, you stumped us. We give up, what's the answer?"

Being assertive is most appropriate when controllers speak fast. Professionals will simply ask the controller to speak more slowly or, use a little humor, and state they are just "student pilots" and need to hear the transmission again. In a Boeing 747 this has awesome impact with controllers. Hopefully, nobody in the passenger section of the Boeing will be listening to the captain's transmission.

HUMULONIMBUS

Pilots who can record their ATC clearances on their intercom system usually have the last laugh. They play back this word sortie into the microphone for their readback. There is usually a pause, then the controller says, "Hey buddy, if you want me to check that clearance, you're going to have to read it a little slower next time."

Developing this quality of assertiveness is best accomplished by modeling the behavior of other professionals. Richard Bem at Stanford University suggests that a person's beliefs and value structures are developed by those they choose as role models. Pilots under the tutelage of a seasoned professional should follow their guide closely. They should study their every move and elicit their strategies for decision making. This is best accomplished by asking questions about why certain decisions are made. Seek to understand the reasoning behind the professional's decision. What were the consequences considered and how were the risks weighed? Therein lies the foundation for developing the command presence found in the wise and experienced pilot.

BE SKEPTICAL

Fourth, instrument pilots should develop a responsible skepticism. It's not in the best interest of aviation safety or longevity for pilots to believe everything they hear, without questioning the source and reliability of the information. Professional aviation thinkers are always asking the question, "Is that information accurate?"

Most have heard the hangar lore about recovering from a spin in a small airplane. "When in doubt, just let go of the controls and the airplane will recover by itself" is a common bit of hangar advice. It's a good bet that if pilots try something like this, they'll be in for a big surprise. Assuming the airplane doesn't have an aft center of gravity, they're likely to recover. But, they'll probably pull out of the dive and create a sonic boom at the same time. Controlling an airplane by letting go of the controls seems about as smart as going to a restaurant without any money, hoping to pay for the seafood dinner with the pearl that may be found in an oyster. Pilots having enough clarity of mind to let go, should have enough clarity of mind to apply opposite rudder or forward pressure on the elevator.

More hangar advice: "When in icing conditions, climb to escape from this peril." This is as faulty a misconception as believing that "Herpes" was a Greek philosopher, or that "Hebrew" is an Israeli macho beer. In a small airplane, if pilots have to rely on climbing to avoid icing conditions, then they had best fly with candles, beads and a little statue of their favorite savior. They're going to need all the heavenly help they can get. Climbing proposes to get the pilot into a layer of warmer air aloft to melt the ice. This assumes there is a warmer layer above that can be easily reached. It's better to make a 180 degree turn, and/or a descent, than to try to climb with the limited performance of a small, iced-up airplane.

CHEER UP?

Not too long ago, the owner of a Cessna 210 presented himself for a Biennial Flight Review. Approaching the runway threshold, he was asked to demonstrate a short field takeoff. He reached over and attempted to raise the gear handle to the retract position while on the ground. My heart stopped; my brain cried for oxygen. I immediately detached his hand and returned it to him. I was unable to speak. The blood flow to the carotid arteries going to the base of my brain was paralyzed. I could only make a primitive, primate sound. He volunteered that he had been told the micro-switches on the gear would keep it from retracting while on the ground, thus allowing an immediate retract upon liftoff. This, he reasoned, should maximize the short field takeoff capability of his airplane. This fellow was about to make a gear up takeoff with me along as witness! Rest assured that my name can't be found in his logbook. Someone had told him that it was safe to raise the gear handle on the ground. He didn't even question the wisdom of that advice.

AUTHOR

Those with the professional flight mentality listen carefully and critically to what is said. When controllers say they are not showing any thunderstorms on their radar, the experienced pro may ask if they have weather radar capability. When pilots returning from a cross country flight say the weather was excellent, the pro finds out what their definition is of "excellent." Professional thinking pilots are wary, cautious creatures, reluctant to take things at face value. They are paranoia personified, with Murphy's Law as a creed. They often believe every airplane was built by the Pandora Aircraft Company.

THINK DEFENSIVELY

Fifth, instrument pilots with the professional mentality think defensively. Several years ago, Tom Wolfe wrote a book about those special individuals having a highly developed survival sense. Wolfe called it the "Right Stuff." Somehow these special pilots could survive situations that would have normally overwhelmed and sacrificed the lives of average pilots. This highly developed survival reflex seems to be rooted in pilots having a keen sense of their own vulnerability.

The esteemed General Chuck Yeager admitted in his autobiography that he was always afraid of dying in an airplane. This man, by all rights, should not have survived the kinds of experiences he had without crippling injury or death, but he did survive. What gave Yeager the advantage was his defensive approach to flying. He made it a point to learn as much about his airplane and himself as he could throughout his flying career. He knew too well that, without this knowledge, he could never have mustered an adequate defense. His autobiography is saturated with subtle clues about his highly developed inner and outer sensing mechanisms. It's quite obvious that Yeager didn't wait for a problem before he tried to solve it. He had already laid the foundation for solution before the need arose.

Sun Tzu, in a book titled, The Art of War, said, "Invincibility lies in the defense, the possibility of victory, in the attack." A pilot's invincibility lies in the mental preparation for every flight. This involves acknowledging one's vulnerability and personal limitations. Sigmund Freud implied that man is the only creature who acts as if he will live forever. Unfortunately, many pilots realize the absurdity of this statement, but act as though they are invulnerable to Mother Nature's predatory creatures and their own physical limitations.

Professional pilots understand that certain inflight problems can be fatal. Their mentality is constantly challenged by contemplating the unexpected. They muse over possible solutions for any imagined occurrence causing them greater vulnerability to the perils of the air. Like the martial artists who protect their vital points, conserve energy and nullify an attack, professional pilots always think in terms of protecting their aircraft structure, airspeed and height above terrain.

The defensive qualities of professional pilots become apparent as they approach an airplane for flight. They look at the airplane from a distance, checking for any

KICK IN THE EMPENNAGE

The aircraft was taken to the wash rack and the static ports were taped up. This was not documented in the log book. I was asked to power up the aircraft for a preflight in the morning. A logbook check and cockpit check showed everything was OK. Our procedures call for an outside check of the struts and tires for inflation and fluid leaks, which I accomplished. I did not notice the static ports were taped up, although I did not make a specific check of them. I will never miss that again. Procedures have been changed to include a thorough walkaround of the aircraft for every preflight after a layover.

I believe anytime anything of a disabling nature is done to an aircraft there should be a logbook item initiated. Of this particular type of occurrence, I believe the indicators should be more prominent, such as long streamer ribbons. I find it very hard to believe that I missed seeing that tape. Human factors: poor visibility (darkness); trust in one's own senses to pick up the unusual; haste.

ASRS REPORT

EVERYTHING'S COMING UP ROSES

This may be minor; but it is possibly a potential hazard. I refueled my aircraft with 35 gallons of 100 octane fuel. I even watched it happen. I went inside, came back, and, out of habit, looked in the tanks and drained a sample. Imagine my surprise at seeing a pink sample! I was ready to yell and scream: then I realized my eye-glasses (brown-rose colored) had changed the color. Suppose I had worn green sunglasses and looked at a clear fuel sample? Moral: Look at fuel samples without sunglasses.

ASRS REPORT

unusual structural problem that wouldn't be apparent up close. They look below the airplane, as it sits on the ramp, looking for oil pools and droppings of important-looking bolts and nuts. They double-check all critical items during the preflight. They remove their sunglasses while straining the fuel, so its correct color can be observed. They look at the nose gear strut and tire compression for apparent shifts in weight that may have gone unnoticed. They feel the airplane as they taxi out for departure, assessing load distribution based on ground handling characteristics. They cup

TAKE A STAND LENTICULARS

I taxied from the military base Aero Club line to the runup area. Another aircraft of the same type (but locally based) had led the way for me, as I was not familiar with the airport. The two aircraft sat there doing our runups. I was finished before the other aircraft. Suddenly, I felt a violent rocking motion. The instructor in the other aircraft had gotten out of his plane and was pulling up and down on my wing tip. He then walked to the tail of my aircraft and removed my rudder gust lock. The gust lock is of the "home-made" wood type with a Velcro fastener. During my walk around pre-flight I had noted the gust lock, but forgot to remove it. Nose wheel steering on this plane worked fine during my taxi. While checking free movement of controls, I had noted slight stiffness in the rudder pedals. I did turn around, did notice some motion and continued the checklist. This incident probably developed because: (1) I was pressed for time, (2) I was upset by the unusual procedures at this base (the pilot must visit the WX office and air ops officer in order to get clearance - phone calls are not permitted); and (3) I was getting sloppy.

ASRS REPORT

hands into their headphones on takeoff, so that sounds of engine aberrations are not hidden or masked. On takeoff, they look out the rear of the aircraft to see if fuel is leaking from the tanks. They constantly monitor the engine instruments. If the oil temperature is going up, they will shorten the flight and if the hobbs meter speed is slowing down, they may give some serious thought to lengthening the flight. These are some of the qualities that make up the defensive mentality of the professional thinking pilot.

It is a fraudulent non-sequitur to equate the thickness of a pilot's logbook with airmanship. While experience, measured in flight hours, may correlate with the trained mentality of a professional pilot, there's no reason that it must. Simply identifying and modeling the cognitive behaviors of professional aviators, will rapidly and purposely mature the mentality of the neophyte. Thinking ahead of the airplane, having choices when flying, being assertive, being skeptical and thinking defensively are the keys to accelerating a pilot's mental development.

With the student thinking like the pros, it's now time to turn to the art of the instrument scan -- the bedrock upon which all instrument skills will be built.

2. THE ART OF THE INSTRUMENT SCAN

Flying instruments is perhaps one of the most challenging and rewarding accomplishments a pilot experiences in aviation. It satisfies and gratifies a pilot's inherent need to be a master of the machine and environment, while offering its own form of entertainment in the process. In fact, instrument flying is analogous to a video game in three dimensions, except pilots don't get to shoot down any Klingons. The pilot's next flight is the "free game" they get for a satisfactory score or performance. Developing a good instrument scan is the fundamental challenge instrument flying offers. Yet, it's in this area that pilots are most deficient.

The trial and error learning of initial IFR training is the genesis of the instrument scan used by most pilots. Most likely, no one told these pilots how to scan their instruments. They just started looking around the panel, groping for bits of information that would allow them to keep their airplane upright. Over the years, instructors see many diverse and amusing scan patterns, from pilots who appeared to follow a fly around the cockpit, all the way to the radical head twister who caused hoods and foggles to fly off.

A PROFESSIONAL INSTRUMENT INSTRUCTOR USES THE LATEST DEVELOPMENTS IN PROFESSIONAL WRESTLING TO TEACH HIS STUDENTS THE PERFECT EYE MOVEMENT FOR A PRECISION SCAN.

ADVANCED IFR SCAN INSTRUCTION

In fact, my initial instrument instructor would insist on tapping the instruments with his metal pointer, his baton leading my eyes in scan. This was about as educational as being at an Amish science fair. He would say, "OK, look here (airspeed); look there (attitude indicator); don't look at that (heading indicator); look at this one (turn coordinator) ..." For a long while, I thought that's what the instruments were called -- HERE, THERE, THAT and THIS ONE.

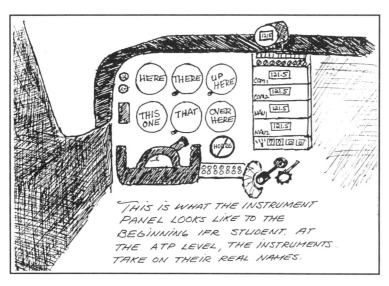

THIS IS WHAT THE INSTRUMENT PANEL LOOKS LIKE TO THE BEGINNING IFR STUDENT. AT THE ATP LEVEL, THE INSTRUMENTS TAKE ON THEIR REAL NAMES.

Many pilots end up having survived, rather than mastered, every IFR flight. For them it may be victory, but it's rarely comfort. Mastering the art of instrument flying is a function of implementing the skills that will allow the pilot to become a good inflight manager. A good instrument scan gives the pilot time to think, plan, anticipate, plot, scheme and stay one step ahead of the airplane. This is what instrument flying is all about: to master the mechanics of flying, to "free up" a pilot's imaginative capacity to be aware of position and what's expected next.

THE THREE STEPS

There are three essential steps in the effective instrument scanning process. They are to be executed every time a major attitude change is made. All three steps should take approximately 10 to 15 seconds to complete. Here are the three steps of the scan, in the order they should be done:

STEP 1. SELECT ATTITUDE, POWER, TRIM & CONFIRM
STEP 2. RADIAL SCAN THE PRIMARY INSTRUMENTS
STEP 3. TRIM USING THE VSI AND MONITOR SCAN THE BIG-6

Essentially, the airplane is put in the desired attitude, power is adjusted and an initial twist of trim is applied to hold the airplane in this attitude. The correct operation of the most critical instruments is checked by a confirmation process. The primary instruments are then scanned in an organized fashion, and small corrections are made to fine tune the airplane to the proper attitude. The final trim adjustments are made, and the airplane's new attitude is monitored on the six main panel instruments, otherwise known as the "BIG-6." This is the big picture of how the instruments are scanned in this three step process. The specific details and reasons for each of the three steps follow.

STEP ONE OF THE SCAN

The first step in the three step scan is to select the attitude, power and trim conditions for the new flight attitude. This first step is executed by focusing on the attitude indicator and selecting, from experience, the attitude that educated approximation says will provide the flight conditions desired. The implication here is that the pilot has, or is acquiring, a knowledge of the predetermined attitudes necessary to make the airplane climb, turn and descend as commanded.

After the first few hours of instrument flying, pilots should immediately decide on an array of specific power settings and flight attitudes that will cause the airplane to do exactly what they wish. These power settings and flight attitudes are values or reference points on the tachometer and attitude indicator. In a light, general aviation trainer, climbs are typically done with full power and a 5 to 10 degree nose up pitch attitude. This will consistently result in a good cruise climb speed. Most turns are accomplished with a 15 to 20 degree bank. This is close to the bank necessary for a standard rate turn at normal cruising conditions.

Remember, a standard rate turn simply means that the nose of the airplane changes direction at three degrees per second. The easiest way to figure out what bank is required for a standard rate turn is to drop the last number off the airspeed and add the number five. If the airspeed is 125 knots, then the bank required for a standard rate turn is 12 + 5 or 17 degrees. If the airspeed is 90 knots, then the standard rate bank is 9 + 5 or 14 degrees. If the airspeed is 600 knots, then the bank required is 65 degrees. This could be real interesting for the passengers! There is a good chance some of the older passengers will experience a dislodging of their uppers. The general rule is never to exceed 30 degrees of bank, under IFR conditions, even if something steeper is required for a standard rate turn.

Besides, someone once suggested that most airline pilots avoid steep turns because of the debilitating effects of G-forces on posture. After spending many years in a flight crew seat, professional pilots have been known to take on the shape of a lazy-boy recliner. The critical stage is reached when pilots start to look like they have just graduated from the Quasimodo posture school.

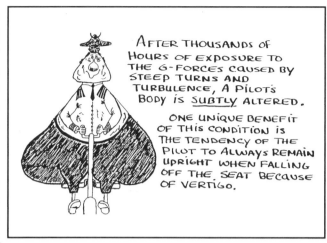

AFTER THOUSANDS OF HOURS OF EXPOSURE TO THE G-FORCES CAUSED BY STEEP TURNS AND TURBULENCE, A PILOTS BODY IS SUBTLY ALTERED.

ONE UNIQUE BENEFIT OF THIS CONDITION IS THE TENDENCY OF THE PILOT TO ALWAYS REMAIN UPRIGHT WHEN FALLING OFF THE SEAT BECAUSE OF VERTIGO.

No VFR pilots worth their weight in slow hobbs meters would deny that looking outside at the horizon is a good thing. The earth's horizon is what allows a pilot to keep the airplane in the correct attitude for flight. In fact, most pilots flying VFR spend upwards of 90% of their time referencing the visible horizon. Why should this be any different during instrument flight? When the earth's horizon is no longer visible, the airplane's attitude indicator (artificial horizon) is a most welcome substitute.

Step one of the instrument scan suggests that the attitude indicator be exclusively observed during major attitude changes. This is certainly contradictory to what many pilots have probably been told about instrument flying. It's always been considered a punishable offense to stare at any one instrument. For the most part, this is a good rule -- except when it comes to step one of the scan.

The Air Force Instrument Flying Manual AFM 51-37 states: "The attitude indicator is the only instrument which you should observe continuously for any appreciable length of time. Several seconds may be needed to accomplish an attitude change required for a normal turn. During this period, you may need to devote your attention, almost exclusively, to the attitude indicator to ensure good attitude control." Since the USAF is in the business of flying aircraft, it's a sure bet that they have given this statement a great deal of thought. Problems with instrument scan often occur when pilots spend too little rather than too much time observing the attitude indicator.

Many years ago, a military study of professional pilots discovered something educationally interesting. When cameras were targeted on the eyes of these professional pilots during their instrument scan, it was discovered they spent 85% of their time looking at the attitude indicator. The only reasonable conclusion that can be drawn is that this behavior has evolved because it is eminently useful and efficient. The implication is, if it's deemed appropriate by professionals, then it is wise to emulate this behavior.

The attitude indicator is a complete instrument. Unlike any other instrument it contains both pitch and bank information. Therefore, it's reasonable to focus on this instrument when changing attitudes. If attitude indicators never failed, there would be no concern with their being the center of a pilot's attention. As an entry instrument, it is the "core" of the scan. But one cannot be obsessed with its presence, nor crippled by its absence. These instruments do fail, often with disastrous consequences for the pilot addicted to the attitude indicator who rejects all other injections of information. Knowing how to detect instrument failure, and correct for it, is the defensive counter measure which balances the emphasis on the attitude indicator.

In the final step of this scan, pilots will compare and validate the results of control input to the response of the attitude indicator. This is the confirmation process which ensures the attitude indicator is working properly. In other words, the attitude indicator should respond according to how the controls are moved. For instance, if control pressure is applied to make a right turn, the attitude indicator should show a right turn deflection in proportion to the amount of control input. A slight amount of back pressure on the controls should show a gradually increasing pitch on the attitude indicator. Any discrepancy between control input and attitude response should then be checked by consulting the turn or pitch "triangle of agreement."*

TURN TRIANGLE OF AGREEMENT

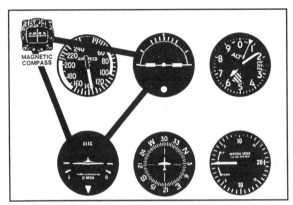

Fig. 1. Turn Triangle of Agreement

A triangle of agreement is when flight instruments, of the same dimension, respond at a similar rate in a noncontradictory manner. For example, the turn triangle of agreement, figure 1, consists of the attitude indicator, turn coordinator and magnetic compass. All three of these instruments respond to a turn. When turning, these instruments should reflect similar rates and similar directions of turn. In the event a discrepancy is suspected in the operation of the attitude indicator, the other two instruments of the triangle should be consulted, starting with the turn coordinator. If the turn coordinator does not reflect the attitude indicator's expected direction and rate of turn, the magnetic compass should be checked for movement. The instrument in disagreement with the other two is probably the one that must be eliminated as "failed." For instance, if the attitude indicator reflects a turn and the compass shows a heading change, but the turn coordinator indicates a constant heading, then this identifies that the turn coordinator is in error. The majority wins. It's just like professional wrestling, which, by the way, isn't real. If it's Wally, the Flying Cadaver Creator or Herbert, the Organ Donor Provider, the wrestler who has the loudest fans usually wins.

On most modern day general aviation airplanes, the turn coordinator is electrically operated, the attitude indicator is vacuum powered and the magnetic compass is blessed and powered by Mother Nature. This means that each of these three turn indicators is operated by an independent power source. Generally, they won't all fail at once. This is why these three instruments make up the turn triangle of agreement. Why isn't the heading indicator part of this triangle? The heading indicator, on most airplanes, is vacuum powered. Since it operates on the same power system as the attitude indicator, a failure of the vacuum system could render both these instruments inoperative.

Several years ago, a high performance, single engine, general aviation airplane entered a repair shop to have work done on the instrument vacuum system. Apparently, the mechanic forgot to put the airfilter on the intake line that allows air to be drawn over the vacuum instruments by the vacuum pump. The aircraft departed IFR and entered a solid wall of precipitation. Water was drawn through the air intake of the vacuum line and into the vacuum system. The pilot stated that he looked up at his instruments and

*Only check the turn or pitch triangle of agreement if you suspect the attitude indicator or any other flight instrument of error. In other words, it's not necessary to check the triangle of agreement every time a major attitude change is made.

saw water filling up the attitude indicator and the heading indicator. Wow! Now that's something his instructor probably never told him about. What would most pilots think if this happened to them? They might think the mechanic installed an auto-timed, self-lubricating, gyro system. Be prepared. Instruments can and do fail.

There is a little used instrument that is actually easier to use than the magnetic compass for detecting turns -- the ADF. It's my opinion that pilots should never fly instruments without having the ADF tuned to a station with a strong signal. In the event the turn triangle of agreement needs to be consulted, ADF needle movement would be a strong indication that the aircraft is turning, and, in what direction the turn is being made. In addition, in the event all the flight instruments fail, the ADF could provide enough information to keep the heading constant.

PITCH TRIANGLE OF AGREEMENT

The pitch triangle of agreement, figure 2, consists of the attitude indicator, vertical speed indicator and alternate static system. The attitude indicator and the VSI operate on separate power sources -- vacuum and static pressure. Neither the airspeed indicator, nor the altimeter, can be used as the third instrument in the triangle, because both these instruments operate on the same static source as the VSI. If a pitch discrepancy exists between the attitude indicator and the VSI, it is possible the static source is blocked. Therefore, the altimeter and airspeed indicator may also be in error. The appropriate action is to eliminate the VSI as source of error. Simply activate the alternate static source and note any change in VSI indication. If the VSI's indication doesn't change with the selection

MIND TWISTER

I was cleared for an immediate departure. I went through the final checklist: Time, Instruments, Transponder and Strobe. When checking the directional gyro with the compass and runway heading, I noticed it was 20 degrees off and made a mental note to keep track of precession.

After passing through about 500 feet, I was told to contact Departure. I acknowledged and hit the flip-flop button on the #1 Com and called. I got no response, so I tuned the #2 Com to Departure to try again. In my airplane, the radios are located beneath the yokes, with #2 on the bottom. This requires a large movement of the head in two axes. When I raised my head, I noted the Attitude Indicator was way off to the right, and I started to follow it. It became clear, almost immediately, that something was wrong, as the airspeed was building and the rate-of-climb was descending. I caught a glimpse of the approaching ground before I got back under control with the turn-and-bank and started to resume a climb. I simultaneously called Departure and declared a no-gyro emergency. The controllers acted with aplomb and reassurance, and a successful no-gyro ILS was accomplished.

What happened? The A.I. had a leak in the case (discovered by the instrument shop the next week) causing it to slow down and tilt and the D.G. to precess. The rapid head movement of retuning the radio caused vertigo, and I started to follow the tumbling A.I. My instrument crosscheck located the defective gyros in time to prevent disaster; partial panel ability, with excellent assistance from ATC, assured a successful landing.

How to prevent similar occurrences? I have raised my personal minimums for instrument takeoff in controlled airspace.

ASRS REPORT

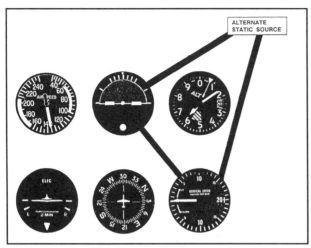

Fig. 2 Pitch Triangle of Agreement.

of the alternate static source, then the attitude indicator is in error. If the VSI's indication does change, then leave the alternate static source open. If the alternate static source is inside the cockpit, there will be a slight jump of the needle due to lower pressure.

What's required if pilots have a pitch discrepancy and don't have an alternate static source? Break the instrument, right? Which one? Break em' all and use braille? Making a small break in the glass in the VSI would be the appropriate choice to create an alternate static source. Pilots should only do this if they are in IFR conditions. Imagine the heart attack the owner of the FBO will have if a student pilot returns from the traffic pattern with the VSI smashed. A controlled impact keeps from smashing the VSI through the firewall into the engine compartment. Remember, the VSI will "work backwards" if static pressure is sensed from the front of the instrument, through the newly created opening. If this were to work the same way with hobbs meters, many students would invest heavily in precision glass smashing equipment. With several means of checking for instrument failure, pilots should now feel more confident focusing on the attitude indicator during major attitude changes.

SETTING POWER IN THE FIRST STEP

After the initial attitude is selected, the power is adjusted for the desired flight condition. If selecting a climb, the power is added as the nose is raised. This reflects the old adage, "Pitch, plus power, equals performance." There is no need to look at the tachometer when entering a climb in fixed pitch propeller airplanes, since the climb is usually with full power. In high performance airplanes, first the propeller and then the throttle control should be moved while the aircraft is entering the climb attitude. The appropriate tachometer and manifold setting can be set by making a quick glance at the engine instruments. Initially, this setting need only be approximate. A more precise setting can be made when the new attitude is finally established. When pilots gain experience, they'll set RPM by sound alone!

To enter a descent, the power is reduced first, then the attitude is adjusted. The more smoothly these two actions become simultaneous, the less indicated airspeed variance will be noticed. It's not necessary to even look at the power gauges when the initial power reduction is made, since the setting can be approximated by experienced feel. Pilots want to keep a keen eye on the attitude indicator during the attitude change, thereby maintaining complete control of the aircraft in the transition.

When any instrument is to be broken, most pilots will select the hobbs meter as their first choice. However, no matter how tempting, this would not be appropriate.

Once an attitude is selected and power is adjusted, trim should be added to keep the selected attitude constant. This initial "Gross" application of trim should be just enough to keep the airplane's attitude from wandering. All "Wheel of Fortune" fans should avoid the temptation of yelling, "Come on, one thousand" when twisting the trim wheel. The final and more accurate application of trim should be completed in step three. Give the trim wheel a couple of good turns as experience indicates, then go on to step two.

STEP TWO OF THE SCAN

Step two of the three step scan procedure is to "Radial scan" the primary instruments. This is done for two very important reasons. First, the primary instruments are those that allow the pilot to fine tune the attitude selected on the attitude indicator. Second, the primary instruments allow the pilot additional confirmation that the attitude indicator is reading correctly.*

Readily identifying, in flight, which instruments are primary for a given flight condition, is difficult for many new instrument pilots. Experienced professionals know exactly what instrument they need to look at to precisely fly the airplane. In fact, skill at instrument flying lies not so much in scanning all the instruments, but learning in which instruments to invest time. When time is spent efficiently, the airplane is easily controlled. This is where instant recognition of the primary instruments becomes very important for successful instrument flying.

There are always going to be three primary instruments for any condition of flight: one for Pitch, one for Bank and one for Power. Primary instruments are those that dispense the needed information to accomplish the intended maneuver. These instruments are "primary" in the sense they reaffirm that the selected attitude is correct. If pilots know which instruments are primary, they will avoid ocular waste while scanning instruments providing them with only redundant information. The best way to understand these primary instruments is to tape the words shown in figure 3, under each instrument on the panel. The FAA considers the word "bank" to be associated with either holding headings or heading change. This makes sense, considering controlling the angle of bank is directly related to the control of the heading.

Figure 3 shows which instruments are primary for specific conditions of flight. For instance, in straight and level flight, pilots should look at the panel and find those instruments listed as "straight" and "level." The directional gyro is primary for bank, or, going straight, the altimeter is primary for pitch and the tachometer is primary for power. In constant airspeed climbs or descents, airspeed is always the primary pitch instrument. In a turn, the turn coordinator is always primary for bank. The primary instruments for a climbing turn would be: airspeed for pitch, turn coordinator for bank and tachometer for power. The primary instruments for a level turn would be: altimeter for pitch, turn coordinator for bank and tachometer for power.

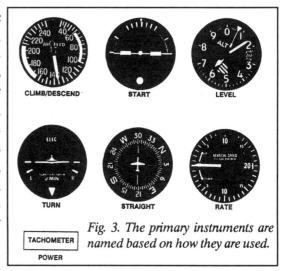

Fig. 3. The primary instruments are named based on how they are used.

*Please see footnote at the end of this chapter on the exception to this observation.

In a straight climb or descent at a specific rate, the VSI is primary for pitch and the heading indicator is primary for bank. Additionally, if a specific airspeed is necessary for the constant rate descent, and it most often is on ILS approaches, then the airspeed indicator will be primary for power. This is one of the rare situations where the tachometer is not primary for power as listed. Think of it this way, "What is the job to be accomplished, and what is primary to do the job?" The job, on a constant rate descent, is to maintain a specific airspeed, heading and rate. The only instrument that can do the job of telling the pilot if the airspeed is correct, is the airspeed indicator. Power is modified to maintain this specific airspeed.

To determine which flight instruments are primary, pilots should seek the words under each instrument for the intended flight condition. This visual prompt precludes the awkward mechanics of having to rigidly memorize which instruments are primary. This can be a difficult task for the neophyte when instrument relationships may not be understood. After pilots have flown IFR with the primary instruments labeled, these will be more easily recognized, and the words can be removed from the panel.

Of course, removing these taped-on words assumes they have not been welded on with "super tape." I think this super tape is made by the same people that make the instructor's "No-peekies." These are the round, attachable items that are placed over individual instruments to simulate partial panel operations. These suction cups are so powerful, they can pull the entire instrument right out from behind the panel. I've often thought a more practical item would be to have a baby octopus in a little container and use it in lieu of a "No-peekie." With all those suction cups, it's not likely they are going to fall off in turbulence. In the event they did fall off, they would leave the appropriate amount of dye over the instrument glass until they could be reattached, thus preventing the student from catching a glimpse of the forbidden instrument. Perhaps three or four of the little critters could be carried along in the flight bag. Imagine the students shock at seeing these multi-legged, throbbing creatures hanging from individual instruments. Perhaps these little guys could be trained to crawl to specific instruments on command, thereby adding a random variable to simulated instrument failure. I suppose if it's important for students to learn anything, they should learn never to fly with an instructor packing an aquarium.

Step 2 directs pilots to "radial scan" these primary instruments. To radial scan means to begin the scan at the attitude indicator, marked "Start." Pilots should then move to the primary instrument, extract information from it, return to the attitude indicator and make some correction in attitude. This is called the radial scan because the visual scanning track is from the attitude indicator out to the primary instrument, then back to the attitude indicator, making what appears to be "spokes" radiating from the attitude indicator to all the primary instruments as shown in figure 4. The attitude indicator is marked "Start" because this is where all attitude changes begin. It's very important that pilots understand how the radial scan is accomplished. A pilot's eyes should move from the attitude indicator to a primary instrument, observe its reading or detect its movement, then return to the attitude indicator and make an attitude adjustment to stabilize the primary instrument.

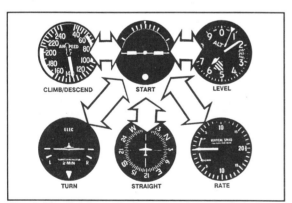

Fig. 4. "Radial Scanning" starts at the attitude indicator.

If straight and level flight is the goal, pilots should radial scan the altimeter, the directional gyro and the tachometer, as shown in figure 5. The secret to radial scanning is to start at the attitude indicator, proceed to a primary instrument, snatch information, then return to the attitude indicator and make a small attitude adjustment to effect the correct performance. Each of the three primary instruments should be quickly radial scanned at least once, before spending additional time radial scanning any one instrument in particular. This scan immediately identifies how close the airplane is to the planned attitude.

Figure 5 exhibits the scan for straight and level flight. Pilots would immediately radial scan the altimeter by observing it, then return to the attitude indicator. If the altimeter was moving, a small pitch change should be made on the attitude indicator to neutralize, then correct, this movement. The heading indicator should be radial scanned next, by observing it and returning to the attitude indicator. If the heading indicator is turning, or is not on the desired heading, a small correction in bank should be applied to the attitude indicator. Use a 5 degree bank correction on the attitude indicator to return to a heading that's not off by more than 20 degrees. It's important to stop a straying parameter, then correct it.

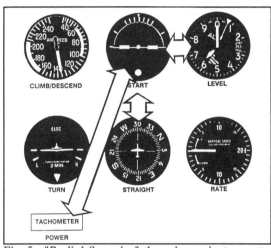

Fig. 5. "Radial Scanning" the primary instruments for straight and level flight.

The tachometer should be radial scanned last. Pilots should look at the tachometer and make any final adjustment in the setting, then immediately return to the attitude indicator. There is usually no need to initially radial scan the tachometer more than once during a major attitude change. If carburetor ice is suspected, or detected, then it should be scanned more often. After radial scanning all three primary instruments, pilots should alternately radial scan the altimeter and heading indicator, making small corrections on the attitude indicator to stabilize these instruments.

Notice how the pitch instruments were radial scanned first, the bank instruments second and the tachometer last. In other words, the primary instruments were radial scanned from the top of the panel in a downward direction. This is effective because pitch changes are more critical, and require more time to correct, than bank changes. Remember, an ATC violation can occur if pilots are off their assigned altitude by 300 feet. Being 30 degrees off an assigned heading for a "very short" period of time, however, does not normally ring bells and whistles. RPM changes are the least critical and take the least time of all to correct.

This is not to suggest that it's proper for pilots to be off their assigned heading. I'm merely pointing out how the ATC system prioritizes flight deviations. I fully realize that some pilots may have some difficulty holding headings. In fact, as an instrument student, I was often tempted to reach up and twist the heading indicator back to the assigned heading when my instructor wasn't watching. Of course, this would have been corrected later. I suggested to my instructor that some pilots might pay handsomely for an electric heading adjustment knob in their aircraft. These little devices could come in handy, especially on IFR checkrides. These observations explain why my first instrument instructor bid for early retirement at the place where all crazed flight instructors go: "El Casa de Burnout." It's been over twenty years, and I think he's still there.

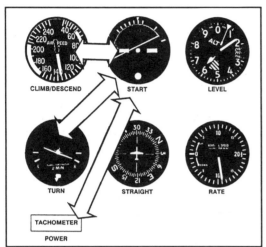

Fig. 6. "Radial Scanning" the primary instruments for a descending turn.

Figure 6 shows the proper instrument scan for a descending turn. The primary instruments for this condition are: airspeed for pitch, the turn coordinator for bank and the tachometer for power. The power is reduced as a right, 20 degree banking turn, of approximately 3 degrees nose down pitch is selected. An initial application of trim is applied to stabilize the airplane, thereby completing step 1 of the scan. The airspeed indicator, turn coordinator and tachometer are initially radial scanned, and small adjustments to the attitude indicator are made to make the primary instruments indicate correctly.

Figure 7 shows the proper instrument scan for an ILS approach. The ILS approach requires that a constant rate descent be maintained, as well as a specific airspeed. The VSI becomes primary for pitch control, the heading indicator becomes primary for bank and the airspeed becomes primary for power. Remember, although the airspeed is not labeled as a primary power instrument in figure 3, it does serve this purpose when making a constant rate descent on an ILS approach. This is the one exception to primary instrument identity as marked underneath the instrument. The throttle position is predicated on maintaining a specific airspeed; therefore the airspeed indicator becomes primary for power.

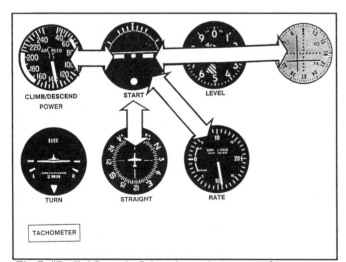

Fig. 7. "Radial Scanning" the primary instruments for a constant rate descent while on an ILS.

STEP THREE OF THE SCAN

Step three, the last step, is to make the final trim adjustments using the VSI and monitor scan (see next page) the new aircraft attitude on the BIG-6 instruments. Step three is accomplished once all the primary instruments have been radial scanned and are indicating the proper values. If rudder trim is available, it should be used first, followed by aileron trim, then elevator trim. For most small general aviation airplanes, the elevator trim will usually be the only one available on the aircraft. To properly trim the airplane for pitch, the VSI should be used. This instrument is very sensitive for "SMALL" pitch changes and will indicate almost immediately the direction of movement. The VSI also has a large, noticeable needle swing that is visually easy to identify. When leveling off, or when established in a climb or descent, trim for a constant VSI indication.

A gradual easing of control pressure will make it evident if the airplane is properly trimmed. There is never any reason to let go of the controls <u>when</u> <u>trimming</u> to see what the airplane will do. This causes pilots more heartaches than it's worth. By letting go of the controls, an untrimmed airplane could rapidly deviate from the planned flight attitude, depending on just how out of trim it was. Pilots must now return the airplane to its previous flight condition before they can re-trim. It's so much easier to ease up on control pressure, observe VSI needle movement and make a corresponding change in the trim. Very small adjustments in trim can now be made without having to recapture a runaway airplane. Another valid reason to hold onto the controls while trimming is turbulence. In turbulent air, pilots can still apply aileron control while trimming for pitch.

Once the airplane is properly trimmed, pilots can use the rudders to control the direction of the aircraft. They simply apply enough rudder pressure to keep the airplane on its desired heading. This frees them to sort charts, tune radios and complete cockpit chores that require the use of two hands. The airplane may wander up and down a trickle, but it won't stray a great deal from the desired flight condition. This is rather consistent with what pilots already know. They "walked" the airplane down a runway for takeoff, and they "walked" a heading with their feet to land. Minor heading changes are easily "walked" enroute also.

HAIL OF AN IDEA!

This story is about when all the lights went out and all those circuit breakers started tripping. The First Officer and I were well equipped with size "D" cell flashlights -- you know, those heavy duty jobbers made of aluminum that the fuel truck could run over and not squash. His was a two-cell and mine a three-cell. We had lots of long-lasting light to supplement the lousy two light bulbs that are supposed to illuminate the instrument panel -- or what is left of the instrument panel when one is operating on emergency power.

We had our hands full. The stabilizer was stuck at 1/2 degree, so the bloomin' airplane was trying to dive into the ground; the auto pressurization had failed, along with the auto temp control and, of course, the autopilot. The captain's heading and attitude indicator circuit breakers had tripped, so heading information was available only from the standby compass which is not illuminated and has to be viewed through two mirrors... but that is another story. What I needed here was one of those little flashlights fighter pilots use that you can hold in your teeth to give you one more hand to fight the airplane. I now carry one in my flight bag as a back-up along with the spare batteries and bulbs that zing the x-ray machines. We made it down OK...and my big ol' three-cell was still running when the last of the passengers walked off, just as the ship's batteries ran down.

So, there you have it folks: the "D" cell flashlight (or its equivalent) is required by FARs for some aircraft. But no matter what bird you fly, some of you may decide that it makes good sense to pack a mini-flashlight as your back-up.   **ASRS REPORT**

After the final trim adjustments are made, the BIG-6, or six main panel instruments, are monitor scanned. This may be done in a sideways fashion, going from the top row to the bottom row of instruments, or in a clockwise, circular fashion. Basically, pilots may select any particular scanning pattern with which they feel comfortable. The objective is to monitor deviations from the established attitude. When deviations are noted, small adjustments should be made on the attitude indicator to maintain the desired flight conditions. Monitor scanning is the condition in which pilots spend most of their time. Therefore, step three is continuously performed until a new flight attitude is desired. All three steps of the scan procedure will, once again, be repeated when a major attitude change is made.

The first two steps of the three step scan process should take about 10 seconds, with each step taking about 5 seconds. There are instances where pilots must return to step two of the scan. In turbulence, or when on an instrument approach, they may find themselves obliged to rapidly radial scan the primary instruments to maintain precise control of the airplane. Remember, radial scanning is a lot of work: visually, intellectually and emotionally. It is possible to radial scan all the instruments on the panel, but this is usually unnecessary and can become very tiresome. Radial scan only those instruments necessary to control the airplane.

TIPS FROM THE PROFESSIONALS

Over the years, some professionals have reported a rather unusual method of detecting instrument deviation once the airplane's attitude has been established and the aircraft trimmed. These pilots focus their vision in the center of the panel, just underneath the attitude indicator. Relying upon only their peripheral vision, they watch for any instrument movement. In much the same way as a speed reader is taught to take in three to four words at a glance, instrument pilots can absorb information from clusters of instruments at a single glance. Developing peripheral vision takes practice, but it does seem to represent the higher art of instrument flying. Until then, when step 3 of the scan is completed, pilots should keep their eyes moving around the panel, looking for attitude deviations.

PITOT HEAT

PILOTS SHOULD NEVER BLOW INTO THE PITOT TUBE, ESPECIALLY IF THE PITOT HEAT IS ON. THEY MIGHT HEAR SOMETHING THAT SOUNDS SIMILAR TO BACON FRYING!

The radial scan is useful for scanning non-control items in the aircraft. Everyone remembers the perilous experience of driving an automobile with an "attack" bumblebee flying about. From the outside, the hand movements look like a hyperexcited person, in convulsions, trying to land a B-29. People didn't crash their car in instances like this, because of the way they allocated their time and attention to the problem. They looked at the road, went hunting for the little critter, then looked back at the road again. While the little varmint was yelling, "Tora, Tora, Tora," the insect was being radial scanned with the road being the starting point. This is similar to how the attitude indicator is used in the radial scanning process.

The radial scan can be relied upon when scanning approach plates, radios, engine instruments or copying clearances. The secret to airplane control, when looking away from the panel, is to return to the attitude indicator every few seconds and make small adjustments to keep the airplane in the planned flight path.

SUBTLE SECRETS

After a certain amount of exposure to instrument flying, many pilots start to notice subtle secrets that make instrument flying easier. Professionals understand that these little bits of information are what add polish to the art of flying instruments. In many cases, these subtle clues are a direct contradiction to what pilots have been taught about instrument procedures early in their flying career.

For instance, does the airspeed indicator have a lag in its response? Many instrument pilots say it does. Experienced professionals know this just isn't accurate. If a pilot walked out to an airplane and blew into the pitot tube, two things would happen. One, all the valves on every mechanic's heart would seize with shock at such a sight. Never blow into a pitot tube, under any circumstance. The delicate pressure sensing mechanism inside the instrument would be immediately damaged. Second, the instant a pilot blew into the pitot tube, the airspeed needle would immediately indicate Mach 3. There would be no appreciable lag whatsoever in this instrument.

The apparent lag in the airspeed indicator is caused by the airplane's inertia, or resistance to changing speed. When the nose is raised, the airplane begins losing speed. It may take a few seconds for the airplane to settle down to a new velocity. This implies that pilots should select a specific attitude, then wait for the airspeed to settle down to its final value. If the airspeed is still off its assignment, then change the attitude and wait for the new indication. Chasing the airspeed indicator is a common error among new instrument pilots, but, it's an error an experienced professional avoids making. That's why the deviation is stopped first, then a correction is applied.

SERIOUS CIRRUS THOUGHTS

Approach called with instructions to use the DME arc to Runway 13 ILS. The weather was ideal. I had never executed a DME arc before. This airport does not have radar. All of my instrument training had been in a radar environment. I flew the arc well; but in retrospect, I realize that I flew it too well. I flew right through the localizer without realizing it, and continued around the arc for a while before I realized my error. There was no danger this time, but I have not been able to stop thinking about just how bad this could have been in real IFR weather. My training and checkride was in a single without DME; now I fly a twin with DME. I made sure when I bought the twin that I knew how to fly it. I should have had instruction on the DME as well. Now I know better! **ASRS REPORT**

When instrument pilots get a few instrument flying hours under their belts, they learn time can be saved by memorizing an array of power settings for specific conditions of flight. Setting 1,900 RPM into the tachometer yields a constant rate descent of approximately 500 feet per minute at 100 knots in a Cessna 172 or Piper Warrior. The difficulty arises when the RPM is set while the airplane is above the intended approach speed. Professionals are aware that when power is reduced from the cruise setting to 1,900 RPM, the higher airspeed will have a "pin-wheel" effect on the tachometer reading. Essentially, higher airspeed will cause the RPM to act like a pin-wheel and vary with a change in airspeed. When the airplane is slowed to the new approach speed, the decrease in wind flowing over the propeller will cause the RPM to settle to a lower setting.

An experienced professional handles this problem by setting the tachometer about 50 to 75 RPM higher than the desired setting when slowing the airplane. Similarly, when increasing speed, the tachometer is set 50 to 75 RPM lower than the desired setting, since the RPM indication will increase with an increase in airspeed.

Experienced professionals know the attitude indicator offers its own brand of instrument error. At the completion of a 180 turn, the attitude indicator will experience the greatest error due to precession, indicating a slight climb and a slight turn in the opposite direction. This precessional error tends to cancel itself out if an additional 180 degrees of turn is made in the same direction. When making a turn of approximately 180 degrees, pilots should be prepared for the attitude indicator to precess and anticipate its reading to be in error. This precessional error varies between instruments and will generally take from 5 to 15 seconds to completely disappear. This emphasizes the value of the primary instruments during this short period.

The vertical speed indicator is an instrument that has not received the credit it deserves. While the VSI does have a slight lag, pilots can quickly learn to anticipate this and become fairly good at flying specific rates. This is what allows a pilot who is considered a "good stick" to fly the VSI on an ILS and keep the indication within 20 to 30 feet per minute of a specific indication in smooth air. When the airplane's attitude is abruptly changed, the VSI will initially show a slight climb or descent in the opposite direction of movement. This is because of the inertia of the needle and inner mechanisms, which vary with change in "G-force." This is why the VSI is a superb "trend" indicator.

The VSI, once mastered, provides useful information for precise control of an aircraft. Taking time to learn to fly the VSI with a great deal of precision will pay off handsomely. Most pilots find the VSI very useful in level flight. Instead of radial scanning only the altimeter during any level flight condition, they additionally scan the VSI. The large swing arc of the needle, and its greater sensitivity, make for an immediate indication of deviation from level flight.

Pilots should practice until they can keep the VSI needle within 50 feet per minute of a specific value during a constant rate descent in fairly smooth air. Pilots who can do this can probably pass the toughest ATP checkride, even if it's with inspector "Pinkslip." I've seen pilots who can keep the needle paralyzed at a specific rate. I thought the instrument was broken! These pilots realize that precision control of the VSI is the key to shooting enviable ILS approaches and maintaining altitudes within the 10 to 20 foot mark. This is certainly a skill worth developing.

There are many boring things to do in life, but instrument flying isn't one of them. The art of flying instruments is a challenging test of a pilot's mettle. Instrument flying offers pilots the opportunity to master their airplane and themselves. A rather sophisticated form of satisfaction results from this combination. Perhaps this is why most instrument pilots are so happy. They realize the scope of their accomplishment. However, pilots should warn their fellow instrument pilots at the airport not to look too happy or someone will make them take a drug test.

My good friend Dave was flying his 727 when the controller came on the radio and asked, "Flight 1313, what are you vacating?" Dave replied, "The last two weeks of September, how about you?" Communication difficulties are a real problem in IFR flight, especially when pilots have problems communicating with themselves. The next phase of instrument flight that pilots are required to master is learning to communicate through the use of self-talk dialogues.

*FOOTNOTE FROM PAGE 15 - The primary instruments, with the exception of the heading indicator, operate on power systems that are separate and independent from the attitude indicator. This implies that a failure of one power system will be noticed as a discrepancy between the primary instrument and the attitude indicator. In many aircraft, the heading indicator operates on the same vacuum system as the attitude indicator. Since the heading indicator is primary for bank when performing any "straight" maneuver (i.e. straight and level, straight climb or descent), there may be concern about how the attitude indicator's accuracy can additionally be determined in this condition. In addition to checking control application against attitude indicator response, there are a couple of ways erroneous bank information on the attitude indicator would be noticed. First, the turn coordinator is in the pilot's peripheral vision when the heading indicator is being scanned. Any failure of the attitude indicator would probably be observed on the turn coordinator, when the heading indicator is radial scanned. In other words, if the heading indicator isn't moving, and the turn coordinator is, the vacuum system may have failed; therefore, the turn triangle of agreement should be consulted. Second, the heading indicator and the attitude indicator, in a failing mode, may indicate conflicting attitude information. This may occur as the gyros spin down and behave in a peculiar manner. Despite the attitude indicator and the heading indicator operating on the same power system, these additional means of detecting vacuum failure should be comforting to the pilot.

3. SELF TALK DIALOGUES

After mastering the instruments with the three step scan procedure, pilots now must learn to master themselves. Psychologists state that people may spend up to 70% of their time talking to themselves. Certainly there is nothing peculiar about this behavior, as long as it's not done out loud, with witnesses. However, at Denny's restaurant around 3 o'clock in the morning, this particular behavior is considered quite normal. Self dialogues are a very important part of the process governing behavior, and it's these dialogues that have a considerable effect on a pilot's ability to learn to fly instruments professionally.

Silently talking to oneself is as much a part of daily experience as eating, drinking and sleeping. If people were to stop this silent, internal dialogue, they would have to respond to the world through mental pictures and visceral emotions. While this may have some interesting psychological results, it wouldn't be immediately useful, since most of a person's more sophisticated behaviors were learned through the coding of the English language. Therefore, behaviors are shaped by the language used to install them.

One linguistics professor reaffirmed the power of language to change people's behavior. The professor said that it's man's ability to use language that makes him the dominant species on the planet. A crusty, older flight instructor at the airport disagreed with this bit of wisdom. This fellow believed that what sets us apart from all the other animals on the planet is that humans are not afraid of vacuum cleaners. I don't particularly share this line of reasoning. Perhaps having 25,000 hours teaching and observing humanity from the right seat of a small trainer alters a person's thinking process in peculiar ways.

GOOD ATTITUDE INDICATOR

Simply stated, one secret to accelerated learning and successful instrument flying is when pilots know what to say to themselves and how often it should be said.

Self talk activity serves to guide flying behavior in reminding pilots to accomplish tasks such as lowering the landing gear prior to touchdown, or closing their flight plans at the destination airport. Used correctly by a student or an educator, this self talk behavior can be a valuable asset in the acceleration of a pilot's learning to fly instruments.

After many years of observing pilots learning to fly instruments, it became apparent that those individuals whose behavior improved most efficiently, in the early stages of instrument training, were responding in a more active, self directed manner. Their behavior was being "self guided" through an internal dialogue consisting of a specific set of questions or statements. These questions or statements offer something similar to an audio checklist, reminding pilots of the order and frequency of behaviors to be performed. The objective of the self talk dialogue is to make a particular behavior so reflexive that the internal dialogue no longer becomes necessary.

THE PANIC ATTACK AND DISSOCIATION

When pilots are overcome by panic, self talk becomes very helpful, if not life saving. This form of communication has been known, for many years, to help people maintain the inertia of proper response while in the throes of anxiety. It's as if the verbal portion of the psyche can command the behavioral part of the mind. Words are symbols having a tremendous power of influence over people's behavior, regardless of whether they say them or someone else says them.

Psychologists have been saying for years, when overcome by erratic behavioral inertia, people should immediately start telling themselves what to do, either silently or aloud. Panic, the inability to function effectively, can best be dealt with by saying, "OK, remain calm, breathe slowly" or "Slow down, relax, look at the problem" or "Wait, let's think before acting." These statements have been known to save one's life when gripped by incapacitating fear, anger or panic.

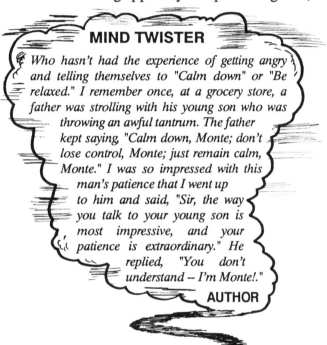

MIND TWISTER

Who hasn't had the experience of getting angry and telling themselves to "Calm down" or "Be relaxed." I remember once, at a grocery store, a father was strolling with his young son who was throwing an awful tantrum. The father kept saying, "Calm down, Monte; don't lose control, Monte; just remain calm, Monte." I was so impressed with this man's patience that I went up to him and said, "Sir, the way you talk to your young son is most impressive, and your patience is extraordinary." He replied, "You don't understand – I'm Monte!."

AUTHOR

The proper self dialogue can be of benefit to help pilots purposefully change their behavior in an airplane. I have always been impressed with those individuals who, in the face of overwhelming odds, continue to perform their emergency piloting duties. Consider fighter pilots who have lost their engine in IFR conditions and still carefully follow the required emergency procedures to the letter, despite their airplane being summoned to earth by gravitational forces. Highly trained pilots can feel almost dissociated, or outside themselves, when in the throes of an emergency situation. This emotional detachment allows them to be intensely involved in solving the emergency problem on an intellectual level and not be distracted by debilitating emotions like fear.

This dissociation effect probably results from two things: 1) pilots having sufficient training in emergency procedures to feel overwhelming confidence in their application; and 2) following a specific internal dialogue that implements these procedures. Essentially, pilots know what to do as a result of their training, then, proceed to direct themselves while performing the required behavior. If pilots were to respond to deep, visceral emotions in the face of an emergency, they would probably be prone to panic.

For some pilots, the first solo was responsible for producing such an anxious and primitive response. When it was announced that they were to solo, they could be seen running from the airplane, through the runup area, while being chased by the flight instructor. When they were finally caught, they wrapped their hands around the instructor's waist and refused to let go. It usually took four firemen and the "Jaws of Life" to separate them. Internal dialogues keep the pilot's mind away from the instinctual, more primitive responses and focused on rational, unemotional solutions to the problem. Pilots do not "go spontaneous" -- it kills!

BIG PICTURE SELF TALK

Directed self dialogue can dramatically increase an instrument pilot's rate of learning about positional awareness during instrument approaches. This offers great value since most instrument students, starting the approach phase of their training, often find it difficult to maintain an awareness of their position. This "big picture" orientation is an absolute necessity for safe flight in the IFR system.

Instrument students often fly through approach courses, forget descents and often have little or no idea of their position. Perhaps this explains why controllers have been heard to ask IFR students questions like, "32 Bravo, where are you going?" Students often reply, "Wherever this thing is pointed, buddy." I have found that the following self dialogue of three questions, develops the "big picture" comprehension necessary for safe instrument flying. The three questions are:

> ## 1. WHERE AM I GOING?
> ## 2. HOW DO I GET THERE?
> ## 3. WHAT DO I DO NEXT?

These questions represent one of the most important internal dialogues instrument pilots can develop. Pilots should be continuously asking themselves these three questions as they are moving in the IFR system. They may be asked silently or aloud, depending on preference, although CFI's prefer having instrument students ask them aloud. I have found that professional pilots automatically seek the same information offered by asking these questions. After many years of training, their behavior is so reflexive, they don't have to prod themselves to ask the questions to get the information. With a little practice, pilots will find this information soliciting behavior will soon become automatic.

The first question, "Where am I going?" helps pilots understand that they are headed toward some specific navigational course and must accomplish a number of tasks in order to get there. It's very easy for instrument pilots to be so occupied with flying, that there is not a spare gray cell left. This is called "paralysis by analysis." Student instrument pilots, in the throes of intense instrument flying, frequently don't envision the end goal of the radar vector or navigational track. They may be vectored to an airway and have a specific radial as the destination end point. They may be navigating on a radial to an intersection, at which point a procedure turn will be accomplished. It's very important for pilots to keep a mental picture of the destination intersection; otherwise, they may not recognize when they have gone beyond this point.

PROPERLY DONE

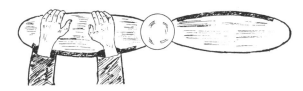

I experienced an engine failure at 3500'. I prepared for a forced landing. There were four types of terrain available: lakes, open swamps, small timber up to 20 feet tall with butts up to five inches, and heavy large timber up to 50 feet tall with large butt size. I chose the small timber and entered it with airspeed in excess of 70 MPH. The aircraft clipped off the small trees for a distance of 85 paces before a wheel touched the ground and then stopped in another 20 paces. Because the small trees brought the aircraft to a stop gently, none of the occupants were injured. The point of this is that the safest forced landing terrain -- other than a hard, smooth long surface like a road or runway -- is in small timber, brush or new growth that is probably not over 20 feet tall.

ASRS REPORT

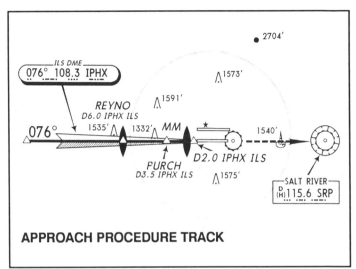

APPROACH PROCEDURE TRACK

Fig. 1. The approach procedure track (thick, black line) is where pilots can expect to be radar vectored.

Remember, pilots are always navigating toward a specific spot during IFR flight. When the controller asked them where they wanted to go, they didn't say, "Oh, it doesn't matter, whatever is convenient for you." Who knows what awful place they would have been sent? During radar vectoring to an instrument approach, the "someplace" pilots are going, is the black, thick line in the center of the approach chart, as seen in figure 1. This maximum thick line is known as the approach procedure track.

Pilots should keep in mind, no matter what is happening during the radar vectoring process, they are going to end up on that thick black line. Radar vectoring would, perhaps, be a more pleasant experience for the controller if he just said, "Hey, 32 Bravo, do you see that big, black line? Well, go get it; 'sic'em boy'." With an end goal like this in mind, pilots would easily get on the course and the controller would probably be happier than a Russian radar man receiving a position report from a Stealth Bomber.

During one IFR day in Southern California, an apprentice controller was given the job of vectoring aircraft to the localizer at a local airport. Her trainer's attention was diverted from the screen and the scope suddenly got very busy. She accidentally vectored one aircraft through the localizer. When the pilot complained she brought the aircraft around and accidentally vectored it through the localizer once again. This happened a third time. She finally got so frustrated that she picked up the microphone and said, "32B, these vectors aren't working, for gosh sakes, take over visually and save yourself!"

Author

Asking, "How do I get there?" allows pilots to develop a navigational strategy to get to the location in the first question. It also permits them to analyze if the current navigational strategy is going to work. There is always a heading, or a route to fly, that will move them closer to the final objective. In the case of an instrument approach, that objective is the approach procedure track. This question develops the positional awareness necessary to identify any incongruities between where they are and where they want to go.

When pilots are being vectored toward the ILS-30 instrument approach, they should always use their navigational equipment to keep themselves oriented to the approach course. Unfortunately, some pilots use their navigational equipment only to tell them when they have arrived, rather than if they will arrive on the approach course. When inbound on the approach, they'll be tracking in an approximate direction of 300 degrees. Therefore, a left needle indication means they must fly some heading to the left of 300 degrees, or they will never get closer to the approach course. A right needle deflection means they must fly some heading to the right of 300 degrees to intercept the localizer. Using their navigational equipment this way will help pilots to determine if their present heading will take them closer to their intended destination.

Proper planning is the result of asking the third question, "What do I do next?" Professional pilots are constantly planning for the next course to be intercepted, the next radio to be set or the next chart to be accessed. With an ATC system that frequently demands complete attention, pilots cannot afford to forgo planning for the next phase of flight. The subtle prodding offered by this question is indispensable to successful instrument flying.

Pilots should keep in mind that there is always something for them to do while in flight, even if it is checking circuit breakers or ammeter indications. When caught up, with nothing to do, there is a good chance that something has already been forgotten. This question keeps pilots thinking. When instrument pilots stop thinking, they are being stalked by the Grim Reaper and are candidates for the Museum of the Permanently Still. In a busy terminal environment, there should be no time when pilots are not asking these questions at least once every one or two minutes. Pilots, with a professional mentality, should never find themselves in IFR flight without the consistent presence of these three questions.

HUMULONIMBUS

FORE!

While returning to the airport, flying about 1,500 feet above a golf course, my engine sputtered and stopped. Since I was at a comfortable altitude, I had plenty of time to choose an appropriate fairway -- facing the wind, with an uphill slope and no people. I spiraled down and made a fine power off landing...no damage, no injuries. While refueling, several golfers told me about their flying days during WWll, and asked if I would please depart as I came in -- without interrupting their game.

And please call out loudly "FORE" before commencing takeoff. **ASRS REPORT**

SEE IT, SAY IT, CHECK IT

Another problem experienced by most instrument pilots is making small but devastating mistakes with numbers (and sometimes letters). All pilots can remember having set their VOR course selector and heading bugs to a number different than desired. Certainly anyone who has ever flown can remember setting the radios to an inappropriate frequency. There is a way of minimizing these mistakes by initiating another self dialogue.

Repeating the words, "See it, say it, check it" provides the key for the proper check and balance to minimize these mistakes. When pilots are involved in any activity using letters or numbers, they should make sure to "SEE" the specific character they are using. They should repeat the words, "SEE IT" to themselves as they're referencing the specific value on the chart, instrument or navigation equipment. This statement should compel pilots to specifically study the number or letter being used. For instance, when setting the OBS to a specific number, they should make sure they see the radial number on the chart, as well as seeing the number as it is set into the VOR equipment. They should look at this number as set into the equipment and compare it to the airway direction seen on the chart. When programming a loran, they should make sure they see the exact three letter airport, navaid or intersection identifier set into the equipment.

Next, pilots should "SAY" the letter or number aloud as they set their equipment. Psychologists tell us that a small percentage of the population, although they are quite functional, sometimes experience dysnumeria. This is similar to dyslexia, but it concerns numbers instead of letters. Now, that's not anorexia-dyslexia, which means that you can read thin books backwards. Dysnumeria is an impairment in sequencing numbers. This can be more than just a nuisance in an airplane.

HOOD WINKED

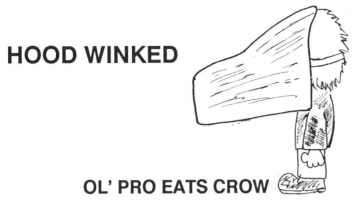

OL' PRO EATS CROW

Upon taking off from the high altitude field (VFR in TCA), I reported to Departure and was instructed to climb to 7000'. I was then instructed to resume my own navigation, so I turned to about 220 degrees and leveled at 7000'. I gave a radio call, "Level at 7000," with no answer. I intended to give another call when the controller asked, "Are you climbing or what? I showed you at 8000 feet." I responded that I was level at 7000'. He replied with a traffic report at 8000 in an area to my right. I spotted it about 3/4 mile to my right, at an altitude of, perhaps, 100 feet lower than I. It passed ahead of me, and I resumed my heading (I had turned left when observing the traffic). When he passed he told the controller, "That guy sure is not at 7000." The controller informed me that I was leaving the TCA, "Squawk 1200." I said, "Thanks, I'll get my altimeter checked." And I was very serious: I thought I was having trouble with my Mode C when he first reported the improper altitude. I was sure that everything was properly set and functioning during preflight and takeoff. We had been having trouble with the Mode C transponder and had had it in the shop. But that was not the problem -- it was ME! After leaving the TCA, I tuned back in on the airport ATIS and heard 30.16. This shocked me, as I was certain it was 29.16 when I set it during preflight. In fact, that was the first thing I looked at when the controller said I was at 8000.

Well, I did a lot of thinking about making such a stupid mistake. You see, I have always prided myself about being a real pro when it came to my flying -- former Chief Pilot, instructor, etc. So, how did Ol'Pro get himself into such a fix? The biggest single cause was, likely, fatigue. I had been involved in a number of serious business issues of late, not sleeping well, got to the airport on a tight schedule, only to find that they had forgotten to ramp my plane. By the time I climbed into the plane, I had set myself up real good: not for flying, but for goofing! And that's what I did. During my preflight, I set the wrong ??.16 on the altimeter. In the long run, this will serve as a good lesson; I now realize that I am not invulnerable. I'd better start listening to some of the advice I have so freely given in the past about not flying when over-stressed, etc., etc. I may even take some vacation...

Perhaps some other perfect pro will benefit from this. P.S. Please excuse the lousy typing job. You wouldn't expect me to have my secretary type it; what would she think of me - a perfect boss?

ASRS REPORT

Under the stressful conditions of instrument flying, the misinterpretation of a letter or numerical value is apt to be more common. Saying the specific heading, altitude or frequency aloud, lessens the chance of error. This visual and aural contrast should allow any discrepancy to be apparent. This is why most airlines require their pilots to repeat "all" numbers back to the controller.

Short term memory retains seven to nine items for approximately 20 seconds, then abandons the antique of the group. This is why some clearances can easily exceed a pilot's ability to retain information without committing it to paper. An additional value of repeating numbers or letters is that short term memory is reinforced 25% to 100% with aural repetition. This increases the chances of the correct value being used. Seeing the correct letter or numerical value, then saying the numbers, is sure to offer the necessary check and balance to minimize errors.

Saying "CHECK IT" offers a final check by prodding pilots to assure the specific value a final time. Looking back at the specific letter or numerical value to be used, disciplines pilots to prevent making regrettable mistakes.

AWARENESS SELF TALK

Maintaining a high degree of awareness is essential during instrument flight. Professional instrument pilots have trained themselves to be highly aware and on the lookout for any problems that could arise. Good pilots are suspicious people! Apathy is pathetic. There is nothing worse than floating along in the system for a couple of hours, then discovering the ammeter needle has disappeared off the left side of the instrument.

The alternator output was so low, it appeared the electrical equipment actually sucked the needle into the wires. This is not the type of problem pilots want to discover during solid IFR flight. At this point, most pilots have been known to start making transmissions without using the radio. It seems the person they wish to communicate with doesn't require a radio to be reached. What they're saying is, "Hello Allah; come in Buddha; speak to me Krishna."

The following questions are so important for maintaining a high degree of cockpit awareness they should be asked reflexively every few minutes. Professional pilots routinely ask themselves some version of the following questions:

> 1. "HOW AM I FEELING?"
> 2. "HOW IS THE AIRCRAFT?"
> 3. "HOW IS THE ENVIRONMENT?"

Asking, "How am I feeling?" should cause pilots enough introspection to allow them to assess their physical and emotional state of well-being. Sometimes pilots just don't attend to these states, thereby ending up highly fatigued, agitated or hungry without even being aware of it. This is certainly not safe. Ask any pilot who hasn't eaten for quite a while. With the liability of low blood sugar, mental capabilities fade quickly. After a few hours without food, they can start to feel like they have an IQ a grade lower than bean dip. They could even start hallucinating, misinterpreting the clock's sweep second hand for the weather radar and every 30 degrees noticing precipitation taking the shape of big numbers.

At the slightest indication of physical or emotional debility pilots must get their airplane down. It takes a pilot's full concentration to handle an airplane in solid IFR. Being out of shape doesn't help much either. I have a friend who is so out of shape that he gets winded putting on a seat belt. In fact, the last time he ran was in 1973, and that was because he didn't hear the bells on the ice cream truck. Pilots have no business flying unless they are in reasonable shape.

KICK IN THE EMPENNAGE

On an IFR cross country flight, in a turbo-charged, small airplane, over-the-mountains, a pilot and his three passengers were all on oxygen. The pilot and the front passenger were on the built-in system and the two rear passengers were on a portable system. The pilot knew the portable tank of oxygen would likely run out before the descent was made below 13,000 feet. He planned to switch the rear passengers to the built-in system. He had instructed the rear passengers to let him know when the tank gauge was at 200 PSI, or if the flow indicator turned red. We were transferred to Approach, who wanted a fast descent. There were heavy cumulus clouds with moderate turbulence and the pilot was concentrating on the busy, turbulent approach. He did not check the rear oxygen tank pressure/flow, as he had been doing regularly during cruise. At about 11,000 feet, the rear passengers "awoke" -- somewhat confused with no flow to their masks. Obviously, the rear passengers ran out of oxygen during the descent and, either because they forgot to check or because of the effects of hypoxia, they did not realize they were running out. The pilot, who had been watching the rear tank, neglected same because of a demanding instrument approach. No apparent damage was done to the passengers. Everyone was thankful for a good outcome, but frightened by what might have been.

ASRS REPORT

Pilots should expect problems with fatigue more at night than during the day. Perhaps this offers a partial explanation as to why there are 10 times more single pilot IFR accidents at night than during the day. These IFR pilots may be so fatigued that they're unable to maintain a high level of awareness, allowing themselves to get caught in dangerous traps. Any sign of drowsiness should be recognized as alien to a pilot's attentive nature. Pilots who find themselves fatigued can do a little trick that may help keep them fresh. They should sit up straight, and take a few deep hits off the oxygen system. This is especially useful before making an instrument approach. Even this little bit of refreshing can keep pilots sharp, giving them an extra edge on safety. Remember, the effects of hypoxia are experienced at lower altitudes at night. The eyes are usually the first organs to experience this deterioration.

There are few things more frightening than falling asleep in an airplane at night, during cruise flight, with the autopilot activated. This only has to happen once, and a pilot will never be the same again. Most, in fact, start flying with religious statues glued to the control column of their airplane.

In 1976, just such an experience was mine to claim. On a flight from Santa Barbara to Orange County airport at 11:30 p.m., my sleek A-36 Bonanza had just leveled off at 7,500 feet. This altitude was chosen to avoid the TCA and stay above an inland overcast. Visibility was not great, averaging only about 5 miles. Without a moon, the sky was exceptionally dark. The autopilot was engaged. Mesmerized by the enchanting hum of the engine, I drifted off.

Suddenly awake, gasping for breath, the reality was shocking. There was absolutely nothing to be seen in front or to the sides of my aircraft. It was pitch, pitch black! California is known for its high terrain and my spastic, pounding heart reminded me of this. Immediately glancing at the clock, it became apparent that thirty minutes of time had elapsed that were unaccounted for. I quickly turned 180 degrees, checked fuel and reestablished my position. Whether I was too dazed to account for this time or fast asleep, will never be known. This is perhaps one of the most frightening experiences pilots can have.

PROFESSIONAL TIPS

WHEN THE PASSENGERS ARE IN THE GREEN, A SEASONED PROFESSIONAL CFI WILL TAPE THE BARF BAG TO THEIR HEAD. THIS FREES THE PASSENGER'S HANDS TO APPLY THE "TIBETAN DEATH GRIP" TO THE FRONT SEAT.

Now my flight bag provides whole sunflower seeds for those long night cross-countries, to keep me awake. No pilot can fall asleep while ferreting out these tiny nuts from their shells. I also make it a point to carry red pistachio nuts for my copilot. This keeps me awake thinking about how much fun I am going to have watching him walk around the airport with big red lips.

Asking, "How is the aircraft?" should prompt pilots to monitor all engine, electrical and vacuum instruments. They should start at the left side of the panel and work their way across, looking at every instrument, making sure it's indicating properly. Are the gauges in the green? Are the passengers in the green? Perhaps smoother air should be found. How's the ammeter doing? Does it show a needle deflection comparable to the electrical demand of the equipment being used? It should. What about the vacuum gauge? If the vacuum pump is lost, then a partial panel must be flown. They call it partial panel because pilots realize just how partial they are to those instruments that aren't working.

Asking, "How is the environment?" should cue pilots to assess any unfavorable changes in the weather. If anything even looks suspicious, they should start asking more questions. In addition, this question is quite valuable for many other inflight situations. For example, when pilots are entering a busy terminal area in VFR conditions, they must concern themselves with traffic vigilance as well as flying the instrument approach. While landing, it's very important for pilots to pay attention to the runway environment. After all, there may be something on it that's not supposed to be there.

Cautious pilots are constantly checking their environment. They carefully monitor the taxiway for obstructions, and visually verify that no one is approaching to land before they taxi onto the runway. Cautious pilots know they only have to let their guard down once to get bitten.

WINGING IT

Dave Gwinn, an airline pilot, and CFI, was taxiing with a student when they saw a helicopter parked right in the middle of the taxi way. The controller came on the radio and said, "35 Bravo, I'm not talking to that helicopter." Dave came back with, "OK, then we won't speak to him either."

EMERGENCY SELF TALK

Handling inflight emergencies can be accomplished by using another self-talk dialogue that compels pilots to use a rational approach to solving the problem. The following four questions should be asked whenever any unusual situation presents itself in the airplane:

```
1. "WHAT IS HAPPENING?"
2. "WHAT ACTIONS MUST I TAKE TO CORRECT THE PROBLEM?"
3. "WHAT LIMITATIONS MUST I NOW OBSERVE?"
4. "WHEN DO I HAVE TO LAND?"
```

The first question, "What is happening?" directs pilots to specifically identify the problem and its effect on their airplane. There are times when pilots hesitate to identify the precise problem, and these precious moments, once lost, cannot be recovered. Asking this question starts the ferreting out process so necessary to immediately solve aviation problems.

Sometimes inflight problems are subtle, and it is difficult to identify precisely what is happening. Inflight icing can be one of these insidious problems. It is possible that pilots with insufficient experience in icing conditions, might not realize they are ice collectors until it's too late. Pilots who have experienced icing at night understand it's difficult to see, unless they're specifically looking for it. This is one reason why IFR pilots carry flashlights (hopefully, that's not the container in which they carry their dead batteries) at night. Illuminating the wing or the windshield with the flashlight will usually identify the icing problem. Icing can go unnoticed until pilots have a full scale, aerodynamic danger on their hands.

Sometimes inflight problems are blatantly easy to identify. If the problem is an engine failure, then, rest assured, these are pretty easy to detect. In fact, passengers are most helpful in pointing out these problems for the pilot. On one charter flight, in a Cessna 421, caution told me to shut down an engine during cruise flight because of an over temperature condition. The throttle was gently eased back, the propeller gently feathered and the plane was trimmed with a minimum of telltale vibration.

WHEN PASSENGERS RENT AN AIRCRAFT WITH TWO ENGINES, THEY EXPECT BOTH OF THEM TO BE USED DURING THE FLIGHT

Suddenly, one of the passengers leans through the curtains and says, "Hey! What's happening, buddy?" as he's pointing to the engine. Trying to use a little humor, my retort was, "Oh, it's just a spare, and we don't use it much in cruise unless the other one stops." He went, "OH...OK." Amazingly, that satisfied him for a few minutes, until the other three passengers discussed multi-engine airplanes and the number of engines they rented. They suspected something was up and I was now forced to explain exactly what was happening.

The second question to ask is, "What actions must I perform to correct the problem?" Essentially, pilots should be trying to discover what must be done to return the situation to normal. With an icing problem, pilots should respond in one of two ways: either get out of the clouds, or go where the temperatures are warmer than freezing. The answer is very clear for this type of problem.

If the problem was an engine failure with some assurance of no internal damage, then the action to be taken is to attempt a restart. Engine failures are usually caused by pilots running out of fuel, or not being able to find the fuel that's onboard. Pilots should reroute the fuel, if this is an option. If no more fuel remains, then they have an entirely different problem and should return to question number one.

Once the problem has been identified and action taken, pilots should ask, "What limitations must I now observe?" With a full load of ice, they must now operate within specific limitations. This would not be a good time for them to practice their commercial maneuvers, such as chandelles or lazy eights. They now have specific bank, altitude and range limitations with a whole host of other limits.

Having some practical experience with the problem is necessary to help pilots identify their limitations. Pilots may want to make an immediate descent away from icing conditions and put their gear down to expedite the descent. If they do this they are probably going to turn their airplane into a gravity test probe. They could easily become one of God's "frozen" people. The gear, blatantly exposed to the airflow, could accumulate ice so quickly it may be difficult to maintain altitude. This is why it pays to learn as much as possible about potential abnormalities and emergency situations that can be experienced under instrument flight.

A catastrophic engine failure under IFR conditions is the pilot's worst nightmare. Given options, my preference would be to parachute into a backyard full of hungry pit bulls than to contemplate a dead stick landing while in the clouds. The first action a pilot must perform under these conditions is to fly the airplane. With the probable loss of the vacuum system, pilots, not current on partial panel flying, will get a chance to practice under solid IFR emergency conditions. Attentive pilots know the location of airports that are within gliding distance. Such attention seems almost unreasonable, considering the rarity of modern engine failure. Nevertheless, pilots with the survival edge know that the only action they can take to correct such a problem is to plan in advance for this type of catastrophic occurrence.

Fortunately, problems with icing can be dealt with on a more strategic level. Pilots can often plot and scheme to manipulate a way out of the problem. There are very few instances when icing will immediately smite an airplane from the sky. Freezing rain is one of these rare occurrences. It demands immediate action. Freezing rain can whittle away lift so fast that there won't be enough time to get an open channel to the pilot's Savior of choice. A 180 degree turn is one of the most immediate actions needed to correct the problem.

The last question for dealing with inflight emergencies or abnormalities is, "When do I have to land?" With an engine failure the answer is quite clear: land now. With partial power failure, or the loss of only one engine in a twin, the situation becomes a little more complex. When pilots have any serious problem, the objective should be to get down as soon as possible. If they had the windshield implode during IFR conditions, they might want to land whether or not there is an airport underneath them. If need be, they could make their own airport by landing on a road or a field. Pilots who have lost one engine in their twin and can maintain altitude must consider other options. If they were to land at the nearest airport, without runway considerations, they might experience a

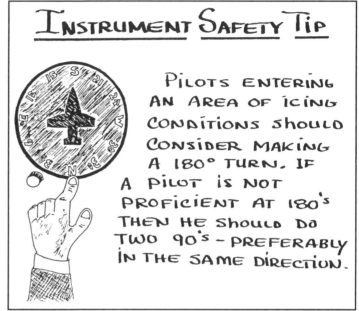

INSTRUMENT SAFETY TIP

PILOTS ENTERING AN AREA OF ICING CONDITIONS SHOULD CONSIDER MAKING A 180° TURN. IF A PILOT IS NOT PROFICIENT AT 180's THEN HE SHOULD DO TWO 90's - PREFERABLY IN THE SAME DIRECTION.

long, long rollout on a short, short runway. With a gear malfunction, they might want to select an airport with emergency facilities to handle possible complications. Having enough practical experience, either their own or the experience of others, is a must for pilots to be armed for solving emergency problems.

THE 6 T's

There is probably no instrument pilot alive who hasn't heard of the 6 T's: TURN, TIME, TUNE, THROTTLE, TALK and TRACK.* Now, there are several variations of this. I once met an instrument student who had 12 T's! I suppose if this student didn't come up for air around the 9th T, he would surely get hypoxia. One of my more nervous students added a 7th T - THROW UP. Nevertheless, the 6 T's are another excellent example of a useful self-dialogue.

Normally, the 6 T's are used at the final approach fix (FAF) of an instrument approach to fly and configure the airplane for descent to the minimum descent altitude (MDA). However, there are additional uses for the 6 T's to make instrument flying easier. When flying holding patterns, pilots will find the 6 T's a useful reminder to: turn to the specific entry heading; start the time upon entering the holding pattern entry; tune the VOR omni bearing selector to track the inbound leg of the holding pattern; throttle to the specific holding airspeed; talk to the controller to report entering holding; and track the inbound course. In fact, the 6 T's should be used when reaching an intersection, regardless of whether a turn or change in direction is required.

*The T's are performed in this order so the sequence can be used for both approaches, holding patterns and other activities. Keep in mind that this sequence is an aural checklist use to remind the pilot. As soon as the turn is started, the time may also be started. Punching the button of a timer is not a workload intensive activity so there should be no delay in starting the time on an approach.. This "T" pattern should be very versatile and work as an effective behavior reminder for approaches, holding patterns, turning at intersections, etc.

FAF SELF TALK

Another internal dialogue can be employed when inbound at the final approach fix. Pilots should ask themselves these three questions:

```
1. HOW LOW?
2. HOW LONG?
3. WHICH WAY?
```

Every instrument approach in the United States has a minimum altitude. It's possible that if pilots descend below this altitude, they may hear three little tire squeaks and notice a housing suburb where the runway should be. One fellow came back from an instrument flight with a television antenna actually impaled on the landing gear of his Cessna 172. Imagine trying to explain this to the FAA. Asking "How low," and reaffirming the minimum altitude for descent while on the approach, is always a good practice.

Asking, "How long," and "Which way," provide useful reaffirmations of critical missed approach and approach direction information. It's all too easy for pilots to fail to start their timers when inbound at the final approach fix on nonprecision approaches. It's also a common error for pilots to forget to make any additional turns required at the final approach fix to track the approach course. These last two questions, while appearing rather obvious, can offer pilots a useful defense against an inattentive mind.

Richard Buckminster Fuller, the engineer, mathematician, and planetary-change guru, once said, "The only way for people to think is by asking themselves questions." Instrument pilots must think well. It's their job. It's their internal dialogues that structure their thinking and compel them to act in the most meaningful and disciplined way. Asking questions and stating directives mentioned in the internal dialogues covered in this chapter will have a profound effect on an instrument pilot's ability to think properly in the instrument environment. It will also help propel the instrument pilot toward the next level of achievement: "Getting it."

4. MANAGING COCKPIT RESOURCES

Think back to the time when ILS approaches were as mysterious as a shaman walking on hot coals and when popping out of the top of an overcast into the blue sky seemed as wonderful as a rabbit popping out of a hat. These were times when, through subtle transformations, a pilot's inexperience and naivete were gradually catalyzed into an uplifting level of confidence, never imagined possible. Often, this shift in newly acquired confidence was subtle rather than pronounced; but when recognized, there was no denying that a valuable perspective had been acquired for instrument flying. In the parlance of New Age psychology,* a pilot can be anointed as having "Got It," and there is no denying that "It", whatever this nebulous, mental quality is, was certainly welcomed, appreciated and needed.

What is this cerebral quality of vague reference that seems so substantial to a pilot's independence in the IFR system? Is it the confidence in knowing that when robbed of visual freedom and cast into an abstract, seemingly imaginary environment of vectors and clearances that pilots can still find their way? Is it the ability to contain claustrophobic claws when a covering hood compacts the universe into a two dimensional, six dial panel? Maybe it's nothing more than, once and for all, learning just what controls airspeed and what controls altitude. Perhaps it's one, two or all three of these; but, if observation serves me correctly, to "Get It" is determined more by a pilot's ability to properly manage cockpit resources than anything else.

SET PRIORITIES

Instrument flying is a continuously shifting environment that rewards those who can adapt to its evolving demands and humbles those with predetermined conceptions. General aviation pilots must be a whole crew: captain, copilot, flight engineer, navigator, mechanic and flight attendant. In satisfying all these functions, they must become masters of allocating their time under IFR flight. Therefore, a good instrument pilot must learn the art of prioritizing items and events that occur in flight.

It's amazing how a deep, modulated and resonant voice is so compelling. When ATC calls, a pilot's first impulse may be to respond immediately, regardless of what it will cost in terms of aircraft control. Who knows what kind of banishment is in store if ATC's edict is not acted upon fast enough? At about this time, it's not unusual to see newly rated instrument pilots, so confounded with ATC requests, start shooting approaches using the ammeter needle -- a truly amazing sight to witness. When this happens, some instructors switch the pitot heat on and off just to see them start doing those S-turns while tracking.

AVIATE, NAVIGATE, COMMUNICATE

When instrument students have completed about 30 hours of instrument training, they may start to question their ability to learn instrument flying. They may start comparing themselves to other students and ask questions like, "Hey, how come Bob can do this, but I can't?" They defensively eliminate all comparative options for this alleged behavioral failure, especially the one where they momentarily

---

*Something I don't completely agree with. However, I should inform the reader that large portions of this book have been channeled by a 35,000 year old pterodactyl pilot named 'Bob.' Through Bob I have become proficient in the ancient art of dowsing for petroleum. This comes in handy at the airport when trying to find a gas truck.

concede that Bob has a bigger and more evolved brain than they have. They may be concerned that their thinking skills may be a little rusty because they attended one too many "Grateful Dead" concerts in the 60's; but, so did Bob, so, they don't place too much stock in this idea. They may be forced to conclude only one thing: "The instrument system is unfair; there just isn't enough time to aviate, navigate and communicate all at once." They now realize they can be gobbled up all at once, faster than they can pray for help or beam up a CFI. Without realizing it, they have surrendered to the first big step in becoming seasoned instrument pilots.

When ATC demands are at a peak, the seasoned instrument professional's priority system immediately goes into effect: AVIATE, NAVIGATE AND THEN COMMUNICATE. Transmitting a "Standby," or a "You're number one for the callback," to ATC may not always endear you to them, but this is not a social club! A pilot's job under IFR is to pilot the aircraft safely. Most controllers applaud and yield to this important credo. Being friendly, being firm, and insisting on flying the airplane first will allow a pilot to more easily manage important cockpit resources.

Savvy pilots are always prepared for ATC to talk at Mach-2 when the system gets busy. Several years ago, my friend, Pete Campbell, was sitting in a Baron waiting to depart IFR at a busy metropolitan airport. Anyone who has had the pleasure of listening to Pete, a professional aviation speaker, knows that he's one sharp cookie, and it's difficult to fool him. The controller delivered a clearance so fast that the radio speaker in the Baron was smoking. Pete picked up the microphone and said with his slow, southern drawl, "Any of that stuff you boys just said important?" The controller came back on and said, "Important? Hey man, that was your clearance." Pete replied, "Well then, why don't ya'll say it like it's important!" This is unconfirmed, but after he got out of the penalty box, he had a good flight but a late departure.

PROPERLY DONE

Perhaps no more important words were ever spoken than by Aviation Accident Specialist, Paul Stebelton, when he said, "Never drop airplane to fly microphone."

In preparation for the instrument rating, a great deal of emphasis is placed on keeping the airplane within an assigned, big tube of air. This tube is 100 feet up or down and 10 degrees either side of a specific heading. On the checkride, if pilots can keep the airplane within the tube, they get a license. If they can't, they still get a license, but it's a pink one. It's a license to attempt to ride in the tube again. In real life IFR, pilots are not so concerned about the tube. As long as the heading and altitude doesn't vary too much, they can use their time to do other things, such as navigate and communicate.

Pilots should not interpret this as validating sloppy IFR flying. Nothing could be further from the truth. I am the number one aficionado of precision aircraft control, but I'm also a realist. Most IFR pilots are not as current as they would like to be and their skills are rusty. To forgo time used to plan, plot and scheme because of altitude variations of 50 feet is ludicrous. Realistically, the airplane should be trimmed and allowed to run its own course within reasonable limits. This will provide enough time to get some of the planning and navigating chores done when things get hectic. Most airplanes are very stable and, with little or no turbulence, will settle down into their own stabilized altitude variation patterns of approximately plus or minus 75 feet. All pilots need do is steer with their feet, leaving their hands free. Sure this may scare the passengers, but they'll soon calm down (although a few may need defibrillation). I guess this adds a whole new meaning to yelling the word "Clear."

ANTICIPATE CHANGE

Another level of instrument resource management occurs when a pilot learns to anticipate change instead of reacting to change. Skilled instrument pilots are never surprised by ATC. They have developed an uncanny sense about what is happening in the system and will be planning for this possibility. Their eyes and ears take the pulse of the Air Traffic Control system. They are actively listening for what's about to happen next, and are constantly formulating mini-plans to accommodate this anticipated change.

When ATC issues the final heading with an approach clearance, the prepared instrument pilot will already have the radios set, the approach chart reviewed and minimum altitudes plotted. All that remains is to slide down the electronic bannister and observe the results of the plan. When they hear approach control issuing warnings of approach delays, they'll contemplate fuel reserves and the possibility of selecting alternates. Throughout the flight, they will find themselves pondering probabilities and possibilities and mentally rehearsing likely scenarios. Herein lies one of the secrets of managing cockpit resources.

The instrument pilot's calling goes far beyond manipulating navigation needles and maintaining altitudes. Instrument training develops and disciplines a pilot's thinking. In much the same way as a flight instructor must simultaneously teach and fly, the instrument pilot must think and fly. Thinking is the high art of instrument flying. Converting a two dimensional world of charts into a three dimensional act of navigating an airplane seems unnatural at best, especially when distractions chip away at the delicate balance between gravity and aircraft control. Instrument training develops a pilot's ability to plot, plan and scheme; in other words, to anticipate.

SERIOUS CIRRUS

The active runway was 19. My former flight instructor was sitting in the back seat, and my almost new instructor was in the right front seat. Both instructors are real kidders and practical jokers. During an ILS Runway 1 approach, jokes were told, and we were talking back and forth pretty freely (me under the hood). I started a non-directional beacon Runway 1 approach; at the Outer Marker, I was about 1/4 mile east of course. Tower then said (I thought), "Turn right at the Missed Approach Point for a circle to land on 19," as we had requested. While trying to get back on course, both instructors were talking about my being off course, my descent to MDA, heading, etc,. etc,. etc. Anyway, afterward I talked to the controller and both instructors, and this is what the tower said, about one mile north of the Outer Marker: "Turn right." I did not acknowledge the transmission from the tower; I was just too worked up by the instructors and with getting back on course, and I guess I just didn't hear the controller say, "Turn right, traffic departing runway 19; turn right NOW!!"

At this time, the instructor in the back seat said, "PUSH THE NOSE DOWN; WE'RE GOING TO HIT THAT AIRPLANE." The instructor in the right seat then pushed the control yoke full forward and most everything in the airplane hit the ceiling. We passed about 180 feet under the airplane, which never saw us. We then circled left to land. **ASRS REPORT**

In a word, a seasoned instrument pilot is cunning. To pilot a small airplane in complex airspace, while at the mercy of carnivorous thunderstorms, predatory precipitation and an unmerciful ATC system, takes skill. But it's a skill unlike the skill required of a commercial airline captain, or a fighter pilot. Both of these professionals must master a highly technical and complex environment, fraught with its own traps and predators. However, insufficient climb power isn't one of them. In a Cessna 172, with four little cylinders, of which only 3 may be working at any one time, there is very little room for negotiations with Mother Nature. When icing summons a pilot to Earth in a small airplane, it's not a question of how to get away; but, how can the problem be fended off long enough to get down. Exposure to the IFR environment can offer the kind of valuable insights that money just couldn't buy. It's this experience that will breed a more mature, street smart mentality for the small airplane driver. It's this valuable resource of experience that must also be managed properly.

EXPERIENCE EVERY FLIGHT

If it were just exposure to the IFR environment that modified an instrument pilot's ability to think, then the quantity, and not the quality, of experience would be more highly prized. One would then assume that a 100 hour instrument pilot would have twice the insights and double the wisdom of a 50 hour instrument fellow. The facts do not prove this to be accurate. Experience is not what happens to a pilot; it's what the pilot thinks about what happened. In other words, what one has been exposed to must be mulled over or thought about to extract the potential pearls of wisdom. If it were only practice that improved performance, then one should assume the average reader should become faster each time something was read. Unfortunately, readers continue to read approximately 250 words a minute for most of their lives, unless a specific attempt is made to improve this performance.

A competent instrument pilot is, therefore, one who has given a great deal of thought to the experience of every flight. When the strengths and weaknesses of pilots are revealed, they are leveraged to obtain better performance the next time they are in command. While this introspective behavior may not always be obvious with the professionals, every competent instrument pilot observes this practice. Don't be fooled into thinking they do not. This is the reason the military can produce a "ready for action" fighter pilot with 250 hours of flight time. After every flight, military students are debriefed, debriefed and debriefed again. All this results in an efficient change in a pilot's behavior. This is the key to pilots becoming highly seasoned and obtaining a cunning mastery over their environment. Just ask any military fighter pilot from the elite Louisiana Air Force known as "Top Gumbo."

ATC AS A COPILOT

Perhaps one of the least used resources in the ATC system is Air Traffic Control itself. Legal IFR flying is never done without the aid of an air traffic controller in controlled airspace. Even in a nonradar environment, ATC is still controlling aircraft separation and providing information to the pilot. ATC is a valuable, untapped resource for the pilot. In essence, ATC can perform many of the functions of a copilot.

A copilot's job is to provide information and oversee the captain's piloting of the aircraft. If copilots are interested in job security, they will also try to make the captain look good. ATC can easily perform many of these same functions of the copilot at the proper time and place, except the part about making the

THUNDER THOUGHTS

The tops were at 8,000 feet with clear and unlimited visibility above; bases were at ground level in the area. A SIGMET was in effect for severe turbulence within 5,000 feet of rough terrain below. I was on an IFR flight plan at 12,000 feet when I encountered severe wind shear and the plane dropped like a stone to 8,000 feet. A fuel tank unported, starving the engine which then stopped. The drop put me in the clouds. Like the one armed paper hanger, I had too much to do. In this order I 1) called "Mayday," got Center and explained the problem; they gave me a vector away from the high terrain; 2) commenced re-start procedure after switching tanks. The tank that unported had only about eight gallons remaining. During the restarting procedure, I lost another 2000 feet, yet Center kept me in a safe area, although surrounded by high terrain in all quadrants; I was in a valley. The engine started, and I got climbing again, IFR, in a large circle, until I broke out on top again. In the clouds it was needle, ball, airspeed, as all gyros went out with the engine. This shows the need for practice on no-gyro procedures. Hats off to the guys at Center! **ASRS REPORT**

captain look good. For instance, in a radar environment, ground speed checks are often available and are of great value to the pilot. From this information, wind direction and velocity can be estimated. The controller can even act as a personal weather service by soliciting PIREP information from aircraft ahead along the airway. This information can prove to be invaluable. I have also requested controllers to ask other pilots what their weather radar was painting and had that information relayed to my aircraft. Imagine sitting in a Cessna 150 and having all the benefits of weather radar and not having to pay for it. Besides, where would a mechanic put the weather radar dish in a Cessna 150? The nose cone? I suspect that the pilot would probably get vertigo watching the picture rotate around and around. With that extra weight, a 10 to 12 thousand foot ground roll would be needed just to get airborne.

When being vectored for the approach, there are several things that can be requested from the controller to better manage the flight. For instance, pilots not familiar with the approach can ask to be vectored two to three miles farther out from the normal course intercept point. The aircraft can then be stabilized and the pilot will have more precious time to plan for the approach. A pilot may ask for a 45 degree intercept vector instead of the customary 20 to 30 degrees. Pilots may want to do a procedure turn in lieu of the radar vector, if they are worried about terrain or losing orientation during the vector. They may even ask for the full route clearance to remove the controller from the navigation loop, thereby avoiding the vector completely. I have even known pilots who ask for wheel checks from tower controllers when landing under emergency conditions, and the potential for distraction is high. Think of this as a professional wake up call! Some pilots with a great sense of humor may ask for a wheel check while in a Cessna 150. The controller can be an important ally in helping pilots manage their cockpit resources. Take advantage of their services.

ORGANIZE THOSE CHARTS

An often neglected area of cockpit management is chart organization. Some cockpits look like they had a paper mill explode inside. The folding and unfolding of charts under the exigency of IFR flight often takes on the semblance of a competition origami meet. The best solution to this problem is to purchase an 11 x 14 inch clipboard along with three strong clips. Place the clips in the middle of each side of the clipboard, as shown in figure 1. This is a ready-made cockpit organizer. Place the enroute chart under the big clip, on the left side of the board. The enroute chart should be folded in such a way that it can be pulled out to examine the route, then let it compress back to the folded position. The approach chart is at the top of the clipboard; and the flight planning information and other charts are clipped to the bottom of the board. The clearance copying paper is on the far right hand side of the board. If the pilot is left handed, put the clearance paper on the left side.

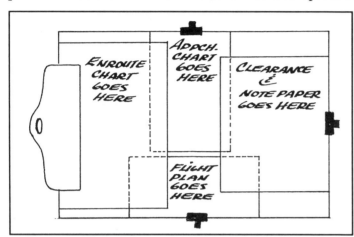

Fig. 1. An IFR lapboard that will help organize the cockpit.

The uniquely useful aspect of this setup is that each chart can be raised and lowered over any other chart making it unnecessary to remove any of the charts for IFR flight. It's often a good idea to glue a little strip of foam rubber under the clipboard to keep it from sliding around. This sure does beat the old knee board, doesn't it? Some pilots get out of airplanes with three or four knee boards strapped to their lower appendages. They looked like instrument gladiators. I don't think they were using them for IFR flying. I believe they wore them at the airport to make people think they were IFR rated. They may have even been worn as some sort of archaic courtship display. Perhaps, in far off and little explored corners of airports, there exists a special breed of instrument pilot that engages in ritual dancing and chanting, hoping to attract an instrument mate. These knee boards may help protect the lower limbs from banging into the rusting hulks of aircraft as they flail their appendages wildly, performing the frenetic, "Dance of the Pheromones." Perhaps not.

FLY BAIT VEST

Several years ago, while walking around the ramp at the local airport, I noticed one of the most unusual things ever seen in an airplane. I saw a pilot wearing one of those bright orange bass fishing vests -- the type with 20 pockets sewn into the lining. Perhaps this wouldn't have been so unusual if the aircraft was a floatplane; however, it was a Cessna 172. I approached this pilot cautiously because he was wearing a red beret. He looked like he could have been one of those Guardian Anglers.

Striking up a conversation with him, we got to talking about his vest and all the things kept in those pockets. There were pencils, colored pens, flashlights -- the standard accouterments of IFR flight. What was so unusual were all the other, nonstandard items this fellow kept with him. For instance, he produced a pair of small, underwater goggles to protect the eyes in case of smoke from an onboard fire.

There was a moist rag, kept in a plastic pouch, in case it was necessary to breath though toxic smoke. He had a dozen large zip lock baggies and a straw in another pocket. The straw could be used to inflate them though a small, unzipped opening. If it were ever necessary to go into the water, a few of those inflated baggies stuffed into his shirt would keep him afloat until help arrived.

What was most impressive about this pilot's preparedness was the fact that in one of the pockets, there was a pair of leather gloves. These were worn for a very specific reason. If a pilot ever had an inflight fire or had to exit a burning airplane, it would be very difficult to do so with burned hands. Several airline pilots I know fly with leather gloves in their flight kit for the same reason. Leather doesn't burn easily. This explains why most people have never seen a cow catch fire. This pilot was perhaps the most prepared and organized aviator I have ever come across. Why, he even had one pocket especially for those orange peanut butter cookies that help keep flight instructors from hypoglycemic unconsciousness. The moral, here, is to be prepared. If using a bass fishing vest would help then, by all means, purchase one. One word of caution about a used bass fishing vest: be sure to clean it out before using it. There's nothing like going hunting for a pencil and pulling out a mackerel.

GET THE LEAD OUT

Always make it a point to have a pencil handy on every IFR flight. Write down all headings, altitudes, frequencies and directions. Don't be concerned about writing on the chart either. It's easy enough to erase all markings after each flight. Air traffic control information should be listed on the chart as the flight progresses. There is nothing more frustrating, and perhaps more dangerous, than missing altitudes and headings because they were not recorded. Some pilots keep their pencils ready for action by wrapping a rubber band around their wrist and putting a pencil underneath. This will certainly keep it handy -- no pun intended.

KNOW THE EQUIPMENT

It's almost impossible to fathom how pilots can manage their cockpit resources properly if they are not familiar with all the equipment on the airplane. A friend of mine was flying his twin Cessna into the very busy New York environment, using his latest loran equipment that included a moving map display for navigation.

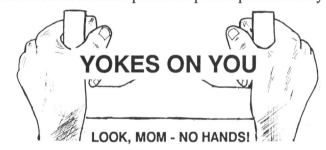

YOKES ON YOU

LOOK, MOM - NO HANDS!

We borrow from England's "Flight Safety Focus" a tale about an airline in the process of installing Autoland equipment in its fleet. Test report:

Log entry from pilot: "Autoland carried out. The aircraft landed very firmly and well to the left of centerline. Most unsatisfactory."

Engineer's entry: "Autoland not fitted (installed) to this aircraft...."

ASRS REPORT

While in turbulence, his hand reached for the radio and accidentally hit the radio master, temporarily shutting off all navigation equipment. When the master was reactivated, an unanticipated problem arose. It seems that the loran system moved to a default mode when the power was cut, and now the system demanded reprogramming. All this was occurring when he was solid IFR, and only 10 minutes from the approach, while in turbulence. Needless to say, M&M's would just about melt in his hand.

Knowledge of the airplane and its equipment is a vital part of managing cockpit resources. Knowing how to turn the equipment on and off just won't do. Sometimes things are just plain complicated and take a great deal of additional study. Ask anyone who has a VCR if they still have that flashing "12:00" in their window. Most people can't figure out how to shut it off, much less program the device. A friend, who is an engineer, put a piece of black electrician's tape over the flashing "12:00" as a solution to the problem. This gentleman is one of the professionals making the commercial airliners in which people fly. This perplexes me!

CHEER UP?

My instructor felt I was ready for my CFI check ride, so he had me fly with another instructor to find any weak spots. While I was going through the pre-start checklist (I was in the right seat), he quizzed me about the pressure switch in the nose gear (the aircraft was a small, retractable gear type). When I indicated that I didn't know how to test it, he said, "You can test it this way," as he turned the master switch on and pulled the gear lever to the UP position. In accordance with Murphy's law, the pressure switch didn't work, and the nose of the aircraft crashed to the pavement.

ASRS REPORT

Today's airline pilots have to spend several weeks in school to learn the operations of their airplane before they are turned loose to fly passengers. Many years ago, when economics were not such a mitigating factor in education, airline pilots would spend many months in school, learning detailed intricacies necessary to fly their aircraft safely. Similarly, general aviation airplanes are often quite complicated and demand the same degree of attention and study to master their mechanical and electrical complexities.

General aviation pilots are more susceptible to moving into the domain of technological ignorance than professional pilots. Airline pilots have to go to school and learn their equipment, but this is not so for small airplane drivers. It is possible, with just 125 hours of flight time, and a newly acquired instrument rating, to jump into a pressurized Cheyenne 400LS, equipped with an EFIS (Electronic Flight Instrument System) and fly cross country at 41,000 feet, being sucked along by the jet stream with ground speeds in the 300 knot range! All this could be done legally, albeit a pilot would probably have trouble getting insurance! But this is a different matter. The pilot would not be required to obtain any education on the particular equipment flown. This lays a tremendous responsibility on pilots to make sure they are knowledgeable enough to fly competently. Fortunately, many pilots are only too aware of the potential for problems and do get the necessary technical education. So, learn the airplane well, study it very carefully and let it help in managing cockpit resources.

Instrument flying is more than just a recreational activity. Instrument flying is an art, requiring sufficient mastery, that it should be raised to the level of a secondary occupation. Its rewards are plentiful, but ignorance is intolerable. Professionals consider instrument flying tantamount to licking honey off a thorn. It's quite sweet, but if it's done carelessly, they know they are bound to get poked. Professionals make it a personal mission to master the management of their cockpit resources and soon find that their luck is just like the capital of Ireland -- Dublin.

Mastering the fundamentals of ADF navigation is quite similar to developing the skill of managing cockpit resources. Both require the application of sound, tried and proven techniques.

5. ADF NAVIGATION MADE SIMPLE

As an instrument student, I was always disappointed with the ADF. Perhaps this was because I originally thought the automatic direction finder was the person in the right seat. It wasn't long before I found an entire covey of students at the flight school who felt the same way. Many of these folks felt they would rather do something less challenging than learn ADF navigation -- like being a chicken dangler at a pit bull fight or, perhaps cliff diving, a difficult sport in which to make a comeback. With ADF navigation, I found myself getting lost so much that the only thing to do was keep changing where it was I wanted to go.

It's no misconception that more people have trouble with ADF navigation than can be counted with a turbo abacus. However, ADF navigation can be easily understood and mastered when the similarity of NDB bearings to VOR radials is understood and by applying two very important rules for navigation.

PICTURE THIS

VOR navigation is done via radials, 360 of them, radiating away from the station, while ADF navigation is done on bearings oriented to and from an NDB. These bearings can be thought of as being similar to VOR radials. However, bearings are unlike VOR radials, in that they are more difficult to picture on the face of the ADF. Pilots know when they are on a specific radial when the needle on the VOR centers. At this point, they would turn the airplane to the heading selected in the course selector and fly either to or from the station. NDB bearings are a little more difficult to picture on the face of the ADF. Pilots can positively determine that they are on a specific NDB bearing when they can turn to the direction of the bearing and have the ADF needle point to the nose or the tail of the ADF.

NOSE OR TAIL

Figure 1 shows two airplanes flying to and from an NDB. Airplane A is on the 090 degree bearing to the station, since it's heading 090 degrees, and the needle is pointed to the nose of the ADF. Airplane B is on the 060 bearing from the station since it is heading 060 degrees, and the needle is pointed to the tail of the ADF.

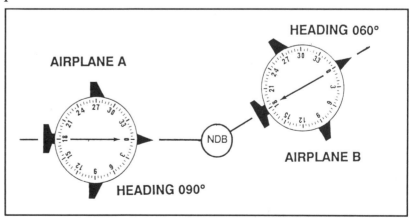

Fig. 1. When the needle is on the nose or tail of the ADF, the airplane is on a specific bearing to or from the NDB

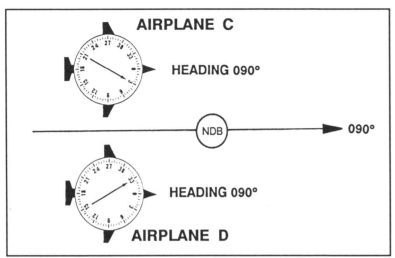

Fig. 2. Airplane C is to the left of the 090 degree bearing to the NDB and airplane D is to the right of the 090 degree bearing to the NDB.

Figure 2 shows that airplanes C and D are not on the 090 degree bearing to the station. Both airplanes are headed in a 90 degree direction, but the ADF needles are pointed to the right and left of the instrument respectively. Therefore, these airplanes are not going to or from the NDB on the desired bearing. For airplane C to be on the 090 degree bearing to the NDB it would have to move to the right, and airplane D would have to move to the left.

Referring to figure 3, would airplane E be on the 300 degree bearing to the station? Is airplane F on the 300 degree bearing from the station? The answer to both questions is yes. Both airplanes are on a specific NDB bearing when they can turn to the heading of that bearing and have the ADF needle point directly to the nose or the tail of the ADF. Airplane E is heading 270 degrees and the ADF needle is pointed 30 degrees to the right of the nose. Turning airplane E 30 degrees to the right will pivot the airplane about the needle by 30 degrees. The airplane will now be headed 300 degrees, with the needle directly on the nose of the ADF, while going to the station on

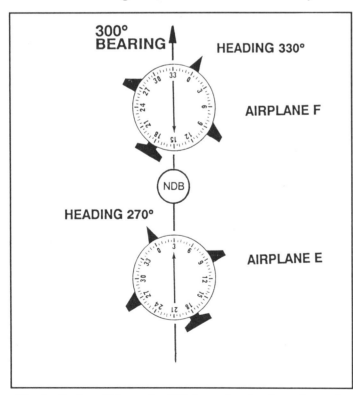

Fig. 3. Airplane F is on the 300 degree bearing from the station and airplane E is on the 300 degree bearing to the station.

the 300 degree bearing. Airplane F is headed 330 degrees with the ADF needle deflected 30 degrees to the right of the tail. Turning airplane F 30 degrees to the left will pivot the airplane about the needle by 30 degrees. The airplane will now be headed 300 degrees, with the needle directly on the tail of the ADF, while going away from the station on the 300 bearing.

Notice that airplanes E and F both have differences of 30 degrees between their headings and the 300 degree bearing. Notice also that the angle between the ADF needle and the nose of airplane E is 30 degrees, and the angle between airplane F and the tail is also 30 degrees. It seems that when the airplane is on the desired bearing, a relationship exists between the angle at which the bearing is being intercepted, and the angle the ADF needle makes with the nose or tail of the ADF instrument. This relationship is VERY, VERY important. To understand this relationship is to successfully comprehend ADF navigation.

Understanding the basic concepts is not only important in ADF navigation, it's also important for all higher knowledge. Einstein talked about relativity or time distortion. I never understood this until a professor said, "The length of one minute depends on which side of the bathroom door you happen to be on." It's also interesting to consider that Einstein is remembered for $E = MC^2$. Now, you would think that a guy who was smart enough to create this formula would understand that: "NO HAIRCUT + BAD CONDITIONER = THE FRIZZIES."

Now that pilots can identify when they are on a specific bearing, they are ready for the two most important rules in ADF navigation:

RULE 1

WHEN HOLDING A CONSTANT HEADING, THE HEAD OF THE ADF NEEDLE ALWAYS FALLS TO THE BOTTOM OF THE INSTRUMENT.

RULE 2

WHEN A SPECIFIC NDB BEARING HAS BEEN INTERCEPTED, THE ANGLE OF INTERCEPT WILL BE SHOWN BETWEEN THE NEEDLE AND THE NOSE OF THE ADF, OR THE NEEDLE AND THE TAIL OF THE ADF.

Rule number one becomes extremely important for identifying the airplane's position in relation to specific bearings. Pilots should try the following experiment on the ground. They should pick a reference spot about 20 feet in front of them, and assume this spot is the NDB station. They should point to this spot with an arm stretched out, while pretending that arm is an ADF needle. Keeping an arm pointed to this spot as they move, they should walk in any direction, maintaining a constant heading while walking. They will notice their arm moves towards their rear, regardless of which way they are walking, as long as they are holding a constant heading, as shown in figure 4. Of course, be real careful while walking.

One time I sent a student home to do this. He showed up the next day with a big bandage on his head. He apparently walked square into his refrigerator. Strangely enough, his understanding of ADF navigation dramatically improved after the collision. My theory is that when a student's head is filled with knowledge, then bumped against something, a permanent synaptic attachment is achieved within the brain cells. Unfortunately, because of a lack of volunteers, I have not been able to replicate this experiment.

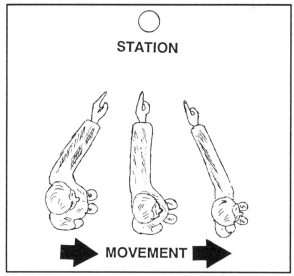

Fig. 4. Maintain a constant heading and all stations in front move to the rear.

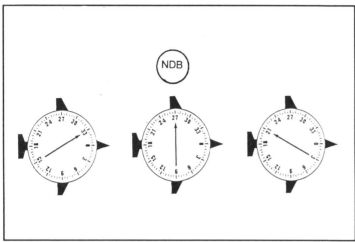

Fig. 5. *When a constant heading is maintained, the ADF needle will always fall (move) to the bottom of the instrument.*

Similarly, while holding a constant heading in an airplane, any station in front of the plane will eventually move towards the tail. Any station already behind the wing will move further toward the tail of the airplane. Thus, the ADF needle always falls towards the bottom of the ADF instrument, while a constant heading is maintained,* as shown in figure 5. This action implies that while maintaining a constant heading, the angle made between the needle and the nose of the ADF instrument will continue to increase. It also implies that the angle made between the needle and the tail of the ADF instrument will continue to decrease.

Rule number two states that pilots have intercepted a specific bearing, when the angle of bearing interception is shown between the needle and the nose, or the needle and the tail, of the ADF, depending on whether it's a bearing to or from the station respectively, as shown in figure 6. If intercepting a bearing to the station, the intercept angle will be shown between the needle and the nose of the ADF instrument. If intercepting a bearing from the station, the intercept angle will be shown between the needle and the tail of the ADF instrument.

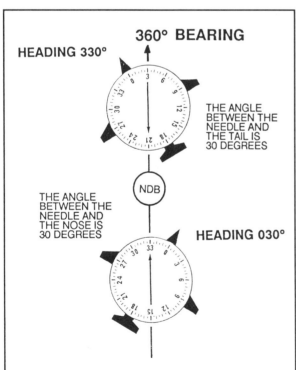

Fig. 6. *The intercept angle is the angle made between the needle and the nose of the ADF, or the needle and the tail, of the ADF. The numbers on the ADF card should be used as 30 degree increment markings.*

BASIC NAVIGATION

Keep in mind that this intercept angle is the angle made between the needle and the nose, or the needle and the tail, of the ADF, and not the numbers to which the ADF needle points on the compass card. As far as pilots are concerned, the printed numbers on the face of the ADF dial should have no meaning during initial ADF practice. There is an appropriate time when these numbers have meaning, but not for basic ADF navigation. Leave the rotatable ADF card fixed, with the "zero" reference set to the top of the instrument. In fact, pilots shouldn't even think of the numbers on the ADF card as numbers; they should think of them as 5, 10 and 30 degree reference marks around the face of the dial. These reference marks make it easy for pilots to tell how many degrees the needle is away from the nose or tail of the ADF instrument. Unless pilots think of the ADF numbers as simple indices, they may have a very difficult time learning basic ADF navigation. They could become so frustrated that they may fall to the cockpit floor and start flopping around like a fish just pulled out of water.

*The only exception to this rule is during very strong wind conditions when the aircraft is very close to the station. For all practical purposes, this exception can be forgotten.

INTERCEPT ANGLES

Figure 7 shows the progressive needle movement of airplane G as it moves toward the NDB approach course on an intercept vector. The intercept angle is the difference between the inbound bearing of 040 degrees and a heading of 070 degrees. An intercept angle of 30 degrees will be shown between the needle and the nose of the ADF, when the airplane is on the 040 degree bearing. Since the NDB station is to the left of the airplane, the intercept angle will be shown to the left of the ADF's nose.

Pilots can immediately tell that airplane G1 is not on the approach course, since the angle between the needle and the nose is only 20 degrees. The intercept angle is 30 degrees, and this angle is not yet shown. The important question to ask here is whether an angle of 30 degrees will ever be shown between the needle and the nose. The answer is yes. As long as the intercept heading of 070 is maintained, the needle will consistently move from the top to the bottom of the ADF, eventually indicating an angle of 30 degrees between itself and the nose of the ADF as shown by airplane G2. At this point, pilots know they are on course and should turn to a heading of 040 degrees to track inbound.

The basics of ADF navigation are quite simple. Unfortunately, unless pilots completely understand these basics, comprehension of ADF navigation is not possible. It's like going into a shoe store. The clerk puts a shoe on and says, "This is your toe." How basic. Most people reply, "Oh, thank you, I've been looking for that."

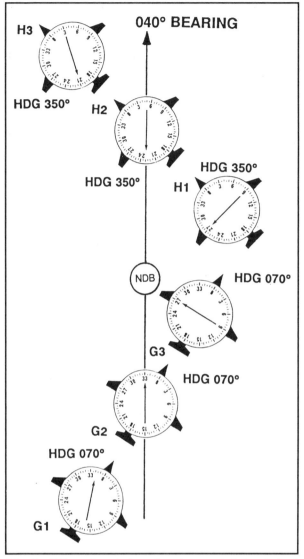

Fig. 7. When the airplane has intercepted the desired bearing, the intercept angle is shown on the same side of the ADF face that the station is on.

Suppose the ADF is showing an angle of 90 degrees between the needle and the nose, as is indicated by airplane G3. Has the airplane gone past the 040 degree bearing to the station? Since the needle always falls, pilots know they will never see an angle of less than 30 degrees (the intercept angle) between the needle and the nose as long as the intercept heading is maintained. When they see an angle greater than the intercept angle shown between the needle and the nose on the face of the ADF, they know they have flown through the approach course and now must turn in the opposite direction to reintercept the course.

Assume a pilot is being vectored to the 040 degree bearing from the station, as shown in figure 7. Airplane H1 is on an intercept heading of 350 degrees. With a needle indication of 90 degrees to the left of the nose, the pilot knows that the ADF needle will continue to fall if a constant heading is maintained. The 040 degree bearing from the station will be intercepted when an intercept angle of

50 degrees (difference between 350 & 040) is shown between the needle and the tail. Since the NDB is to the left of the airplane, the intercept angle will be shown on the left side of the ADF. Airplane H2 shows this intercept angle and, at this point, a right turn to an outbound heading of 040 would be made to track from the station.

Suppose a pilot experienced a major distraction in the aircraft, like finding a stowaway in a Cessna 150, and flew beyond the 040 degree bearing. The pilot would have an indication, as shown on airplane H3. The needle is showing an angle of 30 degrees between the needle and the tail. It's very important that pilots recognize from this indication that they have flown beyond the 040 degree bearing. They should realize that the needle will continue to fall on this heading. There's no way the ADF will ever show an intercept angle of 50 degrees between the needle and the tail, as long as the heading is maintained. The pilot has flown beyond the 040 degree bearing, and the only recourse is to turn back to the right and reintercept the course.

WIND CORRECTIONS

Pilots skilled at intercepting NDB approach courses can easily transfer these skills into making corrections for wind. Once established on the bearing, pilots should maintain the inbound heading and watch for needle drift. Normally, ADF needles have a tendency to wander a few degrees. I've never found a great deal of comfort in this fact. However, passengers like it because this somehow makes the needle seem more intelligent when it wiggles, as if it's thinking by itself. When a full 5 degree deflection from the nose or the tail is observed, then it's time to apply a correction for wind.

Referring to figure 8, it's evident that airplane J1 has drifted to the right of the 270 degree inbound bearing. At this point, pilots should reintercept the course to the left by assuming a 20 degree intercept angle, as shown by airplane J2. I recommend reintercepting at a minimum of 20 degrees because it gets the pilot back on course quickly. Notice that airplane J2 now has a needle deflection of 10 degrees to the right of the nose. If an intercept heading of 250 is maintained, the intercept angle of 20 degrees will eventually be shown between the needle and the nose. Once this intercept angle is shown, pilots know they have reestablished themselves on the course, as shown by airplane J3. At this point, they should turn to a 5 degree wind correction heading of 265 degrees, as shown by airplane J4.

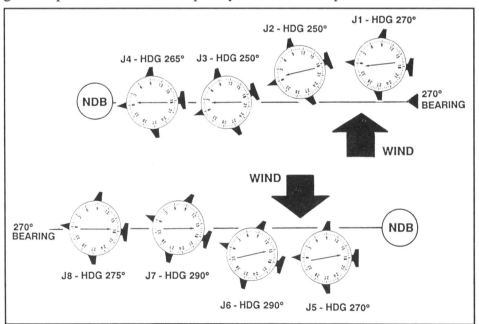

Fig. 8. Wind correction while tracking an NDB bearing.

If this wind correction is sufficient, the ADF should continue to show the wind correction of 5 degrees between the needle and the nose while on a heading of 265 degrees. Remember, the test of whether pilots are on the bearing is if they can turn to the desired bearing and have the needle point directly to either the nose or the tail of the ADF. Turning 5 degrees to the right will have the needle of airplane J4 pointing to the nose, but not for long, since the wind will eventually blow the airplane off course.

Wind correction, while tracking outbound, is done in much the same manner as tracking inbound. Pilots should wait for a needle deflection of 5 degrees off the tail, then turn 20 degrees in the appropriate direction to reintercept the course. Assume airplane J5 experiences a wind deflection while tracking outbound and turns to a heading of 290 degrees to reintercept. The angle between the needle and the tail of the ADF is now 30 degrees, as shown by airplane J6. When the airplane is back on course, the ADF will show the intercept angle of 20 degrees between the needle and the tail, as shown by airplane J7. At this point, a wind correction angle of 5 degrees is applied, as shown by airplane J8. If the wind correction is sufficient, the ADF will continue to show a 5 degree angle between the needle and the tail. If the wind correction angle is not sufficient, or the wind changes, then pilots should reintercept the course at a 20 degree angle and try a new wind correction angle. Always use a 20 degree angle to reintercept the course. This angle is small enough to let things happen gradually, but not small enough to make them happen too slowly.

PROPERLY DONE TIPS

HUMULONIMBUS

ADF navigation, like VOR navigation, becomes more of an art form, rather than a frustrating chore, when instrument students learn to bracket. Bracketing is very easy to learn, and it's what separates the pros from the amateurs. The only difficulty a student may have learning how to bracket is with communications. This is especially critical in Southern California. There is an airport named Bracket Field and this has caused several instrument instructors grief on a few occasions. Once, while in the throes of a lesson on VOR navigation, I looked over at my instrument student and said, "Bracket." He must have thought I was being a bit laconic. Nevertheless, he starts to head off in a direction that wasn't going to center the needle. He was actually headed in the direction he thought would take him to "Bracket Field." I said, "Hey partner, are you going to bracket, or what?" He replied, "OK, I'm doing it now." I said, "That's not the way to bracket." He said, "Do you know a better way?" I replied, somewhat confused, "What about the way I showed you?" He immediately quipped, "You never showed me the way to Bracket before." At this point I decided to use the audio impact theory of learning. This is where, if the student doesn't get it the first time, instructors just say it louder. It didn't take long before we both discovered what had happened and had a good laugh. Shades of Abbott and Costello. **AUTHOR**

Here are a few more important items to consider when tracking an NDB bearing. First, pilots should always make sure the heading indicator is set to the proper magnetic compass indication when doing ADF navigation. I have seen instrument pilots think they are doing a marvelous job of NDB navigation, only to discover they were navigating 30 degrees off course. This is no fun for the pilot, but is sometimes entertaining for the controller. Second, always leave the volume up slightly when doing an NDB approach. Since ADF's have no "OFF" flags, the only way to identify a failed station is if the identification becomes inoperative.

Third, if pilots ever become confused about their position in relation to an NDB bearing, they should turn to the heading of that bearing and look at the needle indication. This will immediately confirm their position in relation to the desired bearing. If the needle is anywhere to the right of the ADF, the bearing is to the right of the airplane. If the needle is to the left of the ADF, the bearing is to the left of the airplane. They should turn in the appropriate direction to reintercept the course at a 20 degree intercept angle. Fourth, pilots should disregard the numbers on the face of the ADF card for basic ADF navigation. These numbers can be used with a rotary ADF card once the basics of ADF navigation are understood.

REVOLTING ACTIONS

ADF navigation can sometimes be misunderstood. The same thing can happen with VOR navigation. Sometimes the results are very unpredictable!

On a recent checkride, a local Southern California designee instructed a student to track to the Seal Beach VOR. The student reached over, set the VOR course selector to center the needle, then proceeded to rotate the DG knob to the same number set in the course selector. The designee said, "Excuse me buddy, what are you doing?" The student replied, "My instructor said that whenever we use a VOR, these two things have got to match!" VOR's can be quite confusing, and it's no wonder people are still getting lost with them onboard.

AUTHOR

ADF navigation is certainly not the most accurate form of navigation available. However, in certain parts of the country, pilots find it is their only umbilical to earth. Because of the abundant supply of VHF navigational aids, pilots in the United States can use the ADF for navigational backup, as well as picking up ball scores when aloft on the airways.

The study of ADF navigation has some practical value. It's not a waste of time. Unfortunately, the same can't be said about holding patterns. Define them for what they are: a waste of time! They are aerial parking lots whose primary purpose is in spinning clocks and watches. They have all the significance of a stop sign. However, as Mohammed Ali might say, "Ain't no big thing!"

6. THE TRUTH ABOUT HOLDING PATTERNS

In all the years I've spent training instrument students, the one subject for which they invariably showed the least enthusiasm was holding patterns. In fact, a pilot's lounge, full of instrument students studying holding patterns is about as animated as a family lying around their living room after a Thanksgiving dinner. It looks like there was a gas leak in the house, or someone stuffed the turkey with thorazine. While holding patterns don't arouse much excitement on the ground, they can cause emotional apoplexy in flight.*

Diabolical flight instructors spend a great deal of their recreational time plotting and scheming about holding patterns. During their after hours, they can be found in a smoke-filled room, huddled over an aged enroute chart, with fingers jabbing at intersections. They are usually attempting to discover just the right combination of holding clearances to cause their students to swoon, limp at the controls. Perhaps this is another reason instrument pilots wear hoods. They act like roll bars protecting the head from banging into the instrument panel and leaving altimeter knob indentations in the forehead after the frustration blackout. What makes holding such a frustrating curiosity to instrument pilots, and how can the problem be dealt with effectively?

Concern over holding patterns usually is divided into two areas: learning how to do holding patterns and then worrying that you may actually have to do one for real. Concern over learning holding patterns is reasonable. However, fear of having to perform them in the IFR system is not. Few instrument pilots see many holding patterns in today's IFR system. According to a study done by NASA in 1980, instrument pilots, on the average, are asked to hold only once a year. Of course, the chances of holding are

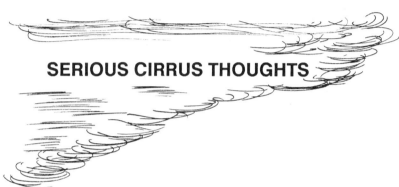

SERIOUS CIRRUS THOUGHTS

Since the briefing called for marginal VFR, an IFR flight plan was filed. I was aware that a V.I.P. was to make an appearance at the destination field, but the FSS knew of no restrictions. The flight proceeded over a solid overcast with tops about 5,500 feet.. Approximately 30 miles from the field we were told to descend to 4,000 feet in preparation for the ILS approach. Moments later we were informed that the field would be closed for approximately 30 minutes. My passenger and I understood the controller to instruct us to track outbound on the localizer so I acknowledged the same. At almost 20 miles out, the controller wanted to know when we would be starting our southbound leg. I informed him I had not received further instructions. He informed me that my instructions had been to hold north of the localizer on the outbound radial.

In a moment of sheer frustration, being concerned about not following instructions, I wanted to be going south. A normal 15 degree bank became a 60 degree bank. I overshot the heading, gained 500 feet, lost 1,000 feet., then came back down to my assigned altitude. A vector was given, only this time it was to establish us on a course which would intercept the ILS for landing. From that point on, I could relax and everything went as smoothly as clockwork through the approach and subsequent landing.

Although I have considerable IFR experience, each actual IFR flight has been without delay at the destination, and therefore, I was mentally prepared for the approach. To be required to hold at any location would have taken a "mental image"...one that I haven't had to deal with since getting an instrument rating. That's a long time between holding patterns. Holding patterns are not a part of my normal hood time practice, but, rest assured, they will be in the future. **ASRS REPORT**

*Webster, in his best selling book The Dictionary, defines NECROMANCY as "the art of communicating with the dead." It seems to me that there are similarities between this and a ground school session on holding patterns.

naturally greater when flying to a major airport in low ceiling and visibility conditions. However, with radar vectoring available in many busy terminal areas, having to hold for separation purposes is rare.

Even when holding is required, it is usually initiated as the pilot approaches an intersection along the route. An uncomplicated, direct entry is typical. The pilot simply crosses the intersection and commences an outbound turn. Yet it's doubtful a pilot will find solace in holding infrequently, since the real frustration with holding patterns comes from learning, not doing.

With all this frustration over holding patterns, it would be nice if there was something meaningful to be gained when learning about them. After all, if a pilot doesn't have to hold often, then why practice these mental conundrums in the first place? Probably no other activity in instrument flying offers such an opportunity to develop a pilot's ability to think while under pressure. Holding patterns can be mastered in the sterile classroom with relative ease. However, after receiving a holding pattern clearance, pilots may find themselves flying about as relaxed as a moth on PCP. Things easily mastered on terra firma can be much more difficult when airborne. Exposure to the multi-dimensional task of holding patterns will mold and discipline a pilot's IFR thinking skills through prioritization of incoming information.

ONE STEP AT A TIME

Psychologists tell us even the most complex task can be mastered if broken down into simple components. When first introduced to holding patterns, pilots often have little or no strategy for approaching the problem. Therefore, the secret to successful holding patterns is to develop an effective strategy for dealing with them. After receiving a holding pattern clearance, it's not unusual for instrument students to continue to fly straight ahead, with their brain caged in an apparent EEG flatline. The first rule of student instrument piloting is, "If you don't look at it, it will go away." At this point, students are usually hoping for something less complex to handle, like major airframe failure, with the engine on fire, during an inverted flat spin. The secret is to attack the holding pattern one step at a time.

THE FIRST STEP

The first step in mastering holding patterns is to realize there is a definite structure to the holding clearance. Look at the following clearance and form a strategy to handle the problem:

THE CLEARANCE

"CESSNA 1215B, RADAR CONTACT EIGHT MILES SOUTHEAST OF THE SEAL BEACH VOR. CLEARED TO PRADO INTERSECTION, VIA HEADING ZERO FIVE ZERO, INTERCEPT VICTOR 363 TO PRADO. HOLD EAST ON VICTOR 16, LEFT TURNS, MAINTAIN 3,000 FEET, EXPECT FURTHER CLEARANCE AT ZERO TWO THREE ZERO." Refer to figure 1.

Upon receiving this clearance a pilot should immediately mentally flash the questions: "Where am I going? How do I get there? What do I do next?"* The destination is PRADO intersection, so a pilot knows exactly where to go. The first priority is to decide how to get to the holding intersection. The clearance said fly heading 050 degrees as a vector to Victor 363.** Immediately, the pilot should turn to a heading of 050 degrees to intercept the airway.

THE SECOND STEP

The next step is quite critical. A pilot should immediately set the navigation radios to identify the airway and prepare to track to the intersection. A pilot may be tempted to start drawing the holding pattern and not even think about the route to be flown to the holding intersection. The inability to prioritize is the greatest chasm a pilot will face to master instrument flying. Pilots must remember to: AVIATE, NAVIGATE and COMMUNICATE, in that order. This is the law of survival in the world of IFR.

When established on an intercept heading of 050 degrees, the Pomona VOR frequency should be selected, the volume turned up to hear the Morse code identification and the OBS rotated to 344 degrees, in this order. Don't worry about identifying the station now. When the airplane is established on the intercept heading, and the OBS has been rotated, then the station can be comfortably identified.

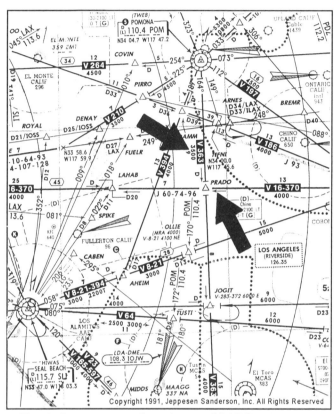

Fig. 1. Jeppesen area chart showing PRADO intersection

THE THIRD STEP

Once pilots know where they are going and how to get there, they should employ whatever free time remains and construct the holding pattern on paper, at least until they get good enough to do it from memory. Draw an actual picture of the holding pattern at the intersection instead of having to store the picture in visual memory. I remember having a student who always had to look up and to the left when he tried to visualize anything. This was a real detriment when taking IFR training. I always thought he was operating under the philosophy that, "One peek is worth a thousand cross checks." It turned out that he couldn't visualize anything unless he moved his head in this direction. This may have resulted from some type of cranial injury caused by the IFR training hood clamped too tightly over his head. Perhaps he bumped his neocortex one too many times against the control column as he attempted to fiddle with the hobbs meter fuse.

Most pilots find it vivid and valuable to draw the holding pattern on their IFR charts. Sometimes, though, pilots are too overly concerned about marking up their IFR charts. Thus, they deprive

*"What am I doing here?" should not be on this list!
**Do not recall the "What's my vector, Victor...?" movie dialogue either!

themselves of a visual tool to make holding easier. There is nothing more difficult than trying to visualize a holding pattern, while in the throes of intense IFR flight. One instant of inattention and a pilot could experience a memory core dump and completely lose the holding pattern picture. It's much easier to simply draw the holding pattern on the chart in pencil and to erase it after the flight.

Pilots can also put their often used charts in plastic pouches and use a grease pencil for marking. If one chart gets too worn, it can be thrown away and another one purchased. The verb "purchased" doesn't sit well with most pilots, especially flight instructors. Perhaps this hyper-frugality explains why

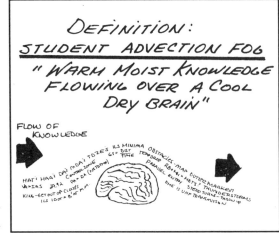

fledgling flight instructors can be heard to say, "What do you mean, you don't want to buy my blood?," and, "Just why am I not eligible for food stamps?" Don't be stingy when it comes to IFR charts.*

THE BUILDING BLOCKS OF THE HOLDING CLEARANCE

Success at deciphering and understanding holding instructions is predicated upon the premise that every holding clearance will contain the following information: a place to hold, a radial, course, bearing, airway or route to hold on, the direction of holding from the fix and, if the pattern is nonstandard, left turns will be specified. Holding patterns are normally performed at intersections, on airways or at VOR stations. Occasionally, they will be at points formed by DME fixes along an airway, route or course, whereby the controller creates an artificial intersection for holding.

THE INBOUND LEG

The most important part of the holding pattern is the inbound leg. The inbound leg is the course on which pilots navigate to get to the holding fix. Figure 2 shows holding patterns at WILMA and LIMBO intersections. Notice both holding patterns have a leg that's inbound to the intersection. A pilot would

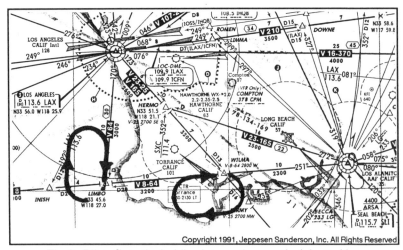

navigate to the fix on this leg. The inbound leg to LIMBO is on the 170 degree radial from LAX VOR, in a direction of 170 degrees. The inbound leg to WILMA, on the other hand, is on the SLI 251 degree radial (or 071 degree course to SLI), in a direction of 071 degrees**. Understand that the inbound leg of every holding pattern must be on some radial, bearing, airway or course -- otherwise, how could a pilot arrive back over the holding intersection? In comparison, the outbound leg of every holding pattern is always a simple heading that is flown for a short amount of time, normally a minute.

Fig. 2. Pilots fly to the holding intersections on the inbound leg.

*One trick a pilot friend of mine uses is to cover her IFR enroute charts with clear, sticky plastic shelving paper. The charts can be drawn on with an oil based marker and easily erased.
**Remember basic VOR navigation here! To track the inbound leg to WILMA on the 251 degree radial, you will have to set the VOR's course selector to 071 degrees.

HOLDING PATTERN SELF TALK

An airline pilot friend of mine told me: "Holding patterns and athlete's foot were two of God's curses upon the world." For instrument pilots, this curse manifests as two separate problems: drawing the holding pattern and deciding upon an entry. After a few perplexing encounters with these demonic mind twisters, it becomes embarrassingly clear that the greater problem is not deciding upon an entry, but correctly depicting the holding pattern in the first place. Unless pilots hold in the proper direction, as instructed in their clearance, the entry they chose will be meaningless.

Following a step by step sequence is the key to dismantling the complex task of drawing a holding pattern. Use of the following internal dialogue, to guide a pilot's mental behavior, will immediately cause little lights to flicker in the pilot's psyche. Soon, more mental flash bulbs will be going off than at a Madonna concert. How utterly simple the process of getting a holding pattern down on paper is when the following step-by-step procedure is followed:

HUMULONIMBUS

Creature Feature

We were issued holding instructions at ABC intersection. A few miles before reaching ABC, a distraction arose in the cockpit -- a very large bug was crawling up the inside of the windshield. I became involved with removing the insect, as I didn't want a distraction during the upcoming approach. The weather was W1X1/4F, and we were expecting an ILS. Shortly after removing the problem insect, the Approach controller called us and asked if we had started our entry into the hold at ABC. I then looked at the DME and noticed that we had passed the holding fix by approximately 4.5 miles. I let an insect distract me, and I flew through a holding fix. **ASRS REPORT**

HOLDING PATTERN SELF-TALK DIALOGUE

1. "WHAT IS THE RADIAL, BEARING, AIRWAY OR COURSE TO HOLD ON?"
2. "WHAT ARE THE TWO POSSIBLE CHOICES OF INBOUND LEGS?"
3. "WHICH INBOUND LEG IS ON THE SIDE OF THE INTERSECTION OR FIX SPECIFIED IN THE HOLDING DIRECTION?"
4. "IS IT A RIGHT OR LEFT HAND PATTERN?"

QUESTION ONE

Asking, "What is the radial, bearing, airway or course to hold on?" identifies the navigable route pilots will fly inbound to the holding intersection. When ATC says to hold on a specific radial, bearing, airway or course, pilots should immediately identify this specific route. Hopefully, they will circle it, point their finger at it, highlight it, or in some way visually identify the place on the chart where they are to hold. Don't do what a student of mine once did. He always used a black highlighter. This is why he had such a tough time passing courses in college.*

---

*Actually, he did graduate "Magna cum lucky." He was originally going to study marketing in college, but decided that spending four years learning how to shop was not proper. He finally ended up in publishing -- he got a paper route.

QUESTION TWO

"What are the two possible choices of inbound legs?"* When holding at an intersection, there will almost always be two apparent choices for inbound legs. This happens because the radial, airway, bearing or course goes through the holding fix. The holding course appears to exist on both sides of the fix. Only one choice will be correct. Figure 3 shows that Victor 16 exists on either side of PRADO intersection. Only one of the two inbound legs is correct. One selection for an inbound leg is to the

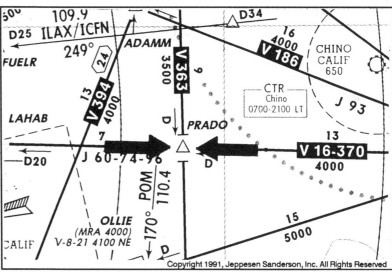

Fig. 3. When holding at PRADO, on V-16, only two inbound legs are possible.

west of PRADO on Victor 16, the other is to the east of PRADO on Victor 16. Determining which inbound leg is correct is the most important point to understand in constructing holding patterns.

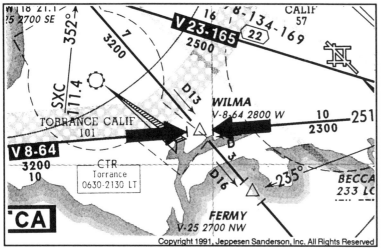

Fig. 4. When holding at WILMA, on V-8, only two inbound legs are possible. One inbound leg will be chosen based on the specified direction of holding.

Figure 4 shows two possibilities for inbound legs when instructed to hold on Victor 8 at WILMA intersection. Notice that there can only be two choices of legs inbound to WILMA when instructed to hold on Victor 8. If pilots can narrow the choice of inbound legs to only two possibilities, this increases the likelihood of selecting the correct one to a 50-50 chance. As an instrument student, I would have considered something in the 50-50 range to be a magnificently attractive risk, considering my track record of confusion. In asking my first instrument instructor about my skills in drawing the holding pattern, he would reply, "Well, you're missing the correct answer closer now." If he had any more warmth and empathy, he could have worked for the Department of Motor Vehicles. The next question will allow pilots to determine which of the inbound legs is the correct choice.

QUESTION THREE

Once the two choices for the inbound leg have been established, how is a pilot to determine the correct leg on which to hold? The answer is revealed by asking, "Which inbound leg is on the side of the intersection or fix specified in the holding direction?" Based on the previous clearance -- to hold east of PRADO intersection on Victor 16 -- the correct choice of inbound leg is the one that's east of PRADO, as seen in figure 5A.

*When pilots become experienced at holding pattern construction, they may elect to skip step two and proceed directly to step three.

QUESTION FOUR

Asking, "Is it a right or left-hand pattern?" will establish whether standard or non-standard turns are made. If right turns were to be made while holding east of PRADO intersection on Victor 16, the pattern would look like that shown in figure 5B. The lengthwise direction of the holding pattern lies east of PRADO intersection <u>along</u> Victor 16. Don't be misled by the holding pattern being offset to the right side of Victor 16. This has absolutely nothing to do with the holding pattern direction. Sometimes a pilot becomes confused, thinking that the right or left hand turns of the holding pattern have to do with the specified direction of holding (i.e., north, south, east, west, etc. of the fix). This is as big a misconception as believing that Pluto is a large dog that orbits the sun or that renting the movie "Caligula" will improve a person's handwriting. Whether the holding pattern is flown with right or left turns has absolutely no bearing on its direction.

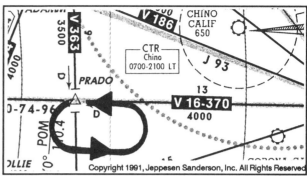

Fig. 5A Holding east of PRADO on V-16, left turns.

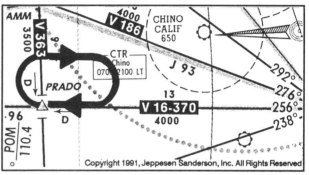

Fig. 5B. Holding east of PRADO on V-16, right turns.

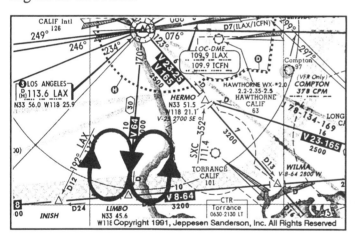

Fig. 6. Both patterns at LIMBO are located north of the fix on V-64.

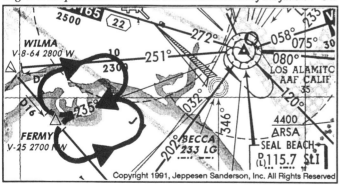

Fig. 7. Both patterns at FERMY are located NE of the fix on V-8.

Figure 6 shows both holding patterns at LIMBO intersection, lying north of the fix on Victor 64. One holding pattern is done with right turns, the other with left turns. Both patterns still lie in the same direction, north of the fix. This is a very important point to understand. I believe it's useful to meditate on this very important point. I recommend pilots take this book, sit on top the roof and ponder this paragraph. The holding patterns shown at FERMY intersection in figure 7 are both oriented in a direction northeast of the fix, on the SLI 235 radial. The only difference is one pattern is standard (right turns) and the other is non-standard (left turns).

Keep in mind, the holding pattern only has to face in the general direction specified in the clearance. At FERMY intersection in figure 7, the SLI 235 radial lies approximately northeast of the intersection. At LIMBO intersection in figure 6, Victor 64 lies approximately north of LIMBO intersection. Controllers will specify the general direction of holding; therefore, pilots shouldn't translate it literally.

Drawing a holding pattern correctly is a task which manages to contribute to its share of inflight stress and failed check rides. Understanding the specific questions to ask will make constructing the patterns a snap, even under the pressures of instrument flight. Perhaps only one area is more difficult than drawing the holding pattern, and that is deciding how to enter it.

RUDDER MUTTER

Many years ago, during an instrument ground school, I asked the class this question, "What is the purpose of a holding pattern?" Several of them, in orchestrated chorus, replied, "To keep us from passing our checkrides." One student, in particular, went on to say that he derived great benefit from the practice of holding patterns. He said that it lead to proficiency in unusual attitude recovery. He apparently had ample opportunity to polish his recoveries during those holding pattern induced synaptic overloads. These entries are not as mysterious as they may seem once a pilot has eaten from the tree of holding pattern knowledge ———— **AUTHOR**

HOLDING PATTERN ENTRIES

Perhaps the most important thing to understand about entries is that in the real world, it makes little or no difference how the pattern is entered. In real life IFR flying, the most important thing to do is to keep the airplane within the protected holding pattern airspace during the entry. It makes absolutely no difference to the controller whether a pilot uses the AIM prescribed entry or an "inverted whifferdill" entry with a full twisting dismount and difficult factor of 4.9.

In the enroute radar environment, ATC's horizontally protected holding airspace is determined by standard radar separation minima. There is no template placed over the intersection beyond which pilots shall not trespass. These templates are reserved for holding in nonradar environments. In the enroute radar environment, air traffic controllers keep airplanes a minimum of 5 nautical miles apart. Realistically, cautious controllers will always use a little more distance as a safety margin. When pilots enter holding in a radar environment, their radar track is expected to conform to something resembling a regular race track pattern. Pilots have a lot of latitude in choosing an entry. Sometimes that's what they use -- a lot of latitude (longitude, too). The point is that they should not stray outside the race track. The only time this really becomes critical is when another aircraft is nearby. Savvy controllers will monitor the aircraft during holding. If the pilot's pattern starts to resemble a large amoeba on the screen, controllers may start to move airplanes.

Of course if the controller has been alerted that the pilot is an instrument student, they immediately acknowledge a greater potential for the radar blip to drift aimlessly.* It's not unusual to see a student blip meandering off by itself, like a puppy dog with a wagging tail on a broken leash. On occasion controllers may have to go fetch these pilots and bring them back.

In a nonradar environment, straying outside the holding race track is more critical since there is no controller <u>visually</u> observing the aircraft. Therefore, pilots must be cautious not to stray too far from the race track.** Additionally, pilots holding on an airway, should be concerned about exceeding the airway's obstacle protection. A 30 degree bank turn at 300 knots will produce a turning radius of 13,800 feet. This produces a turning radius just a little over 2 nautical miles, or, a 4 nautical mile turning diameter. At 300 knots ground speed and 30 degrees of bank, pilots could exceed the 4 NM obstacle protection offered on either side of the airway.*** This explains why the maximum holding airspeed for any civilian aircraft is 230 knots IAS. This speed keeps the aircraft within the safe boundaries of the airway while maneuvering. In a smaller aircraft, moving at 100 knots with 15 degrees of bank, a turning radius of less than 4,000 feet would be expected. Therefore, a pilot's main concern when holding in a small aircraft isn't obstacle clearance, it's bumping into another airplane operating in similar horizontal planes.

*A former USAF navigator friend of mine tells me that ATC use to issue her navigator students a WALRUS clearance. ATC was use to planeloads of student navigators sweating over unfamiliar E6B's, trying to figure out where they were. It was only sometime later she found out this was ATC's informal acronym for "Wandering Aimlessly Lost over the Rural United States."
**Almost every controller I've spoken to says that they provide more than the FAA's minimum holding pattern horizontal protected airspace in a non-radar environment.
***Of course, this becomes even more critical when the aircraft is holding at the minimum altitude for that airway.

HOLDING PATTERN ENTRY METHODS

The following are methods for entering holding patterns and have been found quite useful over the years. Pick one that is the easiest and makes the most sense. Any one will allow easy entry and prevent exceeding the controller's protected airspace.

THE PLASTIC OVERLAY METHOD

This has to be the ultimate solution to deciphering holding pattern entries. Figure 8 exhibits what is internationally marketed in cereal boxes as the "Rod Machado Premier Holding Pattern Entry Decoder." Cut the box out around the dotted lines and have it photocopied on overhead transparency material. Do this at any stationery store* at a cost of approximately one dollar. Of course, most flight instructors will be stricken by painful angina at the thought of spending this quantity of money, but the investment will be worthwhile and the results guaranteed.

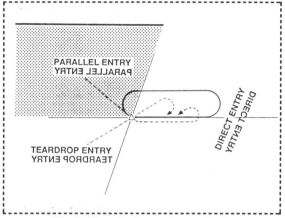

Fig. 8. The plastic overlay method.

This plastic overlay can now be used to decode any holding entry. After drawing the holding pattern on the chart, lay the transparency over the drawn race track pattern. Determine from what direction the holding pattern is approached, and pick an entry based on what the plastic overlay dictates. Non-standard patterns are easily handled by flipping the overlay over. For instance, assume the pilot was instructed to hold at SAUGS intersection as published, and shown in figure 9. Lay the decoder over the pattern depicted at SAUGS, assuring it matches the correct direction of the drawn pattern. If a pilot was approaching SAUGS from the south, on Victor 165, the decoder shows a tear drop entry would be the appropriate way to enter the pattern. Approaching SAUGS from the northeast, on Victor 386, would result in a parallel entry. Approaching from the north, on Victor 165, would result in a direct entry.

Fig. 9. Holding at SAUGS.

This is certainly a lot easier than using the plastic whiz wheel, holding pattern computer to decide upon an entry. Over the years, instrument students have come to me with one or another of these Rubic's Cube offspring, trying desperately to decipher how it's used in flight. One student had real difficulty reading the microprint on the little device. During one intense flight, I asked him what kind of entry he was going to make. He looked down at his cherished new purchase, twisting and turning the cryptic device, then replied, "Ahhh, a copyright 1983 entry?"
The best use for the holding pattern whiz wheel is for determining wind direction at the airport. Just throw it into the air and see which way it blows. It may even be useful as a self-defense device. If a Ninja from another flight school threatened an attack on the flight line, one well-aimed toss would slake his thirst for aggression.

---

*That's "stationery" not "stationary." In California there are very few "stationary" stores because of all the earthquakes. In fact, this is the only state where a hotel room comes complete with a collision damage waiver.

THE SPLIT PATTERN METHOD

Another method of decoding holding entries is to reduce the possible choices to two. When the pattern is drawn on the chart, a pilot should draw a line through the intersection, perpendicular to the inbound leg, as shown in figure 10A. WIGGI intersection has a dashed line drawn perpendicular to the inbound leg, on Victor 220. Pilots approaching WIGGI from the left of the perpendicular line, on the small side of the sliced holding pattern, would simply fly the heading of the outbound leg when crossing the intersection. This heading is flown for one minute, then a 180 degree turn is made to intercept the inbound leg. This turn should be made in the shortest direction back to the inbound leg. If directly over the track of the inbound leg, when it comes time to turn inbound, a turn to intercept should be made toward the side of the pattern where the outbound leg is located. This will keep the aircraft within protected holding pattern airspace. When approaching WIGGI anywhere from the right of the perpendicular line, the pilot should turn right to fly the outbound leg of the holding pattern, when crossing the intersection. Fly thereafter, for the appropriate time or distance, then turn right again and intercept the inbound leg.

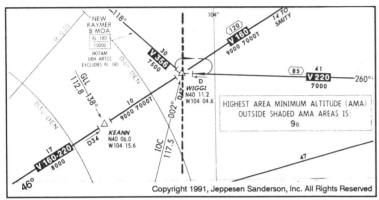

Fig. 10A. Holding at WIGGI using the split-pattern method.

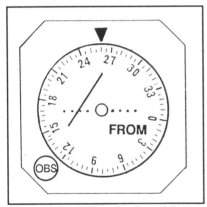

Fig. 10B. VOR indication while outbound at WIGGI.

For instance, approaching WIGGI from the southwest, on Victor 160, the pilot should fly a heading of 080 degrees (the reciprocal of 260) when crossing the intersection. The pilot would probably be paralleling the inbound leg to the north of Victor 220 with a VOR indication, as seen in figure 10B. After the end of one minute, the pilot would observe the VOR indication and make a right turn to intercept Victor 220 inbound to WIGGI. An accomplished pilot would identify the shortest direction to turn to intercept the inbound leg on Victor 220 by looking at the VOR indication.* Figure 10B shows that the 260 radial is best intercepted by flying some heading to the left of 260 degrees. This makes a right turn from an outbound heading of 080 degrees the quickest direction to turn.

Approaching WIGGI from the northeast on Victor 160, a pilot would turn right to a heading of 080 degrees and fly the outbound leg. At the end of one minute, the pilot would turn right to intercept the inbound leg. If the holding pattern were a non-standard (left-hand) pattern, a turn would be made to the left, towards the outbound leg.

The split pattern method is elegant in its simplicity. There is another method for determining holding entries that not only provides the FAA's recommended entries, it is also the quickest and most painless method I have ever experienced.

---

* A course selection of 260, and a left needle indication, implies that some heading to the left of 260 degrees is needed to intercept the 260 radial (V-220). If a 30 degree intercept is chosen, the aircraft should fly an intercept heading of 230 degrees. While flying outbound at WIGGI, on a heading of 080 degrees, a right turn is the quickest way to get to the intercept heading of 230 degrees. This is how an accomplished pilot may think in determining which direction to turn to intercept the inbound leg.

THE HEADING INDICATOR OVERLAY METHOD

Another successful and effective thought process for deciphering pattern entries is called the heading overlay method. This technique is so effective that it can be considered a Rosetta stone for the instantaneous decoding of any entry. The secret of this method is to simply visualize the holding pattern on the heading indicator. Visualize the VOR, NDB or holding intersection at the center of the heading indicator. Locate the outbound heading of the holding pattern along the DG's compass rose. Visualize a line drawn inward toward the center of the DG from this heading. This will be the inbound leg of the pattern.* Continue to draw a turn, either right or left, depending on the direction specified in the clearance.

Figure 11 shows three examples of holding patterns superimposed on the heading indicator. Assume that a pilot is approaching WIGGI intersection, figure 10A, and has been instructed to hold as published. The direction of the outbound leg is 080 degrees. The pilot should now look at the heading indicator and identify where the 080 degree direction is on the DG's compass rose and imagine an inbound leg toward the center of this instrument.

If the inbound leg of the standard holding pattern falls anywhere within an arc of 70 degrees to the right of the aircraft's present heading, a tear drop entry should be made into the holding pattern. Figure 11A shows an approach to WIGGI intersection from the southwest, on V-220, while heading 46 degrees. The inbound leg falls within a 70 degree arc to the right of the present heading, therefore, a tear drop entry would be appropriate for this direction. With just a little bit of imagination pilots can actually see the complete holding pattern with a birds-eye view of them approaching. Looking at figure 11A, assume the airplane is at the center of the heading indicator and has just arrived at WIGGI. A right turn to a heading of 050 degrees (30 degrees to the left of 080) at the holding fix would set the aircraft up perfectly for the tear drop entry.

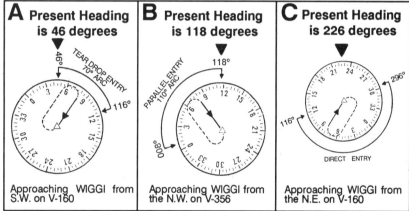

Fig. 11. The heading indicator overlay method for holding pattern entries.

If the inbound leg of the standard holding pattern falls anywhere within a 110 degree arc to the left of the present heading, a parallel entry is recommended. Figure 11B shows an approach to WIGGI intersection from the northwest, on V-356, while heading 118 degrees. The inbound leg falls within 110 degrees to the left of the aircraft's present heading. Therefore, a parallel entry into the holding pattern would be appropriate. Visualizing the complete holding pattern on the DG, as shown in figure 11B, identifies that a left turn to a heading of 80 degrees would allow the pilot to parallel the inbound leg.

If the inbound leg of the standard holding pattern lies beyond the 70 degree right position or the 110 degree left position, a direct entry should be made. Figure 11C shows an approach to WIGGI intersection from the northeast, on V-160, while heading 226 degrees. The inbound leg falls outside both the 70 and 110 degree arc positions. Therefore, a direct entry should be made into the holding pattern.

*For consistency, I will refer to the mental line drawn from the outbound heading to the center of the DG as the "inbound leg." However, DO NOT FORGET that the number to look for on the DG, to identify this inbound leg, is the OUTBOUND HEADING. Sorry this is a little confusing, but it's very important to take a moment to commit this to memory. It will be worth it. Trust me!

Visualizing the complete holding pattern on the DG, as shown in figure 11C, identifies that pilots need only turn right and fly an outbound heading of 080 degrees when crossing the fix to accomplish the direct entry.

If the holding pattern is non-standard, the 70 and 110 degree reference positions are reversed, as shown in figure 12. Simply identify the position of the inbound leg on the heading indicator. If the inbound leg falls anywhere within 110 degrees to the right of the aircraft's heading, a parallel entry should be made. If the inbound leg falls anywhere within 70 degrees to the left of the aircraft's heading, a teardrop entry should be made. If the direction of the inbound leg falls outside the 110 and 70 degree position, then a direct entry is appropriate.

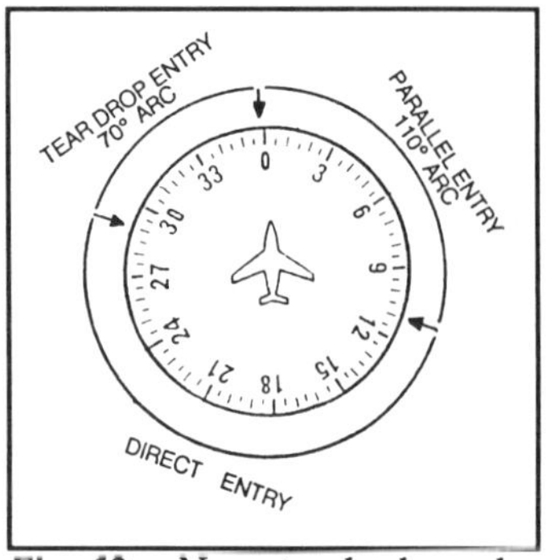

Fig. 12. Non-standard overlay method.

THE MODIFIED HEADING OVERLAY METHOD

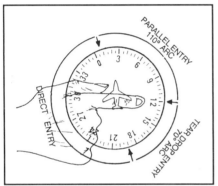

Fig. 13. The modified heading overlay method uses the finger as a heading reference.

The previous method of deciphering holding entries only works when the aircraft is directly approaching the holding fix. However, if the aircraft is not yet directly approaching the holding intersection, then a modified method can be used to determine the entry. The pilot should place a finger, or the heading bug, on the final heading that will be used to approach the holding intersection. From this point of reference, the pilot can determine the entry based on the 70 and 110 degree positions relative to the finger or heading bug location, as shown in figure 13.

I recall many unusual types of holding pattern entries over the years. I have heard of direct drop entries, tearallel entries and even heard of vicinity entries. That's where a pilot just stays in the vicinity of the intersection. None has ever surpassed what one pilot told me during his instrument competency check, many years ago, when I asked him what type of entry he was going to make. He looked at the paper for a while, made a few scratches, then said, "Ah...a silence/no silence entry." Raising an eyebrow, I asked, "Just what is that?" He replied, "Well, you just sort of enter in whatever way feels good and listen to the radio. If ATC doesn't say anything, then you must have done a good job!" This was the fellow I mentioned before who had more knowledge of disconnecting hobbs meters than any person this side of the Anchorage localizer. I suspect he's the type of pilot that would send his NASA ASRS form in before each flight. He probably had a special secretary who had a full time position just filling these reports out for him. Needless to say, it took a great deal of time to straighten him out and to get the FBO's hobbs meter reconnected.

Someone once asked, "What is it that you get when you play a country-western song backwards?" Their answer was, "You get your wife back, you get your house back, you get your truck back and you get out of jail." When pilots apply the rules provided in this chapter, in the proper order, they are going to get a welcome sense of comfort when confronted with their next holding pattern.

A similar sense of comfort and confidence will be felt by pilots when they understand the inner workings of the IFR airspace system.

7. HOW THE IFR SYSTEM WORKS

When the magician, David Copperfield, caused a Learjet to disappear before a large crowd in Las Vegas, he startled and stunned the audience. Right before their very eyes, an object disappeared, in a way which defied reality. Any concept of illusion, or simple distraction, was simply inconceivable. "Where did it go?" his audience wondered. They probably thought it went where all the other airplanes go that disappear -- South America. Summoning the forces of magic, Copperfield pulled off the ultimate, mystical illusion. To many instrument rated pilots, ATC matches this trick every time an IFR flight plan is filed and activated.

Pilots often know little more about how their IFR flight plan is generated, and how the ATC system works, than Copperfield's audience knew about rabbits from hats or disappearing airplanes. Without understanding the intricacies of the ATC system, they must operate solely on faith and the anticipated mercy of ATC's good will and honorable intentions. Knowing the rules and limitations of the IFR system is the key to safe and relaxed instrument flying. It will also keep a pilot's airplane from disappearing for real.

CONTROLLED AIRSPACE

IFR flight in the continental United States is performed in controlled airspace (otherwise known as Class, A, B, C, D or E). Pilots may dare to fly IFR in uncontrolled airspace (Class G) without an ATC clearance and IFR flight plan, but this is about as sane as IFR banner towing. Such action would have fascinated Dr. Freud. First of all, pilots would have to create their own airways, charting their own terrain clearance and VOR reception altitudes.* Of course, since the entire concept of IFR flight in uncontrolled airspace is slightly insane, a bonafide nut shouldn't be troubled with these complications! Second, pilots would never know if someone else is aviating in the same airspace and altitude. Flying IFR in uncontrolled airspace is a daredevil stunt that's best left to those people having metal plates in their heads. Don't do it! Besides, pilots with metal plates are frequently getting lost because the magnetic compass always points to their head!

Controlled airspace is administered by an air traffic controller whose primary job is to assure separation between IFR airplanes. Many of these controllers come together in subterranean buildings called Air Route Traffic Control Centers. Actually, these Centers are not always underground; they are just dark on the inside. Therefore, the belief that controllers work intensely for a while, then someone takes them to the surface, walks them around to revitalize them, then commands them back down into the pit is a fabrication. However, having spent some time watching controllers over the years, I can affirm that, in the high density parts of the country, they often have their hands full.

An inspiring, educating and mesmerizing experience for an instrument pilot is to sit at a radar screen and watch controllers work traffic. Most pilots will get so excited by what they're learning, they'll feel compelled to grab a microphone and help out. This personal insight will allow them to better, and more appropriately, leverage the IFR system to make their IFR flying safer.

*If pilots request, controllers will include routes through Class G (uncontrolled) airspace as per the FAA controller's handbook (7110.65, Par. 5-90(c)). Pilots should be advised that, while it is legal to fly IFR in uncontrolled airspace without an ATC clearance and without an IFR flight plan, such action is not recommended by this author.

In addition, the experience adds substance and a human dimension to those ethereal voices that accompany every IFR flight. Any empathetic exchange between pilots and controllers concerning the other's needs is bound to have positive effects.

THE SYSTEM

There are 21 Air Route Traffic Control Centers in the United States. Each Center is made up of many individual sectors that are manned by one or more controllers. There may even be a low altitude and high altitude controller, if the airspace is very busy. This explains why pilots are always being handed off from one controller to the next. As an instrument student, I always thought it was because my lack of expertise exhausted the previous controller. I'd wear out one, then they would bring up another. I often wondered what would happen if they ran out of controllers before the "used-up" ones could regenerate?

IN A MOMENT OF DEEP FRUSTRATION
CONTROlleR BOB GOES AFTER
A STUDENT PiLoT

Air Route Traffic Control Centers provide radar coverage over most of the United States. At airports where approach control isn't available, Center may provide radar coverage to handle arriving and departing IFR flights. However, there are many areas where no radar coverage exists, or radar is not available on a 24-hour basis. IFR operations in these areas are conducted without radar. These are administered in much the same way they were 40 to 50 years ago. Controllers simply follow an airplane's progress by position reports. If pilots are fortunate enough to have been exposed to non-radar operations, the experience will serve them well. There's little that breeds more confidence and self-reliance in pilots than being completely responsible for their own navigation.

Controllers at the Center are responsible for all the IFR flight conducted within thousands of square miles of airspace. The boundaries of each Center can be quite large. For example, Los Angeles Center handles the airspace from Central California south to the Mexican border and east to around Phoenix, Arizona. Center's primary purpose is to handle IFR enroute traffic.

Air Route Traffic Control Centers normally control the IFR traffic above approach control's airspace. In the Los Angeles basin, the Center starts controlling traffic at approximately 13,000 feet MSL up to Flight Level 600 (60,000 feet). This is the top of the high altitude airspace structure. Above FL600 there is activity by the military, but no one is quite sure what it is. At least no one can seem to stay there, holding their breath, long enough to find out. This is the domain of aircraft like the SR-71, U-2 and aircraft of that ilk. One controller received a call from a pilot requesting FL600. That's 60,000 feet! The controller said, "Hey buddy, if you can get up there, then you can have it!" The pilot responded in his best, laconic, Chuck Yeager voice by saying, "Ahhh, we'll be coming down to FL600." Now that's performance! These guys probably have little TV's with planets orbiting the screen in lieu of altimeters.

Approach control, where available, is responsible for IFR traffic operations below Center's airspace. Approach control handles all traffic approaching and departing local airports. Where approach control's jurisdiction ends, Center takes over. Approach control is sometimes called a TRACON (Terminal Radar Approach Control), RAPCON (Radar Approach Control) or TRACAB (TRACON in Tower Cab) if radar located in the tower. TRACONs are radar facilities usually found in separate locations from Air Route Traffic Control Centers. It's not unusual to find TRACONs located in the tower for one of the airports they serve. Towards the west, Santa Barbara, Monterey, Las Vegas, Palm Springs and Honolulu all have TRACONs located in Air Traffic Control Towers.

TEC FOR FUN AND PROFIT

If an IFR flight is to be conducted entirely within the boundaries of the individual approach control facilities, and doesn't penetrate Center's airspace, a Tower En Route Control (TEC) provision may be made for IFR pilots. This allows them to operate to and from any airports within the airspace covered by approach control.* Where there is an area not covered by these approach controls, Center must assume responsibility for controlling traffic, and Tower En Route Control will not be available.

Tower En Route operations offer pilots a couple of advantages. First, since IFR flights are probably operating closer to radar sites, these flights can be controlled with less horizontal separation. When IFR flights are conducted within 40 miles of the radar antenna, a minimum of 3 miles horizontal separation is authorized. All IFR flights operating beyond 40 miles from the radar site are regulated by a minimum of 5 miles horizontal separation. In fact, the standard separation for IFR traffic in Center's airspace is 5 miles. To pilots, this means that they can get into and out of airports faster when operating in the TEC system because of the smaller required distance between aircraft.

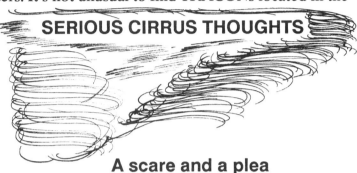

SERIOUS CIRRUS THOUGHTS

A scare and a plea

I was northbound, IFR, above an undercast (8,300') at 9,000'. Approaching an area of puffy cumulus clouds (tops 8,500-10,000), and in contact with Approach Control, I suddenly noticed what appeared to be a large bird above one of the nearer cumulus clouds. I thought it might be migratory birds -- but it was a small aircraft that popped out of the clouds about 1/2 mile in front of me, on a head-on collision course at 9,000'. I turned to the East as this plane turned due South. All of this happened in the space of ten seconds. The cloud conditions were such (and were for the next 120 miles) that the pilot was in the clouds part of the time and skimming in and out of the tops for the remainder. There was NO way he could have made this flight VFR. I immediately called Approach to see why I had not been warned about this traffic. They informed me that they had no other IFR traffic near me and, furthermore, showed no other targets near me on their radar. By this time, I was in the clouds and unable to immediately follow the other plane. I called Approach who tracked a small aircraft that matched the description, but, of course, I can't positively identify it. I filed a near midair report with the suggestion that someone talk with the pilot of the tracked aircraft -- just in case. So, in conclusion, if I had been ten seconds farther along, I'd have hit that plane. Please tell those who would fly in the clouds, without filing IFR, that radar doesn't show all targets -- especially if they don't have a transponder, or don't turn it on. If you MUST fly thorough clouds "VFR," then please have the common courtesy to put your transponder "ON" so that radar will see you and the rest of us can be warned. There really is no excuse for this type of flying!

None whatever! Flying "VFR" in the clouds is stupid and illegal. Don't do it.

ASRS REPORT

*When approach control facilities border each other (i.e. their airspace touches), TEC flight can be made through these individual facilities. This is why it is possible to fly IFR under TEC from Santa Barbara to San Diego, California -- a distance of over 160 NM. At no time is an airplane outside the coverage area of an approach control facility. In fact, there are 5 invididual approach control facilities, all side-by-side, that an aircraft flies through enroute to San Diego.

Second, TEC allows pilots easier access into the IFR system. In Southern California, it's possible to fly from Santa Barbara to San Diego in the TEC System without having to file a "paper type" flight plan with the FSS. Pilots can be sitting on the ground at Santa Barbara, call the tower controller, and ask for a Tower En Route IFR clearance to San Diego's Lindbergh field. No "paper type" IFR flight plan is necessary. When tower controllers are too busy to accommodate them, pilots may be directed to file a flight plan with the local FSS.

FROM: BUR VNY WHP

TO	ROUTE ID	ROUTE	ATC USE
FUL LGB SLI TOA (RWY 29)	BURG1	V186 V394 SLI	J70MPQ50
HHR LAX	BURG2	V186 ELMOO	JMPQ40
LAX (LAXE)	BURG3	VNY SMO	JM50PQ40
TOA (RWY 11)	BURG4	VNY SMO	JMPQ40
SMO	BURG5	V186 DARTS	JMPQ30
CCB CNO EMT HMT L12 L65 L66 L67 F70 ONT POC RAL RIR RIV SBD	BURG6	V186 PDZ	JM70PQ50
CRQ NFG NKX L39 L32	BURG7	V186 V363 V23 OCN	JM70PQ50
MYF NRS NZY SAN SDM SEE	BURG8	V186 V363 V23 MZB	PQ50
MYF NRS NZY SAN SDM SEE	BURG9	V186 POM 164 V208 MZB 320 MZB	JM70
OXR CMA	BURG10	VNY	JMPQ40
SBA	BURG11	FIM V186 V27 KWANG	JMPQ60
SNA	BURG12	V186 V363 V8 SLI	JMPQ50
SAN (SANE)	BURG13	V186 V363 V23 V165 SARGS	PQ50
SAN (SANE)	BURG14	V186 POM 164 V25 V165 SARGS	JM70
NZJ NTK	BURG15	V186 V363 V23 NZJ 162 NZJ	JM70PQ50
AVX	BURG16	V186 V363 KRAUZ SXC	JM70PQ50

FROM: HMT L12 L65 L66 L67 RAL RIR RIV SBD F70

TO	ROUTE ID	ROUTE	ATC USE
BUR VNY WHP	ONTG1	PDZ V186 VNY	JM80PQ60
CMA OXR	ONTG2	PDZ V186 FIM	JM80PQ60
SBA	ONTG3	PDZ V186 V27 KWANG	JM80PQ60
SMO	ONTG4	PDZ V186 DARTS	JMPQ60
LGB	ONTG5	PDZ V16 V363 V23 SLI	J80

FROM: FUL LGB SLI SNA TOA (RWY 11) NTK NZJ

TO	ROUTE ID	ROUTE	ATC USE
SMO	CSTG6	SLI V23 LAX LAX 046 ELMOO	JM70PQ40
SMO (LAXE)	CSTG7	SLI SLI 333 V186 DARTS	JM50PQ40
CCB EMT POC ONT(E)	CSTG8	SLI V8 V363 POM	JMPQ50
CNO HMT L12 L65 L66 L67 F70 ONT RAL RIR RIV SBD	CSTG9	MUSEL SID MUSEL RAVEC PDZ (SNA RWY 19 ONLY)	JM60
CNO HMT L12 L65 L66 L67 F70 ONT RAL RIR RIV SBD	CSTG10	SLI V8 PDZ	JMPQ50
CRQ L39 NFG NKX L32	CSTG11	V23 OCN	PQ50
CRQ L39 NFG NKX L32	CSTG12	V25 V208 OCN	JM70
MYF NRS NZY SAN SDM SEE	CSTG13	V23 MZB	PQ50
MYF NRS NZY SAN SDM SEE	CSTG14	V25 V208 MZB 320 MZB	J110M90
OXR CMA	CSTG15	SLI V23 LAX VNY	M50PQ40
OXR CMA	CSTG16	SXC SXC 295 VTU 160 VTU	J80
SBA	CSTG17	SLI V23 LAX VTU KWANG	PQ40
SBA (LAXE)	CSTG18	SLI SLI 333 V186 V27 KWANG	M50PQ40
SBA	CSTG19	SXC SXC 255 VTU 160 VTU KWANG	JM80
SAN (SANE)	CSTG20	V23 V165 SARGS	PQ50
SAN (SANE)	CSTG21	V25 V165 SARGS	J110M90
CRQ L39 NFG NKX L32	CSTG22	SXC V208 OCN	JMPQ50
MYF NRS NZY SAN SDM SEE	CSTG23	SXC V208 MZB 320 MZB	J110M90
MYF NRS NZY SAN SDM SEE (WHEN SAN IS EAST TRAFFIC)	CSTG24	SXC V208 OCN V165 SARGS	PQ50
MYF NRS NZY SAN SDM SEE	CSTG25	SXC V27 MZB	PQ50

Fig. 1. Preapproved IFR routings for flight within the TEC system.

Essentially, the tower controller requests an IFR clearance for the pilot from the Center's computer. Pilots are then assigned a preapproved routing and altitude. These routings are often available for review by pilots for preplanning purposes and can be obtained at the nearest ATC facility. These are regularly published by the FAA and are depicted, as in Figure 1. Pilots should check with the nearest ATC facility for a listing of these preferred departure and arrival routes for their local area.

Tower En Route operations can be found in many parts of the country. The prerequisite for their availability is that the area be covered by approach control. TEC's intent is to allow nonturbojet aircraft to operate to and from metropolitan areas without entering Center's airspace. It is also intended for relatively short flights of two hours' duration or less. If pilots are filing a "paper type" flight plan using pre-approved TEC routings, they should list the letters "TEC" in the remarks section of the flight plan. This information provides the FSS specialist with a pilot's request to stay within approach control airspace and avoid operations in Center's airspace.

Understand that "TEC" operations may vary slightly across the country as do many local customs. For example, in California, "gun control" is a hot political issue. However, in Texas, "gun control" means holding it with both hands! Similarly, in California it's rare to see a pickup truck with a gun rack in the rear window. In Texas, it's not uncommon to see a gun rack on the back of a motorcycle. Be prepared for slight variations in "TEC" from one ATC facility to the next.

While the Tower En Route IFR flight plan is undoubtedly an easy and efficient way to enter the ATC system, pilots should be aware of a few caveats. When a Tower En Route flight plan is verbally solicited from the tower controller, valuable flight plan information is often not recorded. A tower controller, generating a TEC flight plan, is not required to record the following information into the computer: number of people on board the aircraft, color of aircraft, pilot's name and address, the amount of fuel on board and true airspeed. If an aircraft went down, search and rescue operators would not have the critical data necessary to help them in their search.

When a "paper type" flight plan is filed, this search and rescue information is kept by the Flight Service Station and provided to the appropriate search and rescue operators.

The convenience of filing a Tower En Route flight plan can often lure a pilot into flying IFR without considering an alternate airport. Remember, an alternate is not required for IFR flight when, within plus or minus one hour of the pilot's ETA at the destination airport, the weather is forecast to have a ceiling of at least 2,000 feet above the airport elevation and visibility of at least 3 statute miles. A good memory aid for this regulation is: alternate 1-2-3: 1 hour, 2,000 feet and 3 miles. Flying IFR to an airport 30 minutes away, that has a ceiling of 1,500 feet, requires that an alternate airport be selected for the flight. It's quite easy to call the tower controller and request a TEC clearance to this airport without even considering, or

CAUGHT WITH WHEEL PANTS DOWN

Pilot: *I've been calling you for fifteen minutes. You having radio trouble?*
Tower: *It would seem so.*
Pilot: *Fixed now?*
Tower: *Must be. I hear you.*
Pilot: *Works better when you're in the tower.*
ASRS REPORT

listing, an alternate. Filing a "paper type" flight plan with Flight Service at least forces pilots to contemplate the alternate box on the flight plan form. Hopefully, this visual prodding will motivate a pilot to determine if an alternate is actually necessary.

Even without listing an alternate on a tower-generated TEC flight plan, pilots can still insert an alternate into the systems computer. Tower controllers can list any "pilot remarks" directly into the computer. Asking the tower controller to include the name of the alternate in the "remarks section" of the TEC flight plan will cause this information to print out on the pilot's data strip. The controller can readily identify the pilot's alternate airport from this information. During a ramp check, this should satisfy any curious FAA inspector's concern about whether a pilot selected an alternate when required by the FAR's. (To add a little humor to these FAA ramp checks, a physician pilot friend immediately hands the FAA inspector his license when requested. Unfortunately, it's his fishing license. He always tells the inspector that his medical has just expired, then proceeds to give himself his own medical exam right there on the flight line).

Alternate airport information, once typed into the computer's data base, is kept with other essential search and rescue information. Radar controllers won't see this information on the data strip. In fact, the data strip contains only essential flight information such as: transponder code, true airspeed, route of flight, altitude, etc., as shown in figure 2. If the radar controller needs to know what airport the pilot has chosen for an alternate, he need only ask the pilot. In the event of lost communication, a controller can identify a pilot's alternate airport by calling the Flight Service Station and having them research this information.

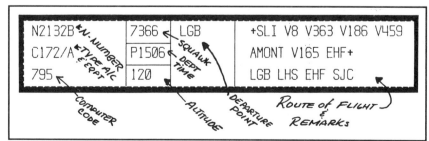

Fig. 2. The flight data progress strip contains only operational information. Search and resuce information is kept by the FSS.

Filing a "paper type" flight plan within the TEC system is usually the wisest procedure when undertaking any IFR flight. At least, a pilot will be led through all the boxes on the flight plan form. This is especially important if the pilot is an IFR student. Many freshly-ticketed IFR adventurers have hastily taken flight without adequate preparation.* The "paper type" flight plan will, at least, motivate the pilot to reflect upon possible routes, fuel consumption and alternate airport requirements. This is minimal insurance for IFR pilots, especially considering they may not yet have the depth of experience that fosters sound habit patterns. It's rather frightening to think that IFR students may obtain an instrument rating without flying in the clouds, selecting their desired routing (by flying TEC), flying without the use of radar monitoring, or having gone more than 51 NM away from the destination airport, (i.e., the 250 nautical mile, IFR cross country is accumulative distance, not airway distance).

ATC's FAVORITE ROUTES

When a "paper type" IFR flight plan is filed with the Flight Service Station, it follows a predictable route. These flight plans are first coded into a computer terminal by the specialist. In essence, the specialist is communicating directly with the computer at the nearest Air Route Traffic Control Center. This computer is responsible for allocating the routes, altitudes and transponder codes given in the IFR clearance.

When a preferred routing has been established for the direction a pilot intends to travel, the computer will select this route automatically, regardless of the routing the pilot has requested. Pilots may slave for hours over charts and select the shortest, most efficient or most elegant routing humanly possible. All this energy may have been for naught. They will get what the computer thinks is logical. This explains why most instrument students can be found in a deep, dark depression just before an instrument flight. They may be heard mumbling something about wanting to fall on their sword to deal with this depression. IFR pilots should know the shortest distance between two points is a curve, a zigzag, even a circle, under the ATC mandated laws of geometry. Euclid, please forgive them! And be careful about getting into an argument with the computer. One may byte off more than one could eschew!** Remember, Euclid never flew IFR!

One of these days, don't be surprised to find that a frustrated student has run a hose from the exhaust duct into the cabin, with a little note saying he surrendered his will to live when ATC gave him a new, full route clearance other than the one he filed. If pilots have a definite need for routes other than what ATC offers them, they can manage the problem in one of two ways. First, they can ask the tower controller to request a different routing directly from the radar controller. This is a simple communication via telephone connections from the tower cab to the radar facility. The radar controller may be able to create a route for the pilot that will satisfy both of their needs. Second, the pilot may elect to negotiate a different routing with the controller when airborne. Of course, this presupposes the pilot will fly the original routing until renegotiated.

GOOD ATTITUDE INDICATOR

To avoid last-minute paper chases, some experienced pilots "script" the most important flight information -- estimated time of flight, estimated fuel burn, expected departure routing, etc. -- well in advance of a departure (the night before, for example). This exercise provides a review of likely scenarios, and can help pilots detect deviations from expected procedures when these do occur. **ASRS REPORT**

*Checking the weather before a local IFR flight is very important. If pilots file IFR to VFR on top, they should have an idea of expected cloud tops as well as the extent of cloud coverage. There's probably nothing quite as chilling as being on top of a cloud deck, with a lost comm problem, and not having any idea where to go to find VFR conditions.
**I had to do that! I may do it again!

The computer's program gives a pilot a clearance based on predetermined routes in one of four categories: preferred IFR routes; preferential departure routings (PDR); preferential arrival routings (PAR); or preferential departure and arrival routings (PDAR).* These preferential routes are based on flow control and traffic management considerations.

Preferred IFR routes can be found in the back of the Airport Facility Directory, as seen in figure 3. The directory stipulates routing between busy terminal facilities. These routes are not normally used between facilities within the TEC system. For operations within the TEC system, preferential arrival and departure routings (PDAR's) are often used. These routings can be found at one of the local ATC facilities in the TEC area.

	LOW ALTITUDE	
	Route	Effective Times (UTC)
SAN FRANCISCO/OAKLAND METRO AREA From SAN FRANCISCO Area: West Bay Airports		
Los Angeles Area	(70-90-110-130-150-170) V27 VTU V299 SADDE V107 LAX	1400-0800
From OAKLAND Area: East Bay Airports		
Los Angeles Area	(70-90-110-130-150-170) V109 PXN V113 V485 V299 SADDE V107 LAX	1400-0800
	HIGH ALTITUDE	
Terminals	Route	Effective Times (UTC)
BURBANK		
Chicago O'Hare	TRM J78 DRK J96 IRK J26 BDF V10 PLANO	0700-2200
	or	
	DAG PGS J64 FMN J110 ALS J102 SLN J96 IRK J26 BDF V10 PLANO	
Detroit Satellites: Detroit City, Windsor, Pontiac, Willow Run, Ann Arbor	[BUR OBH] OBH J100 DBQ BAE MKG LAN V103 CRATR	1100-0300
Metro Wayne Co	[BUR OBH] OBH J100 DBQ BAE MKG V450 DXO342 POLAR	

Fig. 3. Preferred IFR routes can be found in the back of the Airport Facility Directory.

When operating within a busy terminal area like Los Angeles, pilots will experience many PDAR's. For an IFR flight from Van Nuys to Long Beach, the shortest airway routing is via V165 to the LAX VOR, then to the SLI VOR, as seen in figure 4. Pilots filing this routing, even with "please" in the remarks section of the flight plan, are not going to get what appears logical. This routing takes the aircraft directly across the LAX Class B airspace. Pilots would scatter 747's like a covey of quail if ATC permitted them to fly IFR across all those localizers.

The insert, in the bottom left hand corner of figure 4, depicts the preferential departure and arrival route (PDAR) from Van Nuys to Long Beach. This route takes pilots southeast bound via V186 (VNY's 095 radial) to intercept V394 from Pomona VOR direct to the SLI VOR. This route circumnavigates LAX Class B airspace to the east.

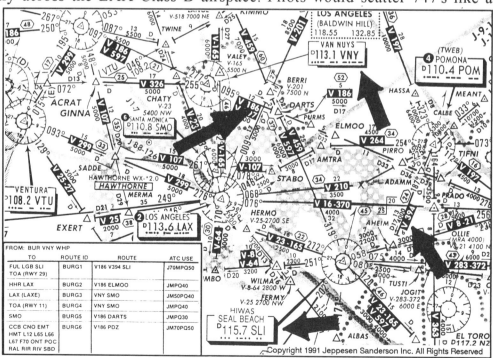

FROM: BUR VNY WHP			
TO	ROUTE ID	ROUTE	ATC USE
FUL LGB SLI TOA (RWY 29)	BURG1	V186 V394 SLI	J70MPQ50
HHR LAX	BURG2	V186 ELMOO	JMPQ40
LAX (LAXE)	BURG3	VNY SMO	JM50PQ40
TOA (RWY 11)	BURG4	VNY SMO	JMPQ40
SMO	BURG5	V186 DARTS	JMPQ30
CCB CNO EMT HMT L12 L65 L66 L67 F70 ONT POC RAL RIR RIV SBD	BURG6	V186 PDZ	JM70PQ50

Fig. 4. Preferential route around LAX Class B airspace from VNYs to SLI

*All these routes are simply the "preferred" type routes that the Center's computers have been programmed to give pilots.

CHANGING THE GAME

Changes in flight planned routes are not uncommon in the ATC system. When a pilot is to receive a route other than the one filed, the initial data strip will code this new routing in red or list FRC (Full Route Clearance) in the remarks section. This alerts the controller that this is a new routing, unexpected by the pilot. Therefore, controllers won't say, "Cleared as filed" to pilots when red colored routing or FRC is shown on the data strip. And, of course, pilots always have the option of requesting a "full route clearance" whenever they are unsure of their clearance. Other controllers working with the pilot will not be clued in that this route is different than the one requested. This occurs because additional data strips are transmitted in the normal black color. This explains why, when a clearance has been modified, there may be some future confusion as to the intended route of flight. It may be that the controller responsible for reading the clearance, with the new routing, didn't deliver it clearly enough. Similarly, the pilot may have misinterpreted what he heard, as opposed to what the clearance was expected to be. In these circumstances, a pilot should immediately request routing clarification from the controller.*

When an IFR flight plan is approved by the computer, a copy of the clearance (in the form of a data strip) is sent electronically to those Air Traffic Control facilities nearest the point of departure. One copy is sent to the nearest tower, or flight service station, and another is sent to the Air Traffic Control facility responsible for handling the departure. In many cases, where tower facilities have the equipment, the computer generates a copy of the flight plan 25 minutes prior to the proposed departure time. If departing from a tower controlled field, pilots can simply call the tower controller, on the clearance delivery frequency, and ask for their prefiled clearance. By receiving the clearance early, the controller has time to verbally practice compressing the words seamlessly together, so they can be spewed out with what a student once called the "Flaming Tongue of Fire."

TONGUE OF FIRE

The best way to handle a rapid fire clearance is to say the words, "Student pilot." As soon as controllers hear this, they immediately become more concerned. When aviators say, "Student pilot," most of the seasoned flight instructors abandon the airport until the student is done flying. I was with a student once who said, "Student pilot" and the controller came back with, "Hey, don't worry, I'm a student controller; we can mess each other up!" When pilots say they are student pilots and they are in a King Air, this arouses suspicion, but, at least the humor of the situation may get across the pilot's message. Of course, if this doesn't work, and the controllers still insist on Mach 2 verbiage, the pilot can simply adopt a foreign accent and mention something about turning off their radio and taxiing around the airport for awhile. This compels the controller's attention. Fortunately, most controllers are quite sensitive to the pilot's needs, and these linguistic sorties do not normally become a problem.

NONTOWER DEPARTURES

Pilots departing IFR from other than a tower controlled airport will find that their IFR clearance will normally be delivered to the Flight Service Station nearest the point of departure. When filing a flight plan with the FSS, pilots should wait approximately 30 minutes before calling to retrieve their clearance. This is usually how long it takes the flight plan to be processed. Many pilots prefer to have

*When activating an IFR flight plan in flight, always request the full route clearance. This could save a lot of grief. There are system quirks that may allow the original data strip containing the red rerouting, or FRC, to be delivered to the wrong sector. Therefore, the controller issuing the clearance may not know that the pilot's routing has changed. The controller may say, "cleared as filed" leading the pilot to believe that his routing is unchanged.

the FSS specialists give them a call on the local phone when the clearance is ready. This may save toll charges and also serves to make pilots look important. After all, when the Flight Service specialist calls, they need only tell their friends that the specialist was calling to get their advice on a weather problem.

When pilots depart an airport without a tower or Flight Service Station on the field, they are usually given a "departure window" with the IFR clearance. The clearance might say, "32B is cleared to ...; clearance void if not off by 10:15; if not off by 10:15, advise Albuquerque, not later than 10:45, of intentions, time now 10:05." When pilots receive a clearance like this, they have 10 minutes to get airborne. If not airborne by 10:15, their IFR clearance is cancelled. Pilots are still under an obligation to notify ATC within 30 minutes that they didn't make the departure window. This is a search and rescue provision; ATC has no way of knowing if the pilot crashed after departure, or just decided not to go on the flight.*

A departure window that is at least 10 minutes from the time the clearance is received is always desirable. Sometimes this isn't possible. Yet, I have received clearances with departure windows of two minutes. Had the clearance been accepted, only two minutes would have been allotted to get the airplane to the runup area, checked out and readied for departure. I'm not that fast. Besides, rushing is the surest way to forget something. A good way to handle this situation is simply to ask the controller for a longer departure window, or a window that would open up a few minutes later. Most controllers are accommodating. If they refuse to negotiate, pilots can always use a psychological ploy of pretending that they are a friend of the family. They may say something like, "Hey, I'd like a longer departure window and your cousin said to say, hello." Of course, they may reply, "My cousin beat me up when I was a kid, so don't even think of leaving this airport."

Pilots should realize that if they don't get what they initially wanted from ATC, they shouldn't give up; they should negotiate! The controller may not want to extend a departure window because of traffic concerns. A good negotiating tactic is to offer to depart and climb in VFR conditions, to an altitude that accommodates the controller, as well as the pilot. This negates the controller's need to apply IFR separation standards, thereby easing the departure window restrictions. Of course, pilots should not depart VFR unless it is VFR.

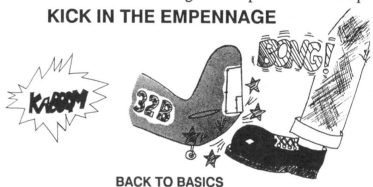

KICK IN THE EMPENNAGE

BACK TO BASICS

I was flying a small plane, on a search for a missing aircraft, in weather conditions that varied from 500 to 1,500 foot ceilings and 5 to 25 miles visibility. My assigned search area included an uncontrolled airport and its associated control zone. I conducted my search at 500 feet above ground level. As I approached the airport to examine the traffic pattern and approach routes, a commuter airline flight, on an IFR approach, heard my position transmission and confirmed with UNICOM that the field was IFR. Upon hearing this, I realized that I was in the control zone illegally and proceeded to leave. I communicated my intentions to the commuter that I was well in the clear and would stay away from the airport. I don't believe there was any danger of collision.

I have to say that I was entirely responsible for the situation. I was using a TCA chart to check for obstructions and to navigate my search track, but failed to notice the control zone symbol. I did see the airport white beacon, but this failed to register. I was flying in good visibility, over flat land and with a definite cloud base. It never occurred to me that I wasn't legally VFR.

Anyway, the basic problem was that I am an airline pilot, and while I am familiar with airline IFR procedures, I had become weak on light airplane VFR procedures. I suggest that more frequent study of AIM, charts and FAR's would have alerted me to the technicalities of VFR rules and procedures. Also, since more and more airline flights are using uncontrolled airports, it might be wise to emphasize the possible conflicts that might arise and the different procedures involved for traffic avoidance.

ASRS REPORT

---

*But beware! Don't takeoff beyond the departure window time! A pilot could end up in trouble with Ned the Fed. A pilot may also have to file a written report and what's really scary about that is trying to spell Albuquerque!

BACKUPS

Flight plan data strips are sent to the nearest Air Traffic Control facility responsible for handling the IFR departure. The radar controller responsible for the departure will have the strip available 25 minutes prior to the estimated time of departure. As the flight progresses within a Center's or TRACON's airspace, each successive controller will have a data strip generated on the flight. At modern Air Traffic Control Centers, a printer at each controller's station generates a data strip for the airplane. This paper back-up is very important. If the cleaning person kicks out the plug on the radar screen, and the entire picture disappears down the electronic tube, at least a paper back-up exists. This would enable the controller to determine who was in the system at the time of the failure. Pilots probably find little comfort in knowing that controllers suspect they're up there, but don't quite know where. This is when the controller starts issuing those, "Y'ALL BE CAREFUL" clearances. This also explains why instructors are constantly nagging students to know their exact position, and be ready to report it to ATC at a moment's notice.

In the days of antiquity, when radar was unavailable, airplanes were provided with 10 minutes of horizontal separation. This equated to approximately 20 to 25 miles distance between airplanes. Today, horizontal separation can be as low as three miles between airplanes.* If radar fails, there may not be a "many-minute" buffer to protect the airplane. Salvation for pilots lies in their ability to immediately identify and broadcast their position to ATC. And when ATC asks pilots where they are, the controller doesn't want to hear, "I'm over my present position now!" They also don't want to hear pilots say, "I'm not lost, I am just temporarily unsure of my present position." That's like saying, "I'm no drunk, I'm an alcohol technician." Pilots need to have a good idea of their position at all times when flying IFR.

WINGING IT

BARREL OF FUN

Possibly, but maybe a bit drastic. Anyway, see and avoid worked again:

Traffic advisory - eleven o'clock, three miles, no altitude given. No initial tally. Additional advisory — eleven o'clock, less than one mile. Sighted traffic at less than one half mile, slightly below. Executed climbing, left barrel roll to avoid. No evasive action by other aircraft.

Pilot probably paralyzed with amazement!

ASRS REPORT

Data progress strips, generated electronically at each controller's position, can inform controllers about something special concerning the flight. The data progress strip contains information a pilot puts in the "Remarks" section of the flight plan. Figure 5 shows a data progress strip containing the remarks a pilot listed on the flight plan. If the remarks are short enough, less than 3 or 4 words, they can easily be inserted into the computer and transmitted on the data progress strip. If they are too long, the FSS specialist may abbreviate them. A pilot could input notations like: "no oxygen on board," to advise ATC that high altitudes are not welcome.

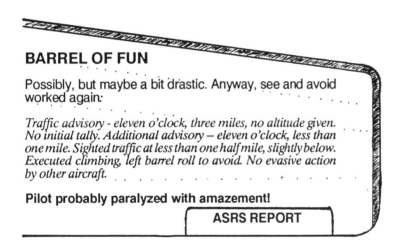

Fig. 5 Flight data strip showing remarks pilots filed in their flight plan.

*This can be less than one minute's duration. That's close. And we wonder why pilots get nervous!

A pilot may also stipulate "no SIDS or STARS." This becomes important when a pilot doesn't have current SIDS or STARS. A friend of mine could never keep his STARS. His wife kept throwing them out because he didn't fly at night. A pilot might also list "student IFR pilot" in the remarks section. This would be important if controller patience is desired. With this remark in the flight plan, if the controller calls and asks, "Hey, 32B, what heading are you flying?", the controller would expect the pilot to say something like, "Ahhhh, all of them!" Nevertheless, a pilot should make use of the remarks section and keep the remarks short to ensure transmission.

At tower controlled airports, it's important for pilots to notify the tower controller, prior to departure, that they are IFR. At many airports, the tower controller must often get permission from the departure controller via the land line (telephone) before they can launch an IFR airplane. Letting the controller know they're an IFR departure will cue them to get this permission, if necessary. Problems can arise when the airport is VFR, but IFR exists in outlying areas. The controller may expect a pilot to be a VFR departure, because there was no mention of an IFR flight plan. The tower controller is often really surprised, but rarely delighted, when the pilot asks permission to switch to departure control after liftoff. Don't make it a point to test the controller's triple by-pass this way!

Pilots running a little late shouldn't fret about losing their flight plan. The length of time the computer keeps the IFR flight plan may vary with different locations, but is usually about 2 hours. When the ATC system becomes very busy, the time parameter may be shortened. Beyond this time, the flight plan is purged from computer memory and pilots must refile. Pilots expecting to be delayed more than one hour should contact ATC or the FSS and notify them of their new departure time. This precludes having to refile.

There's many a slip 'twixt cup and lip

Erasmus

I was working Local Control and traffic was light, so Ground Control (G.C.) was combined with Local. When I accepted the G.C. position, the controller advised me his only traffic was an aircraft waiting to cross an active runway. Once he had crossed, and I had assumed the position, it was almost five minutes before the next ground traffic called. This was a small transport who identified his position on the airport, advised he had the ATIS, and said he was "southbound." When he reached the runway and called ready, I cleared him "...for takeoff; right turn south approved." About three or four minutes later, he asked if I wanted him to go to Departure frequency. This was unusual for a VFR flight, so I asked him if he was IFR. He replied, "Affirmative." As I walked to Clearance Delivery, searching for his slip, which wasn't there, I asked him if he had a clearance, to which he also replied, "Affirmative," and stated his transponder code.

After a quick check with C.D., we discovered the strip at the Ground Control position and scrambled to get Departure Control on the line with an explanation and heading. They found the small transport on radar and requested him "...NOW!" Whether a conflict occurred, I don't know, but the potential was there. Two factors were involved here: primary, of course, was Ground Control forgetting the IFR strip when transferring the position (the strip was not in sight from the Local Control position). The reason for this report, however, is because of the second factor. This was the small transport pilot not telling Ground Control he was IFR. Often, Clearance Delivery will be issuing more than one clearance and it may take time to get the strip to G.C. or L.C. If the pilot informs the other controller he is IFR, the G.C. or L.C. can check with Clearance Delivery to see that a clearance has been issued. We often taxi aircraft out while waiting for a clearance. If the pilot gives his direction of flight only, he is assumed VFR. Also, without an assigned heading (such as "right turn south approved") versus "turn right heading 180 degrees for radar vectors," the pilot should be asking questions: Hopefully, the worst thing to happen with this was a red-faced Local Controller (me) sounding like a complete dummy to the pilot!

ASRS REPORT

POPPING UP

Filing an IFR flight plan in the air is always an interesting experience. Returning from a VFR cross country flight, pilots may unexpectedly find the destination field is below VFR minimums. The AIM suggests that they should contact the nearest Flight Service Station and file a flight plan. This could take 30 minutes and is definitely no fun on the bladder or the fuel tank. In this type of situation, if pilots need an immediate IFR clearance, they might try filing what is known as a "pop-up" IFR flight plan. The pilot would simply call up Center on the local sector frequency, and ask them for an IFR flight plan to the destination airport. If the controllers are busy, pilots might be told to contact the nearest FSS and file with them. My experience has been that most ATC controllers will generally accommodate pilots, if at all feasible.

Popping up with approach control in the TEC system is generally a lot easier. Pilots may be delayed for a short time while ATC accommodates prior requests, but seldom will the delay be long. If anticipating a pop-up into the IFR system, it is wise to do so far in advance of the busiest IFR sector. This assures easier accommodation into the system. Once in the system, pilots are there for as long as they desire. At least ATC is not going to suggest to pilots that they should cancel their IFR flight plan. The only time I have ever heard of something like this was when ATC was dealing with a recalcitrant IFR pilot who thought he was a real comedian. The controller said, "32 Bravo, say altitude." The pilot replied, "Altitude." The controller requested three more times that the pilot say, "Altitude", and each time the pilot said, "Altitude." Finally the controller said, "OK 32 Bravo, say, canceling IFR." The pilot immediately replied, "Ah, we're at 3,000 feet, sir." However, a controller once asked my student what his speed was. My student replied, "One thousand seven hundred....." After a short pause he continued with, ".....RPM, which gives me 90 knots." It's always good practice for pilots to keep tabs on the destination airport weather and, at the first indication of inclement weather, to file immediately.

COMPOSITE FLIGHT PLANS

There are times when pilots know they will be filing IFR to the destination airport, yet do not desire to fly IFR the entire route. Filing a composite VFR/IFR flight plan solves this problem. Pilots simply file VFR to an intersection, or navaid, short of the destination airport and IFR for remainder of the route. Upon reaching the intersection, they cancel their VFR flight plan with the local FSS and open the IFR flight plan with the Center controller. The IFR flight plan can be activated by calling Center on the local sector

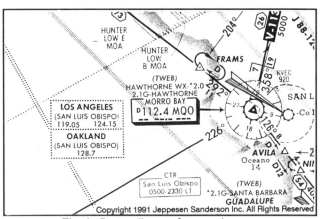

Fig. 6. Sector discrete frequencies.

frequency, shown on the low altitude IFR enroute chart, as in figure 6. This is also an excellent way to ensure that a pilot will have a way into the system, if things get busy.

The VFR/IFR composite flight plan is also useful when pilots desire to fly IFR for the route, yet anticipate departure delays. If it's VFR in the departure area, they may simply file VFR to an intersection outside the area of delays, then pick up the IFR flight plan. This comes in handy when a departure is planned during times when major air carriers arrive and depart the airport. Of course, pilots may elect to forgo the VFR portion of the flight plan. They would file an IFR flight plan to be picked up at some enroute point. In this case, the pilot should list the fix, at which the IFR portion of the flight is to begin, as the departure point on the flight plan.

It's important to understand that, on composite flight plans, the pilot is responsible for canceling the VFR portion of the flight plan with the FSS. The radar controller won't automatically do this. In fact, the radar controller probably doesn't know that the pilot has filed a VFR flight plan for the first portion of the flight. This information is not shown on the pilot's data strip.

Pilots may also elect to file IFR for the first portion of the route and VFR for the latter portion. This allows them to exit an area of bad weather to a VFR area. The IFR portion of the flight plan is then cancelled with the controller, and the VFR portion is activated with the local FSS. This type of flight plan is also useful when pilots are departing an area in which it's difficult to navigate VFR. There are certain areas of the country where a pilot might like to have a pre-programmed route out of the busy terminal area, then continue the flight VFR. Composite flight plans are useful in these instances.

Filing a composite flight plan is done the same way all other flight plans are filed. The only difference is that the VFR and IFR boxes are checked in Section One, under the type of flight plan requested, as shown in figure 7A. The cruising altitude to list in the flight plan box is the altitude pilots will use for the first portion of their flight. If VFR is selected first, a VFR altitude is listed in the flight plan box. If IFR is selected first, an IFR altitude is listed in the flight plan box. In the remarks section, pilots should list what portion of the route will be flown VFR and what portion will be flown IFR. In other words, pilots could list: VFR from SNA airport to PRB VOR, and IFR from PRB VOR to SJC airport, as shown in figure 7B. The order of this information would be switched if the IFR portion were to be flown first.

Pilots should be aware that, when filing a composite flight plan, the FSS specialist may need additional information. For instance, if filing VFR for the first portion and IFR for the remainder, the FSS specialist will need information on the IFR altitude the pilot will fly, the alternate airport (if required), as well as the time the IFR flight plan is estimated to be activated. It's been my experience that some FSS locations are hesitant to accept composite flight plans. They often request that pilots file two individual flight plans instead. If pilots experience this, they should simply file two flight plans with the IFR or VFR portions to be activated at an enroute intersection.

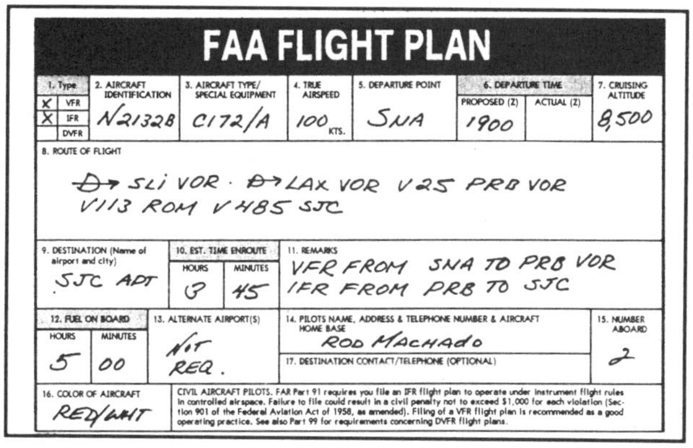

Fig. 7A Both the IFR and VFR boxes are checked for composite flight plans.

Fig. 7B. A VFR/IFR composite flight plan.

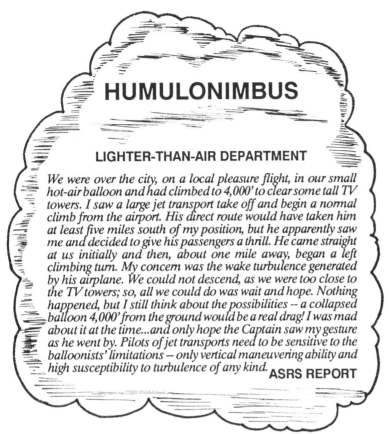

HUMULONIMBUS

LIGHTER-THAN-AIR DEPARTMENT

We were over the city, on a local pleasure flight, in our small hot-air balloon and had climbed to 4,000' to clear some tall TV towers. I saw a large jet transport take off and begin a normal climb from the airport. His direct route would have taken him at least five miles south of my position, but he apparently saw me and decided to give his passengers a thrill. He came straight at us initially and then, about one mile away, began a left climbing turn. My concern was the wake turbulence generated by his airplane. We could not descend, as we were too close to the TV towers; so, all we could do was wait and hope. Nothing happened, but I still think about the possibilities -- a collapsed balloon 4,000' from the ground would be a real drag! I was mad about it at the time...and only hope the Captain saw my gesture as he went by. Pilots of jet transports need to be sensitive to the balloonists' limitations -- only vertical maneuvering ability and high susceptibility to turbulence of any kind. **ASRS REPORT**

Another flight planning option pilots might want to consider is the "VFR-on-top" clearance. This flight is filed just like any other IFR flight plan, with one exception. Instead of a hard IFR altitude being listed in block 7 of the flight plan, the letters "OTP" are substituted. This informs the controller that a climb to "VFR-on-top" is requested for the route. Pilots will receive their IFR clearance with an altitude authorization similar to the following: "32B, climb to and maintain VFR conditions on top. If not on top by (altitude), maintain (altitude) and advise." The "on-top" clearance allows pilots to remain in the IFR system, yet choose their own VFR cruising altitude.

Pilots operating with a "VFR-on-top" clearance must fly the appropriate VFR crusing altitude, comply with minimum visibilities and cloud clearance requirements, follow see and avoid procedures, and adhere to all IFR flight rules applicable to the flight (i.e., MEA's, MRA's, etc.). Additionally, pilots should advise ATC prior to any altitude change to ensure the exchange of accurate traffic information. The unique thing about the "VFR-on-top" clearance is that it's relatively easy to obtain a hard IFR altitude if the weather conditions deteriorate. Simply call the controller and request an IFR altitude. Of course, giving adequate lead time for this request will ensure that a pilot won't be caught in a tight predicament.

Flying IFR with a limited understanding of the airspace system makes as much sense as purchasing deep fried pork skins, then attempting to reassemble the pig. The ATC system exists to serve the pilot. Unfortunately, many pilots don't know enough about the system's structure to use it properly. Knowledge is power. And airspace knowledge is the tool by which IFR pilots gain an advantage over the aviation environment. Abraham Maslow said it best many years ago when he stated, "If the only tool you have is a hammer, then everything looks like a nail." IFR pilots should learn as much about the system as possible, or they will find themselves using their hammer far too often.

Having now absorbed the basics of IFR airspace, the next step is to apply this knowledge in the real world of instrument approaches.

8. THE ART OF THE APPROACH

Most pilots have spent some time pondering the great mysteries in aviation. I'm not talking about mysteries such as, whether D.B. Cooper is still alive and living with Elvis in Memphis, or, whether the two brothers that made it possible for man to fly were really Ernest and Julio Gallo. These are indeed great mysteries, but they are not of the caliber in question. My focal interest is the mystery concerning why many instrument pilots have difficulty mastering the skills of shooting an instrument approach.

Shooting an instrument approach is indeed an art form. As with all art forms, a certain transformation takes place in those who appreciate its more aesthetic aspects. At the completion of an instrument approach, most instrument pilots feel an almost elitist sense of accomplishment. They realize that an instrument approach is a test of a pilot's mettle. The challenge offers them a rare form of satisfaction only the initiated can enjoy.

Acquiring skill in the artistry of the approach means developing an understanding of those subtleties which distinguish pilots with the professional touch. After absorbing some fresh insights and techniques, pilots will soon be ordained "High Priests of the approach." Pilots should remember that when Uri Geller, moves needles with his mind, it's called "magic." Instrument pilots know better. When they move needles with their mind, it's called talent.

BEGINNING THE APPROACH

There are two ways pilots can enter the IFR system: 1) filing a flight plan with the Flight Service Station prior to departure, and 2) requesting a "Pop-up" IFR clearance from ATC while airborne, in VFR conditions. The "Pop-up" IFR clearance is normally requested when an instrument approach wasn't anticipated at the destination. It derives its name from pilots appearing to "Pop-up" on a controller's radar screen wanting an IFR clearance. In many parts of the country, it's frequently used for IFR training. An instructor may be airborne, in VFR conditions, then request his student obtain an IFR clearance for instrument approach practice. "Pop-up" IFR clearances are perhaps the most demanding situation for instrument pilots because the sequence of events occur within a short time frame.

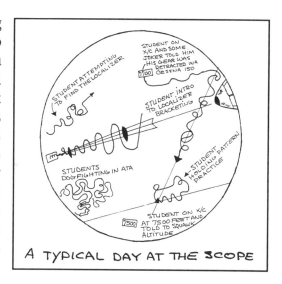

A TYPICAL DAY AT THE SCOPE

Before contacting ATC for a "Pop-up" IFR clearance, pilots should attempt to obtain the ATIS for the destination airport. This arms them with the knowledge of what instrument approaches are in use, the current weather, altimeter setting and NOTAMS critical for the flight. Listening to the ATIS before contacting ATC is especially critical if the weather is reported below minimums for the approach in use. Pilots should ensure that the approach they are using is functioning properly.

After the ATIS is absorbed and the airplane's position is established, pilots should initiate a call to ATC. Perhaps the best way for pilots to stabilize themselves, and the airplane, for the upcoming information exchange, is to establish the airplane in a holding pattern. This makes identification of the aircraft's position easy. Some may consider it cruel and unusual punishment to perform a holding pattern not ordered by ATC. Perhaps it is; nevertheless, this prevents the aircraft from drifting carelessly into another controller's protected airspace. It also ensures adequate time for pilots to review and organize an instrument approach. Another way for pilots to establish

A SHOCKING EXPERIENCE

Books are filled with examples of pilots who chose to fly approaches which were not fully operational. Several years ago, two pilots in Southern California attempted to fly an ILS with an inoperative glide slope. It was a pitch black night when they made a beautiful descent below glide slope and literally landed on high tension power lines several miles short of the runway. While disoriented in an inverted airplane, hanging several hundred feet above the ground, the pilot crawled out onto the wing for a look around. With hands acting like antennae, he felt his way out the door and, to his dismay, felt nothing supporting the aircraft. He immediately crawled back inside the airplane and shut the door. It took a large crane half the night to pluck these fellows from their lofty perch. It is not known whether they actually counted the approach as one of the six necessary for instrument currency. **AUTHOR**

their position is by identifying their location on a VOR radial with a DME fix, or using two VOR cross radials. A transmission can now be made, in an organized manner, without the airplane wandering into a busy area and pouncing on other airplanes like a duck on a June bug.

WORKING WITH ATC

The initial call should sound something like this:

> 32B - Coast Approach, this is Cessna 2132B, request, over
>
> ATC - 32B, this is Coast Approach, go ahead.
>
> 32B - This is 32B. We are a Cessna 172/T over ALBAS intersection at 3,000 feet, request the ILS into Long Beach. We have information hotel, over.
>
> ATC - 32B, squawk 1234.
>
> 32B - 32B, squawk 1234.

The initial call establishes contact. Mentioning the name of the facility on initial contact confirms the correct frequency was selected. Pilots should wait for an appropriate opening in the flow of conversation to make the call. Sometimes, they may have to be a bit assertive and jump right in when an opening presents itself. Remember, I said assertive, not aggressive. Pilots shouldn't pick up the mike and chant, "ATC, breaker-breaker, this' here is triple nickel bravo, you boys got your ears on?" There's a good chance all of the pilot's future clearances will be mid-Pacific once word spreads they talk like this! There are pilots that actually exhibit this type of behavior, which may explain why some animals eat their young at birth.

After establishing contact, pilots should give the controller information on their type of airplane, equipment on board, their position, altitude and type of approach requested. They should also inform the controller they have the ATIS. Air traffic controllers are required to provide pilots with runway information, if they do not affirm they have received the ATIS. Informing the controller that they have the information makes the IFR system function more smoothly and labels the pilot as "cooperative" and "prepared."

Sometimes it's the minor things that influence relationships when communicating with ATC. The pace and tone of a pilot's speech can make quite a difference in the controller's willingness to assist. The plain fact is, people are nicer to those who are nice to them. If pilots don't believe this, the next time they want an instrument approach, they should call the controller and announce, "Hey! Give me vectors and give me vectors now!" These pilots get vectors to boldly go where no man has gone before. Controllers cannot help but make value judgments about pilot skill based on their verbal demeanor. This is the only way controllers have of immediately assessing a pilot's professional ability. When exchanging information with ATC, pilots should speak distinctly and precisely.

Upon arrival into a busy sector, it's not unusual to have ATC request that pilots obtain their own ATIS information and report when they have done so. To handle the situation, request permission to be off frequency for one minute to get the ATIS. When this information is received, pilots should immediately report back on frequency. Pilots will often find ATC quite cooperative in allowing them one or two minutes off frequency. ATC doesn't want the risk of having a pilot rocket through a congested area without constant communication. Therefore, the controller will often provide the pertinent ATIS information.

VECTORS FOR THE APPROACH

Once ATC identifies the airplane, pilots will be given vectors for the approach. The clearance might sound something like this:

> ATC - 32B, your position is 1 mile north of ALBAS intersection,
>   turn left heading 020, vectors for the Long Beach
>   runway 30 ILS approach, descend and maintain 1,600 feet
> 32B - Roger, turning left heading 020, leaving 3,000 for
>   1,600 feet, vectors for the 30 ILS.

The controller initially identified the pilot's position on the radar screen and verified that position. The position report ATC gave the pilot is very important. The controller will identify a target believed to be the pilot. The pilot's job is to suspiciously query the controller if a positional discrepancy exists. This is part of the checks and balances of the initial call up.

It is illegal to intentionally operate an airplane with the transponder set to a code assigned to another airplane. The controller may start vectoring one aircraft, all the while thinking it's another. After the initial contact, listen carefully to the position report the controller gives. If the pilot hears, "32 Bravo, radar contact one-five miles southeast of DAVEY intersection," and the airplane's position is north of DAVEY, immediately correct the controller with: "32 Bravo, is two-zero miles north of DAVEY." Not paying attention to position is an admission ticket to that big runup area in the sky.

SERIOUS CIRRUS THOUGHTS

Think about what could happen if another pilot set someone else's assigned transponder code in their transponder and the controller misidentified these aircraft? I have had this happen before. The other airplane was a Cessna Citation, and ATC was using my call numbers to address him. My student and I were in a Cessna 150 at the time, and I realized something was wrong when the controller asked me to maintain at least 160 knots on final. My student, of course, said, "Roger" and proceeded to lower the nose of the little Cessna. Had I not been there, he would have probably landed with the only delta wing Cessna 150 in existence. I often wondered what the controller must have thought when he saw the Citation making its approach at 70 knots. This is not good!

AUTHOR

GETTING DOWN

As soon as pilots have been given an assigned heading and altitude, they should smoothly and immediately, turn and descend. Things get fast paced when intercepting an approach course, so it's best to head in the proper direction and to get down quickly. Remember: AVIATE, NAVIGATE and COMMUNICATE in that order. A maximum rate of about 600 to 800 feet per minute is a reasonable velocity at which to descend. Speeds in excess of 1,000 feet per minute, during the approach, should be avoided under actual IFR conditions. It's too easy for pilots to become distracted and descend through critical altitudes. Besides, the passenger's popping ear drums will give controllers the impression that pilots are playing the bongos. If it's a long descent, pilots should clear the engine every 500 feet. This is accomplished by a smooth application of "warming" power, then a return to the desired power setting. Remember to use carburetor heat, if required by the operating manual.

NIMBOBIMBUS

SCUD RUNNING

We (in a light twin) had commenced the VOR-DME approach, completing the arc at 19 DME and turning inbound. At 17 DME, 7800' MSL, we began a descent in solid IMC. At approximately 7700' and 16 DME, we were in indefinite precip with down - but no forward - visibility. The copilot said he had the ground; as I looked up, he said he had traffic head-on. I looked out through the left window and saw a small aircraft pass under the left engine; the estimated miss was by only 100-150 feet. He was near the base of the clouds in light precip. Our forward visibility was less than one mile. The small aircraft continued southeast, and we completed our approach, reaching good VFR approximately 6500' MSL. It was an interesting way to start the morning! The small aircraft was scud-running over the foothills, below radar but on the final approach course.

ASRS REPORT

In many small general aviation aircraft, like a Cessna 172 or a Piper Warrior, a maximum descent rate is accomplished at approximately 1,700 RPM at 100 knots. During the descent and level off, the airplane should be slowed to the approach speed. Some pilots may feel more comfortable with a higher speed until established on the approach. This is perfectly reasonable, as long as the pace of the flight doesn't exceed the pace of the pilot's central processing unit -- his brain. Remember, if the airspeed changes more than 10 knots, inform ATC of this change.

Professional instrument pilots will always recall and use the power settings proven to maintain approach speeds. In the 172 and Warrior, approximately 2,300 to 2,400 RPM are required to maintain 100 knots. Of course, this may vary with the condition of the airframe and engine, as well as the number of bird strikes accumulated during the aircraft's history. Upon leveling off, there should be no guess work in finding the proper power settings. Pilots should monitor the vacuum gauge to ensure the descent power is adequate to keep suction values in the green range. If the proper suction isn't maintained, the gyro instruments will spin down and start to precess. Then they go out to recess!

THE SET UP

While being vectored, if the pilot hasn't already done so, the navigation equipment should be immediately set for the approach. This is extremely important. When pilots hear the words, "Vectors for the approach," they should immediately set the frequency in the navigation radio for the approach course.

The frequency for the primary approach navaid is always found in the top, right hand corner of the approach plate, under the type of approach procedure. The identification for this procedure is listed directly underneath this information, as shown in figure 1. Immediately turn up the volume and identify the station.

ILS localizers are directional. Pilots may not be able to receive any identification until they are nearly aligned with the localizer course. If no signal is received, keep the volume up. A reasonable signal must be heard. Above all, pilots must make sure the signal has been identified before tracking on the localizer. Never, under any circumstances, should a navigational course be used unless proper identification is made.

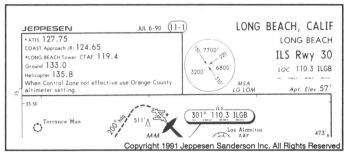

Fig. 1. The frequency for the approach course, along with the identifier, can always be found in the top, right hand corner of the chart.

Pilots should also monitor navigation flags during the approach. If an "OFF" flag appears, they should remove one of the VOR repair kits worn on the end of each leg. One good tap with a shoe will usually solve most of these problems. A good friend of mine was flying IFR in Mexico when an "OFF" flag appeared in the VOR. He tried the old standby and hit it a few times with no luck. Calling the authorities, he found that when it rains, the locals will sometimes unplug the VOR and put the power to a more valuable use. He finally convinced them to plug it in so he could get down. This is a problem pilots will never find discussed in the Airman's Information Manual. Using a shoe is admittedly "tongue in cheek" but, nonetheless, touch and tap "OFF" flags that should not be there.

Is it really necessary to identify frequencies when using the new, sophisticated, user-friendly radios now available? Without a doubt, it is. It's so easy to set in the wrong frequency, even with the best of radios. The consequences can be devastating. Figure 2 lists the Van Nuys ILS and VOR frequencies, 111.3 and 113.1 respectively. They aren't that much different, are they? It would be very easy to juxtapose one frequency for the other, with great potential for disaster. By mistaking the VOR for the localizer frequency at Van Nuys, pilots could come plowing and strafing through nearby mountains, landing with chipmunks and elk horns hooked to the wheels of their airplane.

After pilots have tuned and identified the approach course frequency, they should rotate the VOR course selector to the inbound course direction. Too many times, I've seen instrument pilots tune in the radio for the approach and simply forget to set the approach course on the OBS. The approach course is that maximum "bold," thick black line on the approach plan view, beginning just prior to the final approach fix. The controller won't vector a pilot inside the final approach fix. This wouldn't be logical. After all, to identify the missed approach point on many nonprecision approaches, pilots have to begin timing when crossing the final approach fix. Therefore, pilots will be vectored to a segment of the approach course outside the final approach fix.

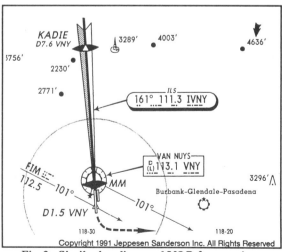

Fig. 2. Similar localizer and VOR frequencies.

YOKES ON YOU

Many years ago, for my ATP checkride, I learned Morse code identification for greater ease in identifying navigation stations. The FAA inspector was a nice enough fellow who watched me like a hawk. When being vectored for the ILS, I tuned in the localizer and listened for the identification. I heard: DIT, DIT, DOT, DIT, DOT, DOT, DIT. I didn't have to look at the chart to realize this was the correct identification because of my newly acquired talent. The FAA inspector looked over at me and said, "OK buddy, what did that say?" I had waited years to do something like this. I replied, "DIT, DIT, DOT, DIT, DOT, DOT, DIT." It was one of those precious moments of brilliant humor. Unfortunately he didn't laugh. I started thinking that maybe I wouldn't do this on my second ATP checkride. Fortunately, I passed. **AUTHOR**

On the initial vector, instrument pilots often become confused when ATC states, "Vectors to the final approach course." In controller vernacular, it's their way of saying that they are vectoring them to the approach segment, located prior to or outside the final approach fix. This is not to be interpreted as being vectored onto the final approach segment, inside the final approach fix.

Figure 3A shows the VOR-A approach for Corona, California. The 078 degree radial from the PDZ VOR is the approach course to which pilots can expect vectors by ATC. The 078 degree radial also serves

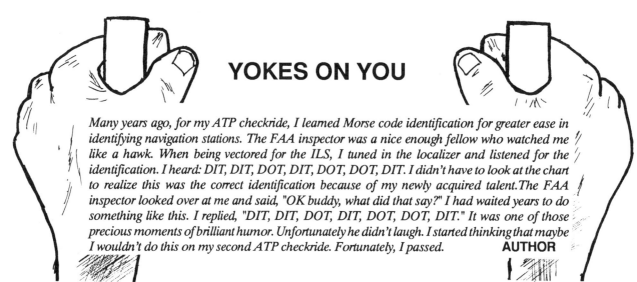

Figure 3A

as the inbound leg of the holding pattern. Pilots will set their OBS to 258 degrees for the inbound track. Figure 3B shows the NDB 34R approach for Sacramento, California. The 344 inbound bearing to Lanee NDB is the approach course. Pilots can expect to be vectored onto this bearing, several miles prior to the NDB. Figure 3C shows the ILS RWY 30 at Long Beach. Pilots should expect to be vectored to that portion of the localizer prior to BECCA intersection. If the approach is an ILS, the OBS should be rotated to the inbound direction of the approach. Even though this has no effect on localizer reception, it is always logical, professional and good housekeeping to set the OBS to the inbound course to be flown.

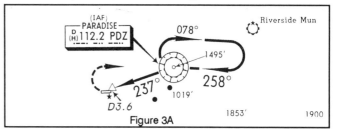

Figure 3B

When pilots are in the process of an instrument approach they should always monitor the navaid frequency. Having the volume up slightly can immediately alert a pilot to a signal failure. This becomes even more critical during an NDB approach. Unlike VOR's and ILS's, ADF's don't have "OFF" flags. The only immediate way to determine ground equipment failure of an NDB is by loss of the identification signal.

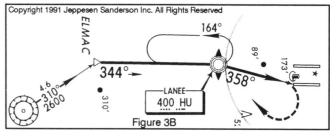

Figure 3C

Fig. 3 A,B,C. ATC uses the term "Final Approach Course" to mean the approach segment to which pilots can expect to be vectored.

Pilots who listen to music while flying should be careful about tuning in a commercial broadcast station. A professional dancer liked to listen to his favorite radio station during training. He said that the music relaxed him. It made me nervous, but I agreed to let him do it nevertheless. Once, while high on the approach to Long Beach, the music finally got to him. I said, "Hey Bob, get down, get down!" Guess what? He started dancing!

POSITION AWARENESS

Pilots should set any other radios in the airplane to receive other navaids shown on the chart. Referring to the Long Beach ILS RWY 30 approach, figure 3C, the number two radio should be set to receive the Seal Beach VOR, and the course selector should be set to 200 degrees, to help identify BECCA intersection, the final approach fix. The Seal Beach VOR can also be used to help identify the aircraft's general position. Pilots should keep in mind that they don't have to know the exact, precise location of their airplane to fly IFR confidently. If they have two radios, one set to the localizer, the other set to the SLI 200 degree radial, they can approximately identify where they are on the chart. There are four quadrants made up of the localizer and the 200 degree radial. Knowing which quadrant they are in is more than adequate as position fixing when pilots know terrain elevation values for that area.

As soon as the ILS and VOR have been properly tuned and identified, the pilot's next job is to activate and use all available navigation equipment in the plane. Start at the top of the communications panel. Turn on and test the marker beacons. Tune in the ADF to any NDB station shown on the approach chart, even if it's not part of the approach structure. In the case of Long Beach, the ADF can be tuned to the BECCA Compass Locator on frequency 233 KHz. This will provide another method of identifying the FAF. During a radar vector, the ADF provides a second indication of position relating to the localizer course. Once pilots have mastered the fundamentals of ADF navigation, the equipment will provide clues to the airplane's position and closure rate to the localizer during intercept.

I remember being vectored to an ILS with a compass locator (NDB installed with a marker beacon). When cleared for the approach, the ADF needle was moving behind the wing of the airplane, indicating vectors inside the final approach fix. The controller had once again mistaken me for another airplane. Having the ADF as an additional source of information helped identify the problem.

THE APPROACH GATE

ATC will provide a radar vector to intercept the localizer at least two miles outside the "Approach Gate." The "Approach Gate" is a portion of the approach course that starts one mile from the final approach fix and extends outward along the approach course, as shown in figure 4. The approach gate has no official ending point. It might be supposed that it extends out as long as the approach course is navigable.

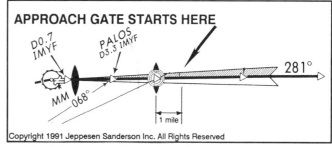

Fig. 4. The approach gate is a reference used by controllers when vectoring aircraft for an instrument aproach.

In no case should ATC vector pilots inside the "Approach Gate," or closer than one mile to the final approach fix. This provides the distance and time to get established on the approach course. Additionally, it also provides pilots with enough time to prepare for the final descent to the airport. If they need to get down quickly, due to a rough running engine or icing conditions, the controller's manual does make a provision for pilots to be vectored inside the "Approach Gate." Just request a "short turn to final" from ATC. Controllers will not, however, vector pilots inside the final approach fix, since they must pass over this point to start the timing needed to identify the missed approach point.

When the reported ceiling is at least 500 feet above the Minimum Vectoring Altitude and the visibility is at least 3 miles, the aircraft may be vectored to intercept the final approach course closer than 2 miles outside the "Approach Gate," but no closer than the "Approach Gate." Essentially this means, when the weather is clear, ATC assumes that pilots don't need all that extra time on the approach course to get set up. Pilots should keep this in mind when they are making an approach to an unfamiliar airport. They may want to request a vector a few miles out on the approach to give them extra time to get comfortably established. Simply ask the controller to be vectored two, three or four miles from the approach gate. Pilots may also request an "Autopilot Coupled Approach" when they desire to be established farther out on the approach course. This allows a pilot time to set navigational equipment for the procedure. Either a 20 or 30 degree intercept vector will be given onto the approach course, depending on the proximity to the final approach fix, as shown in figure 5.

FINAL APPROACH COURSE INTERCEPTION

Controllers will assign headings that will permit final approach course interception on a track that does not exceed the interception angles specified in the Table.*

Table. – Approach Course Interception Angle

Distance from interception point to approach gate	Maximum interception angle
Less than 2 miles	20 Degrees
2 miles or more	30 Degrees

Note. - The intent is to provide for a track - course intercept angle judged by the controller to be no greater than specified by this procedure.

Fig. 5. Angle of intercept relationship to the Approach Gate.

APPROACH CLEARANCE

When nearing the approach course, ATC will issue an approach clearance. Upon receipt, pilots should intercept the course, track inbound and complete the procedure. However, complications could arise prior to being cleared for the approach. If there are conflicting traffic conditions, ATC may want to issue vectors across the approach course for spacing. It is possible the initial vector may take the aircraft through the approach course without ATC issuing an approach clearance to the pilot. Under normal conditions, ATC will announce that this will be a "vector across the localizer or approach course" for spacing. However, there are times when the controller's workload doesn't permit even this brief statement. In the event pilots fly through the approach course during a vector, they should not turn inbound. Continue to fly the assigned heading and immediately query the controller. A turn inbound could upset the controller's minimum spacing requirement between airplanes. The only time they might turn inbound is when they are unable to communicate with the controller and are flying toward higher terrain. In this case, they should assume communications are lost and proceed directly to the approach course in accordance with lost communication regulations.

When the airplane is positioned to intercept the inbound approach course, and traffic is no longer a factor, the controller will issue the infamous approach clearance. This is one of the most confusing times for most instrument pilots because so much is said in so little time. As an instrument instructor, I've seen many unusual responses to these rapid fire clearances. Imagine an IFR student sitting in the pilot's seat, wearing this little hood. ATC issues a clearance so fast the controller's eye teeth can't even see what they're saying. Suddenly, the little hood tilts up at me. I say, "Don't look at me, fly the airplane." The hood looks at the microphone, staring at it, apparently waiting for the video picture to appear. ATC issues another clearance, this time even faster, and, the hood looks over at me again. It's the same expression that history has recorded many times: on the faces of Anne Boleyn and Sir Walter Raleigh. It is common in execution chambers to this day. It does take some time to become at ease with what ATC is saying. The secret to handling these types of clearances is anticipating what the controller is going to say. Essentially, for most instrument students, the approach clearance goes something like this:

> **ATC (rapid fire) -** "32B is four miles from the marker, turn left heading 330, intercept the approach course at or above 1,600 feet, cleared for the ILS 30 approach to Long Beach. Contact the tower 119.4 at the marker."
>
> **STUDENT -** "Huh?"

The "Huh" normally alternates with maniacal laughter, as the final synaptic snap eradicates any ability remaining to function as a rational human being. I once heard a controller simplify the entire process for a frustrated student when he said, "32B, you're four from it, cleared to it and tower at it."

The approach clearance normally contains several standard items. When pilots know what to expect, the anxiety is lessened. First, the controller may issue a position report to help pilots identify and confirm their location. Be alert for discrepancies. If a disagreement exists with the controller's position assessment, a pilot should challenge the controller. The position report also alerts pilots about how fast things will happen. If they are 2 miles from the final approach fix, things will happen much more quickly than 5 miles from the same fix.

Second, the controller will provide the approach course intercept heading. Start turning the airplane to the intercept heading as soon as possible, preferably while the clearance is being given. This will allow more time to set up for the intercept and prevent overshooting. A seasoned IFR pilot has learned to prioritize heading, altitude and airspeed control when the approach clearance is issued. Pilots should remember they can be at most any altitude and still fly the approach course (other than the glide slope). However, if they don't fly specific headings, they'll never find the approach course. After receiving the approach clearance, altitudes then become the next priority, followed by airspeed control.

> **SOMETHING TO THINK ABOUT!**
>
> Said the pilot when minimums fell,
> "Sir, I think we should wait for a spell."
> Said the boss, "I am tired,
> You'll fly or be fired."
> Their estates paid the widows quite well.
>
> **D.G. Scott**
>
> Reprinted with permission of Professional Pilot Magazine

Third, the controller will provide altitude restrictions for the approach. In the above clearance, pilots were instructed to intercept the approach course at or above 1,600 feet. They have the option of maintaining the present altitude or descending to 1,600 feet. If the controller's clearance was to intercept the approach course at 1,600 feet, a descent should be made immediately to this altitude. I would recommend descending to the lowest altitude as soon as possible, unless there are unfavorable conditions below. Reduce power to 1,700 RPM

FLUTTER

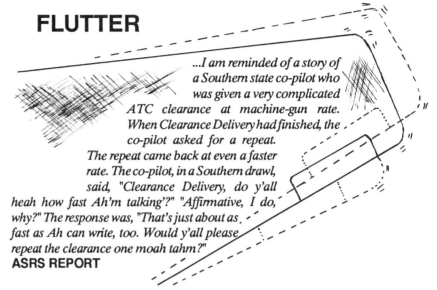

...I am reminded of a story of a Southern state co-pilot who was given a very complicated ATC clearance at machine-gun rate. When Clearance Delivery had finished, the co-pilot asked for a repeat. The repeat came back at even a faster rate. The co-pilot, in a Southern drawl, said, "Clearance Delivery, do y'all heah how fast Ah'm talking'?" "Affirmative, I do, why?" The response was, "That's just about as fast as Ah can write, too. Would y'all please repeat the clearance one moah tahm?"
ASRS REPORT

(or as recommended for the particular aircraft), and descend at the maximum suggested rate of approximately 800 feet per minute to prepare for the next portion of the approach.

When controllers clear pilots for the approach, and do not provide any altitude restrictions, pilots should maintain their last assigned altitude until established on a terminal route or the approach course. Terminal routes and the approach course will always have an altitude, direction and distance listed on

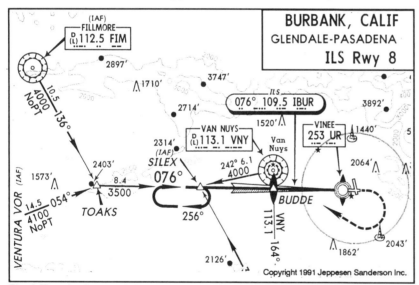

Fig. 6. Terminal routes & the approach course for the Burbank ILS Rwy 8 approach.

the chart. In many cases, they will also be accompanied by a heavy black line with an arrow pointing in the route's direction. These are routes that can be flown without the aid of radar, since they provide information necessary to get to the approach course and avoid terrain. The Fillmore VOR 136 degree radial, the Ventura VOR 054 degree radial and the Van Nuys VOR 242 degree radial are all terminal routes taking the aircraft to the ILS approach course, as shown in figure 6. The Burbank ILS Rwy 8 approach plan view shows 3,500 feet as a minimum altitude on the localizer,

prior to SILEX intersection. When pilots are between TOAKS and SILEX intersection, and they have been cleared for the approach, they may descend to 3,500 feet when they are established on the localizer. If they have been vectored to any terminal route, such as the 136 degree radial from the Fillmore VOR, and they are cleared for the approach, they may descend to 4,000 feet.

The fourth part of the clearance is the official approach clearance to the target airport. Listen very carefully to this. It can be tell-tale. The controller may clear pilots for an approach to a different airport than desired. This is definitely not good! It's been my startled experience to hear this. Pilots may also be cleared for an approach they didn't desire. It's possible to be cleared for the ILS when the VOR approach was requested. This isn't in any way an aspersion on controllers. It's more an example of the natural and expected perturbations in the communication process. This portion of the clearance offers the necessary "checks and balances" to ensure pilots fly the desired approach.

The last portion of the clearance usually ends with instructions to contact the tower at the final approach fix or a specific location. If a second communication radio is available, the tower frequency should be set and the tower called when all the aviating and navigating is completed. However, if there is an instructor on board, my personal recommendation is that no more than one radio be used for communications at any one time. The opportunity for radio confusion is very high when instructors are adjusting volume controls while talking to their students. Pilots might not know which radio is in operation, and could miss an ATC call. Not wanting to embarrass themselves, they would have to think of something creative to say to ATC like, "Ah sir, you were stepped on" or, "Say again, I was on the land line" as center controllers often reply in defense of their absences.

When pilots receive approach instructions in a rapid fire manner, they shouldn't panic! Granted, it appears to be the only logical thing to do, but it just doesn't help. Remember the reasoning behind all that is happening. The pilot is awaiting a clearance for the approach to an airport. Essentially the controller is saying, "Get on the thick black line and go to the airport." When receiving this clearance, listen for the information that is of immediate priority. The heading and the altitude are the most important items to attend to first. Pilots should turn to the assigned heading, and note the altitude restrictions. If they are overwhelmed by the clearance, they should repeat back the heading and altitude only. If they have more time after this, they can state, "Roger, cleared for the approach." If they have additional time, they should state they are to contact the tower at the marker and repeat the frequency given. In other words, pilots should repeat back the entire clearance, if possible. If not, at least turn to the desired heading first, then ask the controller to repeat the clearance.

ESTABLISHING INBOUND

During the vector for the approach, pilots should keep in mind that their objective is to intercept the approach course shown on the approach chart. They should be highly motivated to see that needle centered in the VOR equipment and to fly the inbound course. It's common for students to turn to the intercept vector given by ATC and completely forget to intercept the inbound course. They fly right through the needle because they are so consumed with listening to the controller that they forget the mission. When I was a brand new IFR student, my instructor would tell all the other CFI's that I only saw the localizer needle twice: once when I dove through it on the initial intercept vector and the next time when I recovered at the middle marker. Remember, prioritize: AVIATE first, NAVIGATE second and COMMUNICATE last.

Once established on the inbound approach course, immediately bracket the course to determine the wind direction. Fly the inbound heading of the approach, and watch for needle movement. Make a correction for wind as soon as possible. The sooner determination and correction for wind direction is made, the easier and less complicated the approach becomes.

GLIDE SLOPE INTERCEPT

When flying an ILS into Long Beach, figure 7, pilots should maintain the minimum of 1,600 feet until the glide slope needle centers. Then the descent may begin. The controller's manual states that aircraft will be vectored onto the precision approach course at an altitude at or below the glide slope. This prevents receiving false glide slope signals usually found above the real glide slope.

Notice in figure 7, the glide slope is intercepted prior to crossing the outer marker. This means the glide slope needle will center before the marker beacon is reached, assuming that the marker beacons are not on high sensitivity. The high sensitivity position is for high altitude identification of the marker beacon and should normally not be used for an approach.

Once the glide slope needle centers, a descent should be started. For those pilots with retractable gear aircraft, the lowering of the landing gear at the glide slope intercept point will start the descent. Make sure the landing gear is down by the final approach fix/point on any approach. My personal standard is to have the landing gear down prior to glide slope interception. With this method, only one adjustment of power is needed after glide slope interception.

It's not unreasonable to use the gear to commence a descent upon glide slope interception. This will start a pilot down, but an additional power adjustment is usually required to maintain the desired approach speed. This is a little too much work and poses too great a risk of distraction for my taste. I refuse to let myself be trapped by distractions on an instrument approach and forget to lower the gear. Some pilots may say, "If he is so concerned about forgetting to lower the landing gear, why doesn't he always leave it down?" My response is, "I've considered it." After all, it's not often pilots hear of a gear up landing in a Cessna 152.

Figure 7 shows the glide slope altitude over the outer marker is 1573 feet. This is the only time to check the glide slope for accuracy. Therefore, on the glide slope, at the outer marker, the altimeter should read 1573 feet. If it doesn't, then either the glide slope equipment is inaccurate, the altimeter is in error or the pilot has captured a false glide slope.

FLY THE VSI

Precision control of the glide slope is a thing of beauty to behold. Unfortunately, many pilots don't often see such beauty in their cockpit. That's because their ILS needles often look like sword fights or at least two people fanatically attacking each other with bamboo sticks.

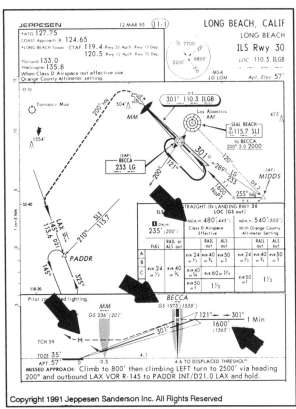

Fig. 7. The Long Beach ILS Rwy 30 approach.

The secret to executing precision ILS approaches is in the use of the Vertical Speed Indicator. Every Jeppesen chart issued for U.S. airports has, in the conversion table in the bottom left hand side of the approach chart, a ground speed-rate table, as seen in figure 8. Pilots using NOS charts will find a similar table in the front of their chart booklet.

With the glide slope inclined at 3 degrees, a descent rate of 538 feet per minute is required to maintain a parallel course with the glide path at 100 knots ground speed. Now, Jeppesen wouldn't put this information here unless it had some value. Pilots can be sure Jeppesen didn't just find

Gnd speed-Kts	70	90	100	120	140	160
GS 3.00°	377	485	538	646	754	861
BECCA to MAP 4.6	3:57	3:04	2:46	2:18	1:58	1:44

Copyright 1991 Jeppesen Sanderson Inc.

Fig. 8. Jeppesen's missed approach table.

a blank space on their chart and need something to put in there. This information is extremely valuable to an instrument pilot. When the glide slope is intercepted, pilots should commence a 538 foot per minute rate of descent using the VSI. This will put them in the ballpark of the glide path. If there is any wind, a different rate of descent will be based on the new ground speed. Remember, this is not indicated airspeed, it's ground speed. In fact, the rate of descent required is indicative of the wind component, which directly affects ground speed. It's a rough "wind check" throughout the approach.

Flying the VSI is a skill, and it takes a little practice to perform any skill well. With a little review, pilots should be able to maintain a descent rate within + or - 25 feet per minute in smooth air. This requires a light touch on the controls. If one has spent a lifetime as a jackhammer technician, some behavior modification may be necessary to attain this piloting finesse. Pilots should understand that the airspeed is controlled by the throttles and the rate is controlled by the elevator controls during an ILS approach. There's no pilot alive who could control the rate, using just the throttles, with the quickness and precision necessary to keep the needles centered under all conditions. Certainly, there's no jet pilot who would consider controlling the aircraft this way. By the time the engines spooled to a new power setting, the glide slope needle would be vacationing against the side of the instrument case.

Consider that the command bars on a Flight Director pictorially direct the pilot to change pitch to hold the glide slope. The command bars do not consider pitch as related to airspeed. In fact, on some Flight Directors, there is a visual warning (the Fast-Slow indicator, for example) letting pilots know the airspeed is off and a throttle change is necessary. Pilots learning to master the VSI develop precision control on the glide path. Remember, at the middle marker, each dot of deflection of the glide slope indicates approximately 8 feet off course. One sneeze and pilots could go below minimums!

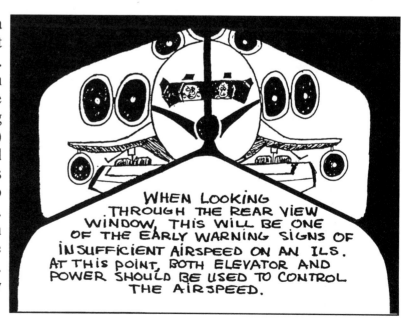

THE 6 T'S

When crossing the final approach fix, the 6 T's should be completed.* At the final approach fix or the outer marker, (on an ILS there is no FAF, there is a final approach point), it should be habitual for pilots to say: **"TURN, TIME, TUNE, THROTTLE, TALK AND TRACK."**

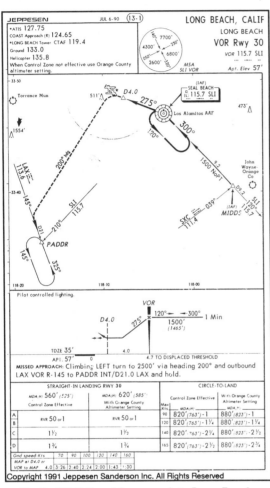

Fig. 9. VOR Rwy 30 approach to Long Beach.

Once established on the ILS, there is no requirement to TURN at the outer marker, since the aircraft is already established on the inbound course. ILS approaches have no turns. In contrast, the VOR approach to Long Beach, figure 9, requires a turn at the final approach fix to a heading of 275 degrees to track the final approach segment.

The TIME should be started to identify the missed approach point. On the ILS, the missed approach point is at Decision Altitude (formerly shown as Decision Height on IFR charts). Nevertheless, pilots should start the time at the outer marker to have options in the event of a glide slope failure. A localizer approach, with slightly higher minimums, can be salvaged from an ILS with a failed glide slope, if the missed approach point, determined by time, can be identified.

My recommendation for turning, rather than timing first, is to make the 6 T's more versatile. It's expected that the pilot is going to time immediately after starting the turn. After all, operating a stop watch doesn't demand a lot of attention. It's easy to <u>start</u> the turn, then punch the timer. This arrangement makes it easy to use the same 6 T's in a holding pattern. When arriving over the holding fix, a turn is made to the outbound heading. Timing can be started immediately to monitor the turn or delayed to measure the length of the outbound leg only.

Pilots have no need to TUNE the course selector for the ILS approach, since this had been done prior to intercepting the approach course. On the Long Beach VOR 30 approach course, figure 9, the course selector should initially be set to 300 degrees. After crossing the final approach fix, which is at the VOR, pilots should TUNE the course selector to 275 degrees and track to the airport.

On the ILS approach, pilots should THROTTLE back when on the glide slope. Pitch to maintain a 538 feet per minute descent rate and adjust power to control airspeed. This sets the aircraft parallel to the glide slope, with a ground speed of 100 knots. A power setting of approximately 1,900 RPM, in many small, general aviation airplanes, will provide approximately a 500 foot per minute descent rate.

*Perform them at the FAF, then repeat the sequence to make sure nothing was overlooked. Also, use the 6T's at every intersection on the enroute structure to be reminded to make time checks and tune new course selections for different airways.

On a nonprecision approach, such as the VOR 30 or Localizer 30 approach to Long Beach, pilots should throttle back to set a descent at a maximum rate of about 600 to 800 feet per minute to the MDA.

In the case of the Long Beach VOR 30 approach, figure 9, the MDA is 560 feet. It's usually best to descend to the MDA as soon as practical, simply because it allows pilots to be prepared to begin scanning for the airport. The most important thing for pilots to remember is not to descend below minimums. The MDA is a minimum altitude, and there's no requirement for the pilot to descend to this minimum altitude. Pilots may elect to stay above it by about 50 feet or so during the initial level off, then creep on down to it, if desired. My recommendation is to level off at the nearest whole hundred foot increment above the MDA because it is easier to visually identify. For precision, pilots may slowly descend the last few feet to the MDA. Even the Practical Test Standards do not expect pilots to go down to the specific MDA for a nonprecision approach. The Practical Test Standards indicate that on an IFR checkride, pilots may remain -0 to +100 above the MDA.

WINGING IT

While waiting for weather improvement in the runup block, in one of the worst thunderstorms, tornado watch, heavy rain, hail and wind conditions that any of us in our cockpit could remember, we heard the following conversation between the tower and an aircraft on approach:

"Tower, Airline 123, outer marker."

"Airline 123, cleared to land; wind 270 at 21, gusts to 29, heavy rain, hail, severe turbulence below 300 feet, RVR 2000 feet."

"Ah, Roger, Airline 123 is cleared to land - and ah, let us know if it gets any worse!!!" **ASRS REPORT**

TALKING is the second to the last task to be completed for obvious reasons. Talking is a low priority item. Talk only when all the other T's have been completed, and the airplane is under control. There are times when ATC may request pilots to contact the tower before arriving at the final approach fix. They should do so only if they have control of their airplane. If they're busy maneuvering or controlling the aircraft, they should request that ATC standby. TRACK serves to remind the pilot to center the needle.

In the event the glide slope is lost while inside the outer marker on the ILS, the localizer approach can be substituted.* The glide-slope-out-MDA, shown on the Long Beach ILS 30 approach chart, figure 7, is 480 feet with Class D airspace effective. The profile view in figure 7 shows a dashed line which represents the "nonprecision" localizer approach. Notice that the 1,600 foot altitude, shown prior to intercepting the glide slope, is to be maintained to the outer marker if a localizer approach is to be executed.

The missed approach point for the localizer "only" approach is determined by time from BECCA compass locator. Pilots can always determine the missed approach point on any nonprecision approach by looking at the conversion box on the bottom left hand side of the approach chart as shown in figure 8.** Additionally, Jeppesen is adding an "M" to the upward curving arrow shown in the profile view of figure 7 to identify the missed approach point on nonprecision approaches.

EXECUTING THE MISSED

If general aviation pilots had the luxury of two pilot crews, piloting an IFR aircraft would be substantially easier. Copilots would raise and lower the gear and flaps, set navigation frequencies and talk on the radio.

*Of course, this assumes that you have not already reached the MDA for the nonprecision part of the approach. If you have glide slope failure after passing the MDA, a missed approach is appropriate.

**The time shown in any conversion box (figure 8) is for nonprecision approaches only. The missed approach point for a precision approach (i.e., ILS), is identified by arrival at Decision Altitude while on the glide slope.

The left seat pilot would exclusively fly and think. Unfortunately, the luxury of dividing chores is not often found in small Cessnas and Pipers. However, there is one activity that copilots perform for their captains that can be mimicked in a single pilot operation -- calling out the 100 foot above DA or MDA mark on the ILS. Pilots should remind themselves when they have 100 feet of descent left prior to DA or MDA. This cues them to anticipate the MAP. Additionally, copilots call out airspeed and sink rate at the 500 foot mark above ground. Aural affirmation of critical performance numbers can jolt pilots into instantly reevaluating whether a questionable approach should be abandoned.

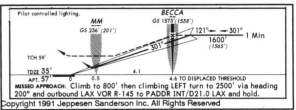

Fig. 10. The missed approach procedure.

Finally, good instrument pilots should have familiarized themselves with the missed approach procedure, prior to committing to the final descent from the FAF. The missed approach procedure, shown for the ILS 30 approach to Long Beach, figure 10, has certain letters and words capitalized. If pilots are ever in quick need of a missed approach review, they need only look at the capitalized information. This is the most important information concerning the missed approach. The first part of every missed approach starts with a climb. Any missed approach that starts with a descent first, should be treated with suspicion. Someone is probably playing a very bad joke on the pilot, or the chart is being read upside down. If this happens, pilots should hunt the guilty author down and ask them about their sick sense of humor.

Many years ago my ancestors became vegetarians after an amazing discovery -- they learned that it's a whole lot easier to sneak up on plants. This makes a great deal of sense. In much the same way, learning the proper procedures to make IFR flying easier just makes sense. Pilots don't have to be a "good stick" to be highly competent in the instrument system. Personally, I am relieved by that last sentence. There is no magic, nor deep mysticism, for competency in IFR flying. It's mostly a matter of obeying a prescribed set of procedures. Nevertheless, it does take enough exposure in the IFR system to reach a practical level of competency. My challenge to the instrument pilot is to learn as much as possible about IFR procedures. This is what is necessary to attain an admirable level of mastery of the instrument environment.

HUMULONIMBUS

FAITH MOVETH MOUNTAINS

A pilot called Approach control stating that the weather ahead was too poor to continue; he was returning. He was radar identified with Mode C showing 2000 feet. When asked if he was in VFR conditions, the pilot stated he was in the soup and requested an IFR clearance. The aircraft was cleared. The pilot stated he did not have the approach plate; I described it to him. During this time, Mode C showed altitudes of 2500 to 4000 feet (assigned altitude was 3000). I warned the Tower that this unit should be watched closely. Sure enough, on a three mile final, still in the clouds, the aircraft started tracking approximately 60 degrees off the final approach course. The tower had to instruct the pilot four times to execute the missed approach. On the missed approach, the aircraft broke out. I told him to pick out a runway and land. Based on Mode C, the aircraft should have hit high terrain. It should be noted that the aircraft is owned and operated by a church; probably why the pilot is still alive.

An approach plate and some instrument instruction might have added a little insurance, just the same. "Trust in the Lord, and keep your powder dry" is still a pretty good motto.

ASRS REPORT

But even attainment of a high level of instrument proficiency does not give a pilot carte blanche to proceed headlong into a thunderstorm.

9. THUNDERSTORM AVOIDANCE

Mother Nature's weather, at its worst, is called a thunderstorm. Its attendant hazards encompass about everything the aviator was taught to fear and avoid: turbulence, hail, lightning, icing and wind shear. It is the 'total cancer' to feed upon pilots and their aircraft. It is the ultimate heat machine, and its fuel is water. The more of it, the more likely this predatory monster will reach maturity. Its energy release has been equated to millions of tons of dynamite, and most certainly only a couple pounds of that product is adequate to "ruin a pilot's day." Encounters are always impressive, memorable and never a pleasure.

Many years ago, Marine Colonel William Rankin had an awesome encounter of the closest possible kind. At 48,000 feet, he bailed out of his disabled jet fighter, deployed his chute and Mother Nature exhibited that he had selected the worst possible patch of sky. Down he went, absorbed into the bowels of a thunderstorm. For over 30 minutes he rode high speed elevators within that cumulo-monster, discovered every turbulent bump and temperature change, explored hypoxia, sampled the icing content and was blessed to be spit from it. He survived it and documented his experience with a book: The Man Who Rode The Thunder. If another book titled Why I Don't Eat Snowcones is seen, I suspect he will be the author.

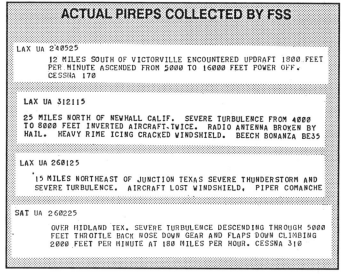

ACTUAL PIREPS COLLECTED BY FSS

```
LAX UA 240525
        12 MILES SOUTH OF VICTORVILLE ENCOUNTERED UPDRAFT 1800 FEET
        PER MINUTE ASCENDED FROM 5000 TO 16000 FEET POWER OFF.
        CESSNA 170

LAX UA 312115
        25 MILES NORTH OF NEWHALL CALIF.  SEVERE TURBULENCE FROM 4000
        TO 8000 FEET INVERTED AIRCRAFT TWICE.  RADIO ANTENNA BROKEN BY
        HAIL.  HEAVY RIME ICING CRACKED WINDSHIELD.  BEECH BONANZA BE35

LAX UA 260125
        15 MILES NORTHEAST OF JUNCTION TEXAS SEVERE THUNDERSTORM AND
        SEVERE TURBULENCE.  AIRCRAFT LOST WINDSHIELD,  PIPER COMANCHE

SAT UA 260225
        OVER MIDLAND TEX. SEVERE TURBULENCE DESCENDING THROUGH 5000
        FEET THROTTLE BACK NOSE DOWN GEAR AND FLAPS DOWN CLIMBING
        2000 FEET PER MINUTE AT 180 MILES PER HOUR. CESSNA 310
```

Many books are written about the three ingredients of a thunderstorm: moisture, instability and lifting action. Few books talk about the threats beneath a thunderstorm, such as: wind shear, downbursts and microbursts. It wasn't until 1947 when a program called, "Project Thunderstorm," determined that thunderstorms had three distinct stages: cumulus, mature and dissipating. About thirty years later (1975), it was first identified that the outflow of thunderstorms had the awesome ability to "out-fly" an airplane. The topic called windshear was born.

The threat is obvious, and what's needed is a discussion on how to avoid thunderstorms. If pilots were to stay on the ground every time thunderstorms were mentioned by Flight Service, they would have little practical use of their airplanes for half of the year. Yet, if they are too bold and don't assess risks properly, they can end up at that big "pilot supply shop" in the sky. Experienced pilots do fly IFR safely, with great confidence, despite these conditions. They do so because they have learned that thunderstorms, like other atmospheric phenomena, must comply with natural law and, therefore, become somewhat predictable.

There is nothing more disconcerting to an instrument rated pilot than looking out the windshield into what was thought to be a benign, stratiform cloud and seeing a ragged flash of lighting directly ahead. This explains why the instrument pilot's most frequently asked question is, "How can I be sure that those are not thunderstorm clouds?" Identifying benign, cumulus type clouds from those with a predatory disposition begins with an understanding of the two basic types of thunderstorms.

UNDERSTANDING THUNDERSTORMS

Thunderstorms come in two basic forms: airmass (general thunderstorms) and severe, usually steady state type storms. The former last from 30 to 90 minutes, and the latter can last for hours. The extreme of the latter is called an MCC (Mesoscale Convective Complex) which can cover states and lasts for hours. Obviously, pilots want to avoid all types of thunderstorms.

Air mass thunderstorms are associated with little or no wind. This is why air mass thunderstorms don't tilt. Their erect nature is one of the reasons they are short lived. During the mature stage, the storm's precipitation falls directly through the center of the cell, shortening its own life through self-induced asphyxiation. The cell stymies and snuffs-out its own updrafts. Air mass thunderstorms are seldom associated with hail, because hail pellets have little time to grow within a doomed body. Most of the thunderstorms that form in Florida are of the airmass type, and this explains why hail is very rare in that part of the country.

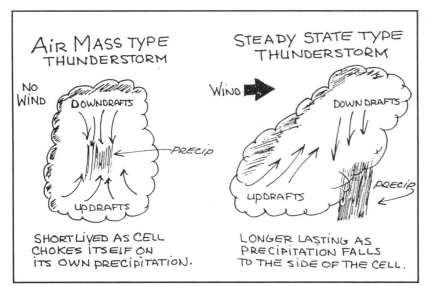

As soon as the thunderstorm starts to tilt, things get a great deal more serious. Tilting of the thunderstorm is associated with faster winds at higher altitudes. These tilting storms generate the steady state type thunderstorms. Precipitation falls away from the center of the tilted cell, therefore, it doesn't choke itself out on its own precipitation. The storm remains in a steady state, with updrafts and downdrafts lasting for a longer period of time, producing more turbulence. As a general rule, if the speed of a thunderstorm is doubled (i.e. more wind), the intensity of the turbulence, and the bad weather associated with it, is quadrupled. In fact, it's not unusual for some Meteorologists to issue hail warnings whenever thunderstorms tilt.

Pilots should pay particular attention to any thunderstorm associated with high winds. These type of thunderstorms usually have tops in excess of 35,000 feet and can be found along frontal lines. They are also associated with squall lines and severe weather watch areas. Pilots should avoid takeoffs and landings in the face of any thunderstorm, particularly a steady state thunderstorm. The maximum outflow measured from a thunderstorm was recorded in Oklahoma many years ago. Thunderstorm generated gusts were identified 18 miles from the storm center. Any aircraft departing or landing within this distance is subject to the effects of wind shear. In fact, many airlines do not permit takeoff or landing operations when thunderstorms are present within 3 nautical miles of the takeoff or landing corridor. It's best to remain on the ground and wait it out. Airmass thunderstorms are easier to avoid because they are stationary; steady state thunderstorms are more predatory -- they come looking for pilots.

HEIGHT IS MIGHT

The 30,000' thunderstorm is considered to be typical, even 'garden variety,' in the Midwest.* One study involving the penetration of 2,893 thunderstorms (where they recruited from the USAF 2,893 young Lieutenants who liked to take vectors and didn't ask questions) concluded some interesting facts.

In terms of probability, the 30,000' thunderstorm has one chance in three of being severe...therefore, one out of three will be! With updrafts of 6,000 - 8,000 FPM, it takes about one minute to reach 37,500' from 30,000', where one in two thunderstorms is severe! In one minute's time, the risk factor for severe thunderstorms went from 33% to 50%!

Meteorologists know that the hail producer exceeds the freezing level by 10,000'. On extremely hot summer days, the freezing level is probably around 20,000' MSL. Therefore, that 30,000' storm, even if NOT severe, is most probably a hail producer.

MAKING THE Go/NoGo THUNDERSTORM DECISION

There is no doubt that thunderstorms are things to be avoided. The preflight weather briefing, therefore, becomes extremely important in answering the question: Is there a potential for thunderstorm formation? Once the potential for thunderstorms has been determined, a rational strategy must be developed to avoid them. Use of rabbits' feet, beads, Tibetan chanting and all varieties of moonrise sacrificial offerings, while comforting to pilots, seem to have little or no effect on helping them avoid thunderstorms. Perhaps this adequately explains why use of these "Voodoo avoidance rituals" has almost completely disappeared on commercial flight decks today. In fact, there are only two ways of avoiding thunderstorm cells: use of onboard storm detection equipment or visual circumnavigation. To blindly fly in solid IFR conditions, when thunderstorms are forecast, without storm detection equipment, is totally unacceptable. However, it's the pilot's job to acquire more information with which to make an intelligent assessment about the potential and location of thunderstorm cells.

The first consideration of a "Go/NoGo" weather decision is based on the consumption of information from several sources. The very first place pilots should start, in assessing the thunderstorm potential of the atmosphere, is with the Area Forecast.

CAUGHT WITH WHEEL PANTS DOWN

Flying a rental airplane, I noticed that a note in the log sheet stated, "#2 Nav inop." The preflight was OK otherwise. Thunderstorms were predicted in the area forecast for XD:00 p.m. I had planned for a XA:30 departure, with 5 hours of fuel, for a 1.5 hour flight. The avionics were "state of the art" with RNAV, LORAN, weather radar, etc. My actual departure time was near XC:00 p.m., so I was pushing it with the weather. Fifteen minutes after departure, I experienced complete radio failure in IMC conditions. Fortunately, I carry a hand-held com radio and was able to maintain contact with Approach. I was vectored to a VFR field 20 nm SW of my home base. The Approach controller was terrific...(in) getting me on the ground.

Rental pilots must insist on equipment being in 100% operating order, but must not blame the aircraft owner/operator for pilot "get-there-itis," no matter how fancy the equipment. I will not get in an airplane again without a fully charged, hand-held radio. **ASRS REPORT**

---

*Thunderstorms are very geographic. In England, a 25,000 foot thunderstorm is simply awsome and seldom seen. At the Equator, 60,000 foot thunderstroms are common. Also, remember that within the U.S. continent, there are two calibers of thunderstorms: the "raining monster" and the "high plains/desert type" storm with high cloud bases. The latter may be accompanied by Virga beneath it and have a remarkably unthreatening appearance. When flying anywhere west of Denver, treat a towering cumulus, especially with rain of any kind, as a thunderstorm. The terrible outflow from this high plains/desert type thunderstorm has followed a common theme: temperature/dewpoint spreads of about 35 degrees or higher. This is the reason for the Virga. The rain is evaporating on the way down and that means COOLING! Cooling means the air is heavy and accelerating downward! This means outflow!

THE AREA FORECAST (FA)

The area forecast provides a pilot with a comprehensive idea about the potential for thunderstorm formation over large areas. It is issued three times daily and contains a 12 hour forecast plus an additional 6 hour outlook, as shown in figure 1A. The HAZARDS/FLIGHT PRECAUTIONS SECTION forecasts thunderstorms when they are expected to be at least scattered in coverage (meaning 25% or more of the area). Severe thunderstorm forecasts are also found in this section. The SIGNIFICANT CLOUDS AND WEATHER section also includes forecast thunderstorms. Figure 1B identifies the percentage of areas expected to be covered, or affected, by thunderstorm activity in the Area Forecast. Additionally, sections of the area forecasts are amended and updated by inflight advisories. The quickest way to determine if an area forecast has been amended is to look at all subsequent SIGMET's and AIRMET's. If these reports are issued after the area forecast was issued, they automatically amend that forecast, until an official amendment to the (FA) occurs. Therefore, knowing the time the area forecast was issued becomes important.

```
SLCH FA 240245
HAZARDS VALID UNTIL 241500
ID MT WY NV UT CO AS NM

FLT PRCTNS...ICG...ID MT NV UT CO AZ NM
          ...TURBC...ID MT WY NV UT CO AZ NM
          ...MTN OBSCN...ID MT WY NV
          ...TNSTMS...ID MT CO
.
TSNMS IMPLY PSBL SVR OR GTR TURBC SVR ICG AND LLWS.
NON MSL HGTS NOTED BY AGL OR CIG

SLCC FA 240245
SGFNT CLDS AND WX VALID UNTIL 241500...OTLK 241500-242100
.
MTN OBSCN...ID MT WY NV
FROM YXH TO GCC TO TWF TO ELY TO 50NE FAT TO RBL TO UKI TO 30SW
UKI TO FOT TO TOU TO YXH
MTNS OCNLY OBSCD IN CLDS AND PCPN.  CONDS CONTG BYD 15Z.
SEE THE SFO FA FOR DETAILS IN THAT AREA.
.
ID
60-80 SCT/BKN 100-120 BKN LYRD TO 240. WDLY SCT RW-/TRW...CB
TOPS TO 350..LWRG CIGS/VSBYS 30-50 BKN/3-5. TSTMS OCNLY IN LNS
OR CLUSTERS. MTNS OBSCD IN CLDS AND PCPN. OTLK...VFR
.
MT
80-100 SCT/BKN 140-160 BKN LYRD TO 240. WDLY SCT RW-/TRW..CB
TOPS TO 350..LWRG CIGS/VSBYS OCNLY 30-50 BKN/3-5. TNSTMS OCNLY IN
LNS OR CLUSTERS.  MTNS OBSCD IN CLDS AND PCPN.  OTLK...MVFR CIGS
RW W OF DVD...VFR ELSW
.
CO
150 SCT WITH BKN CI ABV. SCT TRW NERN CO..CB TOPS ABV 450..LWRG
CIGS 50 BKN..ENDG 04Z-07Z.  OTLK...VFR
```

Fig. 1A. The area forecast.

Adjective	Coverage
Isolated	Single cells (no percentage)
Widely sct	Less than 25% of area affected
Scattered	25 to 54% of area affected
Numerous	55% or more of area affected
OCNL	Greater than 50% probability of the phenomenon occurring but for less than 1/2 of forecast period

Fig. 1B Thunderstorm coverage definitions for the area forecast.

SEVERE WEATHER OUTLOOK CHART

When visiting the FSS, I like to take a look at the severe weather outlook chart after viewing the area forecast. This is a preliminary 24 hour outlook for thunderstorms. It is issued once daily and is shown in figure 2. The left hand panel covers the 12 hour period from 1200Z-0000Z. The right hand panel covers the remaining 12 hours, 0000Z-1200Z. This chart is strictly for advanced planning. A line with an arrowhead delineates an area of probable general thunderstorm activity. Facing in the direction of the arrow, thunderstorm activity is expected to the right of the line. Areas of slight thunderstorm risk have a chance of severe thunderstorms covering 2 to 5% of the area. In the moderate risk areas severe thunderstorms may cover 6 to 10% of the area. Tornado watch areas are also shown on the chart. The information on this chart is based on the same information used in the 0800Z convective outlook. The severe weather outlook is not updated during the next 24 hour period. There is an interesting reason behind this that will be discussed in the next section. Another useful and more detailed description of forecast thunderstorms is the convective outlook.

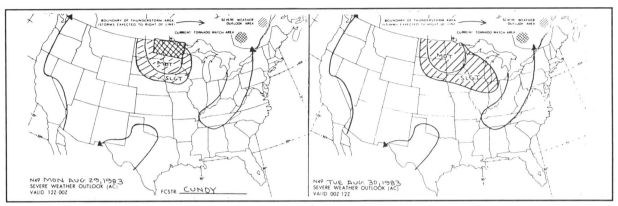

Fig. 2. The severe weather outlook chart has two panels. The left panel covers from 1200Z to 0000Z and the right panel covers from 0000Z to 1200Z.

CONVECTIVE OUTLOOK (AC)

The convective outlook (AC), figure 3, describes the prospects for both general and severe thunderstorms during a 24 hour period. This provides excellent information for anticipating thunderstorm potential later during the day. Much like the severe weather outlook chart, it's used as an advanced planning tool. It's useful in that it describes, in greater detail, the reason and the specific locations of expected thunderstorm activity. Figure 3 indicates that severe thunderstorms and tornadoes near the Great Lakes are expected because of an upper level system that will move rapidly across an unstable airmass where a lifted index of -7 to -10 is forecast (lifted index discussed pg. 99).

Of course, it's possible that the words and terms used by Meteorologists may even add deeper mystery to a pilot's understanding of thunderstorms. When looking at any weather report that appears to contain words from another solar system, it's a good time to hit the books and ask a lot of questions.

```
MKC AC 021500
VALID 021500 - 031200Z

THERE IS A HIGH RISK OF SVR TSTMS BGNG THIS AFTERNOON AND CONTG INTO
THE EVE OVR IL...IND...ERN MO...ERN IA...CNTRL AND SRN WI...LWR MI...WRN
OH...AND WRN AND NRN KY. THE HIGH RISK IS TO THE RT OF A LN FM P02 JEF CID
LSE AWI APN MTC LUK FTK 20 S PAH P02

THERE IS A SLIGHT RISK OF SVR TSTMS TO THE RT OF A LN FM 20 N ROC JST CRW
TUP 30 S MLU SAT SSE DRT...CONT...40 S P07 MAF FSM SZL FRM AXN INL

OUTBREAKS OF SVR TSTMS AND TORNADOES EXPCD FM ERN MO INTO THE GT LKS
AREA AS A VERY STG UPR LVL SYSTEM MOVES RPDLY EWD ACRS A UNSTBL AMS
WHERE SFC LI OF MINUS 7 TO MINUS 10 PROGD.
```

Fig. 3. The convective weather outlook.

Many pilots, attaining what they believe is a working theory of meteorology, often approach new weather knowledge with anxiety. Their concern is that continued exposure to "new" knowledge could punch a hole in their fragile understanding of how things work. Pilots should always be willing to update their theories about weather -- it's their job!

Convective outlooks are updated forecasts transmitted by the National Severe Storms Forecasting Center (NSSFC) at 0800Z, 1500Z and 1900Z. Essentially, weather forecasters combine information from stability charts and many other cryptic weather information sources known only to their high priests of forecasting, and make estimations on possibilities for thunderstorm formation. Pilots, planning flights at 1500Z or 1900Z, can compare the newer convective outlook with the original severe weather outlook chart. This provides them with an idea of how the forecasts are changing.

GOOD ATTITUDE INDICATOR

Alexander Pope wrote: Fools rush in where Angels fear to tread.

IFR moral: Tread not in IMC if you lack qualification.

Along with the convective outlook, the severe weather watch bulletins (WW) define areas of possible severe thunderstorms or tornado activity. Now, it's time to take a look at a chart that will visually identify the locations and reasons behind thunderstorm formations.

SIGNIFICANT WEATHER PROGNOSTIC CHART

The significant weather prognostic chart portrays forecast weather for 12 and 24 hour periods. What's particularly useful about this chart is that it is issued four times daily. The 12 and 24 hour forecasts are based on the 00Z, 06Z, 12Z and 18Z synoptic data. This means that the chart will contain updated and refined information. It's an excellent chart to help identify areas of expected thunderstorm activity. What's especially useful with this chart is the depiction of frontal systems and pressure patterns. Pilots need to know if thunderstorms will be of the airmass type or the steady state type (possibly associated with frontal movement). This chart can provide some information on the type of lifting action responsible for generating the thunderstorm activity. The bottom left hand panel of the prog chart, figure 4, is the 12 hour surface forecast. Thunderstorms and rain showers (R) are expected during the forecast period, in the areas of northern Oklahoma, eastern Kansas and Nebraska and southern South Dakota. By now pilots have a reasonable idea about the likelihood

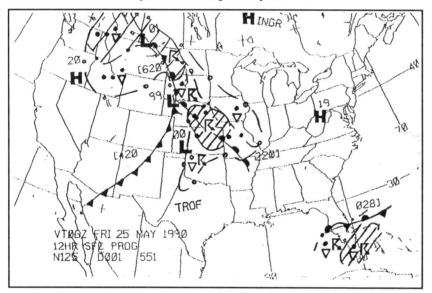

Fig. 4. The 12 and 24 hour significant weather prognostic chart.

of thunderstorm formation. Acquiring a more detailed understanding about why thunderstorms form can be obtained by identifying that the ingredients for their formation exist.

THE COMPOSITE MOISTURE STABILITY CHART

Interpreting how much moisture is in the air, and the degree of atmospheric instability, is very important for IFR flight planning. There is one weather chart that will provide this information to the pilot. The composite moisture stability chart contains four panels, one of which the pilot can use to understand thunderstorm formation. Figure 5 shows the stability chart (sometimes called the "lifted/k-index"). This chart provides direct information on the potential instability and moisture content of the atmosphere.

The stability chart is available twice daily at the Flight Service Station at 0000Z and 1200Z. The information on this wonderful little chart is the result of the two daily Radiosonde ascensions. Pilots should be cautioned that the information on this chart is usually 4 1/2 hours old by the time pilots obtain it for use. Nevertheless, it is still a useful tool.

The two numbers shown above and below the line are referred to as the lifted index and the K-index, respectively. The lifted index identifies the stability of the air, and the K-index identifies the potential for both the moisture content and stability of the atmosphere. Understanding how to use these numbers is a very useful tool for identifying the potential for thunderstorm formation.

THE LIFTED INDEX

The numerical value of the lifted index represents the temperature difference a parcel of air, near the surface, would experience with the surrounding air, if that parcel

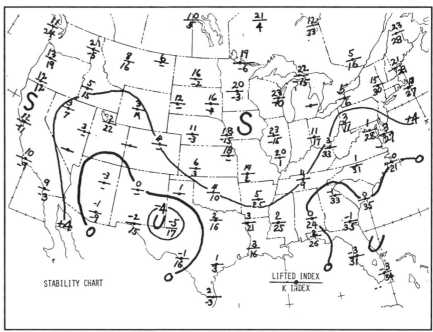

Fig. 5. The composite moisture-stability chart (stability chart shown).

were lifted to 18,000 feet MSL. The value of the lifted index immediately tells a pilot whether the air would be stable or unstable, if lifted. An index with a value of zero indicates that a lifted parcel of air would have the same temperature value as the surrounding atmosphere, making the air neutrally stable. An index number with a positive value indicates that a parcel of air, if lifted, would be colder than the surrounding air, making the air stable. An index with a negative value indicates that the rising parcel would become warmer than the surrounding air, making this air parcel unstable. The index numbers are actual temperature differences in degrees centigrade. Areas with lifted index values of +4, 0, -4, are connected by lines. These lines allow pilots to immediately identify large areas of stability, instability and neutral stability.

Remember, the air must be lifted to experience the temperature differences anticipated by the lifted index. Additionally, lifted index values are for temperature differences based on the air being lifted to 18,000 feet MSL. Lifting the air to a lesser altitude would not result in as great a temperature difference. More intense lifting also means greater stability or instability, depending on the depicted index values. Pilots should note that unstable air does not automatically mean thunderstorms. It's possible to have a negative lifted index with no thunderstorms, because the air simply wasn't lifted high enough for thunderstorms to form.

THE K-INDEX

The K-index is slightly more complex, but it basically indicates the amount of moisture in the atmosphere, as well as the potential for unstable lapse rates. Although the K-index is not a true indicator of stability, it can be used to anticipate the formation of thunderstorms. Basically, the higher the K-index value, the greater the amount of moisture in the atmosphere, and the more likely the air is to become unstable. The lower the K-index, the drier the air, and the more likely it is to be stable.

LIFTED INDEX (LI)	"K" INDEX *	AIRMASS THUNDERSTORM PROBABILITY
0 to −2 weak indication of severe thunderstorms	< 15	near 0%
	15-20	20%
−3 to −5 moderate indication of severe thunderstorms	21-25	21-40%
indication of severe thunderstorms	26-30	41-60%
≤−6 strong indication of severe thunderstorms	31-35	61-80%
	36-40	81-90%
	>40	near 100%

Fig. 6. Thunderstorm probability reference.

Professional opinion has it that with K-index values of less than 20, there is generally just not enough water in the atmosphere to form the most nasty and violent convective phenomena that appear as tornadoes and killer thunderstorm cells. However, K-index values greater than 30, may portend some of the nastiest weather that Mother Nature has to offer. K-index values are more reliable for airmass thunderstorm predictions than for steady state type thunderstorms. Thunderstorm potential is made understandable by referring to figure 6. Comparative clues for the lifted and the K-index allow pilots to assess airmass thunderstorm probability.

USING THE CHART

Armed with this information, pilots can now use the stability chart to identify areas of convective activity. Referring to figure 5, the area around Florida and Georgia have lifted index values of 0 to -3 and K-index values from 33 to 35. This indicates that the air is unstable, and there is enough moisture present to produce some very serious convective weather in the form of thunderstorms and tornadoes. Florida is such a beautiful place. However, on more than one occasion, because of the extreme moisture content of the summer atmosphere, I have felt like I was in attendance at a state-wide humidity festival. On those hot summer days, people can experience the strange sensation that they are actually breathing pound cake. I knew it was hot when I saw two palm trees fighting over a dog!

Certainly, negative lifted values and high K-index values should cue pilots in to the possibility of thunderstorms enroute. Additionally, pilots can use the K-index as a means of identifying thunderstorm severity. Larger K-index values indicate thunderstorm formation is likely to be more severe than with smaller values.

The area around Southwest Texas, Southern New Mexico and Eastern Arizona all have negative lifted index values and low K-index values. This indicates that there will be limited cumulus activity because of the unstable air, but little or no precipitation because of the low moisture content of the atmosphere. These conditions may produce bumpy, but not necessarily hazardous, weather.

The area around the New England states has positive lifted values and very high K-index values. It's likely there may be stratified cloudiness with steady precipitation. These are certainly not thunderstorm conditions. Pilots could generally expect smooth IFR flying conditions and restricted VFR weather. Flying IFR, under these conditions, is perhaps the most favorable way to gain actual weather experience.

The areas around the Northern Plains and the California coast all have positive lifted index values and very low K-index values. The air in these areas is extremely stable and very dry, indicating predominantly fair weather, smooth flying, good VFR and weak thermal activity, if any.

Many years ago, fifty-five general aviation thunderstorm accidents and eighteen airline thunderstorm accidents were examined by a Meteorologist named Modahl. He found that the average lifted index at the time of the accident was -4 for the small airplanes and -7 for their larger brothers. Thus, the stability chart provides pilots with their first warning, during flight planning, of the potential for a convective encounter.

Correlations between the indexes on the stability chart and the resulting weather, may vary with seasons and with different parts of the country. The extent of the instability also depends on other factors, like surface heating or exaggerated lifting from sloping terrain and frontal conditions. Pilots can be sure that any forced lifting from mountains or fronts may exacerbate weather conditions. It's also wise to interpret areas with an index of + 4 as marginally stable air. Experience shows that this air can become unstable due to surface heating, upslope flow, frontal lifting, convergence or inflow of cold air aloft.

When pilots ask the Weather Briefer for lifted and K-index values, they should consider the time the chart was issued.* Stability charts are issued for the early morning hours and the early evening hours. Early morning data can change quickly with surface heating. Using the stability chart, along with the weather depiction chart, allows pilots to sense how likely atmospheric fireworks are to appear.

WEATHER DEPICTION CHART

The weather depiction chart, figure 7, provides an excellent source of IFR and VFR weather, as well as possible sources of lifting. This is a real time chart and not a forecast. Beginning at 01Z, these charts are transmitted at 3 hour intervals. This chart becomes valuable for a current assessment of the atmosphere. Frontal and pressure systems are shown on the weather depiction chart. This information provides pilots with some idea of how likely the air is to be lifted. When this information is combined with the

TOWERING IDEAS

A small aircraft was on a direct flight in a the southwestern United States. The weather was typical for this area in early summer: ceiling and visibility unlimited, except for scattered cumulus build-ups, tending to become broken as the day matured. There are no radio navigation aids available at non-oxygen altitudes along much of this route, and communication with Flight Service is sporadic at best. The aircraft was being handflown, although it was equipped with autopilot. Supplemental oxygen was not on board. The aircraft was operating at maximum available cruise, approximately 160 knots, at 11,500 MSL in smooth, clear air. Considerable cumulus buildup was in the area, but none was within five miles of the aircraft. Then, one sudden, violent downflow was encountered. The pilot, the only Soul on Board, whose seat belt and shoulder strap were secured, struck the top of cabin with his head, partly losing awareness. Sufficient vision and consciousness remained to maintain a (fairly) wings level attitude and to keep the airspeed needle in the only area of the airspeed indicator still in focus – about 80-90 knots. The pilot was able to re-establish control of the aircraft after it had climbed to a little over 22,000 MSL, in solid IMC,...well above the safe non-oxygen altitude.

On arrival at his destination, the pilot was unable to fly a normal VFR pattern due to disorientation in the low-level turns. He finally opted for a five-mile straight-in approach, after three attempts to land from the pattern. On parking the airplane, the pilot fell off the right wing, apparently still suffering a mild concussion. That, plus the intrinsic elasticity of the pilot allowed a considerable upward excursion of the pilot's head! I don't know what can be done to prevent this sort of thing from happening. I certainly don't single out this aircraft as a problem design; clearly a side-glass encounter could happen in any General Aviation type. Putting GA pilots in crash helmets wouldn't do much to instill passenger confidence. In my case, had I lost it, there would have been nothing to indicate the cause of the crash! I do pause to wonder, in how may apparent thunderstorm encounters leading to in-flight structural failures, did the pilot become incapacitated while still flying an intact airframe and, possibly, still in VMC! Perhaps the real points in reporting are that: (a) Pilots should be aware that the hazard exists, and (b) Post-crash investigators should, at least, consider the possibility in otherwise unexplained, and inadequately explained events. **ASRS REPORT**

*When asking for lifted and K-index values, be sure to tell the FSS specialist that the composite moisture stability chart is the one being referenced.

stability chart information, it provides a handy means of detecting how aggravated the air might become. The possibility of frontal lifting implies the likelihood of developing steady state type thunderstorms. If a cold front is approaching an area of unstable air and high moisture content, pilots can be sure that some form of airborne pyrotechnics will be present.

Additionally, pilots can get an idea of the relative amount of cloud coverage by looking at the station models on the

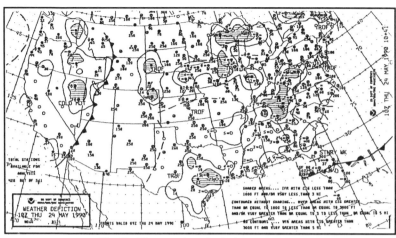

Fig. 7. The weather depiction chart.

chart. Areas of little or no cloud coverage means that, in the absence of frontal lifting, solar heating (convective currents) may cause afternoon thunderstorms to develop. Any pilot who has had the experience of spitting on a griddle knows what can happen when moist air comes in contact with a hot surface. This is Mother Nature's way of cooking up trouble for pilots.

SERIOUS CIRRUS THOUGHTS

Altitude Bust - Pretty Good Excuse!

On a descent, we were given a SIGMET which indicated thunderstorm activity with 2 inch hail and a tornado watch in our area. We were deviating around build-ups, with a clearance to cross 30 miles out at 10,000 feet. At 10,500 feet we could see that 10,000 feet would put us into the tops, between two build-ups, so I requested and received 11,000 feet. As the copilot was leveling off at 11,000 feet, we got hit with a strong updraft that put us at 11,600 feet before you could say it. The copilot was putting forward pressure on the controls just to keep us at 11,600 feet. It was several minutes before we could descend back to 11,000 feet, without putting negative "G's" on the airplane.

ASRS REPORT

Having an idea of cloud coverage is important when thunderstorms are present. Extensive cloud coverage means that thunderstorms may be embedded. If there is anything that should cause pilots concern it should be embedded thunderstorms. Areas with scattered cloud coverage may make visual circumnavigation of thunderstorms much easier. Because of variations in terrain and distance between stations, the weather depiction chart may not completely represent enroute conditions. Nevertheless, it's an excellent chart for obtaining "big-picture" information. Another source of relatively real time information is the radar summary chart.

RADAR SUMMARY CHART

The radar summary chart, figure 8, is an excellent chart for use in testing the validity of thunderstorm forecasts. The chart is provided once every hour and is an excellent source of information on locations of precipitation and severe weather activities. The immense value the radar summary chart offers lies in its depiction of areas of precipitation echoes, echo intensity and the height and movement of the echo.

Radar depicts only water. It's from the amount of water suspended in the weather activity that conclusions are drawn about its severity. Figure 9 shows the radar summary chart's echo intensity/rainfall rate index. The National Weather Service recognizes six thunderstorm intensity levels also known as VIP (Video Integrator Processor) levels. Each level represents a specific echo intensity and rainfall rate in inches per hour as seen on the index. Each contour ring shown on the radar chart represents two intensity levels. For example, the first contour ring bordering the area can represent either a level one or level two storm. The second contour ring can represent either a level three or level four storm.

Notice that there are two rainfall rate columns: one that says stratiform and the other that says convective. Notice also that the rainfall rates in either column, that

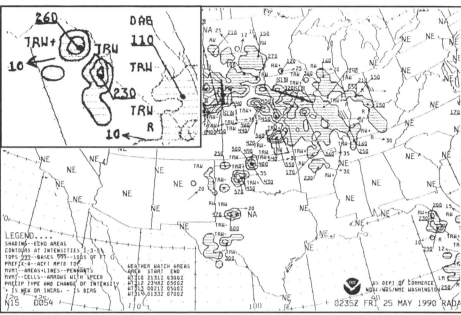

Fig. 8. The radar summary chart.

produce the echo intensity levels, are different. This results from the different pattern of water droplet dispersion between stratiform and convective type clouds. What pilots should know is that the airborne weather radar used in modern day airliners (not the ground based Weather Service Radars, 'WSR,' that produce the radar summary chart) is calibrated to show thunderstorm levels based on the scale used in the stratiform column. In other words, a rainfall rate of .5 to 1.0 inch per hour would be indicated as a level three storm on airborne weather radar. This will produce a red color on the pilot's radar screen. Red is the color airline pilots have been trained to avoid. Therefore, rain fall rates of .5 inch per hour or greater should be regarded as indicating areas of thunderstorms. These areas should be avoided!

Pilots looking at a single contoured area on a radar summary chart may have either a level 1 or level 2 return. This may be produced by stratiform clouds with non-hazardous rainfall rates up to .5 inch per hour or convective clouds with hazardous rainfall rates up to1.1 inch per hour. There is no way a pilot can tell what kind of cloud is producing the return by looking at the radar summary chart. Therefore, in the absence of other information, a single contoured area on the radar summary chart should be regarded as an area of thunderstorms, and should be avoided!

VIP LEVEL	ECHO INTENSITY	PRECIPITATION INTENSITY	RAINFALL RATE in/hr STRATIFORM	RAINFALL RATE in/hr CONVECTIVE
1	WEAK	LIGHT	LESS THAN 0.1	LESS THAN 0.2
2	MODERATE	MODERATE	0.1 - 0.5	0.2 - 1.1
3	STRONG	HEAVY	0.5 - 1.0	1.1 - 2.2
4	VERY STRONG	VERY HEAVY	1.0 - 2.0	2.2 - 4.5
5	INTENSE	INTENSE	2.0 - 5.0	4.5 - 7.1
6	EXTREME	EXTREME	MORE THAN 5.0	MORE THAN 7.1

Highest precipitation top in area in hundreds of feet MSL. (45,000 FEET MSL)

* The numbers representing the intensity level do not appear on the chart. Beginning from the first contour line, bordering the area, the intensity level is 1-2; second contour is 3-4; and third contour is 5-6.

Fig. 9. Radar summary chart echo/rainfall intensity index.

Pilots can rest assured that, if thunderstorms have been forecast and echo formations are seen on the radar summary chart, there is probably some convective weather present. If the echoes or area of echoes are isolated, and not moving, or moving slowly, this may indicate the possibility of airmass thunderstorms that can most likely be visually circumnavigated. If there are many echoes, or areas of echoes, and they are moving quickly, then the possibility of steady state thunderstorms exists.

Stratiform clouds may also contain a great deal of water and provide echo returns on radar. It's possible that, in the absence of forecast thunderstorms, an extensive area of the precipitation associated with stratiform type clouds, may show up as an echo pattern on the radar summary chart. Pilots must use extreme caution in interpreting a radar contour as consisting of benign stratiform clouds with non-hazardous rain. Radars cannot distinguish between stratiform and cumuliform type precipitation. Many other individual sources of information must be consulted to make this assessment. For example, no thunderstorms should be forecast, no PIREPS should show thunderstorms present, there should be an absence of SIGMETS or convective SIGMETS, the stability chart should show stable air, the cloud tops should be similar to those expected of stratus type clouds and the area of echoes shouldn't have tops similar to those expected with convective activity. These are just a few of the informational inputs pilots need to assess, to determine that radar summary echoes are not thunderstorms. The best bit of advice pilots can follow is to assume that any echo shown on the radar summary chart is a potential thunderstorm.

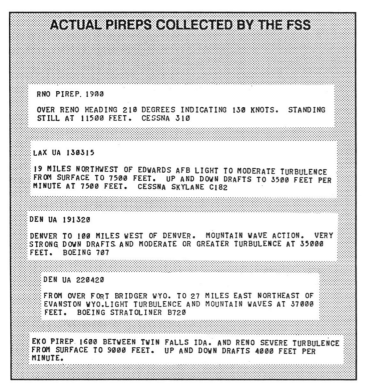

ACTUAL PIREPS COLLECTED BY THE FSS

RNO PIREP. 1900

OVER RENO HEADING 210 DEGREES INDICATING 130 KNOTS. STANDING STILL AT 11500 FEET. CESSNA 310

LAX UA 130315

19 MILES NORTHWEST OF EDWARDS AFB LIGHT TO MODERATE TURBULENCE FROM SURFACE TO 7500 FEET. UP AND DOWN DRAFTS TO 3500 FEET PER MINUTE AT 7500 FEET. CESSNA SKYLANE C182

DEN UA 191320

DENVER TO 100 MILES WEST OF DENVER. MOUNTAIN WAVE ACTION. VERY STRONG DOWN DRAFTS AND MODERATE OR GREATER TURBULENCE AT 35000 FEET. BOEING 707

DEN UA 220420

FROM OVER FORT BRIDGER WYO. TO 27 MILES EAST NORTHEAST OF EVANSTON WYO.LIGHT TURBULENCE AND MOUNTAIN WAVES AT 37000 FEET. BOEING STRATOLINER B720

EKO PIREP. 1600 BETWEEN TWIN FALLS IDA. AND RENO SEVERE TURBULENCE FROM SURFACE TO 9000 FEET. UP AND DOWN DRAFTS 4000 FEET PER MINUTE.

Additionally, the radar summary chart can be a good place to start looking for embedded thunderstorm cells. An area of widespread, stratus type, cloud coverage may seem like a benign weather environment. But, isolated thunderstorm cells within the stratus can be deadly. Be cautious about radar summary charts more than one hour old. Thunderstorms change quickly, and information a couple of hours old will not accurately reflect events in the atmosphere.

If any echoes, or areas of echoes, are detected, then extreme caution should be used when flying IFR in this area. Without storm detection equipment, the only reasonable way to fly IFR in this area is when the individual cells can be visually circumnavigated. This means that pilots have to stay out of the clouds.

WINDS ALOFT FORECAST

The winds aloft forecast can help detect possible convective activity when used in relation with the stability chart and topographical information. If the winds are blowing 20 to 30 knots or more, perpendicular to a mountain range, there is going to be a fair amount of lifting taking place. When pilots compare this lifting potential, with information on the stability of the air, they can make some fairly good assumptions about the possibility of orographically produced thunderstorms.

Pilots can usually develop a sense of how accurate the other available forecasts are by interpreting the existing winds and temperatures. If these are drastically different from what was forecast, then there is a good chance the rest of the forecast will also be wrong.

PIREPS

Checking any available PIREPS and RADAR REPORTS provides the pilot with information on which to decide how much faith to place in current weather charts and forecasts. When making an initial call on Center frequency, ask ATC for all Center weather warnings, PIREPS, AIRMETS and SIGMETS. The closer to real time the pilot report, the more accurate it will be. Pay very close attention to the time of issuance of the report. When ATC says that pilots farther along the airway had a real smooth ride, this may be ancient history unless they are just 30 seconds away. Storms can be new and improved in very short periods of time. ATC's intentions are good, but even their information may be bad.

Pilots should make it a point to return valuable weather information to the FSS and ATC. Giving pilot reports is more than just a casual way to pass time. It's a valuable and meaningful contribution to one's fellow aviators. In a sense, pilots are weather testers, highly trained probes, intellectually geared to verify or deny atmospheric forecasts. Besides, giving pilot reports is an excellent way to find comfort during those late night IFR flights when Center plays the game called, "Let's make the pilot nervous." Nocturnal pilots know that controllers don't speak much at night. Frankly, there aren't too many people flying then. With a little imagination, pilots can get a good case of the "willies" thinking about how their radio has probably failed. Instead of asking for position and time checks, pilots need only offer ATC a pilot report. Pilots make a meaningful contribution and they reaffirm their radio's operation in a dignified way.

Before any weather or operational information is offered to an Air Traffic Control Specialist, pilots should proceed the statement with, "...I have a pilot report for you." A casual remark, no matter how relevant, is considered casual unless "PILOT REPORT" is mentioned. In the Air Wisconsin crash of June 12, 1980, the pilot of the Metroliner was not privy to the previous 7&1/2 minute thunderstorm discussion on Center frequency that abruptly ended when he first reported to the controller. This information would have been invaluable to the pilot, but the previous discussion was not 'officialized' with the mention of "Pilot Report." Therefore, the ATC system wasn't obligated to absorb this information into the communication chain.

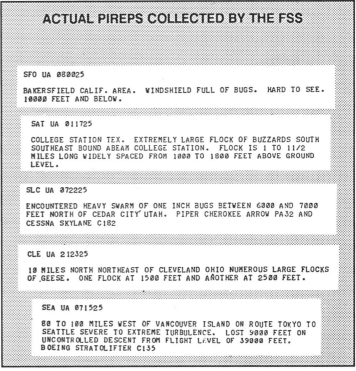

ACTUAL PIREPS COLLECTED BY THE FSS

SFO UA 080025

BAKERSFIELD CALIF. AREA. WINDSHIELD FULL OF BUGS. HARD TO SEE.
10000 FEET AND BELOW.

SAT UA 011725

COLLEGE STATION TEX. EXTREMELY LARGE FLOCK OF BUZZARDS SOUTH
SOUTHEAST BOUND ABEAM COLLEGE STATION. FLOCK IS 1 TO 11/2
MILES LONG WIDELY SPACED FROM 1000 TO 1800 FEET ABOVE GROUND
LEVEL.

SLC UA 072225

ENCOUNTERED HEAVY SWARM OF ONE INCH BUGS BETWEEN 6000 AND 7000
FEET NORTH OF CEDAR CITY UTAH. PIPER CHEROKEE ARROW PA32 AND
CESSNA SKYLANE C182

CLE UA 212325

10 MILES NORTH NORTHEAST OF CLEVELAND OHIO NUMEROUS LARGE FLOCKS
OF GEESE. ONE FLOCK AT 1500 FEET AND ANOTHER AT 2500 FEET.

SEA UA 071525

80 TO 100 MILES WEST OF VANCOUVER ISLAND ON ROUTE TOKYO TO
SEATTLE SEVERE TO EXTREME TURBULENCE. LOST 9000 FEET ON
UNCONTROLLED DESCENT FROM FLIGHT LEVEL OF 39000 FEET.
BOEING STRATOLIFTER C135

Pilot reports are often available at the end of the hourly surface observations. Sometimes these reports indicate the presence of towering cumulus clouds, cumulonimbus clouds, wet downburst, haze and other interesting bits of information useful to the pilot. PIREPS can also be found in a separate listing at the Flight Service Station.

THUNDER THOUGHT

A casual remark, no matter how relevant,is considered casual unless "Pilot Report" is mentioned.

A pilot's best source of the weather that exists between reporting stations will be pilot reports. In flight, make it a point to solicit reports from other pilots on the airway. Airlines do this all the time. I've even had radar equipped aircraft take a look for me on their weather radar. Now that's what they call, "using the system."

ARTCC WEATHER RADAR INFORMATION

Pilots often hear controllers say, "We don't paint weather" or "We have no weather radar display." This misconception may be the result of a training problem or a time problem. Perhaps, it results from controllers not having confidence in, nor understanding the value of, the weather information available on their radar units. Many controllers may feel their weather radar information to be 'inferior' in its depiction. Nothing is inferior if it's the only information available to the pilot.

Airborne X-band radar is about 10,000 mHz in frequency and 3.0 cm, or approximately 1.2 inches, in wavelength. The smaller the wavelength, the better the definition the pilot will see on the aircraft's radar display. Water droplets are small and they tend to absorb energy of a wavelength similar to their own size. This is done in much the same way that long ADF antennas absorb long, low frequency wavelengths and smaller antennas, like DME which is UHF, absorb smaller, higher frequency wavelengths. When these small water droplets absorb radar energy, they radiate that energy back to the radar antenna. The water droplets become thousands upon thousands of little transmitters, after being initially charged by radar energy. Energy is lost in the process of charging these water droplets, and this loss is called "attenuation," or the loss of penetrating capability. Hence, the value of airborne weather radar is "to see weather, to STAY AWAY from weather.*" No airborne weather radar is designed to penetrate water areas. The smaller radar wavelength doesn't make it through all the water droplets without being almost completely absorbed.

RADAR INFORMATION

BAND	MHz	WAVELENGTH	USE
L	1,000	30cm	ATC
S	3,000	10cm	NWS
C	5,500	5.6cm	AIRBORNE
X	10,000	3.0cm	AIRBORNE
K	16,000	1.9cm	MISC

ARTCC radar is about 1,000 mHZ in frequency and has approximately a 30 cm or 12 inch wavelength, which is exceptionally penetrating. This wavelength is so long that it doesn't interact well with small water droplets. The longer wavelengths don't charge as many smaller water droplets with energy. Therefore, ARTCC radar doesn't see water, or weather, returns that well. But ARTCC radars do get a gross return of information due to their extreme power levels (about 5-million watts of power in most cases). When rather large areas of precipitation are present, a slight resistance is felt by the long ARTCC radar wavelengths. This light resistance comes back as crude 'echoes' to the ARTCC receivers. These returns provide valid weather information out to about 125 NM from the antenna.

Within the ARTCC radar system is a computerized enhancement called the Weather Fixed Map Unit (WFMU), and it creates a weather display for controllers. They use two keys: WX-1 which creates

---

*Of course, radar doesn't depict clouds. Only precipitation, or water droplets, are shown. A microwave cooker (similar wavelengths to radar) works by charging the water molecules in food with energy. That energy is absorbed by the food, and the food becomes hot. If no water is present, then little energy will be absorbed and little heat occurs. Radar returns occur in much the same way. If water droplets are not present in the cloud, there will be no absorption of energy to be reflected back to the radar antenna. Therefore, no echoes will be shown on radar.

"slashes" on their display and WX-2 which creates "H's," as shown in figure 10. Controllers are trained to interpret the former as "light precipitation" and the latter as "heavy precipitation." Actually, moderate rain will trigger an "H" and so will a thunderstorm! An "H" is generated at about .2 -.3 inch per hour of rainfall.

Since the controller's radar can't accurately determine the difference between light and heavy precipitation, in the absence of other information, their directives tell them to consider the "worst case" scenario. This might explain why there are conversational conflicts with airliners, with

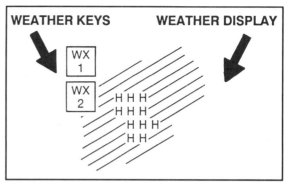

Fig. 10. The slashes and H's as seen on the controllers' radar screen. Slashes indicate light precipitation and H's indicate heavy precipitation.

reasonable good airborne radars, who dispute the controller's analysis that "a thunderstorm" is in front of them. The airliner's radar might be generating a level two (yellow), or specifically "moderate rain," return and the pilot has no indication that a thunderstorm is in front of the aircraft.

Several generalities can be considered here. Even airliners avoid moderate rain if possible. It's noisy, uncomfortable for passengers, restricts vision and is simply water intake in engines that good judgement begs to avoid. Moderate rainfall in light aircraft is especially noisy and distracting.

Pilots should make use of the ARTCC's weather radar capability. Simply ask the controller, "Workload permitting, would you select your WX-1 and WX-2 keys and talk to me about the slashes and H's on my route?" Pilots should then request radar vectors to "avoid the H's."

New Approach Control radars are called ASR-9's. They actually highlight or contour (with circles), all six NWS thunderstorm levels! Older radars had a great deal of weather suppression circuits to preclude weather displays and prevent clutter called MTI-Moving Target Indicators, CP-Circular Polarization, and STC 3-Sensitivity Timing Controls. On the older radars, if controllers saw weather, it was horrid, indeed, to overwhelm all the weather suppression circuitry.

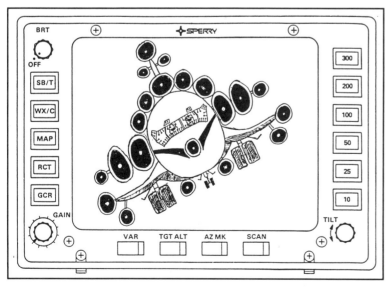

New ASR-9 approach control radars enable controllers (if trained) to provide specific water content weather information to terminal area pilots. Imagine how comfortable pilots feel when they ask controllers if they have one of those ASR-9 radars and the reply is, "Affirmative."

Approach control radars operate in the 10 to 5 cm radar wavelength. These ranges would be ideal for weather display if it were not for the weather suppression circuits. With the ASR-9 'contouring,' these radars become the finest weather displays in the system.

PUTTING IT ALL TOGETHER

Confidence in avoiding convective weather means that pilots should apply the information provided by the National Weather Service, as well as applying common sense principles about weather. When making telephone weather briefings, if the information needed doesn't appear to be available, be persistent. Ask if it's available from other sources or on other charts. When I go to an ice cream parlor and the waiters say they don't have vanilla ice cream, I ask them if they have albino chocolate. The key to obtaining a good telephone briefing is to ask the right questions. The following six points should be considered when making weather assessments concerning thunderstorms:

1. Review the area forecast, convective weather outlook and the 12 hour significant weather prog chart to determine if thunderstorms are likely to occur along the flight planned route. Any indication of possible thunderstorms means that each towering cumulus cloud should be viewed with suspicion. Correlate this information with PIREPS, and what is seen on the radar summary chart, for forecast accuracy. No forecast is 100% accurate, so this correlation will let pilots know how much credence to place in the forecasts.

2. Review the radar summary chart for information about convective activity. If there are echoes, this means that some cell activity already exists. Look for the speed, movement and altitude of these cells. Cells that are moving imply the possibility of steady state thunderstorms. This can mean damaging hail, dangerous wind shear and severe turbulence. If widespread cloud coverage exists, then look for the possibility of embedded convective activity.

3. Review the stability chart and determine its issue time. Be cautious about data more than four hours old. Look for areas of instability and high moisture content as being potential airmass thunderstorm areas.

THUNDER THOUGHTS

BLINDED ERE YET A-WING
Thomas Hardy

We were assigned 14,000 feet by Departure Control, but upon contact with Center, we were told to level out at 13,000 because of turbulence. Passing through about 12,500, we entered an area of turbulence and precipitation and St. Elmo's fire began building up on the windows. It then began to build up ahead of the radar dome. I had never seen this before, and I mentioned it to the First Officer. We both leaned forward to look at it, at which time it discharged in a blinding flash, with a loud sound. At the time, I thought we had been struck by lightning. Because of the turbulence and the effect on our eyes, I flew 500 feet above our assigned altitude before I could see again. I have seen a lot of St. Elmo's fire, but I did not know of the possibility of such a static discharge. I think it would be beneficial if more information could be available to pilots about this phenomenon.
ASRS REPORT

4. Review the weather depiction chart for possible lifting sources. These sources of lift may exacerbate any unstable areas shown on the stability chart. Observe the station models on the chart for areas free of cloud cover. Identify areas where clouds are scattered or broken, in case it's necessary to visually circumnavigate cells. Given the proper geography, and some good sunshine on the surface, thermal activity could develop, providing the necessary lifting to generate convective activity. Remember, the weather depiction chart may have variable weather between reporting stations. It's utility lies in the global information it provides.

5. Review the winds aloft forecast for the direction and velocity of local winds. Determine if there will be a mountainous lifting effect. If so, anticipate a greater potential for thunderstorm formation. Get across the mountains as early as possible to avoid

afternoon instability. Also, be suspicious of winds that change in velocity more than 4 knots per thousand feet. This is usually a sign of some form of wind shear and its accompanying turbulence. If the wind changes direction more than 30 degrees per thousand feet, this might also indicate that some degree of wind shear is present.

6. Comparing texts with charts will help pilots more accurately process weather information. This becomes even more meaningful if a pilot has a visual or aural learning bias. Compare the area forecast (text) with the significant weather prog chart (visual). This provides the pilot with a picture of where the weather -- icing, significant clouds and thunderstorms -- will occur. Compare the convective outlook (text) with the severe weather outlook chart. This, as previously mentioned, helps identify how the thunderstorm forecasts are actualizing. Finally, compare the convective SIGMET (text) with the radar summary chart. Convective SIGMETS are issued for tornadoes, lines of thunderstorms, embedded thunderstorms and thunderstorms with intensity levels of 4 or greater. Comparing SIGMET information with the radar chart provides a more thorough understanding of the convective weather.

LAST WORDS ON AVOIDANCE

Pilots should keep a keen eye out for what the atmosphere is telling them. If thunderstorms are likely to be present, they should make sure they are always in a position to visually avoid them. If possible, pilots should select an altitude on top of the clouds to visually avoid cells. Getting above any haze layer makes it a great deal easier to detect and circumnavigate storm cells. Pilots without storm detection equipment, in visibility less than 4 to 5 miles, should be willing to turn back or land immediately. Be prepared, at all times, to get down. Never fly in solid IFR, with thunderstorms forecast, unless storm detection equipment is aboard the aircraft. Pilots can't count on ATC radar to guide them around storm cells.

At night, watch for lightning. This is a sure sign that there are thunderstorms present. Tune ADF equipment to the lowest frequency and listen for static discharges as a means of identifying thunderstorms. Don't count on the needle to point to convective activity. New ADF equipment will usually suppress any such rapid needle wandering.

I once had a student who had quite a few misconceptions about the ADF. I asked him, "OK, Bob. The air is very unstable, and I have the ADF set to the lowest frequency, and the needle is fluctuating off the right wing. What does this mean?" While looking at the numbers on the ADF dials, he said, "Oh, there are thunderstorms out there. In fact, there are nine of them!" This is not the way to use the ADF.

Pay attention to what the clouds do early in the morning. The earlier the clouds form, the greater the chance of convective activity. Look for altocumulus cloud formations above 10,000 feet. This indicates an unstable layer of air exists at higher altitudes. Any small cumulus clouds reaching this layer could be given the extra energy needed to generate serious convective activity.

For cumulus clouds to form thunderstorms, the cloud tops must penetrate the freezing level. A substantial accumulation of water is necessary to form the downdrafts associated with the mature stage of the thunderstorm. Water formation is dependent on condensation nuclei. Ice crystals, forming when the cloud top penetrates the freezing level, provide the nuclei for water to collect in the mass necessary for thunderstorm formation. Compare pilot reports of cloud tops with current freezing level assessments to get an idea of thunderstorm potential.

Avoid flying at levels where the temperature is 20 degrees Fahrenheit to 35 degrees Fahrenheit. These levels have the most lightning associated with them. Pilots, flying at night, who experience lighting, should lower their seat and turn up all the white lights as bright as they will go. This helps their eyes acclimate to the sudden flashes of lightning. Additionally, to help in avoiding night blindness, pilots should close one eye during periods of strong and frequent lightning strikes. After a strong flash occurs, the other eye can be opened.

Pay particular attention to the dew point. Dew points above 55 degrees Fahrenheit should be cause for concern. This is the magic tornado number. The atmosphere holds more water when it's warmer. High temperature dew points imply a greater degree of atmospheric saturation is possible with lifting. Therefore, more stored energy can be released to create an awesomely impressive parade of severe thunderstorms.

If embedded thunderstorms are suspected, then IFR flight should be avoided unless thunderstorm detection equipment is on board the aircraft, or it's possible to get on top and avoid the cells visually. There is no satisfactory way, in my estimation, to fly in the clouds safely, with the threat of embedded thunderstorms and not have a way to detect them. A combination of Stormscope and a good weather radar is the pilot's best bet in avoiding thunderstorm activity. Pilots should look at the charts, talk to the weather briefer and get a feel for the potential of embedded thunderstorms. Be cautious!

Weather experience means weather confidence. It's an ironic twist of fate that instrument pilots often learn about the realities of weather when they are immersed in the bowels of a thunderstorm, gripped by tentacles of turbulence or dazed by a wing load of ice. Unfortunately, Mother Nature often gives the test before she teaches the lesson. Nevertheless, there is no substitute for experience. Yet, the type of experience pilots need is not how to fly in thunderstorms, but how to detect and avoid this type of weather. It's important for pilots to acquire this experience on the ground, rather than in the air. By following weather development on a daily basis, pilots can acquire the knowledge needed to make critical inflight weather decisions.

Woody Allen once said, "The lion and the lamb shall lie down together, but the lamb won't get much sleep." Similarly, I don't suspect pilots will get much relaxation when flying in areas of suspected icing activity. Understanding how and where icing forms and its debilitating effects on aircraft performance is the key to safely avoiding another of Mother Nature's inflight nemeses.

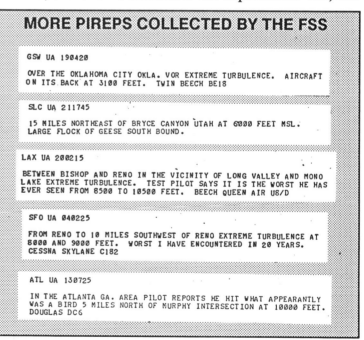

MORE PIREPS COLLECTED BY THE FSS

GSW UA 190420

OVER THE OKLAHOMA CITY OKLA. VOR EXTREME TURBULENCE. AIRCRAFT ON ITS BACK AT 3100 FEET. TWIN BEECH BE18

SLC UA 211745

15 MILES NORTHEAST OF BRYCE CANYON UTAH AT 6000 FEET MSL. LARGE FLOCK OF GEESE SOUTH BOUND.

LAX UA 200215

BETWEEN BISHOP AND RENO IN THE VICINITY OF LONG VALLEY AND MONO LAKE EXTREME TURBULENCE. TEST PILOT SAYS IT IS THE WORST HE HAS EVER SEEN FROM 8500 TO 10500 FEET. BEECH QUEEN AIR U8/D

SFO UA 040225

FROM RENO TO 10 MILES SOUTHWEST OF RENO EXTREME TURBULENCE AT 8000 AND 9000 FEET. WORST I HAVE ENCOUNTERED IN 20 YEARS. CESSNA SKYLANE C182

ATL UA 130725

IN THE ATLANTA GA. AREA PILOT REPORTS HE HIT WHAT APPEARANTLY WAS A BIRD 5 MILES NORTH OF MURPHY INTERSECTION AT 10000 FEET. DOUGLAS DC6

10. AVOIDING STRUCTURAL ICING

The last time my driver's license was renewed, the camera lady insisted upon a smile when she took my picture. I didn't want to smile for the camera because I wasn't going to be smiling when stopped by the police. After all, a picture should reflect how one's going to look when pulled over. This same grimace reflects how I intend to look in the throes of a serious icing condition. The only difference is that my eyes are going to be a lot bigger as they pan the windshield and see large glaciers creeping along the wings. Thank goodness for the optic nerve, which keeps the eyes from popping out and rolling around on the cockpit floor. Icing is serious business, and it's the IFR pilot's greatest nemesis.

THE NASA STUDY

A survey of instrument rated pilots, conducted in 1980 by NASA and Ohio State University, indicated that the single pilot IFR driver's most serious problem was icing. Neither ATC complications, ADF 'crazy needle' approaches, thunderstorms nor other weather conditions caused them more concern than icing encountered in flight.

Despite the obvious perils of mixing small airplanes and icing, these pilots are often unwilling to remain grounded when icing is forecast. The NASA study indicated the following:

"During the daytime, he (the pilot) would go when light icing, light or moderate turbulence, heavy rain, scattered or broken

```
PIREPS COLLECTED BY THE FSS
DEN UA 151420

IN THE VICINITY OF WORLAND WYO. HEAVY ICING AT 12000 FEET.  PILOT
LOST CONTROL OF AIRCRAFT AND RECOVERED AT 800 FEET ABOVE GROUND
LEVEL.  CESSNA SKYLARK C175


MKC UA 140040

OVER WICHITA KANS. AT 0015Z.  PICKED UP ICE AT 4000 FEET.  HAD
TO LAND AS COULD NOT SEE.


BOS UA 032225

40 NORTH OF MONTPELIER VT. WESTBOUND.  ENCOUNTERED VERY LARGE
HAIL.  BROKE AIRCRAFT WINDSHIELD AT 3500 FEET.  PIPER TWIN
COMMANCHE PA30

SEA UA 101415

PORTLAND NORTHBOUND.  LIGHT ICING 7000 TO 8000 FEET.  HEAVY
ICING 10000 TO 12000 FEET.  PICKED UP 8 INCHES RIME ICE.
UNABLE TO MAINTAIN 12000 FEET.  LANDED AT SEATTLE.  CURTIS C46

SLC UA 110500

BETWEEN DILLON MONT. AND DUBOIS IDA.  BETWEEN 8000 AND 12000 FEET.
MOST OF WINGS THICKLY COATED WITH WHITISH ASHY APPEARING SUBSTANCE.
DOES NOT AFFECT PERFORMANCE.  PILOT SUGGESTS THIS COULD BE DAMAGING
TO TURBINES.  SALT LAKE CITY FORECASTER THINKS THIS IS PRIMARILY
DUST WHICH HAS COLLECTED RIME ICE. BONANZA SUPER JET
```

thunderstorms, IFR over mountains or IFR over water were forecast to exist anywhere enroute. He would not go during the day if moderate icing, lines of thunderstorms, heavy ground fog or weather below minimums were reported. At night, he would go when light or moderate turbulence, scattered thunderstorms or IFR over water were reported to exist anywhere enroute. He would not go at night if any of the other previously mentioned conditions were reported."

It's quite apparent from this survey that an educated instrument pilot is willing to proceed cautiously when light icing, as well as other atmospheric hazards are present. But there is a line the pilot won't go beyond. One might assume that the surveyed pilots take liberal risks with Mother Nature's anti-aerodynamic barricades. I think not! Aircraft have to be flown. An airplane is an airplane in a hangar. It's most an airplane when aloft. Staying on the ground everytime icing and thunderstorms are mentioned deprives one of the very freedom that aircraft provide. It's an undeniable fact that flying involves risks. These risks are educated assessments. Safe flying is the calculus of maximizing aircraft utility and minimizing exposure to the elements. Sun Tzu, the famous Chinese general said, "Know the enemy and know yourself; in a hundred battles you will never be in peril." Therefore, understanding how icing forms and how it affects an aircraft, as well as having an out if the weather becomes serious, is the key to properly assessing these risks.

UNDERSTANDING THE ENEMY

Unfortunately, most general aviation airplanes are not qualified for flight into known icing conditions. To do so without this authorization is to glare at all the Gods of doom and dare them to smite thee. One-eighth inch of ice increases stall speed by as much as 16%.* A further one and one-quarter inch of ice will increase the stall speed only 4 knots more. This is why even just a little bit of ice is a very serious matter. In other words, "A little dab will do you (in)!" The odds against pilots, in small airplanes, flying into known icing conditions are just a little larger than the number on the McDonald's sign.

HOODWINKED

We entered an area of unexpected heavy weather, at approximately FL200. During our descent, we encountered moderate turbulence, icing and light hail. We slowed the aircraft and accelerated the descent with speed brakes to our assigned altitude of 11,000 feet. After our level-off, Approach Control reported that their radar readout indicated our altitude was 10,500. We discovered that all three altimeters were still at 29.92. We reset the altimeters and climbed back to our proper altitude. We had been distracted during a very crucial phase! **ASRS REPORT**

When blundering into icing conditions, a pilot's obsession must be to get out. Do something immediately to get the airplane out of the clouds, or away from the freezing level, or both. Don't wait. Act now! Even a slight trace of ice should be immediate catalyst for action. Many pilots have just waited and waited, sometimes an "eternity," so to speak, hoping that the freezing level would change, or the clouds would disappear, only to accumulate so much ice, that they were no longer in control of their airplane. Mother Nature was now inflicting decisions upon them. Whenever pilots forfeit management of their lives or airplanes, they become victims, not pilots.

TWO TYPES OF ICING

There are two basic types of icing with which pilots must contend. Rime ice and clear ice. Take relatively small water droplets, like those found in stratus clouds, and freeze them instantly on a collecting surface. Air will be trapped during the freezing process, giving the ice a milky appearance. This is rime ice. Pilots battle rime ice everytime a glaciated TV dinner is retrieved from their freezer. Rime ice forms more slowly than clear ice, but little solace should be found in this knowledge. Rime ice can radically destroy an airfoil's effectiveness. Instead of the sophisticated air-bending device intended by engineers, this airfoil now punishes laminar flow. Higher stalling speeds are usually the price paid for an encounter with rime ice.

Clear ice forms from large supercooled water droplets freezing on an aircraft surface. Smaller amounts of air are trapped during the freezing process resulting in a relatively clear appearance to the ice. The danger with clear ice is not only that it's heavier than rime ice, but that it forms fast and is very difficult to remove. These large, supercooled water droplets, found in cumulus clouds, are not easily deflected by the curved airflow around the wing and fuselage. Therefore, the rate of ice accretion is higher than with smaller water droplets. I have personally witnessed 1/2 inch of clear ice laminate my

*Up to 1/2 inch of ice on the leading edge of an airfoil can reduce lift by as much as 50%

windshield in less than 30 seconds, while fear laminated my mind. It was nighttime, but there was no problem seeing the ice with the lightning from the thunderstorm lighting up the cockpit. It should be quite apparent with these aerodynamic cryogenics, pilots can't have icing on their plane and fly it too.

HOW ICING FORMS

With the exception of freezing rain, two things are needed to form ice: clouds and freezing temperatures. It's a sure bet that airplanes, in visible moisture (clouds), at temperatures less than freezing, are going to start picking up some form of ice. However, there are several variables that will affect the amount of ice accumulated, as well as the rate of ice accretion.

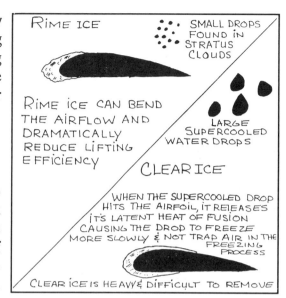

The liquid water content (density) of the cloud is directly related to how quickly ice accumulates. Cloud density varies considerably with the amount of moisture in the air and the intensity of the lifting that's causing the cloud formation. Most pilots have seen clouds that reduce visibility to one or two miles. These clouds are not very dense and won't cause ice to accumulate quickly on the airplane. However, there are clouds, the cumulus type, which are so dense, that it makes it difficult to see the wingtips. With clouds of this density, temperatures near freezing will probably generate more ice than Sir Edmund Hillary would know how to handle.

The intensity of lifting, therefore the rate of condensation inside a cloud, shares a relationship with the amount of turbulence pilots experience. The greater the lifting, the more turbulent the air and the wetter the cloud is going to be. If it's bumpy inside the clouds, and the temperature is at or below freezing, ice will generally accumulate much more quickly than if the air is smooth.

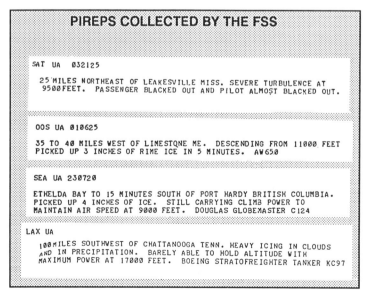

Stratus type clouds have less lifting, therefore, less icing potential. In fact, icing layers 3,000 to 4,000 feet thick are rare inside stratus clouds. The highest moisture content in stratus clouds will generally be found near the top of the cloud. This validates getting as low as possible to avoid the wettest part of the cloud.

The main hazard with icing in stratiform clouds lies in the extensive horizontal area covered by these clouds. Pilots should seriously consider their greater length of exposure to areas of icing when in stratus clouds.* Don't be sedated by the relatively low rate at which ice forms.

*When encountering icing conditions, the main point is to do something! Sometimes an altitude change of 1,000 to 1,500 feet may produce positive results.

Serious icing in stratus clouds is usually found in areas where lifting occurs. Any mountainous lifting, even with stratus type clouds, can produce serious ice accumulation. If the winds aloft forecast indicates winds in excess of 20 to 30 knots, and there are mountains nearby to produce lifting, then unforecast icing should be anticipated. The icing potential will be the greatest in the upwind end of a wave cloud. As a general rule, try to avoid flight parallel to mountain ridges, when mountain wave action is present or suspected.

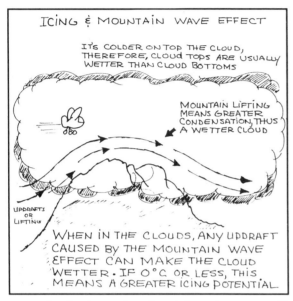

Sometimes it may be difficult to identify the presence of wave cloud activity that may be embedded in an extensive stratus cloud formation. The airspeed indicator may offer a clue to its existence. If airspeed increases, without an increase in power, while holding altitude, suspect mountain wave lifting. Keep in mind that lenticular clouds may be relatively smooth, yet the icing potential can be serious and very difficult to forecast.

Fortunately, the horizontal area of probable icing is smaller in cumulus clouds. Nevertheless, rates of ice collection have been measured in excess of 1 inch per minute for 2 to 3 minutes duration. Icing can occur at all levels above the freezing level in a building cumulus cloud. The most intense icing will generally be found in the upper half of the cumulus cloud. In mature cumulonimbus clouds, icing is generally concentrated in the updraft regions. In dissipating thunderstorms, icing will generally be confined to a shallow layer near the freezing level.

It's well known that cumulus clouds produce clear ice, the most serious type of icing. It's also well known that cumulus clouds are much more turbulent than stratus type clouds. Therefore, the area with the greatest lifting action will produce the wettest cloud and the greatest potential for icing.

Temperature ranges from 0 degrees Celsius to -15 degrees Celsius are prime areas for icing to occur. Certainly ice can occur at lower temperatures, sometimes as low as -40 degrees Celsius, but the rate of accretion at these temperatures is very low. At these temperatures, moisture in the atmosphere is most likely in the solid state and probably won't adhere to an airplane's surface. Temperatures around 0 to -10 degrees Celsius offer the prime temperature range to run afoul of serious icing.

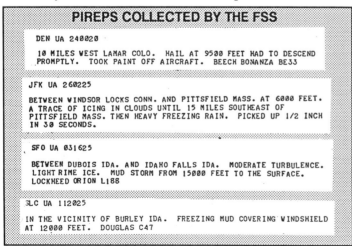

Pay attention to the type of airplane making an icing report. Aircraft flying in excess of 200 knots experience an increase in skin surface temperatures. An increase in skin surface temperatures over 4 degrees Celsius has been measured at 250 knots airspeed.

Pilots of these types of aircraft may not be reporting ice, despite outside air temperatures below freezing. At slower speeds, there may be a serious icing potential.

GETTING OUT OF ICING CONDITIONS

When pilots are in icing conditions, the most important thing on their mind should be to get out of the clouds or get into an area of warmer air. Either way will prevent more ice from accumulating on the airfoil surface. Having an idea of the altitude where the clouds begin and end is a must for any IFR pilot. Pilot reports are usually the best source of this information. Pilots should be local information harvesters, constantly asking questions and ferreting out information. Calling ATC and asking them to query other pilots about temperature and cloud conditions is not only prudent, but a must for the survival oriented aviator. Additionally, pilots should watch the temperature gauge during climbout to identify the temperature profile.

Getting to a lower altitude, where it is warmer, is often a good way to prevent an icing problem. Many times the Minimum Enroute Altitude is not the lowest altitude that can be flown. Pilots should ask ATC for their lowest Minimum Vectoring Altitude. In many cases this may be lower than the MEA.* It often only takes one degree of difference in temperature to make the difference between ice accretion and ice melt down. Therefore, in icing conditions, the thermometer becomes the primary instrument for vertical navigation.

If descending isn't an option, then pilots may consider trying to get on top of ice laden clouds. Asking for a climb to VFR conditions on top, presupposes that pilots have to have a good idea of where the tops are. If cloud tops are unavailable, and the climb will occur in the critical temperature range, then pilots had better have a good escape route. This could be a risky game of roulette.

It's often heard that if the aircraft is picking up ice, then a climb should be made to get to colder temperatures where ice won't form. It's true that at temperatures below -20 degrees Celsius, water normally exists in the form of ice crystals. Ice crystals don't tend to stick to the surface of an airfoil. This is the reason the critical icing temperatures are from freezing to -15 degrees Celsius.

HAIL OF AN IDEA!

Our IFR clearance was as filed, with an initial climb to 6,000 feet. The aircraft was given radar vectors for the climb. Prior to entering potential icing conditions, the crew selected the appropriate anti-icing systems, including pitot-static heat. Freezing rain was encountered at 4,500 feet and heavy icing occurred. At approximately 5,600 feet, the altimeters began to indicate a descent, and an increase in airspeed was also noted. Since the turbulence had been moderate to severe, due to passage of a frontal system, the First Officer, flying the aircraft, assumed a downdraft was responsible and increased the angle of attack. The Captain, noting no increase in indicated altitude or reduction in airspeed, checked to ensure all anti-ice protection switches were on. Confirming this, he then checked the circuit-breaker panel and found the pitot-static anti-ice CB tripped. He immediately switched to the alternate source and noted the actual altitude to be about 7,000 feet. While correcting, the controller asked the altitude and was told 7,000 feet and correcting. We suspect the situation occurred due to water leakage around the F/O vent seal, located above the main CB panel. Waterproofing around this area has been improved. It would have helped in diagnosing the problem to have had more timely information from the controller about our altitude. The aircraft Mode C transponder was operating and accurate.

ASRS REPORT

*Operations below the MEA, while at or above the MVA, require the controller to provide or supplement the pilot's navigation. I don't suspect that any pilot will mind accepting vectors for a while if it will prevent ice from draining the lift from their wings.

Here's a caveat about climbing in icing conditions. Pilots should think before they do anything that elevates them where the clouds are wetter and the temperatures colder. Climbing while in icing conditions, slows the aircraft and increases its exposure to icing. The higher angle of attack, at slow climb speeds, causes more ice to form on the underside of the airfoil. Additionally, climbing while in icing conditions moves the aircraft up where the clouds are wetter. None of these maladies are particularly inviting.* This becomes even more dangerous when pilots are trying to climb through freezing rain to get to warmer temperatures aloft. Unless pilots are flying high performance aircraft, this action is very impolitic. They may have to climb through several thousand feet of freezing rain to get to where the air is warm enough to produce rain. It's probably not going to work in a small airplane.

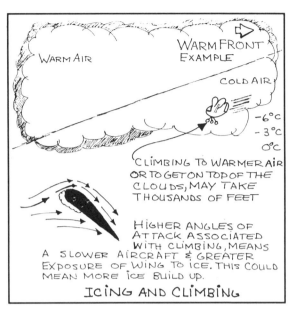

A climb results from excess horsepower beyond that required to sustain level flight. If throttle position is an approximation of the excess power available, then pilots should not feel much comfort. Most of the time, small aircraft are flown with the throttle at 4/5 of its travel position. There's only 1/5 left to climb. It's quite apparent why icing will quickly leach the climb initiative away from small airplanes. One local flight instructor humorously put a makeshift placard above the throttle of a small general aviation trainer that said, "Push in to go and don't pull it back unless you have to."

When encountering icing, pilots should consider all other intelligent options, like making a 180 degree turn, or descending to warmer temperatures. Climbing, without regard for cloud tops and temperatures, in a small, non-turbo, general aviation airplane, is about as safe as running through a pit bull farm, while smothered in steak sauce. Nothing like that makes sense when other options exist. Pilots who fail to consider all the options establish a whole different meaning to the concept of Single Pilot IFR -- no one wants to fly with them.

KICK IN THE EMPENNAGE

Just Trying To Help, Sir!

We were descending to 9,000 feet. We were both looking out the windows to see if the ice was starting to melt. We then noticed that we were at 8,700 and initiated an immediate pullup. At this point ATC said, "Local altimeter is 29.97." The First Officer said, "Sorry about that; we had the correct altimeter setting." If he had just said, "Roger," I wouldn't be writing this report.

ASRS REPORT

THE ICING FORECAST

Armed with the knowledge that icing is best seen in cocktails and not from cockpits, what should pilots look for during preflight planning to prevent an encounter with ice? There are several basic weather charts that should be consulted. These charts help pilots determine three very important things about the air's potential for icing: the temperature of the air, how moist the air is and the potential for the air to lift, or be lifted.

---

*Of course, if a climb can be made to get above the clouds, then, by all means, do so! With the exception of freezing rain, ice won't form when the aircraft is out of the clouds. The moral here is to always be aware of the cloud tops.

WEATHER DEPICTION CHART

The weather depiction chart, figure 1, is an excellent place to start the preflight briefing. It's available once every three hours and provides pilots with a "big picture" understanding of the weather. To help answer the question about the air's potential for being lifted, pilots should make note of any frontal conditions and areas of low pressure. The front, at 1000Z, runs almost vertically from the southern tip of California to the middle of Montana. A trough appears to exist over central Texas, South Dakota and Kansas. These are areas that will have rising air with the possibility of cloudiness and precipitation. Additionally, the weather depiction chart provides an excellent base upon which to overlay other real time weather charts. Pilots should mentally overlay weather information from other sources on the weather depiction chart, to get a more complete understanding of the weather.

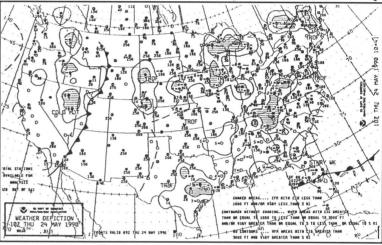

Fig. 1. The weather depiction chart.

AREA FORECAST

The area forecast should be studied to determine forecast icing conditions. This information should be compared with the weather systems shown on the weather depiction chart. Figure 2 identifies areas of forecast icing. The inflight hazards section identifies areas around Idaho, Montana, Nevada, Utah, Colorado, Arizona and New Mexico which are forecast to experience icing. These areas are directly in line with the apparent direction of the cold front.

```
11ØØØ 24025
SLCH FA 24025
HAZARDS VALID UNTIL 241500
ID MT WY NV UT CO AZ NM

FLT PRCTNS...ICG...ID MT NV UT CO AZ NM
           ...TURBC...ID MT WY NV UT CO AZ NM
           ... MTN OBSCN...ID MT WY NV
           ...TSTMS...ID MT CO
.
TSTMS IMPLY PSBL SVR OR GRT TURBC SVR ICG AND LLWS.
NON MSL HGTS NOTED BY AGL OR CIG
.
THIS FA ISSUANCE INCORPORATES THE FOLLOWING AIRMETS STILL IN
EFFECT...OSCAR 1.
....

SLCS FA 240245
SYNOPSIS VALID UNTIL 242100
.
AT Ø3Z...CDFNT EXTDD ALG A MOS-TWF-ELY-LAX-SAN LN MOVG SLOLY EWD.
LOWS WERE NR MSO AND ELY. BY 21Z...CDFNT WILL BE NR A YQL-GTF-
JAC-RKS-GJT-80SW TUS LN. SFC LOWS WILL BE NR YQL AND JAC. DVLPG
WRMFNT WILL CURVE ALG A JAC-COD-CPR AKO-GLDS LN.
```

Fig. 2. The area forecast.

Pilots planning flights in the Idaho, Montana and Nevada area can get a more precise estimate of the icing hazard by looking at the icing and freezing level section of the area forecast, as shown in figure 3. Occasional moderate rime or mixed icing in clouds and precipitation is forecast from the freezing level to 18,000 feet. The freezing level at 0300Z is located at 6,000 to 8,000 feet, west of the TPH-BOI-YXC line, rising to 12,000 to 14,000 feet south and east of the cold front.

FREEZING LEVEL CHART

Pilots should refer to the freezing level analysis, shown in figure 4, to enhance their pictorial concept of the freezing level. The freezing level over Idaho and northwest Montana is 8,000 feet, sloping higher towards the south. Of course, south is warmer and the freezing level is higher. On occasion, pilots will find a surface freezing level that is overlapped by a high altitude freezing level. This indicates the presence of warmer air aloft, with possibilities of freezing rain and other serious icing hazards.

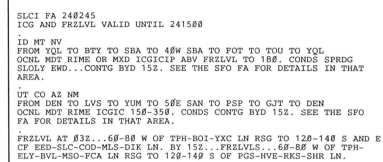

```
SLCI FA 240245
ICG AND FRZLVL VALID UNTIL 241500
.
ID MT NV
FROM YQL TO BTY TO SBA TO 40W SBA TO FOT TO TOU TO YQL
OCNL MDT RIME OR MXD ICGICIP ABV FRZLVL TO 180. CONDS SPRDG
SLOLY EWD...CONTG BYD 15Z. SEE THE SFO FA FOR DETAILS IN THAT
AREA.
.
UT CO AZ NM
FROM DEN TO LVS TO YUM TO 50E SAN TO PSP TO GJT TO DEN
OCNL MDT RIME ICGIC 150-350. CONDS CONTG BYD 15Z. SEE THE SFO
FA FOR DETAILS IN THAT AREA.
.
FRZLVL AT 03Z...60-80 W OF TPH-BOI-YXC LN RSG TO 120-140 S AND E
CF EED-SLC-COD-MLS-DIK LN. BY 15Z...FRZLVLS...60-80 W OF TPH-
ELY-BVL-MSO-FCA LN RSG TO 120-140 S OF PGS-HVE-RKS-SHR LN.
```

Fig. 3. Icing and freezing level section of the area forecast.

Armed with the area forecast and the freezing level chart, pilots will have an educated idea about how to answer questions about the temperature of the atmosphere. Next, pilots should assess how much moisture is in the air by referring to the constant pressure chart.

CONSTANT PRESSURE CHART

Constant pressure charts are depictions of upper air atmospheric soundings made by Radiosonde ascensions. These charts provide pilots with information for several pressure levels in the atmosphere. Pilots should look at the

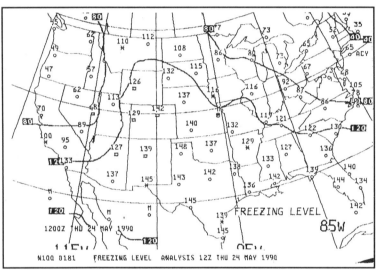

Fig. 4. The freezing level chart.

850mb (5,000 feet) and 700mb (10,000 feet) constant pressure charts to assess atmospheric moisture conditions. Figure 5 shows a 700mb constant pressure chart.

Reporting stations are shown as small circles on the chart, as seen in figure 6. To the left of these circles are two very important numbers. The top left number is the temperature at this pressure level, and underneath the temperature is the temperature-dewpoint spread. Station models for the area around western and eastern Montana can be seen in figure 7. At 10,000 feet, eastern Montana has a temperature of +5 degrees Celsius and a temperature-dewpoint spread of 10 degrees Celsius. Moving westward, the temperature drops to 3 degrees Celsius and the temp-dewpoint spread is now 4 degrees Celsius. Station models are filled in solid whenever the temperature-dewpoint spread is 5 degrees or less, indicating areas of high moisture content. Continuing farther west towards Washington, the temperature decreases to -4 degrees Celsius and the spread is now 1 degree Celsius. This indicates that the air is moist enough to condense and produce visible moisture. Couple this moist air with temperatures between -15 degrees Celsius and 0 degrees Celsius, and pilots can count on some form of nasty icing potential.

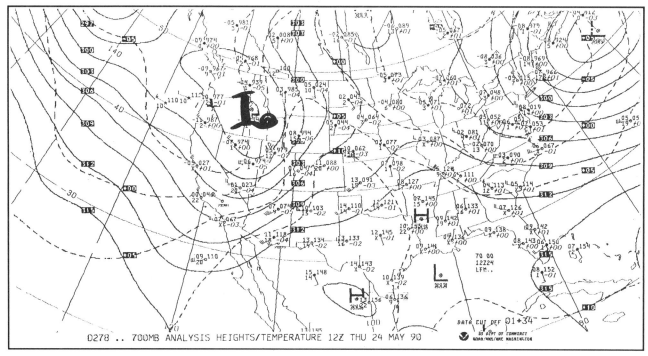

Fig. 5. The 700 MB constant pressure chart.

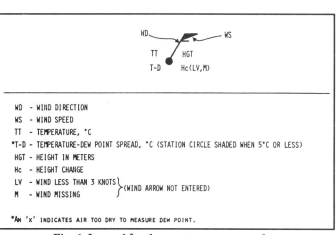

WD — WIND DIRECTION
WS — WIND SPEED
TT — TEMPERATURE, °C
*T-D — TEMPERATURE-DEW POINT SPREAD, °C (STATION CIRCLE SHADED WHEN 5°C OR LESS)
HGT — HEIGHT IN METERS
Hc — HEIGHT CHANGE
LV — WIND LESS THAN 3 KNOTS
M — WIND MISSING
} (WIND ARROW NOT ENTERED)

*AN 'x' INDICATES AIR TOO DRY TO MEASURE DEW POINT.

Fig. 6. Legend for the constant pressure chart.

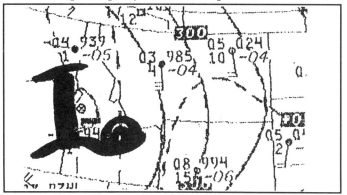

Fig. 7. Close up view of the constant pressure chart.

THUNDER THOUGHTS

Professional pilots survive on two criteria: if in doubt, get out; and if in doubt, don't! They know exactly the outcome of weather, planes and people or they don't play at recess today. It is in their coping makeup to loathe surprise (almost even socially) and to "be surprised," especially by a plane, weather or procedure, indicates a discomfort, a threat, a fact they did not detect. It is this demand for "bland experience" that makes them professionals.

We talk about SAFETY in flying. Well, there's no such thing if safety is properly defined as "the absence of risk." Even an infant in a crib is only as safe as we can make him (bars and all); yet infant death syndrome strikes dramatically.

What we have in aviation is "Risk Management." We can never be entirely safe, but we can eliminate threats, hazards and as much danger as intelligently possible. We try to create a "safe airborne crib." Safety is a myth, but it must always be a goal.

DAVE GWINN

Pilots should compare newer constant pressure charts with older ones to get an idea if the air is becoming wetter or drier. Figures 8A and 8B compare constant pressure charts at 0000Z and 1200Z. The low pressure center has moved eastward by 1200Z, causing the air in the vicinity of northern Idaho to become colder and wetter. This is the reason icing was forecast in the Idaho and Montana area during the forecast period. Couple this with orographic lifting, produced by mountains in the Pacific Northwest, and a tremendous potential for icing exists.

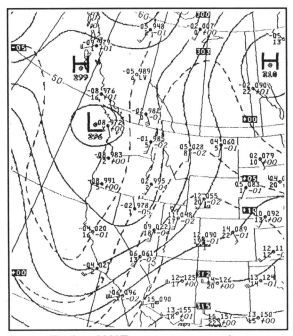

Fig. 8A. 0000Z constant pressure chart.

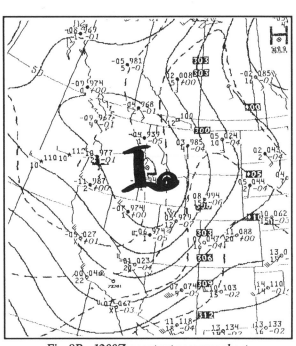

Fig. 8B. 1200Z constant pressure chart.

Figure 9 shows the effect that a moist source region has on the air. Notice the station models located north and south of the low pressure area. South of the low, the air is very moist and cold. Its source region is the Pacific Ocean. These station models show lower temperatures and small temperature-dew point spreads. The area north of the low is drier, since it has already passed over the mountains. This orographic lifting has squeezed a great deal of the moisture out of the air, leaving its remnants dry and perhaps benign. Station models north of the low show greater temperature-dew point spreads, indicating drier air. Pilots should be especially sensitive to the origin of an air mass. The moist air from the Pacific, flowing over the Cascades of Washington, results in some of the worst icing pilots can experience. This also applies to the areas near the Great Lakes. Warm, moist air flowing inland from the lakes can set up the conditions for some pretty severe icing.

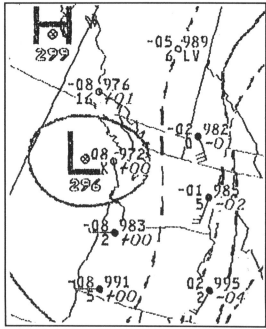

Fig. 9. Effect of moisture on northwest region.

THE STABILITY CHART

The stability chart, shown in figure 10, was originally discussed in Chapter 9. Its immediate value for predicting icing conditions is in determining the amount of moisture in the air and how the air will respond to lifting.

The air around Montana to Northern Utah shows a lifted index of 0 to +2, which is known to be marginally stable. This air can become unstable if there is any upslope flow, convergence or frontal lifting. All three of these have been present, to some degree, during the observation period.

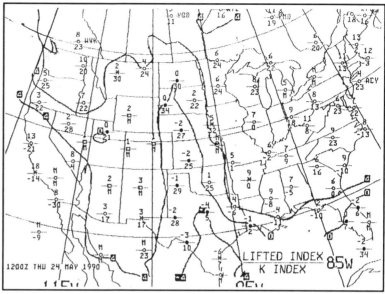

Fig. 10. The stability chart.

The K-index is primarily used by meteorologists, but can be of value to pilots. A large K-index indicates a greater potential for an unstable lapse rate, high moisture content and a high degree of saturation. The K-index value in northern Montana is 30, indicating that the air supports cloudiness and possible precipitation.

Looking ahead of the front in the Central United States, the stability chart indicates the potential for thunderstorm formation. From Texas northward to Kansas, Nebraska and South Dakota, lifted index values indicate potentially unstable air. K-index values are in the high 20's to low 30's, indicating a greater potential for precipitation and cloudiness. Couple this with some lifting, and it's a sure bet that some convective activity will manifest. If a flight is at or near the freezing level in this area, pilots can expect a greater chance of ice associated with cumulus activity.

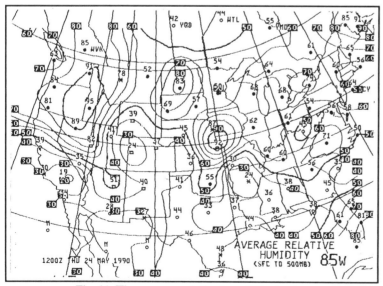

Fig. 11. The average relative humidity chart.

Considering that there is a front approaching, this additional lift can exacerbate any icing potential, as well as help the formation of thunderstorms. There is also a trough in the area, as indicated by the weather depiction chart, implying that the convergence of air will also provide some lifting.

The average relative humidity chart, figure 11, also helps provide some idea of how saturated the air is. The areas around Western Idaho show humidities in the 95% range.* It won't take much lifting to commence the condensation process and create visible moisture. Couple this with freezing conditions at 8,000 feet, and pilots have a reasonable icing potential.

*Remember, the relative humidity is temperature specific. Change the temperature and the relative humditiy changes, but water content is the same.

RADAR SUMMARY CHART

The radar summary chart, figure 12, shows the location of precipitation echoes, indicating their configuration, location and movement. This chart is issued approximately once every hour, making its information current. Pilots should compare the radar summary chart with the weather depiction chart to obtain a complete, 3-dimensional idea of what's happening in the atmosphere.

In northern and southern Idaho, there are signs of precipitation echoes, indicating moisture intense enough to cause a radar reflection. The hazards listed in the area forecast, figure 13, indicate that any thunderstorms imply the possibility of severe or greater turbulence, icing and low level wind shear. Similarly, in the Central United States, there are echoes of varying intensity levels indicating the possibility of nasty thunderstorms and severe icing. Considering the low lifted index and high K-index values in these areas, it's not surprising that precipitation echoes are present.

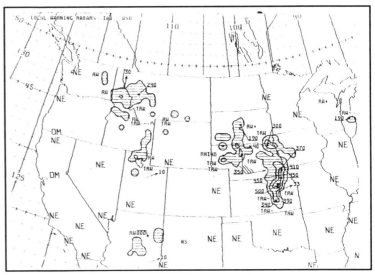

Fig. 12. The radar summary chart.

```
11000 24025
SLCH FA 24025
HAZARDS VALID UNTIL 241500
ID MT WY NV UT CO AZ NM

FLT PRCTNS...ICG...ID MT NV UT CO AZ NM
          ...TURBC...ID MT WY NV UT CO AZ NM
          ... MTN OBSCN...ID MT WY NV
          ...TSTMS...ID MT CO

TSTMS IMPLY PSBL SVR OR GRT TURBC SVR ICG AND LLWS.
NON MSL HGTS NOTED BY AGL OR CIG
```

Fig. 13. The hazards section of the area forecast listing a thunderstorm warning.

Weather that can bite you!

A very good friend was working as a tower controller at Fullerton airport. One day she was glancing at the surface aviation weather reports and noticed something unusual. A New Mexico station had reported the following weather: "R O S N O T." Curious about what this meant, she called the weather station and asked what "R O S N O T" stood for. The weather briefer said, "R O S N O T, let's see. Oh, yes, that observation was taken this morning. It means, Rattlesnake On Step No Observation Taken."

SIGNIFICANT WEATHER PROG CHART

The 12 and 24 hour significant weather prognostic chart provides an excellent pictorial representation of the forecast weather. The top left hand panel, figure 14, shows the weather expected, during the first 12 hours of the forecast period, from the surface to 24,000 feet. The bottom left hand panel, figure 15, shows the surface weather expected during the first 12 hours of the forecast period. Pilots should look at both these panels to determine forecast freezing levels and areas of expected cloud coverage. The bottom panel, figure 15, shows anticipated movements of frontal and pressure systems. Additionally, areas of precipitation, turbulence and thunderstorms are shown on the bottom surface prog panel. Where precipitation and freezing conditions exist, there is the possibility of ice formation.

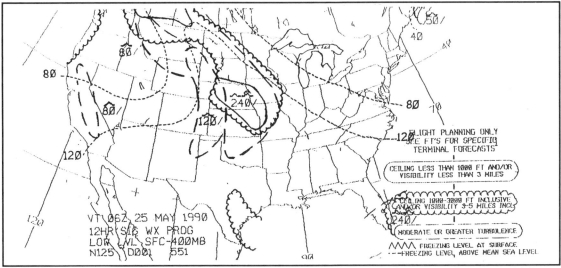

Fig. 14. The 12-hour significant weather prog chart showing forecast weather from the surface to 24,000 feet.

The frontal system is expected to move eastward, with continuous rain showers in the Idaho and Montana area. Pilots operating at, or above, the freezing level in this area should expect the possibility of icing. In advance of the front in the eastern half of Nebraska and Kansas, showery precipitation and thunderstorms are expected to cover more than half the area. Fortunately, the freezing level is greater than 12,000 feet in this area. Nevertheless, pilots should be cautious for icing in cumulus clouds, regardless of the temperature.

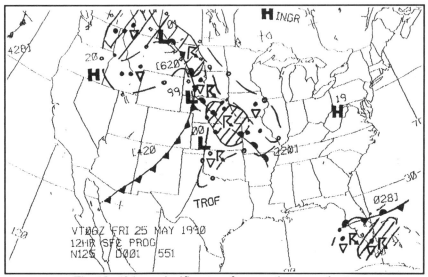

Fig. 15. 12 hour significant surface weather prog chart.

LAST WORDS

I have always been suspicious of technology that's expected to do something and doesn't perform. Recently, I saw a picture of a submarine shooting off a Trident missile which costs taxpayers 3 million dollars apiece. The missile shot a few feet into the air, spun around a couple of times, then dove back into the water. For two mackerel, we can get a dolphin to do the same thing. Similarly, it's unreasonable to expect small, general aviation airplanes, as technically sophisticated as they are, to handle icing conditions. Small general aviation aircraft were not designed for this. Therefore, pilots have to be cunning in their approach to handling icing. The best place to start preparing for the icing nemesis, is with the weather briefing.

The objective of every IFR weather briefing is to discover the temperature profile of the air, how moist the air is and how likely the air is to lift, or be lifted. Therefore, pilots should approach their weather briefing as Columbo would approach a mystery, by looking for clues. Keep asking the Flight Service Specialist, "Excuse me, excuse me, ahhh, just one more thing before I go..." Find those tell-tale clues for the existence of any icing potential. No one chart provides all this information; therefore, it's necessary to consult many different sources. Pilots should study weather charts, even when no flight is planned. This activity helps develop a sense about weather and provides valuable experience from which pilots can make more educated decisions about future weather scenarios.

Surfers are daredevils. These people have been known to go surfing during a hurricane because it produces bigger waves. Why is it that hanglider pilots in the Midwest don't go flying when tornadoes are present? It's unlikely that they will call their buddies and say, "OK, let's go guys, dirts up!" Why? Because they know how to interpret Mother Nature's atmospheric symbols. Similarly, instrument pilots must interpret the symbols on their instrument charts with sufficient accuracy to be able to fly IFR with poise and confidence.

11. UNDERSTANDING IFR CHARTS

Newly rated instrument pilots are proud of their passage beyond the limitations of visual flight. In fact, they are so proud, they are often faced with a unique dilemma: how to let others know of this accomplishment without appearing braggadocio. They certainly don't want to be like Kamikaze pilots who have to do all their bragging ahead of time. Pilots have found some very unique solutions to this problem. First, they can walk about the airport wearing their hood and David Clark head set -- a definite attention grabber. Surely, they will be recognized as a seasoned IFR professional, while strutting the flight line in full instrument headdress. Second, they may attempt to attract attention in the same way a cricket attracts a mate. They can sit around the flight lounge, opening and closing their Jep binders, counting on the distinctive clicks to tip others off about their newly rated status. In a feeble attempt to produce the same effect, pilots of lesser status are, thereby, forced to rub their legs together. Unfortunately, this action produces no discernable increase in popularity.

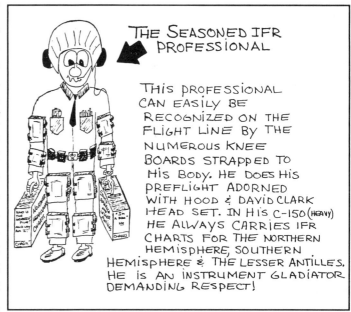

The ultimate solution to this problem is when pilots offer friendly challenges to their IFR rated comrades. Asking their fellow pilots about chart symbology and instrument procedures is a sure fire way to boast membership in this elite brotherhood and produce a rather interesting side benefit. It won't take long for IFR pilots to realize that simply possessing IFR charts doesn't necessarily mean they know how to effectively use them. In challenging fellow IFR pilots with questions, they will begin to realize just how much useful information lies dormant on IFR charts.

Instrument pilots often get by with just a minor, peripheral knowledge about their charts. A seasoned instrument professional makes it a point to utilize all the information available on these 5 1/2" by 8 1/2" sheets of paper. Therefore, understanding how instrument charts are constructed, and the particular meaning of chart symbology, is paramount for competent IFR flying.

THE BIG PICTURE

The information on approach charts has not been organized in a random manner. A great deal of ponderous thought has gone into their construction. The features of the Jeppesen chart format have been carefully thought out to allow easy acquisition of information in the order needed. Figure 1, shows how approach charts are laid out, based upon how the pilot is likely to use this information.

Approach charts are constructed for use from the top down. Pilots will generally use the communication section, along with the heading data first, as they are contemplating a particular approach.

These two sections provide pilots with all the necessary frequencies for communications and navigation. A two-dimensional view of the approach structure is provided in the plan view and is supplemented by the profile view. The profile view adds depth, or a third dimension, to a pilot's understanding of the approach. Keeping with the vertical order of information presentation, the profile view is used when pilots are established on the approach procedure track, at which time critical elements of the missed approach procedure should be reviewed. Finally, the minima section is provided, along with the conversion table, in the lower portion of the chart.

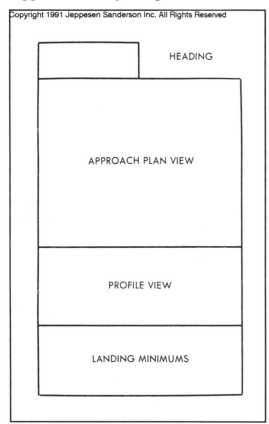

Fig. 1. Approach chart structure.

THE PREFLIGHT CHART REVIEW

The preflight review of an instrument approach procedure should initially center on the currency of the IFR chart. There is very little that's more disconcerting than planning an instrument approach only to find that it has been changed or no longer exists. A pilot buddy of mine, who was never strong with ADF navigation, approached an airport and planned on flying the ILS approach. He was informed that the ILS was not yet in service, and the NDB was his only choice. He carefully weighed the options: either shoot the NDB approach or run out of fuel and crash into the trees. He gave considerable thought to crashing into the trees. After all, he considered the ADF to be about as fine a precision instrument as a cork-screw.

In preparation for using an approach chart, pilots should go immediately to the top portion of the chart and look at the issue date. In figure 2, there are two dates shown on top of the Richland, Washington approach chart. November 10th is the date the chart was issued. The issue date will always be on a Friday. When pilots receive their charts, the changes are already current and ready for use, unless an effective date is also listed. Charts become effective on 0901Z on that date. Therefore, the Richland, Washington, LOC Rwy 19 approach should not be used until November 16th, at 0901Z, its effective date.

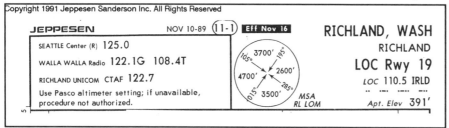

Fig. 2. Jeppesen's issue and effective chart date.

Prudent IFR pilots will not assume that they have the most updated and current information on the IFR system, solely by referencing their Jep manual. It would be unreasonable to assume that no navigational or airport information could change in the two week interval between revision packets. After all, a student pilot may have mistaken an airport's localizer antenna for the arresting device. What a surprise to discover the arresting device is really some fellow, with dark sunglasses, driving a squad car, packing heat.

A quick review of the latest NOTAM information is prudent prior to every flight. This may done with the local FSS or through any personal access to NOTAM information (e.g., DUAT). In addition to the regular NOTAMS, pilots should ferret out the latest FDC (Flight Data Center) NOTAMS. FDC NOTAMS contain the latest information on instrument approach procedures. Since NOTAM information may change, it's always a good idea to obtain a NOTAM update with the FSS while enroute.

Instrument charts are a graphic illustration of Part 97 of the Federal Aviation Regulations. Any change to an FAR requires that an amendment be made. Approach charts are no exception. In figure 3, the

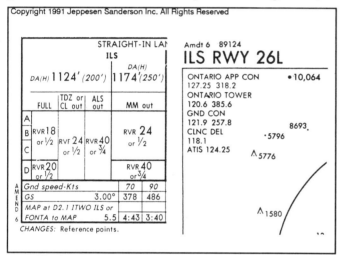

Fig. 3. Jeppesen and NOS chart amendment number.

bottom left side of the Jeppesen chart, and the top left hand side of the NOS chart, show an amendment number. Both these approach charts have had at least 6 amendments since their conception. If pilots have any doubt about chart currency, they should seek out the amendment number listed in the latest FDC NOTAMS. Figure 4 shows the FDC NOTAM for the Burbank ILS Rwy 8 approach. This NOTAM references Amendment No.33, and the chart shows amendment No.33. Therefore, the chart is current. Chart amendment numbers should be at least equal to, or greater than, the NOTAM amendment numbers

Another friend became a believer in chart currency during a trip to Louisiana. He navigated to a VOR, then tracked outbound on a radial for a little over 5 miles. According to the chart, there was supposed to be an airport directly underneath him. There wasn't. He called the tower and said, "Hey! Where are you guys?" The tower replied, "We're down here. If you can't find us, then you must be using an outdated chart. They moved the VOR last month!" How scary. If he was a little earlier, he might have flown the approach while they were actually in the process of relocating the VOR. How unusual it would be to glance downward and see the VOR on a flat bed truck, moving along the Interstate!

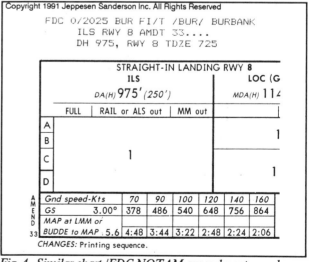

Fig. 4. Similar chart /FDC NOTAM amendment numbers.

THE JEPPESEN FILING SYSTEM

Finding an airport in the Jep manual will be much easier when the filing system used by Jeppesen is understood. All charts are listed under the name of the city in which the airport is located. In figure 5, the instrument approaches to San Diego's Lindbergh, Gillespie, Montgomery and Brown Field, are all listed under the city name of San Diego. Finding an airport in the Jeppesen manual requires that pilots know the name of the city under which it is listed. Often the city name and the airport name will be the same, but when they are not, pilots should refer to the low altitude enroute chart to identify the city name. The enroute chart will show the city name, on top of the airport name, when these two are different, as is seen in figure 6. The communications section, located on the outside panel of the enroute chart, also lists all four airports under the San Diego name, as seen in figure 7.

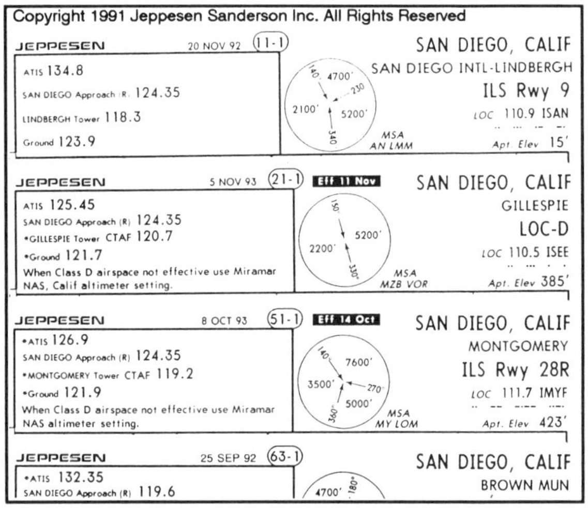

Chart index numbers, listed in the stretched oval at the top of the chart in figure 8, reflect three different forms of chart organization. The first number is the airport identification number. It identifies the numerical sequence of airports listed under the city name. In the case of Denver, Colorado, there are 5 airports listed under the same city name. Four are shown in figure 9. Numbers missing from the numbering sequence are usually military airports, which will be found in a separate military subscription.

The second digit represents the type of instrument approach available. Generally, the lower the number, the lower the minima. Figure 10 shows different chart types, based on variable numbers. The codes for different chart types are as follows:

0 - Area charts, SID's, etc.
1 - ILS, MLS, LOC, LDA, SDF
2 - PAR
3 - VOR
4 - TACAN
5 - HELICOPTER
6 - NDB
7 - DF
8 - ASR
9 - RNAV, Vicinity chart, Visual Arrival or Departure chart

The third digit is the number of approaches, of that particular type, available at the airport. Figure 11 shows that Stapleton International Airport at Denver has several ILS approaches for all those runways.

Fig. 5. Approach charts are listed under city name.

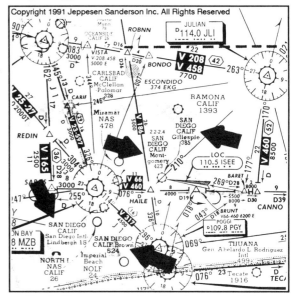

Fig. 6. Enroute chart showing city name of airport.

SAN DIEGO, CALIF.   KSAN p6C
  Brown *ATIS 132.35. **San Diego App(R)**
  119.6. **Dep(R)** 125.15. **Brown *Twr**
  126.5 128.25 (Rwy 08L/26R 128.25).
  Gnd/C 124.4.
  Gillespie *ATIS 125.45. **San Diego**
  App(R)/Dep(R) 124.35. **Gillespie *Twr**
  120.7 123.8. **Gnd** 121.7. **C** 125.1.
  Montgomery *ATIS 126.9. **San Diego**
  App(R) 124.35. **Dep(R)** 128.0.
  Montgomery *Twr 119.2 125.7. **Gnd**
  121.9. **C** 128.55.
  San Diego Int'l-Lindbergh ATIS 134.8.
  San Diego App(R) 124.35 (TCA:
  Areas A & J 119.6; B & K, M, N, O, L
  (E of VFR Corridor) 124.35; C & P & Q
  125.15; D & A, B, C, D, F, L (W of
  VFR Corridor) 128.0; F & S (W of MZB
  R-353) 125.3; H & E, G, H, I, R, S (E
  of MZB R-353) 132.2. **Dep(R)** 128.0.
  Lindbergh Twr 118.3. **Gnd** 123.9. **Cpt**
  125.9.

Fig. 7. Com section on back panel of enroute chart

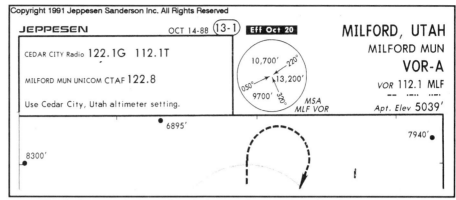

Fig. 8. Jeppesen's three chart index numbers are found in the stretched oval.

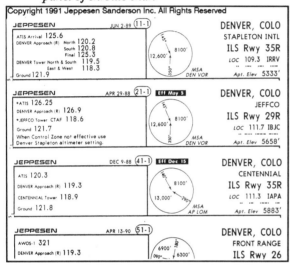

Fig. 9. Jeppesen's first index number for airport city name.

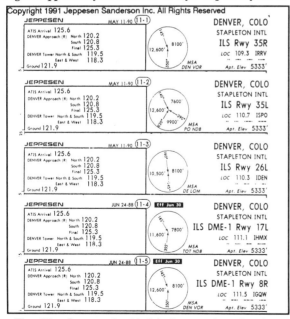

Fig. 11. Jeppesen's third index number showing number of approaches of similar type.

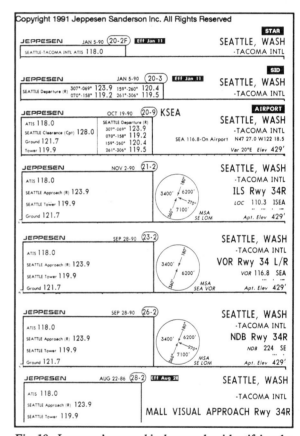

Fig. 10. Jeppesen's second index number identifying the particular type of chart.

IFR WISDOM

An IFR pilot named Jack
Thought himself sharp as a tack
But he missed his last vector,
Wandered into the wrong sector,
And into a mountain did smack.

Mick Capouch

Reprinted with permission of Professional Pilot Magazine

COMMUNICATIONS DATA

The frequency box, at the top of the chart, lists the communication frequencies in the order that they would be used when making an approach. The Sacramento ILS Rwy 16R approach chart, figure 12, shows the ATIS frequency, followed by approach control, tower, then ground control frequency. The reverse side of the chart, also known as the departure side, shows the frequencies in the order of use when departing.

Figure 13 shows a few variations on the communication information section. The Tipp Toe Visual approach to San Francisco shows three different ATIS frequencies. Essentially, there are a few different ATIS transmitters sending out the same information at San Francisco. The San Francisco airport is quite large, having many buildings, as well as a mountain range, that may prevent departing and arriving aircraft from receiving ATIS information. Therefore,

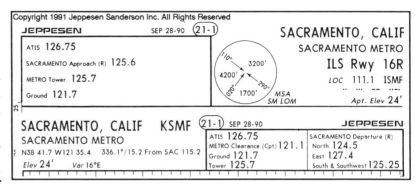

Fig. 12. Jeppesen lists frequencies in order of their use.

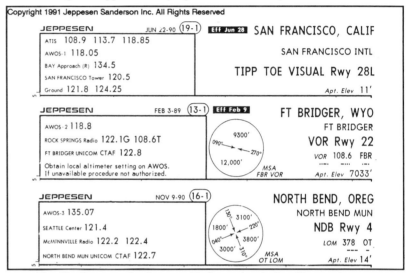

Fig. 13. Communications and information in heading section.

these ATIS transmitters are located in strategic locations around the airport to enhance reception in all quadrants. Additionally, Fort Bridger, Wyoming and North Bend, Oregon have an AWOS (Automatic Weather Observing System) on the frequencies listed.

Altimeter setting information may also be listed in the communications box, shown in figure 14. When the altimeter setting is derived from a remote source, more than 5 miles from the runway threshold, an altimeter setting limitation will be listed. In some cases, approach procedures based on remote altimeter sources are not approved. Altimeter setting restrictions may be applied to an approach procedure when precipitous or highly variable terrain in the area contributes to an unreliable altimeter. Altimeter settings derived from remote sources more than 5 miles from the runway threshold, will generally result in higher obstacle clearance. For every mile in excess of 5 miles that the remote source is from the threshold, an increase of 5 feet is applied to the MDA. This is reflected in higher approach minimums, shown in figure 15.

However, an instrument procedure, based on a remote altimeter source, probably won't be approved in precipitous terrain, or in any other area where reasonably homogeneous weather conditions cannot be determined. This prevents erratic and erroneous altimeter readings caused by the venturi effect in mountain-type terrain.*

---

*Air flowing over precipitous mountain terrain can cause local pressure variations that could create altimeter errors.

An (R) in parentheses next to the approach or center frequency, indicates that radar vectoring is available for this approach. Pilots must not assume that this radar service is available on a 24-hour basis. Small asterisks next to the frequency indicate that radar services are only available part time. Similarly, pilots can't tell if this is ARSR (Air Route Surveillance Radar), meaning only vectors to the final approach course, or ASR (Airport Surveillance Radar), or PAR (Precision Approach Radar), meaning vectors are available on final. The correct way to determine what type of radar is available is by referring to the Airport Facility Directory.

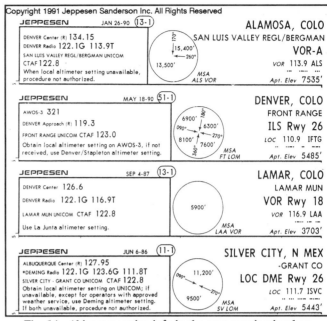

Fig. 14. Altimeter setting info in the communication box.

Pilots reared in today's modern airspace system can often become too dependent on the use of radar for navigation. It is possible that radar service will not always be available even in very active areas. I once heard a pilot receive a clearance for an approach that he was certainly not expecting. It was 11:30 p.m., and radar wasn't available at that hour. The controller gave the pilot a clearance to the VOR, which required him to execute the procedure turn for the approach. The pilot, in a concerned voice, said, "Hey, could you boys run that by me one more time?" The controller reiterated the clearance, at which time the pilot said, "Hey, how about one of those nice little vectors to the ILS? What da ya say, partner?" The controller said, "Sir, radar service is not available, so you're going to have to do this one by yourself." The pilot said, "Hey, you boys down there don't understand. I don't do procedure turns." The controller replied, "Well, then sir, just what is it that you do?" The pilot replied, "Ah, radar vectors and visuals, mostly." The controller paused for a second, then stated, "OK, why don't you just hold at the VOR until it clears up." With little or no hesitation the pilot said, "Well, what the heck, I think I'll try one of those nice little old procedure turns." Pilots should always be prepared to improvise without the use of radar.

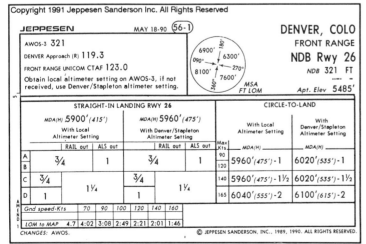

Fig. 15. Minima variation with altimeter source.

MINIMUM SECTOR ALTITUDES

The MSA, or minimum sector altitude, is centrally located in the middle of the heading portrayal, as seen in figure 16. The MSA is a vital bit of information for pilots, if they know how to use it. First, the MSA provides 1,000 foot obstruction clearance within 25 nautical miles of the facility shown on the lower right side of the circle. If the protected distance is other than 25 nautical miles, the protected radius will be listed beside the facility identifier, as shown in figure 16 for Carlsbad, New Mexico. Additionally, the MSA has not been flight checked for navigation, nor communication capability. Therefore, there is no guarantee that primary navigation signals, nor ATC communications, could take place at MSA altitudes.

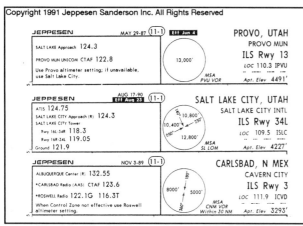

Fig. 16.. The Minimum Sector Altitude (MSA).

Just when should pilots use the MSA? It should be used only as general information or in an emergency. Suppose that a pilot is flying a multi-engine airplane. The left engine quits, and he can't get the right one started. This is definitely an emergency! At this point, the pilot's only interest is in terrain avoidance. There is little or no concern about receiving navigation or communication signals. Besides, there's a good chance the pilot can't even talk! He's in the left seat making a sound like a seal begging for a fish. The MSA provides a quick reference altitude for those command decisions requiring an immediate descent.

While being vectored below the MSA during an instrument approach, pilots should immediately click into high terrain awareness. MSA's cover large chunks of airspace. Tall obstacles in one quadrant of this airspace can disproportionately raise the MSA value, while other quadrants may have lower obstacles. Because the controller's MVAs (Minimum Vectoring Altitudes) cover smaller portions of airspace, these altitudes will often be much lower than MSA values. Nevertheless, when descending below the minimum sector altitude, pilots should take out their sectional or area chart, and keep a keen eye on their height above the terrain. The MSA provides the cue to become terrain sensitive.

One recurring misconception is that when pilots are cleared for the approach, they can descend to the MSA. A clearance for an instrument approach should contain an altitude at which to intercept the approach course. In the event no altitude is mentioned by the controller, pilots should maintain their last assigned altitude until they are on a published, terminal route, shown on the plan view. If pilots aren't sure of what altitude they are expected to maintain, they should ask ATC. They should simply put aside their pilot pride, pick up

CAUGHT WITH WHEEL PANTS DOWN

I was annoyed that Approach Control kicked me off a practice ILS approach (inside the Outer Marker) for following traffic and gave me extensive delaying vectors. I roundly cursed the controller, thinking only my safety pilot could hear me. After several minutes, Approach Control asked us, rather pointedly, "...,have you heard someone on the frequency doing a Lot of cursing--using a lot of profanity?" "Ah, negative," I stammered, immediately wondering, (silently, for once), if I'd had an intermittent stuck mike. Moral: ANY aircraft can have a stuck mike, If you're gonna cuss in the cockpit, do it at your own risk. As I told my safety pilot, in a diatribe liberally salted with invectives, I thought the separation vectors, though prescribed by ATC rules, were not necessary. I also had roundly cursed the flight crew of an arriving airliner. Again, this is a hobby I enjoy in the, (so I thought), privacy of my own cockpit. I was flying with a hand mike, which I usually drop into my lap when busy. Might I have squeezed the side button on the mile with my thighs? Might I have unconsciously depressed the mike button on the yoke and thus activated the hand mike?" I don't know. **ASRS REPORT**

the microphone and ask. I've done this on several occasions. I just call ATC and say, "Sir, listen, I have a student here who doesn't understand what altitude he's supposed to maintain. How about filling him in, OK?" This is one of the unexpected navigational benefits of being a flight instructor.

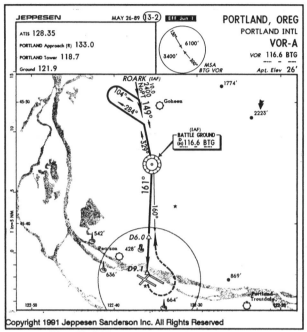

Fig. 17. MSA not centered at the airport.

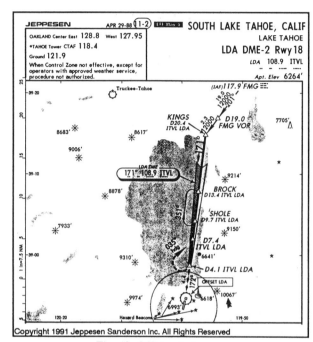

Fig. 18. MSA missing.

Pilots should keep in mind that the MSA may not be centered at the airport. Figure 17 shows the MSA for Portland, Oregon. The MSA is centered at the Battle Ground VOR, which is over 9 miles from the airport. The South Lake Tahoe LDA DME - 2 approach, shown in figure 18, doesn't list an MSA. This occurs when no omnidirectional navigational aids are present on the plan view. These omnidirectional aids are either a VOR or NDB. The localizer doesn't provide omnidirectional information, and it would be meaningless to have an MSA around a point that can't be referenced with bearing information. Additionally, MSA's are not provided on RNAV or radar approaches because they don't have omnidirectional navigation facilities.

A well-known comedienne once said, "More than all else, men love maps." Comedy often has a way of boldly serving up basic truths, and there is no exception in this case. It's not uncommon to see pilots sitting around the pilot lounge, poring over IFR charts, vicariously reliving adventures and tall tales. Just what is it that pilots find so satisfying in their perusal of lines on paper? Perhaps maps allow them to act out a basic, primal, nomadic need. As top flight Neanderthal navigators might portray locations of valued hunting sites on animal skins, modern man satisfies his primal needs in a more technically convenient manner. When looking at a matrix of airways, roads and wires, modern man still conjures visions of respected battles and courageous mastodon kills. Given anything even resembling a map, most men are immediately compelled to test its utility as a pictorial guide. "Can we get somewhere with it?" they ask. "Let's try," they grunt. Perhaps this over-enthusiasm is why so many decorative maps have written on them, "Not to be used for navigation." This may explain why pilots feel a kinship with their IFR charts. Pilots trust these maps because they guide them safely to their destination. Therefore, they are worth further detailed study to fully understand the performance, equipment and procedural requirements of instrument approaches.

KICK IN THE EMPENNAGE

COMPOUND ERROR

All of a sudden it hit me that I was tuned to XXX and not to YYY as I should have been. I retuned, and found I was slightly left of course and between the two intersections. Frankly, I was stunned. I really didn't have an opportunity to completely assess what had happened until I got home. For 7 or 8 miles, I had inadvertently descended below the MEA of 14,000' between the two intersections. I do not know whether I was below the minimum radar vectoring altitude for this area. The whole series of events started when I retuned my radio at altitude, prior to descent. I misread my high altitude chart. I put the right radial in the window, but the wrong frequency on the selector, and then I failed to check the ident. This put us 15 miles father West than I thought we were, even though we were just slightly left of course. The first thing I'm going to do, to prevent recurrence, is to check the ident on every VOR change. Secondly, I think that one or the other of those two VOR frequencies should be changed so that they aren't both 116 point something. It's just too easy to misread the chart and confuse the frequencies.

ASRS REPORT

12. EQUIPMENT FOR THE APPROACH

A older, seasoned pilot, once taught a valuable lesson about the perils of ignorance. This gentleman had been a ship's captain during World War II and had spent many a foggy night at sea. On one particularly foggy night, he saw what appeared to be the lights of another ship heading in his direction. His signalman was instructed to contact the other ship by signal light.

He sent the message: "*Change your course ten degrees south.*"

The reply came: "*Change your course ten degrees north.*"

The captain responded: "*I am a captain. Change your course ten degrees south.*"

The response was: "*I am a seaman first class. You change your course ten degrees north.*"

The captain was outraged. He commanded his signalman to reply: "*I am a battleship. You change your course ten degrees south.*"

The reply was: "*I am a lighthouse. You change your course ten degrees north.*"

Similarly, in aviation, pilots should not be ignorant of the approach procedures they must use. There are several instances where pilots can find themselves in trouble by not understanding the performance, equipment and procedural requirements of instrument approach charts.

LEARNING LENTICULARS

Zapped by the little green men

I had been playing "Space Invaders" for about two straight hours when an experienced co-pilot and I were launched to find a man believed to be injured, who was lost in dense underbrush. After we got to the search pattern, only 100 to 200 feet above the ridgeline we were searching, I started "seeing" (imagining) the "Space Invaders" descending down the windscreen. I gave the helicopter to my co-pilot, who continued the search at a higher, safer altitude. It took me about two minutes to de-program the "Space Invaders" out of my vision. Why did this happen? Two hours of self-induced, strong visual programming, plus mental exhaustion from a normal day and intense game "arcade fever," combined to catch me off guard in a quiet moment in the cockpit, where I had become a little complacent. The knowledge that I was dangerously close to hard "granitus," and a well-developed ability to concentrate on the instruments and facts pulled us out of the situation. Needless to say, I don't spend extended time periods in the arcade any more! **ASRS REPORT**

HEADING DATA

The heading data for all instrument approach charts identifies the type of equipment needed to complete that particular approach. Figure 1 shows the ILS 24 approach procedure to Carlsbad's McClellan-Palomar airport. The procedure identification, located below the airport name, will always indicate the equipment necessary for guidance on the primary approach facility. In the case of Carlsbad, localizer, glide slope and marker beacons (or allowed substitute) are required. Specifically, this is the minimum equipment necessary to shoot the approach; however, having the necessary equipment to transition to the approach structure can be an entirely different matter.

Suppose a pilot is at Oceanside VOR and has been cleared for the ILS Runway 24 approach to Carlsbad, California. Radar is not operating because maintenance technicians have played too many games of "Space Invaders" on it during off hours. Now it's in disrepair. When cleared for the approach, pilots should track outbound on the 83 degree radial from Oceanside VOR. This is the only terminal route available. When the DME indicates 18.3 miles, the airplane is at HOMLY intersection, and the pilot commences a right turn. Suddenly, he realizes he doesn't know what he's supposed to do after turning right. About this time, M&M's start to melt in his hand. From Homly intersection, the procedure requires that the pilot track the 195 degree bearing inbound to the EKG (curious letters, eh?) NDB. Without the availability of radar, or operable ADF equipment aboard, a pilot would be in violation of the FAR's for attempting to fly this approach.

In the upper, left hand side of the profile section, in figure 1, Jeppesen has inserted a small note stating that ADF, or radar, is required to shoot this approach.

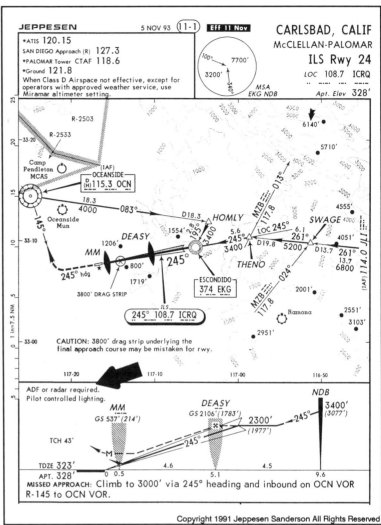

Fig. 1. The ILS Rwy 24 to Carlsbad, CA.

Careful examination of the approach shows there is no VOR transition directly onto the localizer. A short NDB track is required to turn the airplane onto the approach course. Normally, some form of procedure turn would be established to allow the pilot to reverse course on the approach. This is not feasible, in this instance, because of the higher terrain east of the airport. Therefore, the procedure requires that the pilot be turned around onto the localizer by the approach transition.

A KICK IN THE EMPENNAGE

A pilot called and advised he was in zero-zero weather. He was asked to verify whether he was IFR rated or not. The pilot said, "No." His altitude was 1,300 feet MSL, and he was headed for towers 1,320 feet high. He was given a climb to 2,500 feet and a heading for the airport. A second turn for a base leg was given. When the aircraft was three miles south of the airport, a heading for final and a descent to 1,500 were given. The local controller reported the aircraft in sight, one half mile off the approach end of the runway. The pilot sighted the airport and landed without incident. He took off again later and had problems again at his destination!

ASRS REPORT

FAA flight procedures require, where practical, at least one terminal route be provided to ensure transition from the enroute structure onto the approach structure, in the event of radar or communication failure. VOR is the most common form of navigation chosen for this routing. Where this is not feasible, an approach restriction will usually be found on the chart.

The two terminal routes for the Carlsbad ILS are the 083 degree radial from Oceanside and the 261 degree radial from the Julian VOR. The Julian (JLI) transition is flyable by VOR only. Unfortunately, this easterly transition onto the localizer is inaccessible from the heavily traveled shore route. Therefore, the approach requires radar or ADF availability.

Unless pilots suspect that there may be problems transitioning onto the approach structure, they may one day get caught with their wheel pants down. It's always a good idea to look in the profile section for approach limitations. Pilots using NOS charts (National Ocean Service) will usually find these restrictions in the plan view, as seen in figure 2. It's a good practice to run a finger over the terminal routes to be flown, making sure that the airplane has the necessary

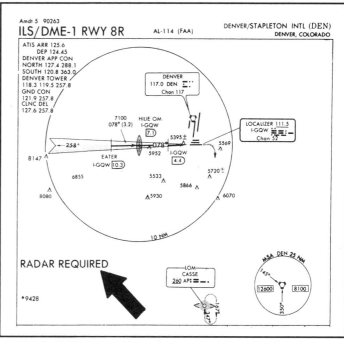

Fig. 2. NOS chart, with equipment restrictions, in plan view.

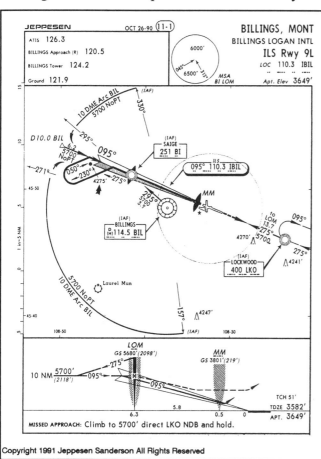

Fig. 3. ILS at Billings MT with additional equipment required to identify the missed approach holding fix.

equipment to get onto the approach structure. One word of caution. Pilots should avoid making the engine noise when running their finger along the chart routing. Although this adds an extra dimension of reality to the simulation, it has been known to quickly erode passenger confidence in the flight crew. Expect ADF or DME to be the most common type of additional equipment necessary for approach transitions.*

IDENTIFYING THE MISSED APPROACH HOLDING FIX

Perhaps the least attractive time to find an aircraft in need of additional equipment is during a missed approach. The ILS Rwy 9L at Billings, Montana, figure 3, and the LOC (BACK CRS) Rwy 2 at Idaho Falls, Idaho, figure 4, both have missed approach holding fixes requiring additional equipment not listed on the approach chart. The ILS Rwy 9L approach to Billings requires ADF to identify the LOCKWOOD NDB, which is the missed approach holding fix. UCONN LOM, the missed approach holding fix for the LOC (BACK CRS) Rwy 2 into Idaho Falls is identified by using

*Approach transitions are synonymous with terminal routes. They are the same thing. They provide a means of self-navigation onto the instrument approach course.

ADF equipment.* Before beginning an approach, it's good idea to make sure the airplane has all the equipment necessary to proceed to the missed approach holding fix and hold, if necessary. Additional equipment required for identifying the missed approach holding fix will not be listed as an approach restriction. It's the pilot's job to identify if this equipment is necessary, prior to the approach.

ADDITIONAL EQUIPMENT FOR THE APPROACH

Instrument procedures will often require additional equipment for approach course guidance. Figure 5 identifies approaches requiring VOR DME, NDB DME and ILS DME equipment. The double listing specifically indicates that more than one type of equipment must be used to execute the approach procedure. DME equipment is required on these approaches to help identify intersections, as well as the missed approach point. When an ILS approach requires DME, this is usually needed to help identify the FAF (Final Approach Fix).

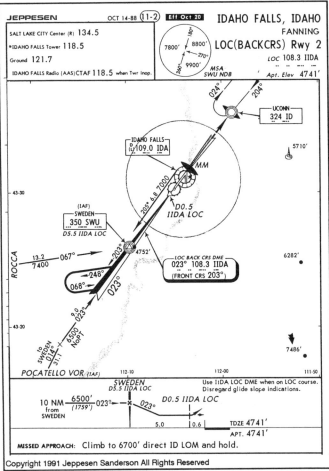

Fig. 4. LOC(BACKCOURSE) at Idaho Falls, ID with additional equipment required to identify the missed approach holding fix.

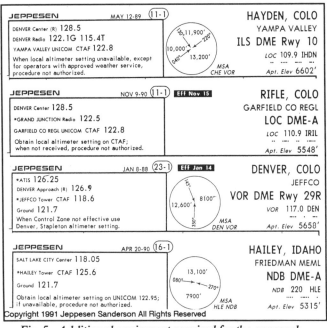

Fig. 5. Additional equipment required for the approach.

When building an approach that requires the use of DME to identify intersections, chart builders determine to what extent ATC can and will be willing to provide radar identification of those intersections. If the ATC facility can provide radar identification on a 24 hour basis, then the approach procedure may not require the addition of DME. If ATC cannot guarantee radar identification of intersections on a 24-hour basis, then DME may be required on the published procedure. Of course, if the Missed Approach Point on the procedure is designed to be identified only by DME, then chart builders will not be allowed to use Air Route Surveillance Radar (ARSR) as a substitution.**

*A marker beacon exists at UCONN and it can help identify the missed approach holding fix. However, pilots should use ADF and not the front course localizer for missed approach navigation because the holding pattern direction is 204 degrees inbound and the localizer's direction is 203 degrees inbound.
**ARSR is any type of radar other than Airport Surveillance Radar (ASR) and Precision Approach Radar (PAR). Both ASR and PAR can be used as instrument approach aids and to identify the missed approach point.

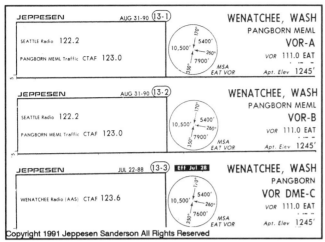

Fig. 6. Circling approaches identified by letters vs. numbers.

CIRCLING PROCEDURES

There are times when approach procedure identification will not have runway numbers, but will have letters instead, as shown in figure 6. Runway numbers indicate that the final approach course is aligned to within 30 degrees or less of the runway direction and has an acceptable descent angle. This is called a straight-in approach and lists straight-in landing minima. Letters indicate that the approach is to an airport instead of a specific runway. This type of approach would list circle-to-land minima.

Figure 6 lists three different circling approaches to Wenatchee, Washington. They are normally listed alphabetically, in the order of increasing minima. All these approaches have circling minima, since they are directed toward an airport and not a specific runway.

DESCENT GRADIENTS

Why are some approaches of the circling type and some of the straight-in type? There are several reasons for the differences. When the final approach course is misaligned more than 30 degrees with the runway centerline, the approach becomes a circling, rather than a straight-in approach. However, this doesn't explain why the Santa Monica VOR-A approach, figure 7, is circling rather than a straight-in type. A close look shows that the final approach course is almost perfectly aligned with the runway centerline. Santa Monica's circling procedure is based on an excessive rate of descent (Approximately 405 feet per nautical mile) required on final approach. A 300 foot per nautical mile rate of descent is considered normal for the final approach segment on a straight-in approach. The maximum permissible descent gradient is 400 feet per nautical mile. When the descent gradient exceeds 400 feet per nautical mile, from the final approach fix to the runway threshold, the approach becomes a circling procedure. This doesn't preclude a pilot from landing straight in, if the aircraft is in a position to do so. However, a circling procedure, aligned with the runway centerline, should cue pilots to expect a steeper than normal final approach.

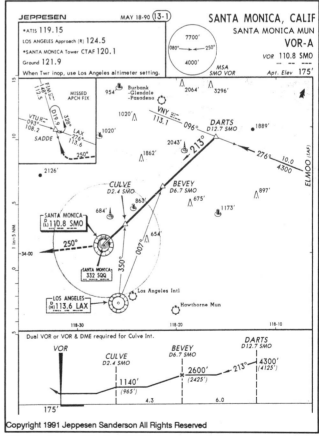

Fig. 7. Santa Monica VOR-A approach has a steep descent gradient on final, requiring circle-to-land minima.

CHARTED VISUAL PROCEDURES

Charted visual approach procedures are unique entities in the IFR system. Technically, they are paper versions of the visual approaches that controllers verbally issue. Despite being created specifically for airline operations, they can be used by anyone having access to the procedure.

The procedure identification will usually specify some prominent geographical reference point to be used in navigating to the airport. Figure 8

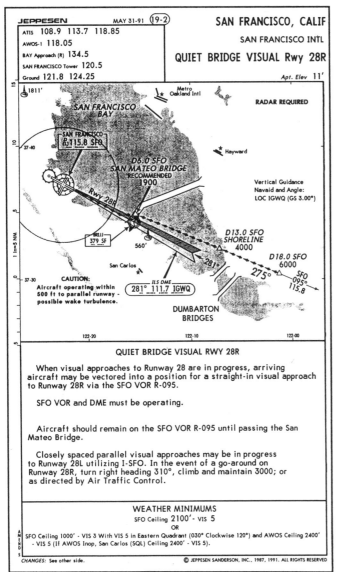

Fig. 8. Charted visual approach procedure.

KNOW YOUR EQUIPMENT!

Several years ago, while on an IFR flight, I overheard a pilot having radio trouble. Apparently he was having trouble receiving the transmissions of Burbank approach, although his transmitter was working fine. Finally, in a moment of confusion, the pilot said, "OK Burbank, if you can hear me, signal me on my transponder!" Apparently, the pilot thought that the little flashing light on the transponder was somehow under the control of the controller. It was all we could do to keep our aircraft upright when several airliners in the vicinity called and said, "Oh, Burbank, could you signal me on my transponder too, please? The moral here is to know how the equipment in the aircraft works, especially its limitations.   **Author**

shows the Quiet Bridge Visual approach to runway 28R at San Francisco. As a word of caution, it's not called the Quiet Bridge Visual because pilots are expected to go under the bridge! The bridge is a visual reference to aid in finding the airport. As with all visual approaches, basic VFR or better is required at the airport to fly the approach. In some cases, because of local geography, higher than normal VFR weather conditions are required. The visual approach into San Francisco depicts these higher minimums.

A charted visual approach is not an official instrument approach procedure. This approach is not considered an official instrument approach procedure because there are no provisions made for an IFR missed approach. In all practicality, an IFR missed approach isn't expected, or required, because at least basic VFR weather (1,000 feet and 3 miles) must exist at the airport for visual approaches to be assigned. Using a charted visual won't cancel an IFR flight plan; however, neither will it provide all that a regular instrument approach procedure would: namely, protection to the missed approach point. Perhaps the most important thing to remember about visuals is that if a go-around is necessary, it should be done in VFR conditions.

YOU CAN'T GET THERE FROM HERE

Every instrument pilot of reasonable experience has, at one time or another, had the experience of being cleared for an approach and realizing that there was no apparent way to get from one point to another on the approach chart. This is very similar to the feeling I got in philosophy class when the professor gave me the essay test question, "What is courage?" I pondered this for a while, then wrote, "This is," on the paper and handed it in. He wrote back, "What is summer school?" Oops! To avoid any sort of similar discomfort, pilots need to understand how terminal routes are flown in the IFR system.

The plan view of an instrument chart depicts terminal routes to be used in the event radar is not available as an instrument approach aid. These flyable routes, called terminal routes, all have one thing in common: pilots can navigate on them without the use of radar. Flyable terminal routes are always revealed by the presence of at least three separate items: altitude information, direction and distance. In the majority of cases, they will also be associated with a dark line and an arrow. This information allows pilots to transition from the enroute phase to the approach phase of the flight, without being radar vectored.

Figure 9 shows the Santa Barbara VOR Rwy 25 approach. The depicted routing from the San Marcus VOR shows the 145 degree radial listing altitude, direction and distance. This approach transition is the terminal route that can be flown without the aid of radar vectors. When cleared for the approach from over the San Marcus VOR, pilots should track outbound on the 145 degree radial, descend to 6,000 feet (unless altitude restrictions were mentioned in the clearance) and, in 8 miles (or 4 minutes at 120 knots ground speed), expect to intercept the 099 degree radial of the SBA VOR. At this point, a procedure turn is required since it is not officially precluded by the designator: "NoPT."

Notice that the San Marcus 145 degree radial is thicker than the other two radials coming off of the VOR. This extra bold line identifies the routing as a terminal route. A careful review of the Jeppesen chart plan view reveals lines of three variations of thickness. For some pilots, variations in line width may be difficult to identify. I recommend investment in a good pair of magnifying glasses. Some glasses are so powerful, they can be used to sight small planets circling distant stars, as well for impromptu spot welding jobs on aircraft. The thinnest lines on the approach chart (the San Marcus 173 and 119 radials) are used for identification of intersections. These radials will not be used as terminal routes (with one exception to be noted later). These thin lines always have a small arrow tip on them, pointing to the intersection they identify.

The medium thick line will always be accompanied by altitude, direction and distance. Therefore, it can be flown without the use of radar for guidance. A closer look at the 145 degree radial from the RZS VOR reveals both a minimum and medium thick line. In addition to serving as a terminal route, the radial also serves to identify ZACKS intersection.

The maximum thick line is called the approach procedure track, and it's the place the IFR pilot is always headed. Figure 10 identifies the approach procedure track for the ILS Rwy 3 at Carlsbad, New Mexico. Altitudes to be flown for the approach procedure track are listed only in the profile view of the approach chart.

Figure 11 shows the NDB Rwy 19 approach at Richland, Washington. Three variations in line thickness can be seen on the plan view. Routes coming from OLFUS, BAKCA and MARLI intersections, as well as from the PSC VOR at the

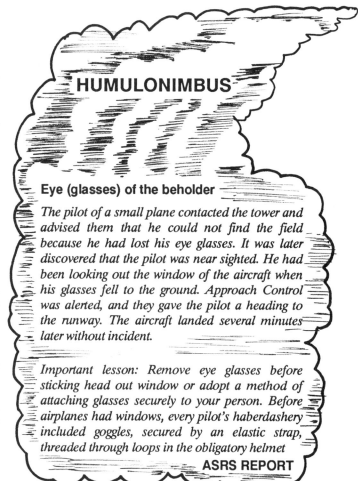

HUMULONIMBUS

Eye (glasses) of the beholder

The pilot of a small plane contacted the tower and advised them that he could not find the field because he had lost his eye glasses. It was later discovered that the pilot was near sighted. He had been looking out the window of the aircraft when his glasses fell to the ground. Approach Control was alerted, and they gave the pilot a heading to the runway. The aircraft landed several minutes later without incident.

Important lesson: Remove eye glasses before sticking head out window or adopt a method of attaching glasses securely to your person. Before airplanes had windows, every pilot's haberdashery included goggles, secured by an elastic strap, threaded through loops in the obligatory helmet.

ASRS REPORT

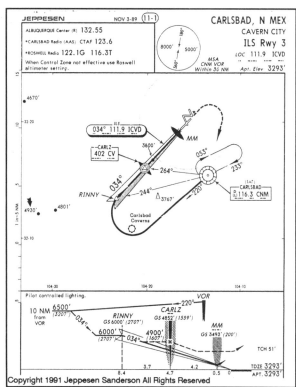

bottom of the plan view, are all terminal routes. They all have altitude, direction and distances listed on the medium thick lines. All these routes point toward the approach procedure track.

Pilots must use caution when established on the approach procedure track. Commencing the procedure turn from over the RIBOO NDB requires that the profile view be consulted to identify the procedure turn altitude. The profile shows 2,100 feet for the procedure turn. It's conceivable that a pilot may look at the altitude, listed inbound from BAKCA intersection, and think 1,600 feet is the minimum altitude to be used for the procedure turn. Doing this would require that IFR flight plans be filed with the Department of Parks and Recreation, because 1,600 feet is too low an altitude for a course reversal. Unless otherwise noted, when pilots are established on the maximum thick line, they should refer to the profile view for the altitudes to be flown.

Fig. 10. Approach procedure track for the Carlsbad, NM ILS Rwy 3 approach.

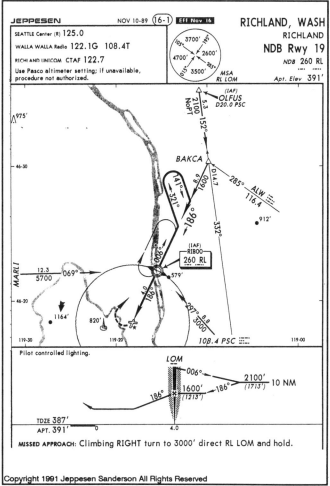

Fig. 11. Three variations in line segment thickness shown on approach chart.

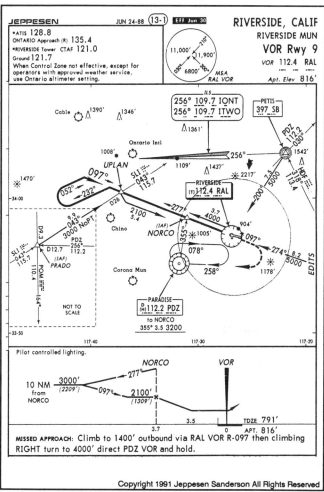

Fig. 12. Approach transition coincidental with approach procedure track.

The VOR Rwy 9 approach to Riverside, California, figure 12, shows a terminal route coincidental with the approach procedure track. This is one exception pilots may find concerning use of altitudes in the profile view. The offset routing outbound from RAL VOR is established for clarity. When the approach is commenced from over the Riverside VOR, pilots should fly outbound on the 277 radial and descend to 4,000 feet. The offset routing takes the aircraft to NORCO intersection, where the procedure turn begins. The procedure turn would then be flown using the altitudes listed in. the profile view.

HE WHO LAUGHS LAST!

Several years ago, at a local Southern California airport, a controller and an airline pilot had a tense encounter. It seems that just after the airline pilot rotated for takeoff, the controller mentioned that the pilot took a little too long on the runway and created an aircraft spacing problem. The pilot wasn't in any mood to hear this and said, "Hey buddy, if you think you can do it any better, why don't you come up here and fly this thing?" The controller didn't respond. About 10 seconds elapsed then the controller issued the pilot a new clearance. The pilot said, "Hey, I can't accept this clearance, it will take me to the airport I just departed from. What's the matter with you guys?" The controller replied, "Well, what do you expect? If you want me to fly that thing, you're going to have to bring it back here!"

AUTHOR

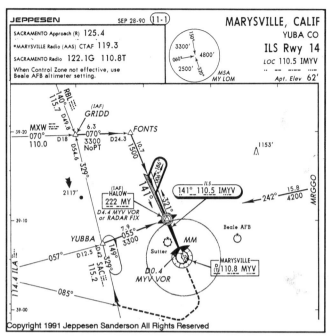

Fig. 13. Comparison of Jeppesen chart to NOS chart.

NOS charts use symbology similar to Jeppesen, but with subtle differences. Figure 13 compares two approach charts for Marysville, California. NOS charts have three variations of thickness for their routings, however, it's very difficult to distinguish between the minimum and medium thick lines. All routes taking aircraft to the initial approach fix are identified by medium thick lines. Additionally, all routes on NOS charts, from the initial approach fixes inbound, are made up of maximum thick lines.

MRGGO intersection, shows a terminal route to HALOW LOM (IAF). Despite the difficulty in separating medium from minimum thickness on NOS charts, a specific line can be identified as a terminal route, because altitude, direction and distance will be listed. The route from MRGGO intersection, along the 242 degree bearing to HALOW LOM, lists the three criteria for flyability.

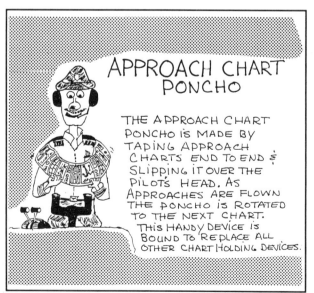

DECIPHERING TERMINAL ROUTES

Government authorities use metal strips to band certain birds. The strips are inscribed: "Notify Fish and Wildlife Service, Washington, D.C." Previously, the strips read, "Wash. Biol. Surv." This was an abbreviation for Washington Biological Survey. The strips were changed after a Vancouver farmer complained to the U.S. Government. He wrote: "Dear Sirs: I shot one of your crows a few days ago and followed the instructions attached to it. I washed it, boiled it and served it. Worst thing I ever ate! You folks shouldn't be trying to fool people with things like this..." It seems that the government, even though unintentionally, is still fooling people, especially those in the aviation community.

A pilot, shooting the ILS Rwy 29R approach into Stockton, figure 14, might be in for a surprise similar to what the Vancouver farmer experienced. Suppose a clearance for the approach was received while over the Manteca VOR. Assume that radar service is not available. What would be the correct procedure to follow? Cancelling IFR is not one of the options. There doesn't appear to be a routing from the VOR to the approach procedure track. At least, there is no medium thick line to indicate a flyable route. A closer inspection of the Manteca VOR indicates that the minimum criteria required for a terminal route is listed underneath the frequency box. Although not easily identified, the altitude, direction and distance to the Locator Outer Marker is depicted. This is an acceptable terminal route onto the approach course, even though a medium thick line is not shown.

When artistic clarity is important, routing information will be listed under the navaid in question. Clearly, a medium thick line, drawn from the VOR to the LOM, would not be visually apparent. NOS charts may show something different. Figure 15 reveals a medium-thick line routing from the Manteca VOR with the altitude, direction and distance listed. Jeppesen apparently considered this just too much of a strain on the pilot's eyes to draw it the same way.

It's often easy to be visually deceived. A gambler at a racetrack once bet on a horse named "Boy George." This horse came in last. Unfortunately, it wasn't a horse, it was a cow dressed up like a horse! Approach charts can fool someone in a similar way. If pilots are confused about the routing for their approach clearance, they should first look at the navaid box nearest their position. Terminal routes may be listed without being accompanied by darker, medium-thick lines.

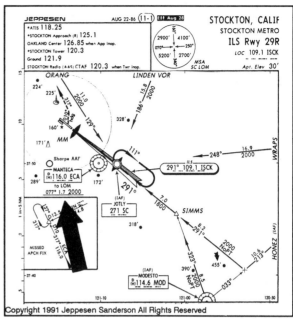

Fig. 14. Jep chart showing terminal route listed under ECA VOR frequency box for Stockton ILS.

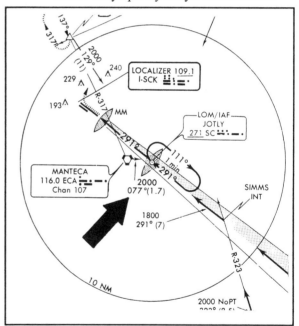

Fig.15. NOS chart variation of terminal route depiction for Stockton ILS from ECA VOR.

DEAD RECKONING ROUTES

In addition to altitude, direction and distance, terminal routes usually specify the means of navigation to be used to get on the approach structure. Normally, this will be via VOR or NDB

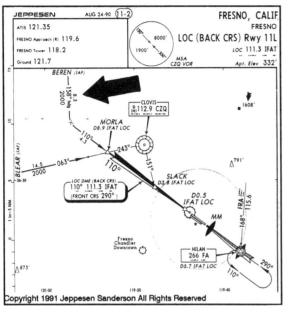

Fig. 16. Dead reckoning route from BEREN intersection.

navigation. On occasion, no electronic means of navigation is used. That's right, nothing! It's possible to have a terminal route that has no means of electronic navigation. Figure 16 shows the Fresno LOC (BACK CRS) Rwy 11L approach. Pilots located at BEREN intersection and cleared for the approach would fly a 158 degree heading, as shown by the letters "hdg" next to the route direction. Essentially, pilots are flying via dead reckoning. Other than radar vectors, this is the only time it's legal to fly IFR without some navigable signal to follow. A heading of 158 degrees is flown until intercepting the localizer. Should any attempt be made to correct for wind? This is normally not necessary.* Pilots should fly the heading and wait for approach course interception.

Dead reckoning routes will be approved only for short distances (10 miles or less). They are also limited to areas where, even with serious wind conditions, drift into higher terrain is unlikely. To facilitate course interception, and further minimize the effects of wind drift, dead reckoning routes will intercept the inbound approach course at angles between 45 and 90 degrees.

NOS charts depict dead reckoning routes by default. In other words, there will not be any apparent means of navigation available on that route. Figure 17 shows the same dead reckoning route for the Fresno LOC (BACK CRS) Rwy 11L approach. From BEREN intersection to the approach structure, there is no electronic means of navigation apparent. On NOS charts, when a route exists without any navigational support, a pilot can assume that it's to be flown via a heading until intercepting the approach course.

DME ARC'S

There are occasions where terminal routes exist, yet cannot be identified from looking at the approach chart plan view. At first, the Paso Robles VOR DME-B approach, shown in figure 18, appears rather benign. At least, until pilots ask themselves why the DME arcs start

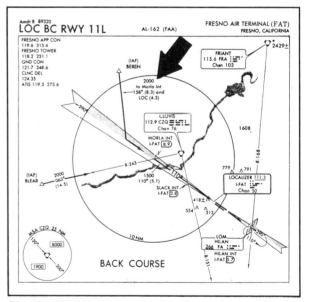

Fig. 17. NOS chart showing dead reckoning route from BEREN intersection.

---

* The USAF's instrument flying handbook (AFM 51-37) suggests that their pilots should attempt to fly the depicted ground track by correcting for wind. Nothing definitive is written for general aviation on this issue. However, every approach designer I talked to said that the protection on either side of the dead reckoning route is so extensive that there is little or no chance of ever being blown into unprotected airspace.

at the beginning of the 077 and 179 degree radials of the Paso Robles VOR. This appears unusual, considering that the DME arcs meet all the criteria for flyability (i.e., they have altitude, direction and distance), yet the radials do not. These arcs appear to start out in the middle of nowhere. The answer lies with the Low Altitude Enroute chart.

Figure 19 shows the 179 and the 077 degree radials to be Victor 113 and 248 respectively. These airways are certainly flyable routes, yet they are not listed that way on the approach chart. Whenever a radial marks the beginning of a DME arc, that radial is always an airway. Airways are always, flyable, terminal routes. Many pilots, when operating within the border of the approach chart plan view, put aside their low altitude enroute charts. Sometimes they fold them up into little globes and orbit them into the back seat of the airplane, thinking that they no longer need them. This may not be the case when flying a DME arc approach. The enroute chart depicts MEA's for these airways and is now a necessary complement of the approach chart.

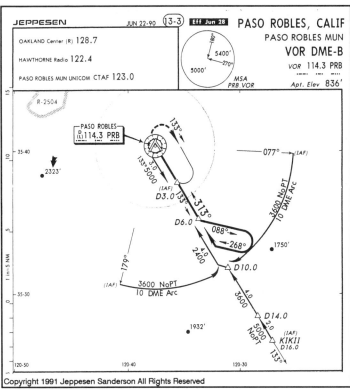

Fig. 18. DME arcs start at radials that are always airways.

DME arcs are a frequently misused means of navigation. Consider that in a non-radar environment, a pilot coming in from REDDE intersection on V-248, figure 19, would have to proceed to the VOR, then complete a procedure turn, before executing the VOR DME-B approach. Requesting the DME arc transition from ATC, and receiving approval, a pilot could now intersect the 10 DME arc off V-248, circle southeast and intercept the inbound course without making a procedure turn. This is certainly an option worth considering in the interest of saving time.

In the Gulf of Mexico one hot, summer afternoon, in 1974, the Coast Guard discovered a man floating on two bails of marijuana. He was taken aboard for questioning. He said,

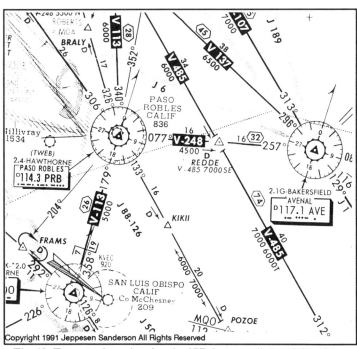

Fig. 19. Enroute chart showing the 077 degree radial and the 179 degree radial as an airway.

"Man, you guys aren't going to believe this, but I was out in my boat when it blew up. I thought I was going to drown, but all of a sudden these two bails of marijuana came floating by..." Nice try buddy! There are very few times when excuses are of any value. This is especially true when flying instruments. Pilots need to be as knowledgeable about their charts as lion tamers need to understand the hunger patterns of their animals. A pilot's skill in deciphering terminal routes is extremely important in handling a no-radar, "Do it yourself" type of approach. Skill in deciphering chart symbology, as well as a deeper understanding of the three-dimensional plan view, will also serve a pilot well.

CAUGHT WITH WHEEL PANTS DOWN

CFIT - ALMOST!
(Controlled Flight Into Terrain)

A conscientious and alert Center controller was still observing an aircraft on radar, after handing it off to a non-radar equipped Approach Control. It was given vectors to intercept the LOC-DME (BACK COURSE)-B approach and told to maintain 10,000'. When the aircraft was established on the radial, Center instructed it to go to Approach. Approach instructed the aircraft to maintain 10,000' until 21 DME, then it was cleared for the Back Course approach. Everything was trimmed up, with the plane tracking inbound right on the button. The autopilot was switched to the ILS (and ILS DME), and the pilot verified he had a few miles to go at 10,000'. He flipped the autopilot on, and blithely went about cleaning up the cockpit (putting away maps, other approach plates, etc.) He diverted his attention for at least a full minute. When he next glanced at the DME readout, he was just inside the 21 mile checkpoint, and he began the profile descent.

What he failed to observe is that he had placed the autopilot in "normal" tracking instead of "reverse" or "back course" tracking. While his attention was diverted, the autopilot took the aircraft through a beautiful coordinated 180 degree turn. He was now heading due wrong!

The Center controller noted the course reversal on radar and phoned Approach, who contacted the aircraft to verify the incorrect heading. The Approach asked, "Give me your best rate of climb immediately...", very calmly. The back course approach is characterized by very high terrain within very close proximity to the profile descent.

The pilot was taught a great lesson and fortunately survived to remember it.

Never, never divert your attention from the instruments once you are on an approach!

ASRS REPORT

13. SECRETS OF THE FRONT SIDE

The captain of a great ocean liner had begun his career as a cabin boy, years earlier, and gradually worked up to his respected position. He had become one of the most respected men on the high seas. His assistant, who had served under him for many years, observed and emulated his every move. But one thing about the captain puzzled him: every morning before assuming his duties, the skipper went to his cabin, opened the top drawer of his desk, took out a small slip of paper, read it with intense concentration, returned the paper to his desk and locked the drawer. After many years, the captain retired and his assistant took command. The first thing he did was open that drawer to discover what was on that slip of paper. The paper had but one sentence on it: "Port is left: starboard is right."

Man has always used crib sheets to help remind him of critical information. In the 1930's, when Captain Jeppesen started keeping a small book of those little paper notes for airports he frequented, little did he realize how technically sophisticated his cache of information would become. Instrument approach charts, and Jeppesen charts in particular, are the end product of many years of trial and error evolution. Considering that an IFR chart's worth lies in its ability to convey a 3-dimensional understanding of the approach environment, a deeper understanding of chart symbology will be of great value to pilots.

THE PLAN VIEW

The Plan view (the bird's eye view) is perhaps the most misunderstood and yet one of the most useful sections of the approach chart. Pilots get their first sense of the approach structure by perusing the plan view, noting altitudes and distances of navaids along the routes to be flown. The plan view provides pilots with immediate information upon which to judge the pace of events during the approach.

Jeppesen's plan view, figure 1, is drawn entirely to scale. This allows pilots to estimate their position and mileage relative to the destination airport. Therefore, an airplane located in the bottom portion of the plan view will have more time to get set up for the approach than an airplane closer to center of the chart. Distances of 5NM or 7.5 NM per inch are the most common scales used by Jeppesen on their plan view.

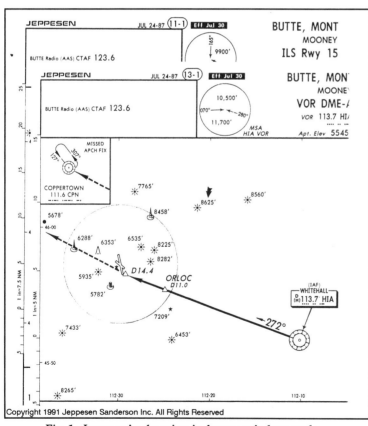

Fig. 1. Jeppesen's plan view is drawn entirely to scale.

NOS charts, figure 2, only provide information to scale within a solid ring that's usually centered on the plan view. Outside this ring, where chart information is unscaled, pilots should not try to guess their distances relative to the destination airport. Ring distances generally vary between a 10 and 15 nautical mile radius.

Jeppesen's scaled plan view provides an additional safety factor often not considered by pilots. Airports depicted on the plan view provide optional landing spots for inflight emergencies. Having a good feel for relative distances, therefore, gliding potential to these airports, provides pilots with valuable landing options in an emergency situation.

Pilots can make rough estimations of arrival over fixes by using their knowledge of chart scale. The average pilot's thumb tip is 4NM's in

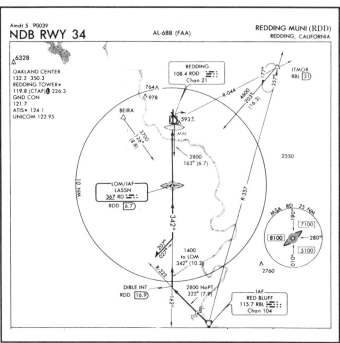

Fig. 2. NOS charts provide information that's to scale within the solid ring in the plan view.

width on a 5NM/inch scale. At 120 knots approach speed, the airplane will travel 4NM's in 2 minutes. Therefore, the average airplane will travel one thumb's width in 2 minutes. When ATC asks for an estimation over a certain intersection, pilots only need count up the digits and tell them they'll be there in 5 thumbs (10 minutes). Of course, pilots who have a great deal of previous experience using power tools may not be able to use this nifty technique. Remember, this technique is not all that accurate; it's only a rule of thumb!

VFR AND IFR AIRPORTS ON THE PLAN VIEW

Jeppesen's plan view shows only those airports having IFR approaches. There's one exception to this rule. When a VFR airport is within one mile of either side of the approach procedure track (maximum thick line), it will be depicted. Gallaher airport, figure 3, located just to the right of the Visalia LOM, is a VFR airport. VFR airports, located this close to the approach procedure track, are shown for use in the event of an emergency. Pilots appreciate having knowledge of any airport's location when flying at the lower altitudes used for the approach. It's comforting to know there's someplace to glide if an engine fails. The 5 point star located above the DME arc is a rotating beacon for Mefford, a VFR airport. These stars may be useful in identifying the location of any VFR airport with a rotating beacon.

One time I pulled the throttle on a student while on a VFR practice instrument approach. The student had the hood on, and I wanted to test his ability to navigate to a VFR airport near the approach course. To my amazement, he precisely navigated to the center of the airport and said, "OK, we're there." I said, "Wonderful, perfect! How did you do that so well?" He replied, "Oh, I could see it out of the corner of my hood." I should have known something was funny when, during one intense instrument flight, ATC called traffic for us, and he said, "Contact." From then on I made him wear foggles underneath the hood.

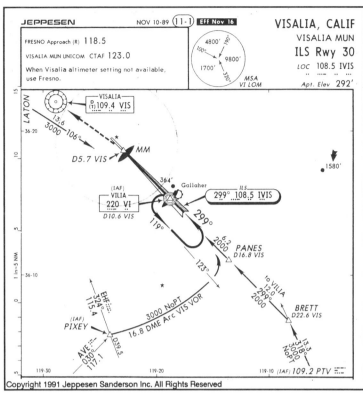

Fig. 3. *Jeppesen's plan view shows all airports having published instrument approaches. Sometimes a VFR airport will be shown, like Gallaher, when it is located within one mile of the approach course.*

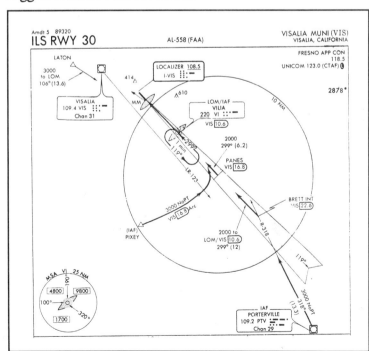

Fig. 4. NOS charts don't depict any airports on their plan view.

Figure 4 shows an NOS chart covering the same area of Visalia. Unlike Jeppesen charts, pilots using NOS charts won't find other airports depicted on the plan view. Only the primary airport which supports the instrument approach is shown. Therefore, when using these charts, it's important to have a low altitude IFR enroute chart or area chart available, which shows the locations of additional airports.

TERRAIN FEATURES

As approach charts are being revised, Jeppesen will be providing terrain information on selected plan views, as shown in figure 5. Approach chart plan views, having obstructions more than 4,000 feet above the primary airport elevation, will contain terrain contour information. Contour information

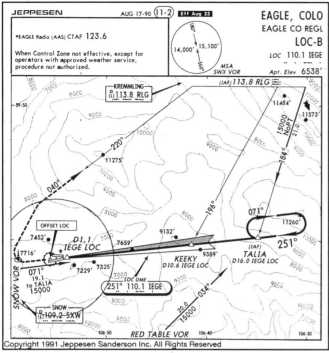

Fig. 5. Terrain information portrayed on Jeppesen's plan view.

will be provided on all approach charts for that airport. This information is presented in contour increments of 1,000 feet. Jeppesen is very specific in stating that this is advisory information only and cannot be relied on for terrain avoidance. The terrain depiction is only intended to be symbolic of the existence of unusual terrain features.

Relief contours are not the only useful terrain information presented on the chart. A large black arrow identifies the highest thing that either man or God has made in the plan view's coverage area. The highest obstruction shown on the Eagle, Colorado, plan view, figure 5, is an 11,573' mountain peak in the top right border of the approach chart. Additional terrain information is shown, throughout the plan view, in the form of natural and man made obstructions.

No IFR chart, either Jeppesen or NOS, will show all obstructions, either man-made or natural. As disconcerting as this sounds, pilots must remember that NOS and Jeppesen can only chart obstructions made available to their charting department. It's quite possible that antennas, wires or other obstructions may have been constructed without this information being made available to the authorities in a timely manner. Pilot's are naturally concerned about this, since the unwritten rule in instrument flying is to avoid bumping into things with an airplane.

The only way a pilot can be assured of avoiding all obstructions, when using an approach chart, is to fly the specified terminal routes, which always provide altitude, direction and distance information, or, at the controller's MVA (minimum vectoring altitude). These terminal routes, which pilots fly using their own navigation, assure at least 1,000 feet of obstruction clearance* until the aircraft is established on the approach procedure track. This is perhaps good motivation to ask ATC for permission to fly the published terminal routes whenever possible, especially when pilots are unfamiliar with the airport and surrounding terrain. These routes are constantly being flown, as well as flight checked, and can be assumed to be free of obstructions. A little more time may be spent flying the approach, compared to being radar vectored, but it could also save a pilot's empennage.

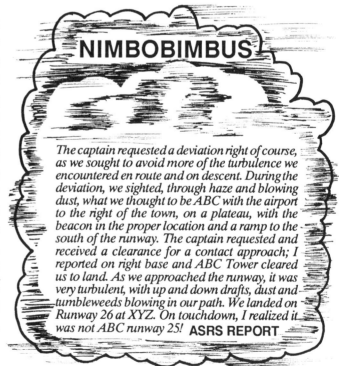

The captain requested a deviation right of course, as we sought to avoid more of the turbulence we encountered en route and on descent. During the deviation, we sighted, through haze and blowing dust, what we thought to be ABC with the airport to the right of the town, on a plateau, with the beacon in the proper location and a ramp to the south of the runway. The captain requested and received a clearance for a contact approach; I reported on right base and ABC Tower cleared us to land. As we approached the runway, it was very turbulent, with up and down drafts, dust and tumbleweeds blowing in our path. We landed on Runway 26 at XYZ. On touchdown, I realized it was not ABC runway 25! **ASRS REPORT**

*The obstruction clearance for initial approach segments is 1,000 feet. For feeder routes, which can lead aircraft to initial approach segments, enroute airway obstruction clearance applies: 1,000 feet in non-mountainous terrain and 2,000 feet in mountainous terrain.

Where pilots get themselves into serious trouble is when they attempt to use terrain information on IFR charts to fly visually to an airport. These charts weren't designed for this. If pilots elect to depart from the established approach procedure, and make a visual or contact approach, they should realize they are responsible for seeing and avoiding any and all obstructions. This is why flying the full procedure at unfamiliar airports, including adherence to MDA's, is usually a good idea.

Terrain becomes a greater concern at night. Statistics indicate that there are 10 times more single pilot IFR accidents per flight hour at night than during the day. I once did a seminar and asked pilots what they thought was the reason for this. One fellow said, "Because pilots, in general, can't land smoothly at night." I asked him why he thought he couldn't land smoothly at night. He replied, "Because dark air has less lift in it than light air does." This wasn't the reason I was looking for. To put it kindly, this gentleman was just a few fries short of a happy meal. Nighttime is a time when pilots are more likely to fall victim to visual illusions.

KICK IN THE EMPENNAGE

The captain looked down to change the frequency, called the Tower, then checked the VOR indicator. He noted that the First Officer had flown through the final approach course and was making no correction toward the plainly visible airport. He checked the First Officer's ILS indicator which showed "FLY LEFT," with the airport to the right of the aircraft. The Captain tuned his ILS which also showed "FLY LEFT." The First Officer made a visual turn to the final approach and executed a smooth, easy approach visually. The Captain rechecked the identifier of the ILS. It identified the nearby military base, not our intended airport. No airspace was violated; there was no violent maneuvering; but it is frightening to contemplate the situation had the flight conditions been less benign. The least repulsive result could have been a landing at the wrong airport. Clearly the wrong ILS was tuned and incorrectly identified. This is probably due to the long night, the early morning, CAVOK and complacency syndrome. We hear what we expect to hear. More self-discipline against complacency and greater division of attention between cockpit and outside are plainly in order.

ASRS REPORT

THE VASI

STUDENT: I understand what red over white, red over red and white over white means. But what does it mean when you see green?

INSTRUCTOR: It means that you are so low that the light is filtering through the grass!

There are many visual illusions that can snare a pilot when it's dark. The "black hole" effect is one of the more predatory of these illusions. Pilots, making an approach where the terrain underneath is unlit, feel as if they are considerably above a normal glide slope. The resultant action is for the pilot to descend prematurely and strike the terrain. One study indicated that pilots, lured by the "black hole" illusion, may feel they are twice as high as they should be on the approach. They compensate by getting lower than normal on the approach. This is why pilots should always honor and respect glide slopes, visual descent points, MDA's and VASI's.

AIRPORT REFERENCE CIRCLE

My dear friend's grandmother loved to go to Las Vegas and gamble. She was 94 years old and, to put it gently, some of her spark plugs were no longer connected. One day, she got uncontrollably excited about a particular machine that always paid off. She claimed she never lost money. The family found out later that she had been playing the dollar bill change machine. This was certainly a safe gamble. Pilots can similarly make a safe gamble with other instrument pilots if they bet on the precise name and function of the circle surrounding the primary airport on all Jeppesen plan views, as show in figure 6. Nine out of ten times, other pilots will say the circle is Class D airspace (the old airport traffic area). Instant success, you win big bucks! Surrounding the primary airport on the Jeppesen plan view, is a circle, 5 miles in radius. Called the "airport reference circle" this ring highlights all obstructions starting at 400 feet or more above the airport elevation.

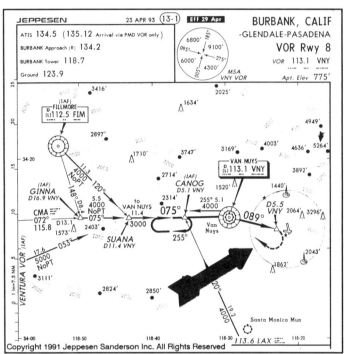

Fig. 6. The airport reference circle shown on Jeppesen's plan view surrounding Burbank airport.

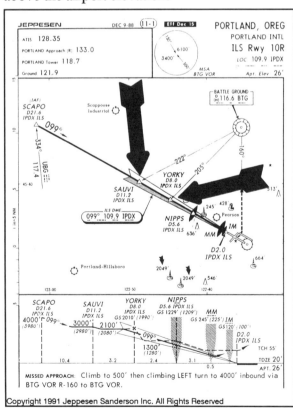

Fig. 7. Cross radial intersection identification using the plan view.

The airport reference circle was originally intended to help pilots more easily identify the airport on the plan view. Unfortunately, it was often confused with other types of airspace. Jeppesen, therefore, decided to begin removing it from their charts as of October 1993. Jeppesen now shows known obstacles standing 400 feet or more above the airport elevation over the entire plan view coverage. This information, coupled with Jeppesen's portrayal of terrain features, adds greatly to a pilot's terrain awareness.

OFFICIAL INTERSECTION IDENTIFICATION

Knowing how to read chart symbols is very important. It's much like going to Disneyland and identifying the rides that offer the greatest thrill. Simply read the signs. The sign for the Matterhorn (one of the most intense rides) says, "NO PEOPLE WITH HEART PROBLEMS, NO PREGNANT WOMEN, NO HIGH BLOOD PRESSURE." Underneath the sign someone wrote, "And no toupees."

The last words told the story. In much the same way, it's the little things on the chart plan view that tell the story about intersection identification.

The plan view and the profile provide the official means used to identify intersections along the approach procedure track. The plan view shows cross radial or bearings used for intersection identification. The profile view shows all means, other than cross radials or bearings, for intersection identification. The ILS Rwy 10R to Portland, Oregon, is shown in figure 7. The plan view depicts SAUVI and YORKY intersections, identified by both VOR cross radials and DME from the localizer. NIPPS is identified by marker beacon and DME information from the localizer.

The identification of intersections on the plan view can often be a little tricky. Figure 8 shows how IBEAM intersection is defined. VOR or NDB identification of an intersection is always accom-

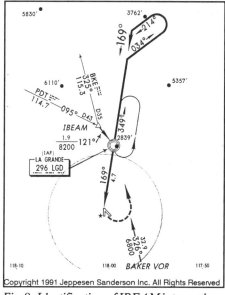

Fig. 8. Identification of IBEAM intersection.

panied by thin arrows. VOR identification of an intersection will have thin arrows coming from the VOR used in identifying the intersection. NDB identification will have thin arrows going to the station identifying the intersection. IBEAM intersection is identified by the 325 radial from BKE VOR and the 095 degree radial from PDT VOR.

Figure 9 shows GANGS intersection and LYNSY intersection. GANGS intersection shows a terminal routing to the NDB via the medium thick line and arrow. Additionally, beyond the thick line, there is a thin line and arrow running to the TKW NDB. This implies that GANGS is defined by the 032 bearing to the TKW NDB and the 344 degree radial from ONP VOR. LYNSY intersection is also defined by a bearing to the NDB and a radial from the VOR station. Pilots having DME onboard can use this to identify both intersections off the 344 radial, since a small "D" is present.

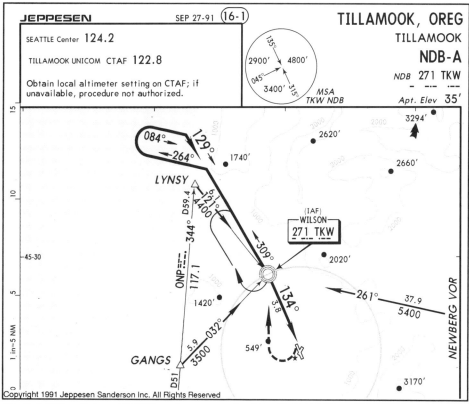

Fig. 9. VOR radials and NDB bearings are used to identify GANGS and LYNSY intersections.

Armed with this knowledge, some interesting observations can be made about intersection identification. Figure 10 shows the ILS Rwy 19R to John Wayne-Orange County airport. Notice the terminal route from the Seal Beach VOR. The 105 degree radial heads the airplane directly towards 1.1 DME fix on the localizer. At this point, a turn would be made outbound, along the localizer, towards the holding pattern. It's tempting to think that the 105 degree radial can be used to identify the 1.1 DME fix, which is one way of identifying the MAP (missed approach point) for the localizer approach. However, since there is no thin line accompanying the transition, this radial cannot be used to identify this intersection. Besides, VOR radials are never used to identify missed approach points. When the aircraft is at the MAP, it's usually at too low an altitude to guarantee undistorted reception for a VOR cross reference. Therefore, time or DME, from the primary approach navaid, is used for identifying the MAP.

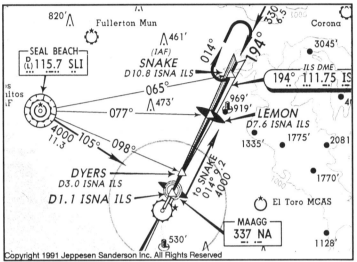

Fig. 10. *The approach transition from the SLI VOR cannot be used to identify the 1.1 ISNA ILS DME fix.*

Additionally, use of VOR cross radials to identify the MAP may involve a higher workload for pilots. Reading clocks or DME indications is a great deal less distracting than twisting course selectors when close to the ground. This is why DME or time is used for identification of the ILS 19R MAP. It involves minimum workload for the pilot. However, VOR radials can be used to identify all other intersections along the approach track.

DME SOURCE IDENTIFICATION

Figure 10 shows a small, spoked circle, that looks very much like a sprocket, at the end of the runway at John Wayne Airport. This looks very much like the Harley sprocket that Hells Angel's motorcycle bikers would use to comb their hair. However, it is not. This is Jeppesen's symbol for the DME transmitter. This transmitter is located on the end of the runway, where the localizer transmitter is normally placed. Figure 11 shows the LOC DME (BACK CRS) - A approach to Santa Maria, CA. Notice that the DME antenna is now located at the beginning of the runway. It's very important to notice these subtle differences to help make sense of DME readings during an approach.

It's easy to make silly mistakes when flying IFR that can cause a great deal of grief. On one flight, while being vectored to the localizer at Santa Maria, my student tried to tune in the Guadalupe VOR frequency to receive DME information. Notice that there is no sprocket symbol inside the VOR, in figure 11. Gaviota VOR, (at the bottom of figure 11), has a sprocket inside the compass rose, in addition to having a small "D" in the frequency box. The sprocket symbol and the "D" both indicate that DME is available on this navaid. It's not available on the Guadalupe VOR. To prevent this problem, the profile view states that pilots should use ISMX DME when on the localizer course. My student was unaware of this and was making a classic, but unforgivable mistake.

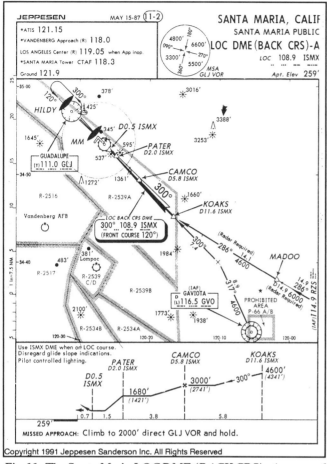

Fig. 11. The Santa Maria LOC DME (BACK CRS) -A approach.

As a fight instructor, I often wait and see what the student is going to do in these unusual situations. Often, these types of dynamic lessons are the most valuable they'll ever experience. They are also some of the most entertaining experiences instructors can have. As an educator, fortune was on my side. The DME started picking up false signals. My student thought it was working perfectly. Since it was VFR, I unplugged his headset from the intercom, then called the tower and requested a low pass with a straight out departure. I then reconnected the plug of his headset. He didn't have a clue what I was doing. He became so involved with the approach, focusing on variable DME information and tracking a back course, that he experienced temporal distortion and lost track of time. After 13 minutes, I asked him to look up. He lifted the hood and stared out at the Pacific ocean. In fairness, I have never heard as cool a remark from a student in my 21 years of flying. He calmly and slowly turned his head towards me, lifted the hood a little further, and with the composure of Mr. Spock said, "Flood?" He then tried to put the hood back on and hide like an ostrich, but I wrestled it away from him.

One word of caution is in order when using DME to identify intersections. The Crescent City ILS DME 11 approach is shown in figure 12. Notice that SLAMM intersection is identified by the 5.0 DME distance from CEC. What is CEC? It's the VOR located on the field. This could catch the unwary pilot who thinks that the DME reading is taken off the ILS. The ILS doesn't show the letters "DME" on top of the frequency box. In addition, any DME identification, taken off a localizer, will have an "I" listed next to the three letter navaid identification, as seen in figure 11. At Crescent City, pilots will have to tune their DME equipment to the CEC VOR and simultaneously receive the ILS frequency, as indicated in the profile view.

OVERHEARD IN CHICAGO

ATC: 32B, are you a Cessna Skymaster?

32B: Oh, no sir, I'm just a student pilot!

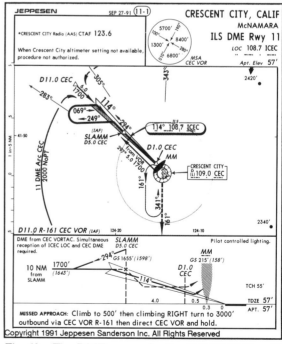

Fig. 12.   The DME source for the ILS DME Rwy 11 approach is located at the CEC VOR.

MINIMUM, MAXIMUM AND MANDATORY ALTITUDES

Altitude information for terminal routes and the approach procedure track is shown on the plan view and profile view respectively. Pilots should keep in mind that, the altitudes shown on terminal routes and in the profile section, are minimum altitudes, unless otherwise noted. When cleared for the approach, without altitude restrictions, a pilot's only obligation is not to go below these altitudes. Nothing says that pilots must descend to them either. This is especially important to consider during an instrument check ride. The PTS (Practical Test Standards) state that a pilot must not go below the minimum altitudes. If these altitudes are MDA's, found inside the FAF, then a descent must be made to within 100 feet of them, but, at no time, should the pilot go below them. A good practice is to descend to the closest hundred foot increment of the MDA and level off. If the MDA is 867 feet then level off at 900 feet. Once established at this altitude, the pilot can carefully nurse the airplane down to the specific MDA.

Figures 13 A and B, show Jeppesen's and the NOS's methods of depicting altitude restrictions on the charts. Jeppesen depicts the words "MANDATORY" or "MAXIMUM" next to the restricted altitudes, seen in figure 13A. NOS charts put a line over and under the restricted altitude when it's mandatory, as shown in figure 13B. Maximum altitudes are shown with a line above the altitude. IFR pilots are always a little

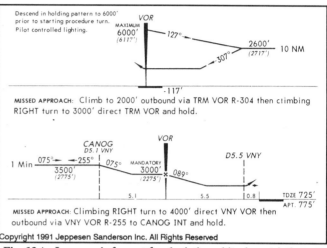

Fig. 13.A. Jeppesen's format for depicting altitude restrictions.

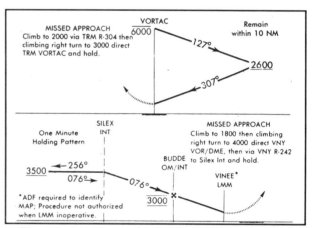

Fig. 13B. NOS format for depicting altitude restrictions.

nervous when altitude restrictions become critical. But this is a "good" nervousness. It keeps the senses sharp, as Mother Nature intended. A fellow pilot once had a little puppy dog that experienced a "bad" type of nervousness. It would wet the carpet everytime the phone rang. He was going to give it to the pound. I love animals, so I took the little fellow home. Then he started calling me every afternoon to see how his dog was doing. I made him buy me a new carpet!

PLAN VIEW ORIENTATION

The plan view is oriented to true north. Lines of latitude and longitude can be seen on the borders of the plan view, in figures 14 A and B. This becomes especially important when considering that Jeppesen's airport diagram is also oriented to true north. Consider the Dillon, Montana, VOR DME-B approach, as shown in figure 14A. If a decision was made to circle south of runway 21 for landing,

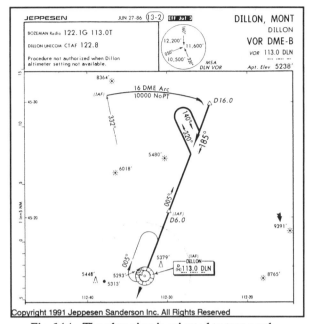

Fig. 14A. The plan view is oriented to true north.

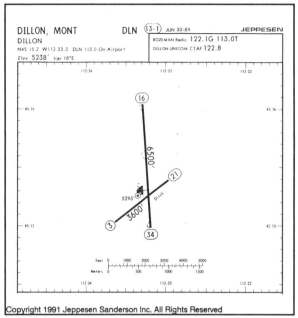

Fig. 14B. The airport diagram is oriented to true north.

the pilot could turn the chart over and look at the airport diagram on the reverse side. Figure 14B shows the airport diagram for Dillon. Since both charts are oriented to true north, pilots could mentally superimpose the approach direction onto the airport diagram. Therefore, approaching from the top right hand side of the approach chart means that pilots would be approaching from the top right hand side of the airport diagram chart. This type of orientation makes it easier to identify how to plan the approach for landing.

NOS charts provide the airport diagram in the lower right hand corner, on most of their approach charts. All of the NOS airport diagrams have a small, thin arrow indicating the final approach course path towards the airport, as seen in figure 14C. These arrows are small and difficult to see, but are very useful in helping orient pilots to runway configuration. Perhaps this is one good reason why medical examiners thoroughly examine a pilot's eyes during the medical

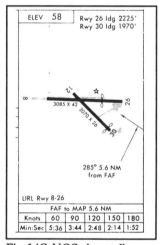

Fig. 14C. NOS airport diagram.

exam. This is one part of the medical exam that makes sense. However, as a student pilot, the one thing I couldn't understand was the part of the exam that had me hopping around on one foot for 20 seconds. I thought this was some unusual inflight maneuver, used to help dislodge stuck gear. For the most part, if pilots can see lightning and hear thunder, they need never worry about failing a medical examination.

THE PROFILE VIEW

Profile views provide pilots with a perspective of depth, when reading an instrument approach chart. The main purpose of the profile is to convey altitude information for letdown on the approach procedure track. This is why profile information is not to scale. Altitude limits need only be conveyed between fixes. This altitude information is provided in the profile, until pilots are positioned to use MDA's and DA's found in the minima section.

The profile view is used when pilots are established on the approach course and are positioned for either the procedure turn or the final descent for landing. Figure 15A shows the profile for the ILS Rwy 25R approach to Las Vegas, Nevada. A minimum altitude of 3,800 feet is shown as the glide slope intercept altitude. On NOS charts, the zigzag arrow, located above 3,800 in figure 15B, identifies the minimum altitude used to intercept the glide slope. If the localizer, or nonprecision portion of the approach is desired, 3,800 feet is the minimum altitude used to the Final Approach Fix at CONDY.

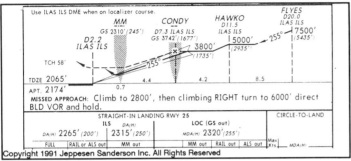

Fig. 15A. Dashed lines inside the FAF on Jeppesen charts mean that a nonprecision procedure exists on an ILS approach.

Jeppesen depicts the availability of a localizer approach on the same chart by a dashed line inside the FAF, as seen in figure 15A. Where this dashed line isn't present, no localizer or glide slope out procedure exists on that particular chart. An example of this can be seen in figure 15C for the Reno, Nevada, ILS Rwy 16R approach. There is a localizer approach available for Reno, but it requires using a different chart. Different charts may be required when approach course intercept altitudes or missed approach routes are substantially different between procedures. On NOS charts, a pilot can identify the availability of a localizer approach when localizer minima is listed in the minima section, as seen in figure 15B.

Holding pattern altitudes and glide slope intercept altitudes are sometimes shown together in the profile view. The ILS Rwy 9 approach to Riverside, California, figure 15D, shows both altitudes in the profile view. If pilots were instructed to hold at SWAN LAKE, the LOM, a minimum altitude of 2,800 feet would be maintained. This allows protection from obstructions, while circling in the holding pattern. When cleared for the ILS approach, pilots could descend to a glide slope intercept altitude of 2,500 feet, when established inbound on the localizer.

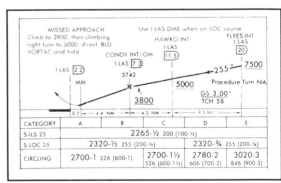

Fig. 15B. NOS depiction of glide slope intercept altitude.

While it's legal to intercept the glide slope at a higher altitude, there is always a possibility of intercepting a false signal. False glide slope signals may exist above the established signal. Intercepting from above is a good way to get snared by one. It's possible that the false signal may have an angle as high as 12.5 degrees. Additionally, there may be erratic needle movement and some reverse sensing. When students first start shooting ILS's, erratic needle movement appears quite normal to them. In fact, most student's ILS needles look like little windshield wipers clearing condensation off the inside of the glass. Pilots should always intercept the glide slope from below, at the

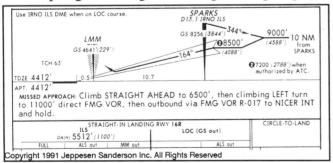

Fig. 15C. A nonprecision procedure doesn't exist when dashed lines are absent on the profile of an ILS approach.

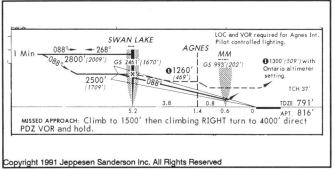

Fig. 15D. Holding pattern and glide slope intercept altitudes shown in the profile view.

recommended intercept altitude, whenever possible. The areas below a glide slope have been flight checked and shown to be free of false glide slope signals. This is the reason the Air Traffic Controller's Manual suggests that controllers give pilots vectors that lead to glide slope interception from below.

There is a way to detect entrapment by false glide slope signals. If the passengers throw their hands up over their head during the approach, as if they are riding a roller coaster, while yelling, "Wheeeee," this is usually a good sign a false signal is being flown. Using the glide slope crossing altitude, shown at the outer marker, is the best bet for identifying this false signal. When on glide slope, at the outer marker, the altimeter should show the glide slope crossing altitude, depicted in figure 16. At USTIK intersection, the glide slope crosses the marker at 4,020 feet MSL. With a centered glide slope needle, the altimeter should show this altitude. Performing this little check will prevent problems with false signals. Besides, this is a nifty way to check the glide slope for accuracy during an ILS approach. An altitude discrepancy means one of three things: interception of a false glide slope

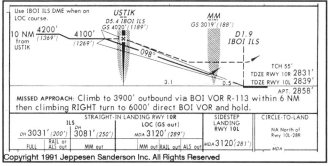

Fig. 16. Glide slope crossing altitudes shown at the outer and middle markers.

signal; the glide slope receiver is malfunctioning; or the selected altimeter setting is incorrect. It's interesting to consider that the VOR equipment in the aircraft has to be checked for accuracy, within 30 days of IFR flight, but there is no similar requirement for the glide slope receiver to be checked.

I look at flying an unverified glide slope in much the same way I do a "good deal" when bargain hunting. It's easy to purchase a microwave oven with cracked glass for just a few bucks! What one gets is a warm TV dinner and leukemia! It's not that great of a deal after all. Monitor those glide slopes to ensure flight safety.

THE CONTROLLER'S PRAYER

Our controller, thou art in the tower, minimum delay be thy name. Thy vector be done, as will be done, on the airway as it is on paper. Give us this day, our daily delay, and forgive us our altitude variations, as we forgive those who delay vector us, and lead us not into the mountains, but deliver us from the granite, amen.

The glide slope crossing altitude at the middle marker can help pilots with identifying their missed approach point. The glide slope crosses the middle marker at 3,019 feet MSL, in figure 16. With a Decision Altitude of 3,031 feet, aircraft on the glide slope will arrive at the missed approach point, just a little before reaching the middle marker. Remember, the missed approach point on an ILS is Decision Altitude, not the middle marker, even though they are located close together. With marker beacons operating on low sensitivity, pilots should anticipate hearing the marker at, or after, the time a decision is made about landing the airplane.

There are times Decision Altitude will be reached after passing the middle marker. Figure 17A shows the profile view for the Pueblo, Colorado, ILS Rwy 8L approach. Decision Altitude is reached after passing the middle marker by 50 feet. Pilots anticipating Decision Altitude, collocated with the marker beacon, might deprive themselves of getting as low as possible on an ILS approach.

Most pilots use the middle marker the same way they use a hotel operator -- for wake up calls. The middle marker is intended to alert pilots they are somewhere near Decision Altitude, and that it's

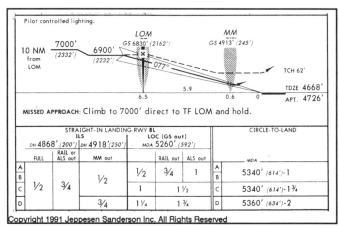

Fig. 17A. Pueblo, CO Rwy 8L ILS profile view and minima section.

time to pay close attention. A friend of mine has an unusual way of handling wake up calls in a hotel. Because wake up calls can be so intense, he gets a wake up call for the fellow in the next room. At least the ringing isn't as loud, and the slamming of the phone gently prods him out of bed.

It's not coincidence that the closer the pilot gets to the ground, the louder and more intense the marker beacon becomes. OM's are blue and have dashes, MM's are yellow and have dots and dashes, IM's (used for CAT 2 approaches) are white and have dots. Perhaps white was chosen to reflect the basic color of a pilot's knuckles when only a few feet off the ground and still in the clouds.

STRAIGHT STUFF STRATUS

Abracadabra

Twenty miles from our destination, we were instructed by Center to intercept the localizer and descend to 4,000'. Five miles outside the outer marker, Center said, "The other aircraft on the approach in front of you has landed; you are number one for the approach." We were level at 4,000'. For some reason, both my First Officer and I thought we were cleared for the approach and left 4,000' on the glide slope. Two miles outside the marker, we were at 3,600 feet and asked Center if we could switch to Tower. Center said, "You were only cleared to 4,000 feet," and informed us that another aircraft was departing. We then held at the outer marker, at 4,000 feet, until we were "cleared for the approach," after the other aircraft departed. This situation occurred because we did not hear the magic words, "Cleared for the approach," but were under the assumption we were cleared, because we were told we were "number one for the approach" and not told to hold, or expect any delay. The way to avoid this situation in the future sounds very basic, but you just do not leave your last assigned altitude on the approach until you hear the exact words, "Cleared for the approach," no matter how misleading everything and anything seems to you. **ASRS REPORT**

It's a good idea to keep the marker beacon switch set to the low sensitivity position when running any type of glide slope check. This allows a more precise determination of aircraft position over the marker. Many pilots, however, operate their marker beacon on high sensitivity, so the wider reception range gives them an earlier warning when nearing Decision Altitude.

INSIDE THE PARENTHESIS

Betting on the numbers in parenthesis can always be counted on to win something free to drink or eat at the airport. This is such a sure bet that it is possible to win an entire house and, possibly, a few acres of land. Figure 17A shows the procedure turn altitude of 7,000 feet, with (2,332) feet in parenthesis. Most pilots will immediately state that numbers in parenthesis are height above ground level. Well, prepare to move into a new house and farm the land. On the Jeppesen charts, numbers in parentheses are never heights above ground. They are either, heights above the airport elevation (HAA's), or heights above the touch down zone elevation (HAT's). The TDZE (touch down zone elevation) is the highest elevation in the first 3,000 feet of the runway surface.

Pilots flying straight-in approaches are concerned with their height above the landing runway. Therefore, numbers in parenthesis, on straight-in approaches, show HAT's. If 2,332 is added onto the TDZE of 4668 (shown in the profile), this will tally to an MSL altitude of 7,000 feet.

Pilots flying a circling approach, or using circling MDA's, are concerned about their height above the airport elevation. Numbers in parenthesis for all circling approaches, or circling MDA's, are HAA's. For a circling approach, or any circling minima, numbers in parenthesis are heights above the airport elevation. The logic here is that the airplane will be circling around the airport and not a specific runway; therefore, the airport elevation is used. Category A circling minima is 5,340 MSL, with an HAA of 614 feet. Adding 614 to the airport elevation of 4726 totals to 5,340, the circling MDA.

Glide slope crossing altitudes have additional uses. A quick check of the outer marker glide slope crossing altitude, in figure 17A, indicates an airplane will be 2,162 feet above the TDZE, when on the glide slope, at the outer marker. With a 500 foot per minute rate of descent, and 2,162 feet to descend through, the airplane tires can be expected to touchdown in a little over 4 minutes. Certain air carriers set their altimeters to read "0" feet upon touchdown. Numbers in parenthesis are very important for these carriers, since one or more of their altimeters is always set to read the HAT and HAA number values.

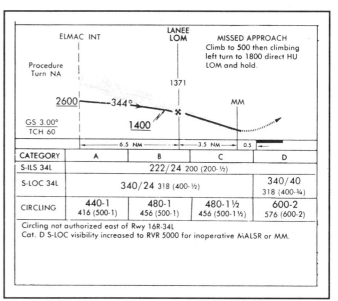

Fig. 17B. NOS charts don't depict HAT and HAA in the profile view nor are they depicted in parenthesis.

On NOS charts, HAT's and HAA's are only found in the minima section. Unlike Jeppesen charts, the HAT's and HAA's are not found in parentheses. They are identified by small numbers near the MDA's and DA's, as shown in figure 17B. For a straight-in ILS 34L approach, an aircraft will be at 200 feet HAT at Decision Altitude. A category A circling approach will put an aircraft at 416 feet HAA at the MDA. Numbers in parenthesis are military minima. Pilots shouldn't use these numbers, unless they are in the military. It's possible that some flight schools may make a pilot feel like they are in the military, but this doesn't count. I had a military instructor who almost made a fortune off me during my first instrument lesson. He said, "Well, let's see, you came in at eight hundred hours and left at ten hundred hours, so that's a difference of two hundred hours. At $10 per hour, you owe me $2,000." I felt a large aorta going to my wallet.

THE FINAL APPROACH FIX

Personally, I have never liked the term, "Final Approach Fix." This always sounded a little too pessimistic for me. Neither do I like the term, "Terminal forecast" or "Final controller." Combine these with terms like "Nonprecision approach" and pilots can easily get the willies. Use of these terms can be quite

discomforting during an approach when the controller states, "32 Bravo, turn left, intercept the FINAL approach course and when at the FINAL approach fix, contact the FINAL controller and tell him you're doing a NONPRECISION approach and would like a TERMINAL forecast." If student pilots hear this, they are going to start showing up for their flights wearing dark robes with hoods. Since pilots are stuck with these terms, they should make it a point to understand a few of them in depth.

The Maltese Cross, at the outer marker, identifies the final approach fix for a nonprecision approach. This is where the final descent to landing is made. Technically,

there is no final approach fix on an ILS approach. Because pilots start down on the glide slope at different altitudes, the final descent for landing takes place at variable locations along the localizer. Therefore, the final approach point is wherever the glide slope is intercepted and the final descent started.

This technical definition is important for instrument pilots to comprehend. When flying a localizer approach (nonprecision), the airplane should start down upon reaching the Maltese Cross. On a precision approach (ILS), the final descent is made when the glide slope is intercepted. This will normally occur before reaching the Maltese Cross. Most inexperienced instrument pilots make the mistake of flying to the Maltese Cross before starting down on the glide slope. They usually end up way above the glide slope and must commence a steep descent to intercept the needle. As soon as the glide slope needle centers, and they have been cleared for the approach, they should commence their final descent.

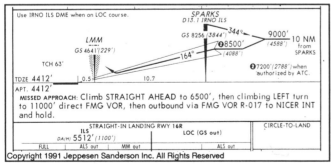

Fig. 18A. No nonprecision approach procedure is established for the Reno ILS 16R approach.

Figure 18A depicts the profile and minima section for the Reno, Nevada, ILS Rwy 16R approach. Notice that there is no Maltese Cross shown in the profile. This indicates that there is no nonprecision (localizer only) approach associated with this procedure. The minima section only depicts a Decision Altitude. It doesn't depict an MDA for a straight-in localizer (GS out) procedure, or circle-to-land operations. ATC should not request pilots to circle-to-land on this approach, since there are no minima allowing this procedure.

Figure 18B depicts the profile and minima section for the Van Nuys, California, ILS Rwy 16R approach. The profile shows a Maltese Cross, despite the minima section showing that no LOC (GS out) minima is available. The presence of a Maltese Cross means that some portion of the approach culminates in a Minimum Descent Altitude, rather than a Decision Altitude. The presence of circling minima is the clue. If pilots are cleared for the ILS Rwy 16R to Van Nuys by approach control, and are requested to circle-to-land on another runway, they should fly the glide slope down to the circle-to-land MDA. When leveling off at this MDA, they should continue to the missed approach point. Since the

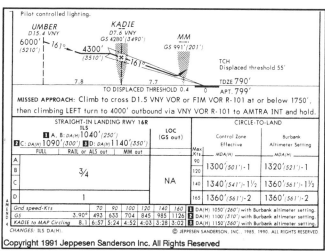

Fig. 18B. The Van Nuys ILS Rwy 16R approach.

circle-to-land missed approach point is not based on DA, it must be determined by time from the FAF. At the bottom of the Jeppesen chart, the conversion table shows the time from KADIE to the MAP. Because the Jeppesen procedure states, "GS out NA," glide slope out operations are not authorized. Pilots are required to use the glide slope when descending to the circling MDA at Van Nuys. The "GS out NA" is Jeppesen's method of depicting that pilots are required to use the glide slope while descending to MDA on this approach, despite its culminating in an MDA vs. a DA.

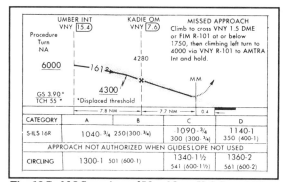

Fig. 18C. NOS version of Van Nuys ILS Rwy 16R approach.

Figure 18C shows the NOS version of this chart. It states, "Approach not authorized when glide slope not used" in the minima section. The reason the glide slope must be used for this procedure, and others similar to it, is to keep the airplane above the dangerous obstructions depicted along the approach procedure track. I really can't speak for other pilots, but, I would certainly feel a little discomfort if I looked out my window, while in the clouds, and caught a glimpse of a mountain goat! All the more reason to respect glide slope information. When ILS procedures list localizer minima, and don't show (GS out) restrictions, pilots experiencing glide slope failure can descend to the MDA and complete the approach as a non-precision procedure. This is a good reason to always start timing when over the FAF on an ILS.

STEP DOWN FIXES

A stepdown fix is found between the FAF and the MAP. It's associated with nonprecision approaches and serves a double purpose. First, a final approach segment can have excessive length. FAA requirements state that when the final approach segment exceeds six miles, the MDA must be increased by five feet, for each one-tenth of a mile over six miles. The intent is to protect pilots from flying long segment lengths, at very low altitudes. Errors in timing, navigation reception and weather related phenomena, could present unusual hazards at low altitudes for long periods of time.

Second, when obstructions are present along the final approach segment, a step down fix may be established, inside the Final Approach Fix, allowing lower minima for the procedure. These step down fixes will be established when at least an additional 100 foot descent can be achieved. Figure 19A shows the LOC Rwy 36L approach at Napa, California. ROOSE intersection is a step down fix, shown inside the FAF. An altitude of 600 feet would be maintained until reaching ROOSE, then a descent to 360 feet is allowed with Class D airspace effective. Pilots with a single VOR could legally identify the step down fix by tuning the 076 VOR cross radial, identifying ROOSE, then returning to the localizer. Things would get busy on this approach, while changing frequencies to identify the step down fix. In fact, the pilot's hands are going to be moving so fast it will be like watching a Bruce Lee, whop and chop, karate movie. Figure 19B shows the NOS version of the same approach chart.

There are times when additional equipment is required to identify a step down fix. When instrument procedures are flight checked by the FAA, the procedure specialist carefully studies pilot work load. A decision is made on the practicality of identifying a step down fix requiring a frequency change, while using a single radio.

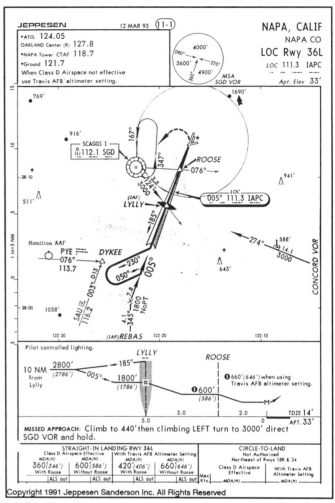

Fig. 19A. The localizer Rwy 36L approach to Napa, CA.

Where pilot work load is too intense to do this safely, a requirement for additional equipment will be listed. Figure 20A shows the ILS Rwy 9 approach to Riverside, California. AGNES intersection is the step down fix, identified by the 032 radial from the Paradise VOR. A note in the profile view states that LOC and VOR are required for AGNES intersection. Pilots without dual equipment cannot descend lower than 1260 feet on this procedure. Jeppesen makes a note in the profile of any additional equipment required for the step down fix. On NOS charts, the separate listing of minima will contain any requirements for additional equipment. Figure 20B shows the NOS depiction of the Riverside ILS minima. The slash (/) between LOC and VOR indicates that separate equipment is required to identify the stepdown fix. Figure 21 identifies other ways step down fix minima are listed on NOS charts.

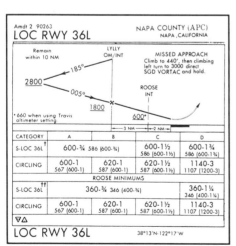

Fig. 19B. NOS version of the localizer Rwy 36L approach to Napa, CA.

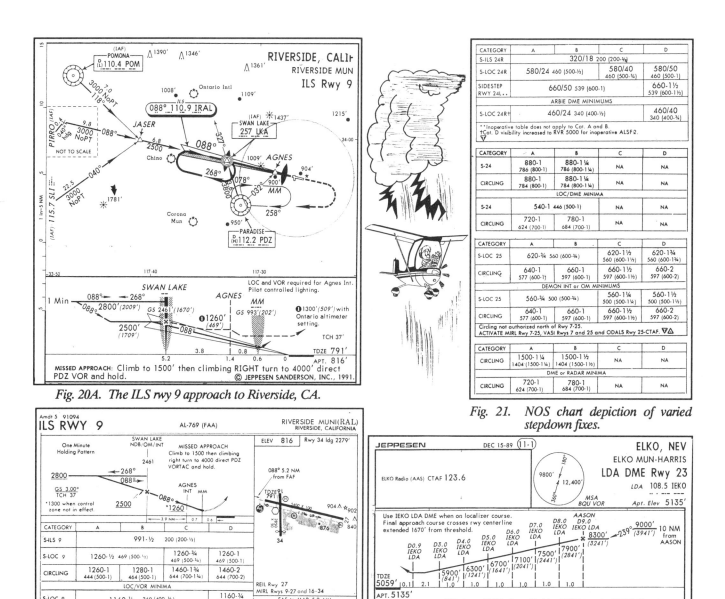

Fig. 20A. The ILS rwy 9 approach to Riverside, CA.

Fig. 21. NOS chart depiction of varied stepdown fixes.

Fig. 20B. NOS depiction of ILS Rwy 9 to Riverside CA.

Fig. 22. The Elko, NV LDA DME Rwy 23 approach.

When approaches are constructed, they are limited to only one step down fix inside the Final Approach Fix. The reason for this limitation is pilot workload. However, there are always exceptions to the rules. The Elko, Nevada, LDA DME Rwy 23 approach, figure 22, shows 6 step down fixes inside the FAF. This procedure had to be approved by the Great Kahoona in Washington before it was charted. Fortunately, DME makes defining the intersections on this approach easy and doesn't involve much pilot work load. All the pilot need do is fly the approach and watch the DME count down while making descents accordingly. In fact, this is such an easy approach that pilots are going to have to engage themselves in fake cockpit activity to maintain the respect of the passengers. The last thing pilots can afford, is to have the passengers find out how easy it is to fly. Experience shows that simply saying, "Roger, Houston" on the radio, is an effective way of impressing passengers during those lean workload times.

THRESHOLD CROSSING HEIGHTS

Pilots flying a wide-body (that's not a passenger, by the way) should be very interested in the threshold crossing height (TCH) shown in some profiles. Because a wide-bodied aircraft is so long, the glide slope antenna is going to cross the threshold at different altitudes than the rest of the airplane. The TCH, listed in figure 23, is 54

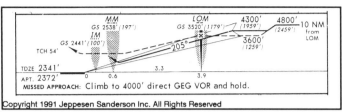

Fig. 23. The threshold crossing height (TCH) listed in the profile view.

feet, which means that the glide slope will cross the runway threshold at 54 feet. If any part of the wide-body happens to be more than 54 feet below the glide slope antenna, the passengers will land before the captain does. There's a good chance that half the lavatories, in the rear of the 747, will be ground down during the landing. Anyone, unfortunate enough to be using the lavatory at the time, will experience a whole new meaning to the phrase, "flying by the seat of the pants."

MISSED APPROACH INFORMATION

The profile view also contains valuable missed approach information. The most important consistency in all of aviation is that missed approaches always begin with a climb. If the missed approach begins with a descent then the pilot is probably reading the approach chart upside down. This is one of the FAA's 13 warning signs that a field sobriety test should immediately be issued to the pilot. Jeppesen makes their missed approach instructions easy to read by capitalizing the most important information. Figure 24 shows 5,000', 9,000', SLC VOR R-249, STACO INT/D20.0 Fix. Pilots should thoroughly understand the missed approach instruction. But, when the missed approach is started, a quick review can be made by looking at the capitalized information.

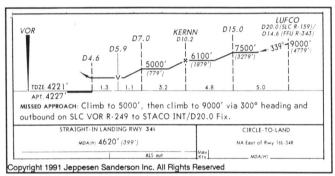

Fig. 24. Critical missed approach information is capitalized.

Talmudic Scholars study the Dead Sea Scrolls* because it's their business to know all about them. IFR pilots study their instrument charts for similar reasons. It's their business to know how to use them. These pilots realize that IFR charts are paper passports through inclement weather. Therefore, they deserve scholarly attention. Pilots should study their approach charts with the same intensity that cats study fish in an aquarium. Understanding the details of chart construction is sure to reward a pilot with the ability to better leverage the IFR system for safe flight operations.

Procedure turns are additional areas pilots should spend time studying. Understanding how to make an unaligned transition, from the enroute structure to the approach structure, is vital for survival in a non-radar environment.

---

*According to Woody Allen, the authenticity of the Dead Sea Scrolls is now seriously in doubt. Apparently the word "Oldsmobile" appears several times in the text.

14. PROCEDURE TURN SECRETS

Two telephone company crews were sinking telephone poles. At the end of the first day, the company foreman asked the first crew how many telephone poles they had put in the ground. "Fifteen," was the answer. "Fifteen?" the foreman replied. "That's excellent!" He asked the second crew how many telephone poles they had put in. "Four," came the answer. "Only four?" the foremen exclaimed. "The other crew did fifteen, and you guys only did four?" "Yes," said the leader of the second group. "But look how much they left sticking out of the ground."

A misunderstanding of the instructions can have humorous implications on the ground; in the air, it can be very dangerous. Pilots are sometimes required to make procedure turns during instrument approaches. Knowing when a procedure turn is required (it's not always obvious) and how to do it, depends on a pilot's ability to interpret the instructions on the approach plate.

If radar vectoring was available at all airports, 24-hours a day, procedure turns would not be required. Pilots would simply be vectored onto the approach course and left alone to complete the procedure. Even when radar is available, there's no guarantee it will continue to work. Therefore, instrument pilots are required to have some means of manually transitioning onto the approach course.

The procedure turn is aviation's version of a gymnast's full twisting dismount. Its purpose is to allow a transition from the enroute to the approach structure, in much the same way a transition is made from the parallel bars to the floor mat. In addition to course reversal, procedure turns allow pilots to lose unwanted altitude in preparation for the approach procedure.

THREE TYPES OF COURSE REVERSALS

Procedure turns* come in three basic types in the United States: the high altitude teardrop penetration, the 45/180 course reversal and the holding pattern course reversal, used in lieu of a procedure turn. Figure 1 shows all three of these types of course reversals. The high altitude teardrop penetration is perhaps the most rare, existing at only a few airports across the country. Its primary purpose is to permit a considerable loss of altitude, within limited airspace, during course reversal. High performance military aircraft frequently use these types of course reversals at military bases.

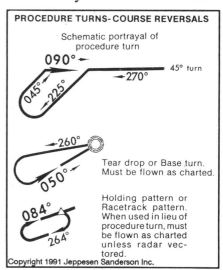

Fig. 1. Three types of course reversals.

*Procedure turn, as used in this book, means either a 45/180 reversal, a teardrop reversal or a holding pattern reversal.

Because of its unique design, pilots are required to fly the tear drop procedure exactly as charted. The most popular type of procedure turn is the 45/180 degree course reversal, with the holding pattern type coming in a close second.

YOKE'S ON YOU

The controller asked the wide-body for an orbit. The Captain replied, "Do you realize it costs 500 dollars every time we turn this aircraft through 180 degrees?" The unperturbed controller simply responded, "Well, give me a 1,000 dollar turn then."
ASRS REPORT

Considering that the 45/180 and the holding pattern reversals both serve the same purpose (course reversal), why would one be preferred over the other? The 45/180 type procedure turn allows a pilot greater ease in reversing course. Descents to minimum approach altitudes are accomplished with fewer turns compared to holding pattern reversals. However, the 45/180 procedure turn requires considerably more space than the holding course reversal. This could

present a serious problem if a procedure turn were to interfere with another airport's airspace. In addition, the longer 45/180 procedure turn could project into higher terrain, causing an unacceptable increase in procedure turn altitudes. This could make the procedure impractical by requiring abnormally steep descent rates during the approach. A solution to the terrain and airspace problem is to use a holding pattern for course reversal. This consumes much less space and accomplishes the same objective. However, it generally involves a higher workload for the pilot.

AIRPORTS WITHOUT COURSE REVERSALS

Some approaches, like the VOR-A to Tracy, California, figure 2, don't show any procedure turn at all. The lack of terminal routes available for transitioning aircraft onto the approach course, often limits the need for procedure turns. There is only one terminal route onto the approach course at Tracy, and this comes directly from the Manteca VOR. Of course, this means that pilots may have to go a great deal out of their way to get to the Manteca VOR to complete this approach. This routing requires no procedure turn to align the aircraft with the approach course. Herein lies the value of procedure turns. They allow pilots to approach the airport from many directions and easily reverse course.

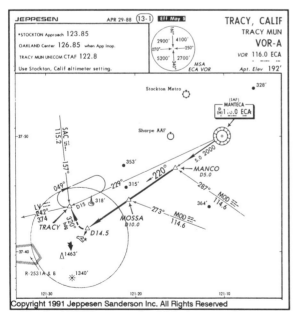

Fig. 2. A VOR approach which does not show a procedure turn.

WHEN IT'S REQUIRED

There are times when pilots must do certain things and not do others. At Miami International, pilots can signal the tower that they are being hijacked by going to the end of the runway after landing, leaving their flaps down, engine(s) running and not talking to anybody. The tower would call the police over to shoot out the tires of the airplane. When student pilots land at any airport, what do they usually do? They usually go to the end of the runway, leave their flaps down with the engine running, and they don't talk to anybody. It's possible that the police could show up and shoot out the student's tires. These students would naturally start thinking to themselves, "Well, I'm sure not coming back here anymore. These folks aren't very friendly!" Fortunately, experienced pilots do the right things because they know the rules. Knowing the rules for procedure turns is a must for instrument pilots.

Many approach charts have several terminal routes approaching from all different directions. Not all these terminal routes require that a procedure turn be made. Terminal routes that are approximately aligned with the approach procedure, and have a small descent requirement, don't require that a procedure turn be made. Terminal routes inbound to the approach procedure, not requiring a procedure turn, are easy to identify. Figure 3 shows two terminal routes from the Pomona VOR and the Seal Beach (SLI) VOR. Both go directly to JASER intersection. These routes are labeled with the letters "NoPT," meaning no procedure turn is required, or allowed, unless permission from ATC is obtained. Therefore, pilots cleared for the approach from either of these two VOR's would be expected to proceed inbound from JASER, without using the holding pattern, and complete the approach. Obviously, there would be no need to reverse course, or lose altitude, on this segment.

If a procedure turn is not allowed, why might a pilot desire to do one? There are times when an approach is commenced from a higher than normal altitude. Making a couple of turns in the holding pattern, or flying a 45/180 course reversal, would be a comfortable way to lose this additional altitude.

The route from the Paradise VOR to the ILS poses a different problem. There are no letters indicating "NoPT" on this route. Lack of these letters means that the procedure turn is required. If a clearance was received for the approach from over the PDZ VOR, the pilot should track outbound on the 327 degree radial, and descend no lower than 3,800 feet. When reaching SWAN LAKE intersection, a parallel entry should be made into the holding pattern, to reverse course and lose altitude. During the parallel entry, a descent to 2,800 feet could be made, as shown in the profile view. After paralleling the localizer outbound for one minute, a 210 degree left turn is made to intercept the localizer. When established inbound on the localizer, a minimum 2,500 foot glide slope intercept altitude can be used.

Most instrument students, when seeing a holding pattern, might want to make a 180 degree turn and head back to their departure airport. They act like Chicken Teriyaki -- the world's oldest, living Kamikaze pilot. Pilots should be brave, like Jacques Cousteau. This could be a wonderful adventure. However, I did mention this at a seminar one time, and a student carefully pointed out that he has never seen Jacques Cousteau actually go into the water. He always seems to be sending his crew into the ocean to talk to the killer whales and man-eating clams.

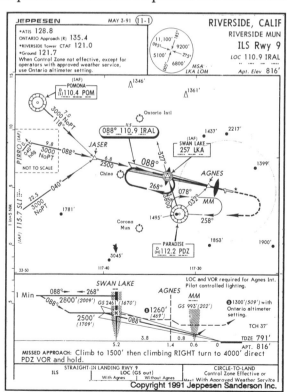

Fig. 3. Terminal routes from the POM and SLI VOR don't require that a procedure turn be made.

Figure 4 shows the Ontario, Oregon, NDB Rwy 32 approach. All the routes on the plan view leading to the Ontario NDB require that a procedure turn be made. One of the unique responsibilities for pilots is deciding what direction to turn, to intercept the outbound procedural course, upon reaching the IAF. There is no requirement that a pilot must turn in any specific direction to fly the procedural course outbound. However, common sense dictates that the aircraft be turned toward the side on which the 45/180 reversal is made. Greater obstacle protection is offered on this side of the course reversal. Logically, pilots approaching from HOVEL and HOSTS intersections would turn right, intercept and track out outbound on the 155 degree bearing from the station. A right turn at the IAF (Initial Approach Fix), when approaching from these intersections, is the shortest direction to turn to align the aircraft with the procedural course outbound.

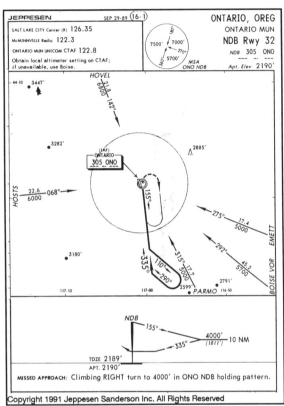

Fig. 4. All routes leading to the Ontario NDB require that procedure turns be made.

Pilots approaching from Boise VOR, or PARMO and EMETT intersections, can make either a right or left turn to intercept the procedural course outbound. A right turn would keep the aircraft on the side that the 45/180 reversal is made. This side offers greater obstacle protection. However, turning left would be the quickest way to intercept the procedural course. Pilots have the option of turning in either direction to intercept the procedural course, upon reaching the IAF. Adequate obstacle protection is provided for either a right or left hand turn, at the IAF to intercept the procedural course outbound.

The area of obstacle protection is always slightly greater on one side of the procedural course. This is designed to protect pilots when they depart the outbound procedural course at a 45 degree angle, then make a 180 degree turn, after one minute, to reintercept the course inbound. Additionally, it also protects pilots flying a holding pattern with turns being made to one side of the procedural course.

OBSTACLE PROTECTION

Procedure turns guarantee pilots a minimum of 1,000 feet of obstruction clearance in the protected airspace of the primary area, as depicted in figure 5. The boundaries of the protected airspace are created by radii from two points, which are offset to the side of the procedural course on which turns will be made. Starting 1 mile to the side of the fix from which the procedure turn starts (usually the IAF), two radii are drawn, one 5 NM's and the other 7 NM's. Moving outbound the allotted distance of

AIRCRAFT LIMITATIONS

Controllers work aircraft with a wide range of performance. Several years ago a Center controller was handling an SR-71. This is one of those aircraft whose turning radius is calibrated in time zones instead of miles. The SR-71 pilot reported on frequency and said, "Ma'am, this is Blackbird 431-Charlie, we're going to Randolph Airforce Base, and ma'am, we don't do turns!" I often wondered what any instrument students may have been thinking after hearing this? Perhaps one of the students, in a Cessna 172, looked over at his instructor and said, "Hey, I'm going to tell them that we don't do turns either!" I can assure all pilots that this statement won't be found in the AIM.
Author

the procedure turn, a spot 2 miles on the turning side is established. Radii of 6 NM's and 8 NM's are established at this point. These radii create inner and outer arcs that are connected by tangent lines. The area inside these tangent lines establishes the primary and secondary boundaries of protected airspace. The primary area provides 1,000 feet of obstacle clearance. The secondary area provides 500 feet of protection at the inner edge, tapering uniformly to zero feet at the outer edge. It's apparent that slightly more obstacle protection area is established on the turning side of the procedural course. This is called the "Maneuvering Zone."

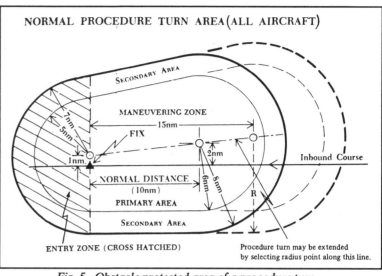

Fig. 5. Obstacle protected area of a procedure turn.

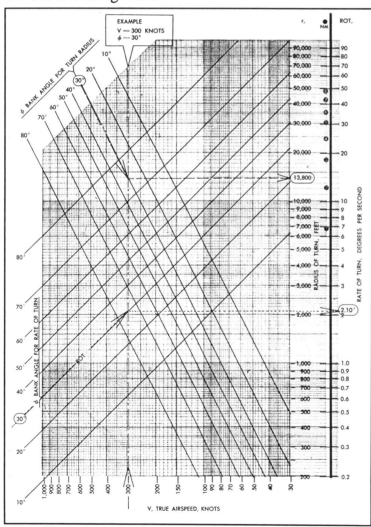

Fig. 6. Bank angle for turn radius and rate of turn chart.

AIRCRAFT TURNING RADIUS

Pilots should always have a good idea of the turning radius of their aircraft. This allows them to feel confidence in knowing they will not exceed the protected airspace of procedure turns, airways and circling areas. Figure 6 shows how to determine the radius of turn for a given bank angle and true airspeed. Assuming a no wind situation, an aircraft with a 30 degree bank* and true airspeed of 250 knots, would have a turn radius of approximately 9,700 feet, approximately 1.6 nautical miles (1 NM = 6,080 feet). The aircraft's diameter of turn would be (2 x 1.6) 3.2 NM. The primary area of the procedure turn, extends four nautical miles on the non-turning side of the procedural course, as shown in figure 5. Even at 250 knots of groundspeed, an aircraft inbound from PARMO, figure 4, making a left turn outbound at the IAF, would be .8 NM from the boundary of the secondary area. In other words, the aircraft would still remain within the primary area of protection as it turns outbound on the non-turning side to intercept the procedural course.** Considering that procedure turns are designed to be flown at speeds less than 250 knots IAS, general aviation aircraft, flying at lower speeds, will remain well within the primary protected area of the procedure turn.

*30 degrees is the maximum used (25 degrees for aircraft using flight directors) when a standard rate turn requires a steeper bank.
**The non-turning side is technically called the non-procedure turn side of the course reversal. However, this doesn't mean that pilots can't do their course reversal on this side. Personally, I prefer to do all my turns on the procedure turn side of the course reversal, whenever possible.

Exceeding the protection of the primary area and entering the secondary area of the procedure turn is very risky. Obstacle protection diminishes rapidly in this area. This is very similar to the danger a man experiences when his wife approaches him and asks, "Honey, would you ever tell me if I was getting fat?" Real danger exists here! A lady friend once asked me this and I said, "Sure honey, and maybe you would tell me if my brain is not getting enough oxygen!" This linguistic counter move is real nifty for staying away from the serious danger associated with truthfully answering this question. Men should avoid these questions if they like to sleep indoors. With similar caution, pilots should avoid the danger associated with the entering the secondary area of protection.

TURNING INBOUND

When a holding pattern type procedure turn is shown, it must be flown as charted. No variations are allowed. Additionally, standard entries should be used to enter the pattern for course reversal. When a procedure turn, other than a holding pattern or tear drop course reversal is shown, pilots may fly any variation of the turn they desire, as long as it's done in the maneuvering zone, figure 5. Do not make the 45/180 reversal on the side opposite of the maneuvering zone. Pilots could easily run out of obstacle protected airspace if they attempted to do so. It makes a lot more sense to fly what is published, instead of being creative and making up a brand new version of the procedure turn. Besides, the act of flying is 99% discipline and 1% creativity. However, don't despair. Talking about flying is just the other way around. A pilot's creative need is best met by taking an art class. In fact, I enrolled in a Pablo Picasso correspondence art course to help meet my creative needs. Unfortunately, I didn't do that well. While sketching, I kept putting an eye on each side of the face.

While outbound on the procedure turn at Ontario, figure 4, pilots could descend to a minimum of 4,000 feet. When inbound, they can descend to the minimum altitude shown in the profile. The Ontario NDB Rwy 32 approach is peculiar in that it doesn't have a Final Approach Fix. Therefore, the final approach is started when pilots are established inbound on the 335 bearing. At this point, a descent to the MDA can be made.

MISSED APPROACH HOLDING PATTERNS

Pilots often become confused about the purpose of the thin line holding pattern shown at the Ontario NDB, in figure 4. Thin line holding patterns are used for the missed approach. They are not part of the procedure turn. An aircraft making a missed approach at Ontario would proceed to the NDB and hold as published. Many years ago, when a missed approach holding pattern was established on the procedure turn course, the FAA would place the following note on the IFR chart: "Approach from holding pattern not authorized, procedure turn required." This restriction has disappeared from many IFR charts.

The FAA assumes that pilots, holding at the NDB after a missed approach, would execute the complete procedure turn, if cleared for another approach. In the case of Ontario, while it's not illegal to start an approach from the missed approach holding pattern, doing so may require excessively steep descent rates to arrive at the MDA prior to the MAP. Therefore, it's best, in similar instances, to fly a complete procedure turn, when cleared for the approach, from the missed approach holding pattern.

WHY IS IT REQUIRED?

Often, it's not at all clear why a procedure turn is necessary, even though one is depicted. The VOR-A for Colusa, California, figure 7, shows a terminal route from RUMSY intersection, located at the bottom, left hand side of the plan view. This routing requires a procedure turn be made. However, it appears that it would be so much easier to turn straight in from over the VOR and descend to the MDA. Pilots doing this would be sharing descent profiles similar to those used by the space shuttle. The minimum altitude from RUMSY to the VOR is 5,000 feet. The profile shows 2,000 feet for crossing the VOR. This is an extra 3,000 foot drop!

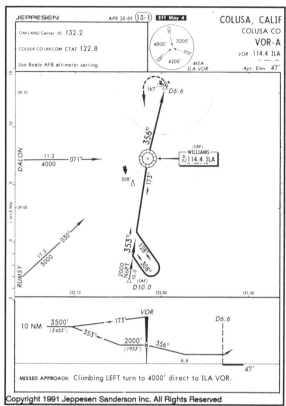

Fig. 7. *Terminal routes from RUMSY and DALON require that procedure turns be made.*

Charting criteria require that a procedure turn be established when excessive altitude and angles are necessary to turn onto the final approach segment. The Williams VOR serves as both a Final Approach Fix and as an Initial Approach Fix. The VOR acts as the Final Approach Fix, when pilots descend to the MDA from over its position. When the procedure turn is started from over the VOR, then Williams is acting as an Initial Approach Fix. If the approach were allowed from RUMSY without a procedure turn, a 34 degree turn would be required to align the airplane with the final approach segment. Charting criteria require that a procedure turn be made when the difference between the terminal route and the final approach segment is greater than 30 degrees. Additionally, when there is a difference of more than 300 feet between the minimum terminal route altitude and the FAF crossing altitude, then a procedure turn is required. Pilots trying to descend from 5,000 feet over Williams VOR, down to an airport elevation of 47 feet, will probably land so fast that they will have all three of their tires disappear in a puff of smoke. Controllers may get whiplash watching the aircraft land.

ALL THREE WHEELS COULD DISAPPEAR IN A PUFF OF SMOKE IF PILOTS DESCEND TOO QUICKLY ON AN INSTRUMENT APPROACH.

Figure 8 shows the San Luis Obispo VOR-A approach. A terminal route from FRAMS intersection doesn't require a procedure turn. Notice the difference between the inbound course to the VOR and the final approach segment. It is 28 degrees. Also, there is no difference between the minimum altitude along the inbound routing and the FAF crossing altitude at the VOR. Both these minimum altitudes are 2,800 feet. Therefore, no additional descent, nor turn of more than 30 degrees, is required to align the aircraft with the final approach segment.

Procedure turn distance limits are predicated upon the amount of altitude required to be lost before turning inbound. Procedure turn distances vary from 5 to 15 miles. The most frequently used distance is the 10 NM procedure turn, as shown in figure 9. A 3,000 foot procedure turn altitude is shown, followed by a 2,700 foot glide slope intercept altitude. Once established inbound on the localizer, pilots may leave 3,000 for 2,700 feet. Pilots are not required to fly the entire distance shown in the profile when completing the procedure turn. They should remain within the depicted distance shown in the profile, and turn when they are ready. I usually fly procedure turns at 90 knots IAS. Assuming no wind, the aircraft is covering 1.5 nautical miles per minute. Traveling outbound for 4 minutes would put the aircraft 6 miles from LASSN. This keeps me within the maximum distance and gives me enough time to lose any unnecessary altitude.

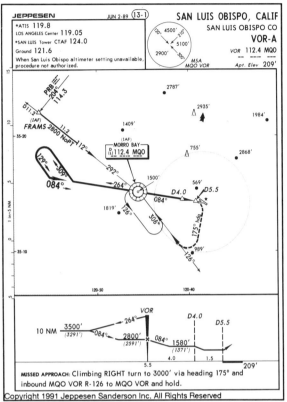

Fig. 8. The terminal route from FRAMS intersection doesn't require that a procedure turn be made.

PROCEDURE TURN DISTANCES

Pilots flying a holding pattern, in lieu of the 45/180 procedure turn, don't have the liberty of varying the distance flown outbound. Holding patterns, used for course reversal, must be flown as charted. Figure 10 depicts a one minute holding pattern at the VOR. Pilots should take no liberty in modifying the time. Figure 11 shows a variation of the holding pattern. At Red Bluff, California, the VOR DME Rwy 15 approach, shows a holding pattern with 4 NM legs. This presents no equipment problems for the pilot, since the approach requires DME equipment.

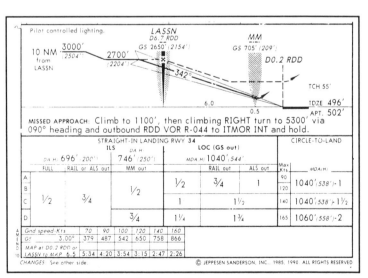

Fig. 9. Procedure turn distances and altitudes.

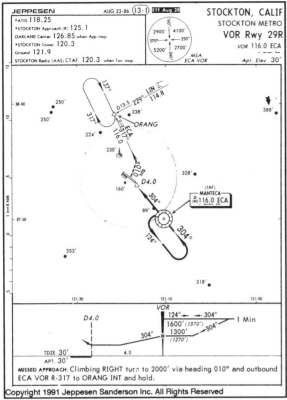

Fig. 10. *Holding patterns used for course reversal must be flown as charted.*

RACE TRACK PATTERN CONFUSION

There are times when a holding pattern, used for course reversal, can offer its own brand of confusion. The VOR-A approach to Corona, California, in figure 12, portrays only the holding pattern in the plan view. What is missing are the terminal routes. A pilot's first impulse is to question how an airplane can transition to the approach structure if there are no terminal routes depicted on the approach chart. Radar vectoring is one way to transition from the enroute structure to the approach structure. However, in this instance, there are approach transitions available, but they are not portrayed on the plan view. The answer lies with the low altitude enroute chart or the area chart.

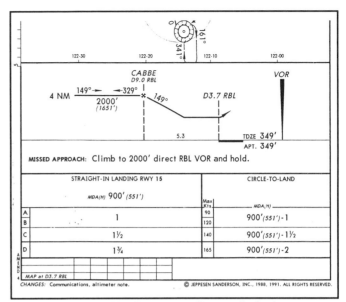

Fig. 11. *Holding pattern distance limitation.*

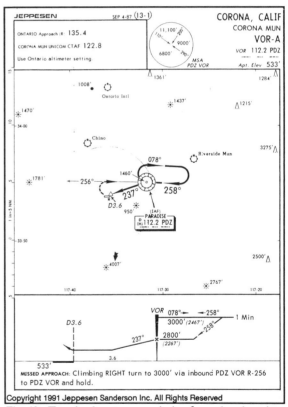

Fig. 12. *Terminal routes are missing from the plan view.*

Low altitude airways are not shown on the approach chart plan view, yet they are a viable means of transitioning to the approach course. The FAA doesn't require that airways be depicted on approach charts since they are already portrayed on low altitude enroute charts. Additionally, when an IAF is established on an approach chart, it is generally intended to be a fix that's common to the enroute structure as well.* This allows a pilot to more easily transition from the enroute to the approach

*There are exceptions to this. Therefore, pilots shouldn't depend on finding all the IAF's listed on the approach chart, as intersections on the enroute chart. Additionally, area charts, because of their greater detail, may have to be consulted to find these intersections.

structure with less ambiguity. Certainly, this is the case at the Paradise VOR. The VOR provides airway guidance and acts as the starting point for the procedure turn. The low altitude enroute chart, figure 13, shows eight separate airway segments converging on the Paradise VOR. It's likely that a pilot may be on any one of them when being cleared for the VOR-A approach into Corona.

Fig. 13. Airway segments leading to Paradise VOR.

Assume an airplane is inbound from the northwest on V-197, and radar vectoring is not available. When the aircraft is a few miles from the VOR, ATC issues a clearance for the VOR-A approach to Corona airport. Is the pilot required to execute the procedure turn (i.e. enter the holding pattern for course reversal), or can the pilot turn inbound to Corona on the final approach segment? There is no depiction on the airway or the approach chart which waives the procedure turn. The FAA's position, in these instances, is that the procedure turn is always required, unless "NoPT" is noted on the approach chart.* Therefore, pilots approaching the Paradise VOR from any direction, either by airway or direct route, are required to make an entry into the holding pattern for course reversal. Of course, when radar vectored, pilots are not expected to make the procedure turn unless they specifically request this from the controller. After all, the purpose of vectoring is to align the aircraft with the approach course. Therefore, there will be no need to fly a procedure turn.

The rationale behind the rule requiring the holding pattern to be used for course reversal is based on pilot workload. Pilots may be approaching the VOR from many different directions and altitudes, similar to what's experienced at Paradise. Aircraft transitioning from the enroute structure may need time to prepare for the approach. Pilots, caught high and fast on the approach, should wear scuba watches because of all the pressure they are going to be under to get their aircraft down! Fortunately, the course reversal allows aircraft to be slowed and configured for the instrument procedure. Additionally, course reversals are required whenever transition routes take aircraft to the point where the procedure turn begins (this point is always an IAF). This is required because the aircraft is either converging on the approach course at too great an angle, or must make too steep a descent on the course.

ALTO SERIOUS CIRRUS

Drip, Drip, Drip...

It was a gloomy day with a steady light rain falling. It was also a good day to practice IFR holding and approaches and also get some actual. The instructor waited inside while his student preflighted the small aircraft. Observing that the student had finished the preflight, the instructor ran outside and quickly got in the plane (to avoid the rain). He asked the student how the oil and fuel looked. Both were reported as full. After about 45 minutes of IFR airwork, the instructor noticed the fuel gauges were almost on empty. He knew the tanks had been full before takeoff, so he flicked the gauges with his finger in disbelief, hoping they were only stuck. When they stayed on empty, the instructor headed back to the airport and landed safely. After landing he checked the tanks, and both were nearly dry. What went wrong? During the hurried preflight, the student pulled up on the lever to drain a fuel sample. The lever did not snap back into the closed position, as usual. As it was raining, the student did not notice that the fuel was still draining out. Pretty lucky.

ASRS REPORT

*Reference: AIM Par.371b(3): "When a holding pattern replaces the procedure turn, the standard entry and the holding pattern must be followed except when RADAR VECTORING is provided, or when 'NoPT' is shown on the approach course."

For example, a procedure turn will help align the aircraft, when approaching Paradise VOR from the northwest, on V-197. The position from which the airplane is approaching would require a radical change in direction, if a turn was made onto the final approach segment into Corona. Therefore, a parallel entry into the holding pattern should be made for course reversal. Notice that the MEA on V-197 is 4,500 feet. A difference of 1,500 feet between the MEA on the airway and FAF crossing altitude exists. This is an additional 1,500 feet that must be lost in descending to the MDA. The procedure turn prevents the pilot from having to make steep descents on final approach.

Practical experience indicates that Air Traffic Controllers may not always expect pilots to make procedure turns, when approaching the IAF from enroute airways. Air Traffic Controllers are very efficient people. They are enchanted by the practical. Controllers, observing* an aircraft heading to a VOR (IAF), on an airway, may expect the aircraft to turn inbound at the fix and shoot the approach. After all, this seems like the most practical thing a pilot could do. This becomes even more likely an assumption when the airway has altitudes and directions, similar to the approach course. Of course, pilots are not allowed to do the practical in these rare instances. They are required to make a procedure turn. This type of confusion is more likely to occur in a radar environment, when the aircraft is not being vectored, but flying under its own navigation.

The reason this type of problem seldom results in conflict is that controllers usually ask about pilot intentions when they are not obvious. As a student, when they heard my voice, I was bombarded with requests for my intentions. Unpredictable Machado! The secret to avoiding these problems is to communicate with the controller. When making airway transitions to procedure turns, in situations similar to the Corona approach, pilots should always let the controller know what they plan to do.

When use of the holding pattern is required for course reversal, controllers expect pilots to make only the entry to establish themselves inbound on the approach course. They are not expected to make additional turns. If pilots desire to make additional turns in the holding pattern, they should obtain a clearance to do so from the controller. A few extra turns may be necessary to lose excessive altitude or to allow more time to prepare for the approach. Making additional turns without requesting permission could cause a traffic conflict. It's possible that ATC may clear someone else for the approach, thinking the airspace is clear. There could be few things worse for pilots than looking out the window and seeing themselves in a tight formation with a Boeing 747. The only good thing about this is they may get to watch the inflight movie while in formation with the airborne whale. Remember, Confucius say, "Pedestrian have the right of way, but rickshaw have more momentum."

How poor are they that have not patience!
Shakespeare (Othello)

After a hurry up dispatch on a Sunday morning, we flew to the destination airport. After being assigned the wrong altitude by the controller three times and having the frequency blocked by a scudrunner, our patience was running thin. We were finally cleared for the approach and completed the procedure turn. We were instructed to relay our landing time to the next aircraft holding to shoot the approach. We cancelled and got the airport in sight and landed: six miles short of the correct airport! The airport layout was just as depicted, and the runway heading was the same too. After landing and realizing the mistake, we completed the flight without any further inconvenience. Factors: Frequency congestion; confusing altitude misassignments; not staying on the approach; hurry up-itis. We hope, by way of this letter, we can help another flightcrew avoid this type of error.
ASRS REPORT

---

*That's observing, not vectoring. In many cases, pilots may be cleared for the approach in a radar environment and left alone to do their own navigation. Controllers would naturally monitor these aircraft to detect potential traffic conflicts.

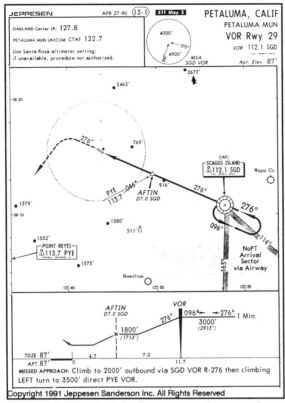

Fig. 14. NoPT arrival via airway sector, shown on chart plan view.

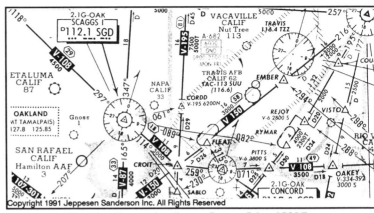

Fig. 15. Airways leading to Scaggs Island VOR.

Certain approach charts' plan views will contain restrictions to procedure turns. Figure 14 shows the VOR Rwy 29 approach to Petaluma, California. In the bottom, right hand side of the plan view, the chart lists: "NoPT Arrival Sector Via Airway." Arrivals on airways from this sector should proceed straight in to Scaggs Island VOR and not make an entry into the holding pattern. Figure 15 shows the airways leading to Scaggs Island VOR. NoPT arrival sectors are shown to clarify when procedure turns are not required because of adequate alignment and altitude compatibility with the procedure.

Knowledge is of value only when put to use. Many years ago when I was in the 8th grade, I was approached by the school bully. He walked up to me and said, "I'm going to punch your nose in." Having a reasonable command of the English language, I replied, "Don't you know that you're not supposed to end a sentence with a preposition?" He grunted, looked at me quizzically, then attempted to "punch in my nose." Knowledge is important, but it must be applied. Unlike the bully who wasn't smart enough to understand his grammatical faux pas, pilots need to be smart enough to apply their knowledge of procedure turns when radar is unavailable for navigation. Likewise, acquiring and applying knowledge of instrument approach segments is of equal importance for pilots.

15. APPROACH SEGMENTS

Whenever anyone in an airplane looks over and says, "Hey, want to see something really neat?," be suspicious! In the late 1960's, a student pilot departed a Fresno airport with his instructor. Fresno is located in the San Joaquin Valley, a large flat, agricultural area with miles of railroad tracks stitching the cities of California together. It was early evening, and the sun was just setting. The instructor leaned over to his student and said, "Hey, Bob, want to see something really neat?" Bob said, "Yeah, sure." The instructor said, "How would you like to see some sparks, Bob?" Not wanting to disappoint his instructor, Bob said, "Yeah, sure, let's see some sparks." The instructor leveled the airplane 15 feet above the railroad tracks as a train was approaching. He turned on the landing light and alternately

pushed the right and left rudder pedals. Looking straight ahead at the train, Bob at last managed to croak, "Eee gads! Look at all those sparks!" And somewhere, in the San Joaquin Valley, to this day, there is still a train rolling around with flat spots on its metal wheels.

It wasn't long after I heard this story that I was on an instrument training flight with my instructor. He looked over at me and said, "Hey, Rod, want to see something really neat?" I said, "NO, NO, NOT ME, NO WAY, FORGET IT, ABSOLUTELY NOT, NO, NO, NO!" He replied, "You mean you don't want to see this neat little thing I learned about approach segments?" I replied, "Oh, I thought you were...never mind." And so, I almost missed the opportunity to learn something really interesting about approach segment

composition. Learning goes that way; sometimes a pearl of wisdom is captured from the oyster, sometimes it's just "Aw, shucks." Little did I know how meaningful these pearls of wisdom about approach segments would become in enhancing my confidence about instrument approach procedures.

Instrument approaches consist of five parts: feeder routes, initial approach segments, intermediate approach segments, final approach segments and missed approach segments, as shown in figure 1. Each segment is designed to allow the pilot to safely, and comfortably, accomplish the specific objective of approaching an airport in IFR conditions. In much the same way that a staircase allows pedestrians to descend one step at a time, instrument approaches lower pilots in an orderly and progressive fashion. Each segment has a specific purpose. Pilots having an understanding of what each segment provides will better understand how to execute a specific instrument procedure.

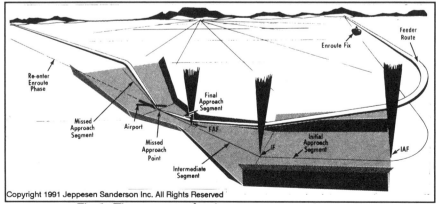

Fig. 1. The segments of an instrument approach procedure.

The basic idea of all these segments making up an instrument approach, is to take pilots from wide, expansive airways to fine, precision-like navigational tunnels that gently coerce reluctant aircraft from their minimum altitudes. Vertical and horizontal tolerances, speeds and margins of safety all become more critical as pilots approach the runway. The various segments are designed with this in mind. They take pilots from "lofty-above" back to their "surly-bonds." And they do it step-by-step, with forgiveness for excursion growing evermore stingy.

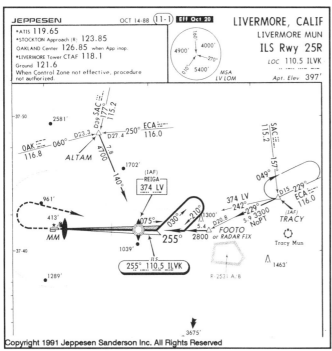

Fig. 2A. The approach segment from ALTAM is a feeder route, and the approach segment from TRACY is an initial appprach segment.

Approach segments are flown in a specific sequence. Starting with the feeder routes, the aircraft is taken to an initial approach fix (IAF). IAF's are identified on the plan view of the approach chart. Initial approach segments start at the initial approach fix (IAF), and proceed to the intermediate fix (IF). While IAF's are labeled with the letters (IAF), intermediate fixes are not labeled on U.S. approach charts. The intermediate segment takes the pilot to the final approach fix (FAF). When the FAF exists,* it is identified by a Maltese Cross in the profile view of the chart. When the missed approach point (MAP) is reached, the missed approach segment takes the pilot to the missed approach holding point.

INITIAL APPROACH SEGMENTS

Feeder routes are designed to transition airplanes from the enroute structure onto the approach procedure. These routes take aircraft to the place where the approach officially begins -- the initial approach fix.** Feeder routes are identified on charts by medium thick lines with arrows,*** minimum altitudes, distances and directions. Figure 2A shows an approach with its various segments for the ILS Rwy 25R at Livermore, California. Pilots can identify the route from ALTAM as a feeder route, since ALTAM is not labeled as an IAF. Figure 2B shows ALTAM as an enroute fix where pilots can transition onto the approach structure. If cleared for the approach over ALTAM, pilots should fly the 140 degree bearing to the locator outer marker and execute the procedure turn.

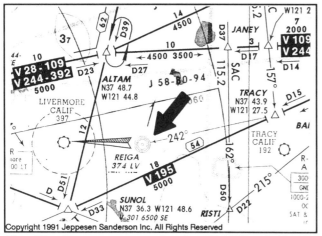

Fig. 2B. Enroute structure showing TRACY and ALTAM intersections and REIGA NDB.

*When there is a lack of navaids available for identifying an intersection on an approach, that approach may be constructed without an FAF. These procedures usually require the navaid to be located on, or near, the field and that the approach incorporate a procedure turn. (Ref:TERPS Par.400)

**A terminal routes is any route that has altitude, direction and distance accompanying it. A feeder route is any route that has altitude, direction and distance and takes the aircraft to the IAF. The distinction is made here for academic purposes. Pilots will have no problem if they just assume they are the same thing.

***As has been mentioned in Chapter 14, the medium thick line and the arrow could be missing from a terminal route, if there is not enough space to graphically portray this line.

Initial approach fixes can also be used to help an aircraft transition from the enroute to the approach structure. TRACY intersection, figure 2A, is an IAF and is also part of the enroute structure, as shown in figure 2B. Pilots, cleared for the approach from TRACY intersection, can proceed outbound on the 229 degree radial of ECA VOR to FOOTO intersection, then proceed inbound on the approach. When an IAF is a fix in the enroute structure, an approach made from this intersection will not normally require that a procedure turn be flown. But, this rule doesn't apply when the IAF is the point where the procedure turn begins. For instance, REIGA (an IAF), figure 2A, is the point where the procedure turn begins. REIGA is part of the low altitude enroute structure, since it's used as a navaid on the low altitude chart, figure 2B. Pilots approaching REIGA NDB, receiving a clearance for the approach, would be required to execute the procedure turn.

Procedure turns are a coarse (as well as, course) alignment maneuver, and hence, are always part of the initial approach segment. As such, they begin at the IAF. They lower the aircraft and turn it around, thereby aligning it with the intermediate segment, or the final approach segment. These two will be differentiated shortly.

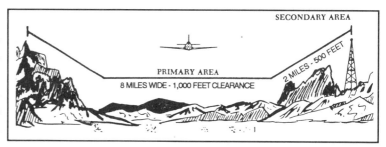

Fig. 3A. Primary & secondary protected areas of an initial approach segment.

When an aircraft is on the initial approach segment, it has departed the enroute phase of flight and is maneuvering to enter the intermediate segment. The initial approach segment can be flown as a DME arc, radial, course, heading, radar vector or any combination of these. While feeder routes provide the same obstacle clearance as airways, initial approach segments provide only 1,000 feet of obstacle clearance in both mountainous and non-mountainous terrain. The 1,000 foot terrain clearance, along the initial approach segment, is provided in a primary area extending 4 nautical miles on either side of the route, as seen in figure 3A. A secondary area of terrain clearance, extending 2 miles beyond the primary area, provides 500 feet of terrain clearance at the inner edge, tapering to zero at the outer edge. Figure 3B shows the required obstacle clearance for the initial segment, as well as other segments of the approach.

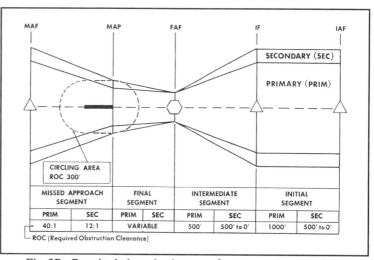

Fig. 3B. Required obstacle clearance for approach segments.

There is no standard length for the initial approach segment, but it seldom exceeds 50 nautical miles. When any portion of the initial approach does exceed 50 nautical miles from the navigational facility, the width and obstruction criteria for enroute airways apply to that portion.

The purpose of the initial approach segment is to align the aircraft with the intermediate segment. During this segment, pilots can make adjustments in heading and altitude in preparation for the final descent to land. This explains why the initial approach segment doesn't provide 2,000 feet of obstacle clearance in mountainous terrain, as do feeder routes. Far too much altitude would need to be lost in preparation for the approach.

Initial approach segments are not as restrictive with turns and descents as are other segments of the approach. Descent gradients for all approach segments are shown in figure 3C. The optimum descent gradient for the initial approach segment is 250 feet per nautical mile, and the maximum descent gradient is 500 feet per nautical mile. At 120 knots ground speed (2 nautical miles per minute), a pilot could expect descent rates of 500 to 1,000 feet per minute to reach the lower minimum altitudes along the

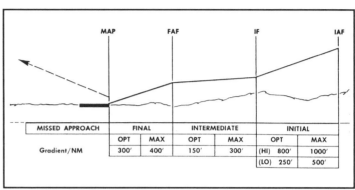

	MISSED APPROACH	FINAL		INTERMEDIATE		INITIAL	
		OPT	MAX	OPT	MAX	OPT	MAX
Gradient/NM		300'	400'	150'	300'	(HI) 800'	1000'
						(LO) 250'	500'

Fig. 3C. Descent gradients for approach segments.

route segment. This is a compelling reason to slow the airplane below cruise speeds while on the initial approach segment. Lower speeds will prevent excessive descent rates.

Of course, pilots flying IFR in the Goodyear blimp don't worry about excessive approach speeds and descent rates. Several years ago the Goodyear blimp made an approach into Long Beach airport, while being followed by a Boeing 727. The controller asked the blimp pilot if he could speed it up a little. As the blimp's pilot keyed the microphone, the flight crew could be heard laughing in the background. Once the pilot recovered his composure, he said they would be glad to perform a side-step maneuver to let the jet pass them, then reattach themselves to the approach. Now, the controller could be heard laughing in the background. Once the controller regained his composure, he stated, "Roger, cleared for a VFR 'side bag' maneuver." The controller, obviously amused by the situation, additionally cleared the blimp for a "bag and go" at the airport. He warned the crew about the wake turbulence, saying he wouldn't want them to do an unauthorized "bag over" while on final approach. Unless pilots desire only to fly aircraft like the blimp, they need to become more aware of descent rates required on the approach structure.

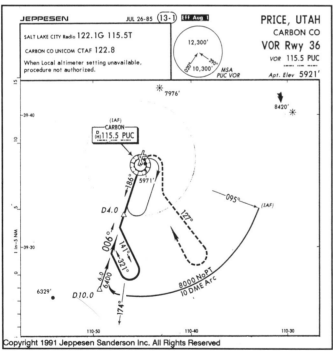

Fig. 4A. A DME arc intercepting the approach course at 90 degrees.

When an initial approach segment is based on a DME arc, that arc will have a minimum radius of 7 miles. The angle of interception between the DME arc and the intermediate segment shouldn't exceed 120 degrees. The VOR Rwy 36 approach to Price, Utah, figure 4A, shows a DME arc intercepting the approach course at 90 degrees. Jeppesen's version of the chart shows the 174 degree radial from

Carbon VOR acting as a lead radial. This provides pilots with a two nautical mile warning when nearing the approach procedure track. At this point, they should prepare to turn in the direction of the inbound course. Figure 4B shows the NOS version of the same chart. The letters "LR" are depicted next to the lead radial.

THE INTERMEDIATE SEGMENT

The intermediate segment's purpose is to blend the initial approach segment into the final approach segment. It's specifically designed with the pilot in mind. Whereas, the initial approach segment puts the aircraft roughly on course and on altitude, the intermediate segment allows pilots to get their aircraft configured for landing and lets them "fine-tune" themselves onto the final approach course. The intermediate

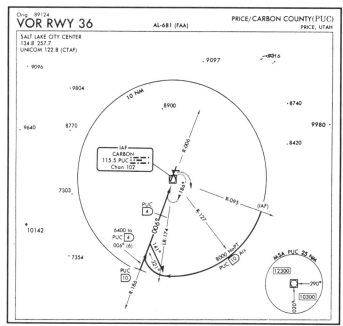

Fig. 4B. NOS version of chart 4A, with DME arc intercepting the approach course at a 90 degree angle.

segment begins at the intermediate fix and ends at the final approach fix. It's found along the approach procedure track, just prior to the FAF.

Figure 5 shows the NDB Rwy 20 approach for Cedar City, Utah. VELDE intersection is the intermediate fix. The route from VELDE to MEGGI is the intermediate segment. The intermediate segment is specifically designed to be a minimum of 5 miles and a maximum of 15 miles in length, with 10 miles considered optimum. It's on this segment that pilots normally complete the final landing checklist. Since the IF isn't marked (as previously noted), the easiest way to identify the intermediate segment is to start at the FAF and work backwards along the procedure. The first fix encountered within 5 to 15 miles of the FAF, while working backwards, is usually the intermediate fix.*

Chart builders make the approach easier for pilots by designing the intermediate segment with only minute changes in heading and altitude. That's why it's there! It's the calm before the storm. Pilots have one last stretch of minimum workload before they grapple with the hard work

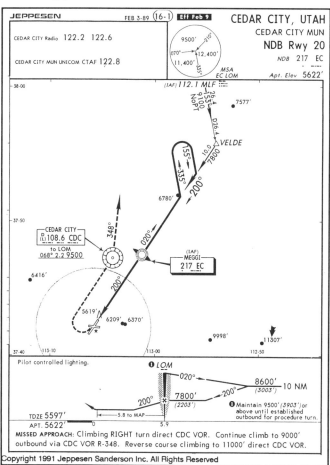

Fig. 5. VELDE intersection is an intermediate fix.

*MEGGI intersection acts as both an IAF and FAF. When the procedure turn is being made from MEGGI, it's an IAF. When the aircraft crosses MEGGI, and is inbound to land, it's an FAF.

of navigating the final approach segment precisely. In fact, the intermediate segment normally doesn't contain a descent. This is of immense value in reducing pilot workload. The intermediate segment is designed to be aligned to within 30 degrees of the final approach course. Descent gradients are designed not to exceed 300 feet per mile, with an optimum of 150 feet per mile desired, as shown in figure 3C.

With shallower descent gradients, pilots can expect descents of 300 to 600 feet per minute at ground speeds of 120 knots. This is considerably less than the 500 to 1,000 feet per minute descent rates expected on initial approach segments, based on similar groundspeeds. Normally, the intermediate segment is aligned with the final approach segment, as is seen in figure 5. However, figure 6, the VOR Rwy 26 to Lewiston, Idaho, shows a VOR approach where the intermediate segment is misaligned by 17 degrees from the final approach course. The maximum difference allowed is 30 degrees. Chart builders consider that pilots who are getting close to the point where the final approach is made could be distracted by high descent rates or sharp turns. Therefore, they carefully consider degrees of turn and descent rates as part of the chart construction process.

Of course, as with all things, there are exceptions to every rule. The Imperial Valley, California, VOR-A approach, figure 7A, is a case in point. The intermediate segment is angled 59 degrees with the final approach segment. This approach was waived by the high priests of chart regulations in Washington. The reason for the waiver was to keep pilots out of Mexican airspace. After all, the aircraft might have to make a forced landing in Mexican territory, after being mistaken for an airborne piñata. Imagine having to explain that one to the FBO!

Figure 7B shows the Chino, California ILS Rwy 26 approach. Proceeding backwards from the FAF, the first intersection encountered is LINDN. LINDN is the intermediate fix. The route from LINDN to SWAN LAKE LOM is the intermediate segment. Notice, that the intermediate segment is less than 5 miles in length. Intermediate segments, on ILS approaches, are treated with a special provision. When the initial approach segment intersects the localizer at shallow angles, the intermediate segment can be less than the minimum of 5 miles in length. Figure 8 shows how the length of this segment is computed.* For example, interception of the intermediate segment, at a maximum angle of 45 degrees, requires a minimum segment length of 3 miles. The initial approach segment from KNDAL intercepts the localizer at 40 degrees, so chart makers apply a minimum segment length of 3 miles. It happens that 3.5 miles works better at Chino, because of other variables. From LINDN to SWAN LAKE, 700 feet of altitude must be lost. At 3.5 miles distance between these intersections, a descent gradient of 200 feet per nautical mile is required along this segment.

INTERMEDIATE SEGMENT MINIMUM ALTITUDE CLEARANCE

I once read a sign that said, "Sheep skins half off." I thought, "Wow, that must really hurt!" Similarly, there's something else that could really hurt, and that's not paying attention to altitude deviations when flying the intermediate segment. Unlike the initial approach segment, the intermediate segment provides a minimum altitude clearance of only 500 feet, figure 3B. When stopping to consider the implications of this minimum altitude, pilots may be taken aback. This segment, from 5 to 15 miles in length, found prior to the final approach fix, could provide obstruction clearance that may be less than the MDA's to some airports. This is a rather sobering thought, considering how nonchalant some pilots are with altitude deviations of a couple hundred feet. Imagine the dangerous possibilities resulting

*Only the technically minded need finish this paragraph. For some, these next few sentences could provide information so dry that it might cure their asthma. It's possible that reading these next few sentences could traumatize their cortex, taint their retina and truncate their corpus callosum. Proceed with caution down this path of esoteric knowledge.

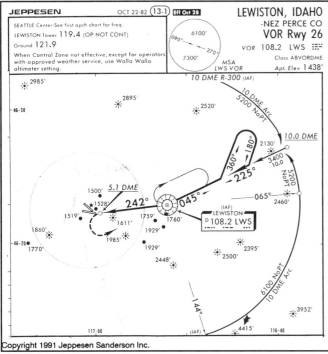

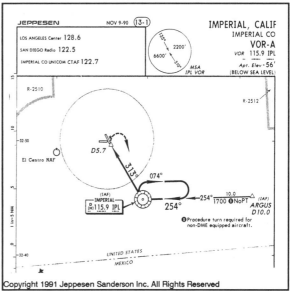

Fig. 7A. *Intermediate segment angled 59 degrees with the final. This approach required an FAA waiver.*

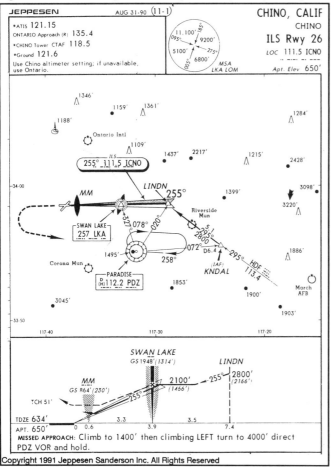

Fig. 6. *Intermediate segment misaligned with final by 17 degrees.*

Fig. 7B. *LINDN intersection is the intermediate fix.*

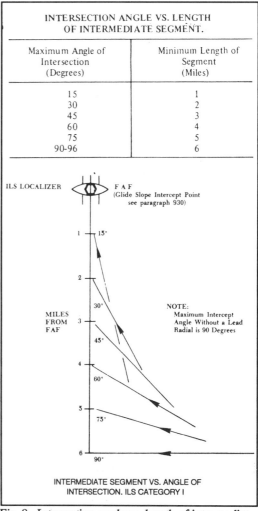

INTERSECTION ANGLE VS. LENGTH OF INTERMEDIATE SEGMENT.	
Maximum Angle of Intersection (Degrees)	Minimum Length of Segment (Miles)
15	1
30	2
45	3
60	4
75	5
90-96	6

Fig. 8. *Intersection angle vs. length of intermediate segment.*

BALLOONY!

On a clear, hazy day with the sun at our backs, we were being vectored for an approach at 6,000' MSL. Approach advised us of converging IFR traffic at 10 o'clock, 5,000', NE bound. After several checks in that position, I finally spotted him, maybe 10 seconds before he passed beneath us. When I looked up again, I saw the small cross-section and very bright landing light of a jet fighter at exactly 12:00, at very close range, at our altitude. I overrode the autopilot and pushed the nose over sharply. As I was pulling back the thrust levers and cursing loudly, the "fighter" turned into a silver mylar balloon with a blue ribbon hanging from it! I could see what it was when it zipped just over our heads and the sunlight no longer reflected directly back into my eyes (the landing light). I was convinced it was a military fighter, complete with the usual trail of dark smoke coming out the back (the blue ribbon?)!

Then - I remembered the traffic directly below us! I pulled the nose up just as sharply as before. Fortunately, everyone was seated in the back, and there were no injuries or damage. Our total altitude deviation was no more than 200'. **ASRS REPORT**

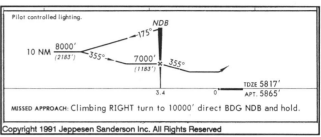

Fig. 9A. Initial approach segment altitudes and intermediate approach segment altitudes.

from an improperly set altimeter, coupled with slack piloting skills, while navigating the intermediate segment. This presents a scenario for a Category 3C touchdown, many miles short of the airport. The reason for the limited obstruction clearance is to keep the airplane as close to the airport elevation as possible, thereby preventing excessive rates of descent on final approach. The tradeoff is that pilots have to pay close attention.

The difference between the initial approach segment obstruction clearance of 1,000 feet, and the intermediate segment obstruction clearance of 500 feet, explains why variations exist in altitudes listed next to the procedure turn, in the profile section. In figure 9A, the altitude for the procedure turn (which is always an initial approach segment) is 8,000 feet. When the procedure turn is completed, and the airplane is established on the inbound course, 7,000 feet becomes the intermediate segment minimum altitude. The lower altitude guarantees 500 foot terrain clearance in the "primary area" of a trapezoid having diminishing and variable dimensions, as defined in figure 3B. This tapers to "zero" altitude protection along a converging secondary boundary.

Figure 9B shows differences in altitudes listed next to the holding pattern in the profile view. When circling in the holding pattern, a minimum of 3,500 feet should be used. Holding pattern entries are considered to be part of the initial approach segment, providing a minimum of 1,000 feet obstruction clearance. When inbound for the approach, a minimum altitude of 3,300 feet can be used. The lower

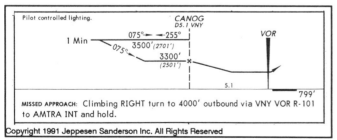

Fig. 9B. Initial approach and intermediate segment altitudes for a holding pattern course reversal.

altitude is the intermediate segment altitude. Remember, intermediate segment altitudes should not be used for procedure turns. If the pilot was inbound to the FAF at 3,300 feet and, for some reason,* another turn in the holding pattern was required, a climb to 3,500 would be necessary to assure adequate obstacle clearance.

*This is an unlikely situation; nevertheless, it serves to make the point that the intermediate segment altitude offers less protection than the initial approach segment altitude. Therefore, the higher altitude should be used for holding.

FINAL APPROACH SEGMENT

The final approach segment begins at the final approach fix, or point,* and ends at the runway or missed approach point. The FAF is usually identified in the profile view with a Maltese Cross, figure 10. Some instrument approaches don't have final approach fixes. Figure 11 shows a procedure turn, an inbound descent and a missed approach point at the VOR. The procedure turn makes up the initial approach segment. There is no intermediate segment on these types of approaches. The final approach segment commences when established on the 282 degree inbound course. In this instance, pilots may leave the procedure turn altitude and descend to the MDA as soon as they are established inbound. The missed approach point is identified by VOR passage. Therefore, there is no requirement to time this approach. Most likely, in this case, a final approach fix wasn't established, because there are no navigational facilities close enough to use as an intersection cross reference.

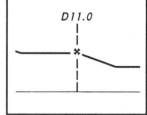

Fig. 10. Maltese Cross identifies the FAF.

Approaches, of the type shown in figure 11, are not uncommon. They are technically referred to as "ON-AIRPORT VOR or NDB (NO FAF)," approaches. What's interesting about them is that they provide a means of establishing an instrument approach, when the VOR or NDB is situated within one mile or less of the airport. Approaches of this type are constructed when there are no other navaids that could be used to establish a final approach fix intersection along the approach course. Therefore, these types of approaches always have procedure turns. The VOR or NDB must be within one nautical mile of the landing runway for straight-in minima to exist. The navaid must be within one mile of the nearest portion of the usable landing surface at the airport for circling minima to exist. Basically, when the navaid is more than one mile away from the airport, an approach with an FAF is more likely to exist.**

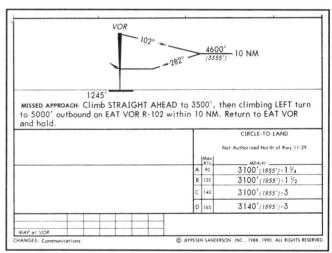

Fig. 11. An approach without a final approach fix.

FINAL APPROACH DESCENT RATES

As an experienced pilot, I look for assurances whenever boarding a commercial aircraft as a passenger. I want my captain to have gray hair, even if he or she keeps it in their flight bag. One time, I looked up the aisle into the cockpit and saw someone, shaking and obviously very nervous, with their arms wrapped around the captain's waist. The captain was saying, "Let go, let go!" Then I realized it was the copilot who had his arms wrapped around the captain's waist. The captain was saying, "Let go and go back to your seat, it's your turn to fly today." Despite this rare exception, most experiences in aviation are reassuring. However, instrument pilots must use caution when feeling reassured by the minimum altitudes shown on approach charts. While these altitudes may protect pilots from encounters with terrain, there are exceptions to their protective coverage.

*ILS approaches have final approach points in lieu of final approach fixes. The final approach point on an ILS is where the glide slope is intercepted.
**More detailed information about ON-AIRPORT VOR or NDB (NO FAF) approaches can be found in TERPS:Par.400 and 600.

There is one situation, although difficult to get into, that could present an obstacle clearance problem. Pilots deciding to make the steepest possible descent to the MDA, after passing the final approach fix, could end up plucking a mountain climber off a cliff. This adds a whole new meaning to the concept of having a "wing man." Figure 12 shows an area where obstruction clearance is not provided in a 7

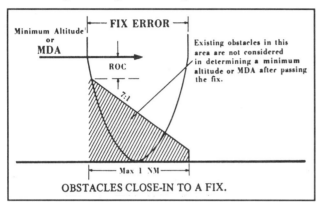

Fig. 12. *Obstacles close-in to the FAF where protection is not provided.*

foot forward to 1 foot downward sloped plane, starting at the final approach fix. This sloped surface <u>starts</u> a minimum of 500 feet <u>below</u> the minimum altitude that crosses the FAF. A descent rate of 857 feet per mile, or 1285 feet per minute at 90 knots ground speed, would be required to parallel the downward sloping surface while approaching the MDA. Keep in mind, the airplane would have to exceed these rates in order to penetrate this 7 to 1 plane. Remember, the airplane is starting at a minimum height of 500 feet above this sloped surface (the minimum obstacle clearance required on the intermediate segment). This is why the descent rates, mentioned above, would have to be exceeded to penetrate this downward plane. However, it's not unreasonable to exceed a descent rate of 857 feet per mile in today's modern airplanes, especially those capable of sprouting aluminum anchors like speed brakes, flaps and landing gear (that mountain climber would add drag, too). So don't forget this caveat entirely.

When obstructions along the final approach path become a serious consideration, the FAA may provide other means of obstruction avoidance. Figure 13 shows the ILS Rwy 16R approach at Van Nuys, California. The procedure states that the approach is not authorized when the glide slope is not used. Therefore, flying the localizer, without using the glide slope, is not approved. One reason for this is the 2046 foot obstruction located just past the outer marker. A likely scenario, that might spell danger for pilots at Van Nuys, is one where they are cleared for the ILS Rwy 16R and requested to circle to runway

34L. Pilots might assume that the clearance for circling would mean they could forgo adhering to the glide slope and just descend at any arbitrary rate to the circling MDA. On other similar approaches, this policy may be acceptable. It is not acceptable at Van Nuys. In this instance, the glide slope would have to be used, while descending to the circling MDA. Once the aircraft levels at the MDA, it would proceed to the missed approach point which is determined by time,* or to the point, where the circling maneuver was begun if the runway was sighted. It's possible, without using the glide slope, that a radical descent to a circling MDA of 1,300 feet would cause a collision with the obstacle located just inside the outer marker.

*It's a common misconception that when the aircraft rides the glide slope down to the circling MDA, a missed approach must be made. In other words, pilots may think that the circling MDA becomes the new DA. This is not correct! Pilots are expected to start their time at the FAF, level at the circling MDA and fly to the nonprecision missed approach point.

VISUAL DESCENT POINTS

Everyone knows that flight instructors are not slaves to fashion. When CFI's walk out of the house, they may think they are dressed nicely, but, someone always stops them and asks, "Hey Bob, going fishing?" The CFI, obviously confused, says, "No, I'm going to work!" Certainly, most pilots have had flight instructors approach them and ask, "Hey, does plaid go with a propeller hat?" Pilots have learned to avoid making any premature assumptions about CFI's based on their clothing. This is wisdom. Other aviation wisdom can be much harder to come by. Take descent rates, for example. Descents to the MDA can be orderly, progressive and a prelude to a flawless and well planned landing. Or they can be fatal. The difference is understanding how to use the VDP.

To help pilots come somewhere between weed-cutting and high-altitude fly-bys, chart builders have established something known as a Visual Descent Point (VDP), as shown in figure 14. The VDP is located along the final approach segment of a straight-in, non-precision approach. The main purpose of the VDP is to prevent a premature descent from the MDA, after visual contact with the run-way or approach lights has been established.

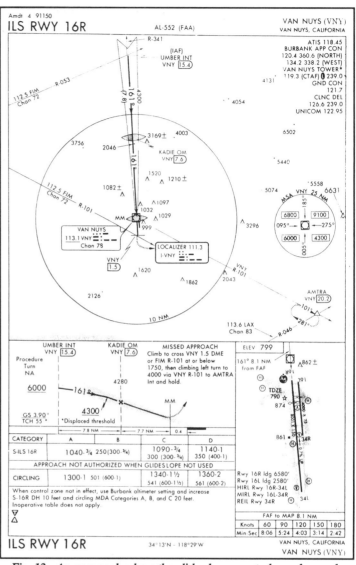

Fig. 13. *An approach where the glide slope must always be used.*

It's also a clue that descents commenced beyond the VDP may require higher than normal descent rates to make the runway. Descents from the VDP provide a descent of 300 to 400 feet per nautical mile (approximately a 3 to 4 degree angle) to the first 3,000 feet of the landing surface.

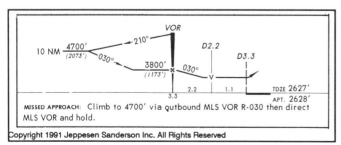

Fig. 14. *The visual descent point (VDP).*

VDP's are navigation references that are usually identified by marker beacons or DME readings. When a VDP is established on an approach, and pilots have the equipment onboard to identify the VDP, they must wait until reaching the VDP before descending from the MDA. Therefore, even if the runway is clearly in sight, they should not descend below the MDA prior to reaching the VDP. Pilots, not having the equipment to identify the VDP, should fly the approach as if no VDP has been provided.

MISSED APPROACH SEGMENTS

Every instrument approach procedure has a missed approach segment. This explains why charted visual approaches are not considered official instrument approach procedures. They do not contain a provision for an IFR missed approach. The missed approach shall be initiated at Decision Altitude for a precision approach or at a specified missed approach point on a nonprecision approach. Missed Approach Points (MAP) for any nonprecision approach are not obvious from either the plan or profile views on Jeppesen charts, but can always be found in the conversion table, located on the bottom, left hand side of every approach chart, as shown in figure 15.

NOS charts show missed approach information under the airport diagram and in the profile view, as shown in figure 16. If the missed approach point is determined by time, the NOS charts will show this information under the airport diagram. Additional means used for identifying the missed approach point will be found in the profile view. The profile view, in figure 16, shows the missed approach starting at 9.6 DME from the FAF (the VORTAC). Either time, or a DME reading, may be used to identify the MAP. When no time is listed under the airport diagram on NOS charts, the profile view is the only place to find the missed approach point, as shown in figure 17. In this instance, the missed approach point is where the solid line stops and the dashed line curves upward at the HZN 11.6 DME fix.

A M E N D 1	Gnd speed-Kts		70	90	100	120	140	160
	GS	3.00°	377	485	539	646	754	862
	MAP at D1.8 IFTG or							
	SKIPI to MAP	4.7	4:02	3:08	2:49	2:21	2:01	1:46

CHANGES: AWOS.

M E N D 18	Gnd speed-Kts	70	90	100	120	140	160
	MAP at D1.1 or						
	LOM to MAP 3.9	3:21	2:36	2:20	1:57	1:40	1:28

CHANGES: CVO VOR approach transition altitude.

M E N D 1							
MAP at D11.7							

CHANGES: Communications.

M E N D 1							
MAP at NDB							

CHANGES: Holyo Int redesignated & transition.

M E N D 1							
MAP at VOR							

Fig. 15. Jeppesen's conversion table.

BYTE THE BULLET!

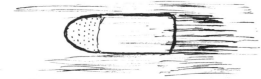

Beware the hackers

I noticed the First Officer was wandering back and forth down the airway. It was worse as we approached nearer our destination. The Center gave us headings to fly for vectors to the ILS approach. It was difficult to track the localizer and glideslope, as both indications were erratic. The weather at the destination airport was about 400' and 2 miles. We broke out at 400', and we were too high to make a normal landing, so, we executed the missed approach. I asked the Flight Attendant if anyone had an FM radio, computer game or other electronic device in use. She checked the passengers, while we were being vectored for another approach. She found a passenger in Row 4 using a portable computer in his lap. He was asked to turn it off. After it was turned off, all ILS and VOR indications became normal again. I believe the computer was generating signals that interfered with our nav instruments. These devices should be banned from use on aircraft during IFR conditions, unless the manufacturer can prove that the unit will not interfere with navaids. It could create a serious problem. **ASRS REPORT**

FLYING THE MISSED APPROACH

Altitude protection along the missed approach segment is not as fantastic as pilots might think. The missed approach protected area consists of an upwardly sloped plane that ascends uniformly at the rate of 1 foot vertically for each 40 feet horizontally (40:1), as shown in figure 18. This sloped surface starts at the missed approach point. It extends outward 15 miles for a "straight-out" missed approach. This climb plane translates into a 152 foot per nautical mile climb gradient. Regulations require that no obstacles penetrate this upward sloping surface. When the missed approach is initiated, pilots are expected to climb, so as to remain above this 40:1 sloped surface. At 120 knots ground speed, or 2 miles per minute, this equates to a 304 foot per minute rate of climb required to maintain a parallel path above the missed approach climb plane.

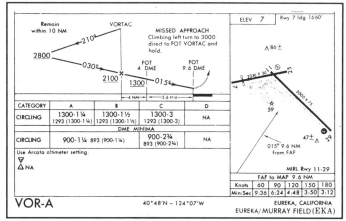

Fig. 16. NOS chart depiction of missed approach information.

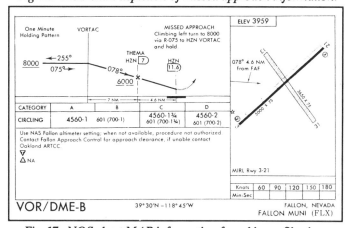

Fig. 17. NOS chart MAP information found in profile view.

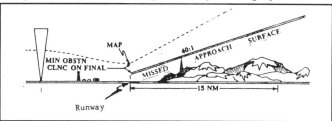

Fig. 18. Missed approach segment protected airspace.

The altitude protection along the missed approach segment, is based on the Minimum Descent Altitude for the particular approach procedure being used.

For example, a straight-in VOR approach provides a minimum of 250 feet of obstacle clearance on the final approach segment. Therefore, if pilots climbed parallel to the 40:1 sloped plane, they may only have a minimum of 250 feet of altitude protection. Fortunately, airplane performance allows most aircraft to outclimb the 152'/NM upward sloping surface. The implication here is that if pilots descend below the MDA, then commence a missed approach, they may have less altitude protection above obstructions along the missed approach segment. Perhaps this is another compelling reason for pilots not to descend below the MDA or DA unless they meet all the requirements of FAR 91.175.* The missed approach protected area requirements may also vary when turns are specified as part of the missed approach procedure. Pilots should·be aware that there isn't a great deal of room for error when operating close to the ground. Therefore, missed approach procedures should be thoroughly studied prior to making the approach.

When it comes to approach charts, pilots should be real nosey. Dive into the chart and ferret out the critical missed approach information. Be like a friend of mine; he's a real nosey pilot. He even admits that he's nosey, at least that's what he says his wife writes about him in her diary. Pilots should carefully consider the problems associated with executing a missed approach, prior to the missed approach point. Missed approach protected areas are based on a minimum climb, starting at the missed approach point. It's conceivable that an early turn, prior to the missed approach point, could put the aircraft dangerously close to obstacles. Therefore, unless otherwise advised by ATC, pilots should always proceed to the missed approach point before executing any turns on the published missed approach procedure.

If a missed approach is desired on an ILS, prior to reaching Decision Altitude, pilots should start a climb and proceed to the missed approach point before making any turns. The missed approach point on an ILS is based on being at Decision Altitude while on the glide slope. If a missed approach is started on an ILS, prior to reaching DA, there will be difficulty in defining the missed

*This regulation deals with the legal requirements for descent below the MDA or DA. It is thoroughly covered in Chapter 16.

approach point. The solution lies in understanding that the glide slope normally (not always) intersects the middle marker at Decision Altitude. Therefore, pilots should climb, overfly the middle marker, and then make any required turns. Additionally, if marker equipment doesn't work, or isn't installed on the aircraft, pilots could approximate the position of the ILS missed approach point by time. Pilots need only start their time at the FAF and fly to the nonprecision missed approach point. While this point will be inside the middle marker, closer to the runway threshold, by 2,400 to 4,200 feet, it's a reasonable reference to use when all else fails. This is a compelling reason why pilots should always start a time reference at the outer marker (FAF) when flying an ILS. Despite this not being required, it's a prudent, defensive action.

Several years ago, an eastbound airliner at 37,000 feet, received a clearance from an air traffic controller that was quite unusual. The controller said, "Transliner 1234, turn right 360 degrees for noise abatement." The pilot was a bit confused and questioned the controller by stating, "Noise abatement, at 37,000 feet? How can that be?" The controller responded with, "Have you ever heard the sound of two 727's crashing into one another?" It seems that there is a reason for almost everything that's done in aviation. Similarly, instrument approach charts have reasons behind every facet of their construction.

A pilot's aviation intelligence quotient results from having established relationships between ideas and concepts where no relationship is immediately apparent. It's this aviation intelligence that could someday, while in the throes of an emergency, allow them to survive or perish. In every pilot's career, there comes a time when they may have to bend the rules. An emergency may dictate that they prematurely leave minimum altitudes or perform an aviation version of "jay-walking" on an approach procedure. Comprehending how approach segments are stitched together and how they precisely lower an approaching aircraft, provides pilots with the knowledge to handle these unusual situations intelligently. This deeper wisdom of approach chart architecture offers pilots a sublime sense of comfort and confidence. In much the same way, when pilots understand how to identify the runway environment, and determine inflight visibility, they will experience greater confidence and comfort in making landings from instrument approaches.

16. DECISION ALTITUDE AND MDA'S

If a Cessna 150 was equipped with a radar altimeter, HSI, dual ILS and a 3-axis, sophisticated autopilot providing for coupled approaches, there would never be a need to worry about legal visibility minimums required for landing. Pilots would simply push a button and watch the Cessna Landomatic

successfully complete a Category 3-C autoland approach. Unfortunately, a Cessna 150 with all this equipment would take 12,000 feet of runway just to get airborne, and would probably blow it's tires during taxi. Therefore, pilots must have a good understanding of how legal minimums are determined for landing.

Assessing inflight visibility is a skill more likely to be used by general aviation pilots than airline pilots. Airline pilots are not allowed to start an approach unless the reported visibility is at or above landing minimums. This rules doesn't apply to Part 91 operators. General aviation pilots have "look-see" privileges. Regardless of the reported ceiling or visibility, Part 91 operators may fly the approach to minimums and assess the conditions. If they have the required inflight visibility, and meet the other requirements for descent below DA or MDA, they may land. Perhaps one of the reasons air carriers are restricted in this way is because of the higher approach speeds of the modern airliner. Assessing visibility near Decision Altitude at 140 knots is slightly more critical than at 90 knots. Additionally, the prime directive of all commercial regulations is to protect the passengers. Therefore, starting an approach with adequate visibility reported, offers the airline pilot a higher probability of a successful landing. Nevertheless, general aviation pilots must be careful not to abuse this privilege of "look-see." The easiest way to violate landing minimums is to have little

What! No autospeak?

I was practicing a CAT ll approach. I decided to continue the approach to an auto-land. We became involved and never switched from Approach Control to Tower. After we landed and cleared the runway, Ground Control informed us we had forgotten to contact the tower. The approach and landing is automatic, but the flight crew has duties the system can't do. We made a mistake!   **ASRS REPORT**

or no knowledge about how these minimums are assessed during an instrument approach.

The Federal Aviation Regulations (91.175) specify two separate requirements to be met for pilots to descend below the published MDA or DA. First, pilots must have the minimum required flight visibility, as shown in the published instrument approach procedure. Second, one of ten individual references for the intended runway of landing must be distinctly visible and identifiable by the pilot.

DETERMINING INFLIGHT VISIBILITY

One of the most perplexing questions facing most IFR pilots is deciding whether they have the required legal flight visibility for landing. To make this determination, pilots need to understand how approach procedures are constructed. Knowing where and why marker beacons are placed along the approach path, as well as knowing the function approach lights serve, will allow pilots to make a more accurate visibility determination at the missed approach point.

ILS ARCHITECTURE

Most ILS glide slopes are inclined at a 3 degree angle. Glide slope antennas project this beam outward on the approach, so that the glide slope beam intersects the middle marker at approximately 200 feet above the touchdown zone elevation. A HAT of 200 feet is the average Decision Height for most

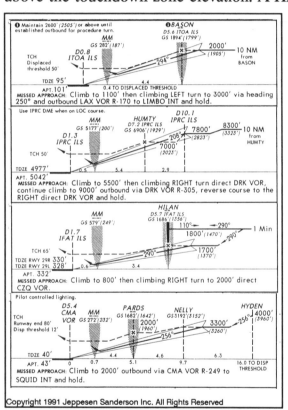

Fig. 1. Middle marker distances from the runway threshold can be found in the profile view.

Category I ILS approaches. It's no accident that middle marker beacons are placed, at or near, the Decision Altitude point. The intent here is to provide the pilot with a visible and audible warning when nearing Decision Altitude. It's important to note that most middle markers are physically located between .4 and .7 nautical miles from the runway threshold. With one nautical mile equaling 6,080 feet (6,000 feet will be used for convenience), this equates to approximately 2,400 to 4,200 feet of distance. A close look at the profile views, as seen in figure 1, reveals the variable distances of the middle marker from the runway threshold. This distance provides the means for determining inflight visibility.

PREAPPROACH SELF-BRIEFING

Before flying an ILS approach, pilots should always have an accurate idea of the distance, in feet, from the middle marker to the runway threshold. Chart distances are always depicted in nautical miles. Therefore, converting nautical mile distance to feet, allows the accurate assessment of inflight visibility. The approach chart profile, in figure 2, shows a middle marker approximately 2,400 feet (.4 x 6,000) from the runway threshold. At Decision Altitude, which is near the middle marker, a sighting of the runway threshold lights establishes an inflight visibility of at least 2,400 feet. It's very important for pilots to understand that inflight visibility minima is always measured in statute miles or in feet. The minimums section shows the required inflight visibility for this ILS, with all the components working, is 1/2 statute mile or 2,400 feet. Therefore, with the threshold lights sighted, and the inflight visibility requirement met, the aircraft is now legal to descend below Decision Altitude.

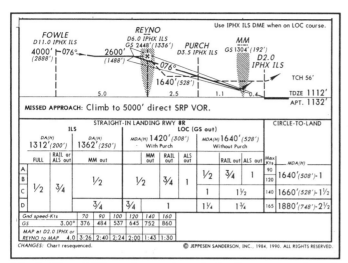

Fig. 2. The middle marker at .4 nautical miles or approximately 2,400 feet from the runway threshold.

Visibility determination on an ILS is based on the assumption that Decision Altitude is reached when the middle marker is crossed. This is a reasonably accurate assumption for ILS approaches. Additionally, when marker beacons are operated in the "low sensitivity" mode, beacon reception will more accurately approximate the transmitter location. This makes for a more accurate, inflight visibility assessment.

On a localizer approach, the middle marker is used to estimate the visibility in the same manner as used on an ILS approach. The only difference is that localizer approaches are flown at a Minimum Descent Altitude and not to a Decision Altitude, as are ILS approaches. When the marker activates on a localizer approach, the pilot makes an initial visibility estimation, then the aircraft overflies the middle marker to the missed approach point. The missed approach point is located at the runway threshold and is often determined by timing from the FAF. This means that pilots flying localizer, rather than ILS approaches, will have a little more time to estimate the inflight visibility prior to reaching the missed approach point.

APPROACH LIGHTING SYSTEM

Suppose the runway threshold, or runway references beyond the threshold are not in sight at the middle marker? How would pilots make an estimation of inflight visibility in this circumstance? The secret lies in understanding the architecture of the approach lighting system. Airports with instrument approaches may have approach lighting starting at the runway threshold and extending into the approach area. These lights may extend a distance of 2,400-3,000 feet for precision instrument runways and 1,400-1,500 feet for nonprecision instrument runways. These approach lights are shown in figure 3. The differences in these approach lights will be discussed later; however, right now it's extremely important to notice that every approach lighting system has one very important thing in common -- a decision bar located 1,000 feet from the runway threshold.

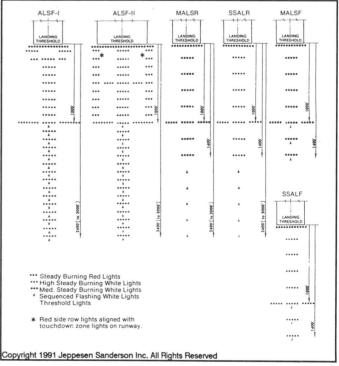

Fig. 3. Approach lighting systems common in the U.S..

THE DECISION BAR

The sideways row of lights that are placed perpendicular to the approach light system is called the decision bar, as shown in figure 4. The decision bar is located 1,000 feet from the runway threshold

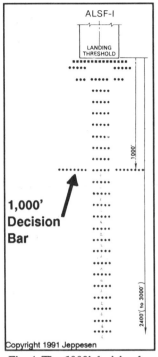

1,000' Decision Bar

Fig. 4. The 1000' decision bar.

and all U.S. approach lighting systems have them. It serves several purposes. First, the decision bar creates a reference to the horizon that's useful when making a visual transition from instruments. While the threshold lights may be off in the distance, the decision bar is closer to the airplane. It acts to help pilots keep their airplane wings level during a low visibility landing.

When the aircraft is on the glide slope at Decision Altitude, the decision bar will usually be seen going underneath the cowling. This may at first appear quite contradictory. If the decision bar is located 1,000 feet from the threshold, and Decision Altitude is located near the middle marker (.4 to .7 NM from the threshold), how can the decision bar appear to be going underneath the cowling? The answer lies in the pilot's observation angle. While looking in a forward and downward angle from this height, based on the average arrangement of aircraft cowling, panel and pilot sitting height, it will appear that the decision bar is just disappearing below the dashboard.

Second, the position of the decision bar explains why sequenced flashing lights, found on some approaches, stop at the decision bar. These balls of light, flashing twice per second, could be a real distraction during the transition from Decision Altitude to touchdown. Fortunately, the sequenced flashers end at the decision bar. Therefore, at DA, these strobes disappear underneath the cowling and no longer distract the pilot. Prior to Decision Altitude, the sequenced flashing lights will help point pilots in the direction of the runway.

This explains why some pilots ask controllers to turn off the flashers when they have spotted the runway, prior to Decision Altitude. The professional jargon to use in asking the controller to turn off the sequenced flashers is, "Kill the rabbit." I had one gentleman in a seminar, several years ago, who thought it was actually, "Kill the parrot." I had to inform him that he was killing the wrong thing. He said, "Oh, maybe that explains why they never turned it off." I wonder how many parrots needlessly died because of this communication failure!

ALTO SERIOUS STRATUS

Too much pushing

We were a scheduled air carrier trying to get in with enough time to turn around and make it out again by the takeoff noise abatement curfew. The Center Controller asked for our best forward speed. The Approach Controller turned us in at the marker. Due to the weather conditions, I was planning a coupled approach. When the autopilot captured the glideslope, the aircraft pitched over about 7 degrees and then began oscillating to capture it. I didn't like the way the autopilot was handling the glideslope, so I disconnected it and flew it manually. At the same time, the autopilot was oscillating, I SEEM to remember the First Officer switching to the Tower, and I remember the wind was given as 120 degrees at 7 knots. When I was stable on the localizer and glideslope, I called for and completed the landing check. When that was done, we broke out to see a jet still on the runway. I was concerned about him clearing the runway before we landed. He turned off the runway as we crossed the approach lights, and we landed. The problem is that I'm not sure whether or not I ever heard, "Cleared to land." The F/O said he was 99% sure that we were. We should have been ABSOLUTELY sure!!! That's one problem. The other is that we were pushing, the company was pushing, and the controllers were pushing. I hope I've learned that this is no way to run the airplane!!!

ASRS REPORT

Third, the decision bar is a valuable aid in helping pilots identify inflight visibility. If the aircraft is at the middle marker, and the runway threshold cannot be seen, pilots should look for the decision bar. If the middle marker is .6 miles (3,600 feet) from the runway threshold, and the decision bar is visible, then the visibility from the cockpit is 2,600 feet. If the approach minimum calls for 2,400 feet, the minimum visibility requirement for landing is met. Similarly, if the middle marker is .5 miles (3,000 feet) from the threshold, and the decision bar is spotted, the estimated inflight visibility is approximately 2,000 feet. Based on this estimate, the approach minimum of 1/2 mile visibility (2,400 feet) would not be met.

A word of caution is appropriate here. FAR 91.175 C2 specifically requires that, to descend below DA or the MDA, the flight visibility may not be less than that prescribed in the approach procedure being used. Another regulation in the same section, FAR 91.175 D, specifically states that no pilot may land an airplane if the flight visibility is less than that specified in the procedure. Having the required visibility at Decision Altitude is no guarantee that it won't change as the pilot approaches the runway. Such an occurrence is not unlikely with a runway threshold that may be an much as .7 nautical miles from the ILS missed approach point. If, upon reaching the runway, the flight visibility has decreased below that required, then a missed approach should be made.

Pilots should always be prepared for a change in visibility when approaching the runway. The most likely cause for such a dramatic change in visibility is variable cloud density near the touchdown zone. This is one reason why professional pilots pay special attention to varying RVR values. This usually indicates the possibility that visibilities near the runway could be much different from those found at Decision Altitude.

Pilots can make a more refined estimate of inflight visibility by using the distance between the individual approach light bars. Figure 5 shows two of the basic approach light structures available in the U.S. The ALSF type has light bars, separated by 100 feet, along the lighting system. The MALS, and other approach lighting systems, have light bars separated by 200 feet. The number of lighting bars pilots can see, beyond the decision bar, will help them more accurately estimate their inflight visibility. If, at the middle marker, using an ALSF system, pilots can see three light bars past the decision bar, they have an additional 300 foot visibility.

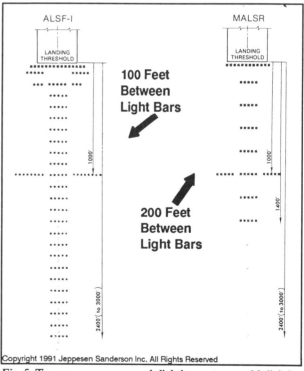

Fig. 5. Two common approach lighting systems, with lighting bars spaced at 100 foot intervals for the ALSF-1 and 200 foot intervals for the MALSR.

At this point, most instrument students may be wondering to themselves, "Do I have enough synaptic connections to handle estimating inflight visibility?" Unless the pilot has taken too many fizzies in the 60's, the answer is a qualified, "Yes." Determining visibility is a perceptual skill. It's similar to learning how to scan for traffic. It requires practice to develop this ability to perceive. It's much like a class I took in college on culture aesthetics. We studied beginning taste and learned new and wonderful ideas like: how to tell a painting from a sculpture. Instrument students should have no difficulty acquiring this perceptual skill. However, if an instrument student is attending flight school on a mud wrestling scholarship and has been known to nod his head at the speakers of a hamburger stand, I'd be a little less optimistic about his potential for success.

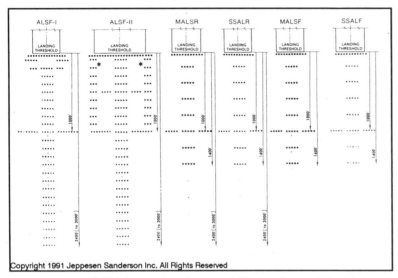

Fig. 6. Approach lighting systems have variable lengths, and it's this length that can help pilots determine their inflight visibility at or near the MAP.

Another method of determining inflight visibility is to make an estimate based on viewing the entire approach lighting system, prior to Decision Altitude. The ALSF I and II approach lighting systems, as seen in figure 6, are anywhere from 2,400 to 3,000 feet in length. Seeing the entire length of the lights, while on approach, identifies the inflight visibility as 1/2 mile or greater. Lighting systems like MALSF, SSALF and MALS are 1,400 feet in length. Approach lighting systems, like the MALSR and SSALR, have RAIL (strobe lights) extending the length of the lighting system beyond 1,400 feet. With sequenced flashers, these lighting systems can extend to 3,000 feet. If sequenced flashers are available, but not operating, and the visibility is low, it's best to have the controller activate them. I suppose the pilot could ask ATC to, "Resurrect the rabbit." Perhaps this explains the origin of the Easter Bunny.

APPROACH LIGHTING AVAILABLE

Pilots should be intimately aware of the approach lighting available to them during an approach. It's unusual to have a full approach light system available for other than ILS or localizer approaches. In fact, a quick check of instrument charts will show that it's uncommon, for airports with nonprecision* approaches, to have an ALSF I and II, MALSR, SSALR, MALSF or SSALF approach lighting system. There is only one airport in all of California without a published LOC or ILS approach that has an approach lighting system, and that is Montague, California. Montague has an NDB-A approach equipped with a SSALR. Airports with nonprecision approaches may have lead-in lights (LDIN), omni directional lead-in lights (ODALS), runway end identification lights (REIL) or runway alignment indicator lights (RAIL).

*Other than localizer only approaches.

THE AIRPORT DIAGRAM

Pilots using Jeppesen charts can identify what approach lighting system is available by referring to the airport diagram. This may be found on the reverse side of the approach chart, or on a separate airport diagram chart. Figure 7 shows the airport diagram for Hobbs, New Mexico. Runway 3 is equipped with an MALSR approach lighting system, as identified in the runway information box and shown at the beginning of the runway on the airport diagram. The MALSR system is 1,400 feet in length, as identified with 7 wide slashes, each slash representing 200 feet of distance between lights. Additionally, there are 8 dots farther out along the lighting system. These dots represent the RAIL lights. These are the strobes that help point the pilot to the runway. Each RAIL light is spaced 200 feet apart, adding 1,600 feet of lights to the system. Therefore, the entire approach lighting system is 3,000 feet in length. When pilots are at Decision Altitude, with the MALS and the RAIL system in operation, they should see 3,000 feet of approach lights. If the RAIL system is inactive, the length of the approach lighting system will be shortened by 1,600 feet.* Since all of Jeppesen's airport diagrams are drawn to scale, identifying the lengths of individual approach lighting systems will be quite easy. Simply measure the specific picture with the scale provided on the chart.

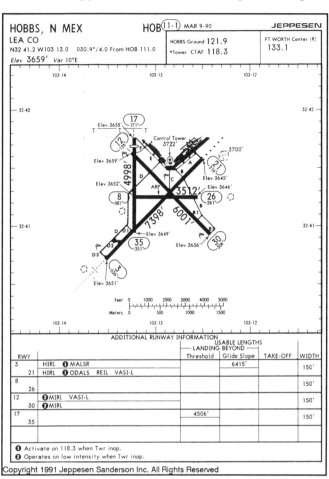

Fig. 7. Jeppesen's airport diagram.

Figure 8 shows the most common approach lighting systems available in the U.S. These are the pictures of what is shown on the airport diagram, as well as the form of the lighting as seen from the cockpit. It's important to become familiar with these pictures. There have been many accidents relating to pilots misinterpreting freeways and other illusory lighting for the approach lighting system. Perhaps this becomes even more of a concern when strong wind exists while on approach. If the crab angle is not anticipated, and mentally corrected for, pilots may tend to visually home-in on what looks like approach lighting. Therefore, always have a good idea of the variable shapes and lengths of the approach lighting available.

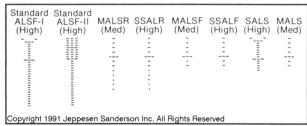

Fig. 8. Approach lights that are similar in size and shape to what pilots will see on Jeppesen's airport diagram.

*Sequenced flashing lights can be deactivated by the controller. However, RAIL, when part of an approach lighting system, may not be able to be deactivated by the controller. In other words, when the controller turns the MALSR on, he or she may not be able to isolate and deactivate the RAIL portion of the lighting system. The controller's ability to isolate the RAIL depends on the particular wiring system of the tower.

The airport diagrams available to NOS chart users are smaller than what is provided on the back of Jeppesen's approach chart. NOS provides smaller airport diagrams on the front of every approach chart. The smaller airport diagrams, found in the right hand corner of the approach chart, contains a

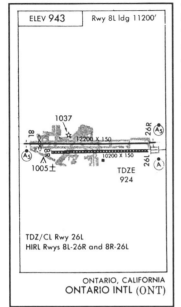

Fig. 9. NOS airport diagram.

picture of approach lighting for that airport, as well as a reference to the lighting legend, as shown in figure 9. The picture shows very small depictions of the approach lighting systems. Little circles, to the sides of the runways, are symbols for the approach lighting that's available at the airport. Because the actual pictures of the approach lights are difficult to see, it's necessary to go to the airport lighting legend, in the front of the approach booklet, as shown in figure 10. This information will help pilots identify what type of approach lighting to look for when landing.

NONPRECISION APPROACH VISIBILITIES

Nonprecision approaches, of the VOR and NDB type, require a different method for estimating inflight visibility. If the approach is a straight-in type, then the MDA is maintained to the missed approach point. This is usually found at, or near, the runway threshold. Any approach lights, if installed, can still be used to estimate distance, based on the length of the lighting system. The secret of estimating inflight visibility is to begin looking for signs of these approach lights well before reaching the missed approach point. Without an approach light system available, it's possible to use the length of the runway to estimate inflight visibility. The difficulty with this technique is that the aircraft must be close to the missed approach point to actually estimate the visibility. This could get a bit sticky. This will put the airplane directly above the runway, at the MDA. Chances are not good that a safe descent for landing could be made when this close in to the landing surface. Besides, FAR 91.175C(1) states that an aircraft cannot descend below the MDA unless, "The aircraft is continuously in a position from which a descent to a landing on the intended runway can be made at a normal rate of descent, using normal maneuvers." There is a better way of estimating inflight visibility on nonprecision approaches.

If a nonprecision approach is timed, then a visibility reference point can be created to help estimate visibility. Figure 11 shows the VOR 21 approach to Laurel, Montana. The missed approach point is based on time from the VOR. At 90 knots (1.5 nautical miles per minute) ground speed, the time to the missed approach point is 5 minutes and 24 seconds. The required visibility is one statute mile. Approximately 40 seconds are required to cover a one nautical mile distance at 90 knots. Therefore, a visibility reference point can be determined by subtracting

Shocking situation

An aircraft executed the missed approach due to restricted visibility, caused by snow, and the inability of airport to properly adjust the intensity of the high intensity runway lights (HIRL). Due to a new tower being installed at present, the runway light intensity is adjusted by twisting bare wires together! In this instance, the airport operators refused to increase the intensity because of the jury-rig setup which caused this aircraft to divert. **ASRS REPORT**

40 seconds from the 5:24 total time.* At 4:44, the aircraft will be one nautical mile from the runway. At this point, pilots should anticipate sighting some visual reference associated with the runway. This would indicate that, at least, a visibility slightly greater than one statute mile exists at Laurel. Remember, this is only a rough approximation of visibility, since the measured ground distance is in nautical miles, which is a little larger than the statute mile visibility requirement.

Additionally, if DME is available along the approach course, it may be used to identify the position where pilots should expect to see some runway visual reference. Remember, DME reads in nautical miles and minimum visibility requirements are in statute miles. The small difference between nautical and statute miles is, again, an error on the conservative side. It gives the pilot a little more visibility than required. These are the types of errors that allow pilots to get by with less than perfect judgement. Not like the town veterinarian and part time taxidermist who put a sign in the window that read, "Either way, you get your dog back!" This was a big error in judgement! People got upset! Perhaps this is

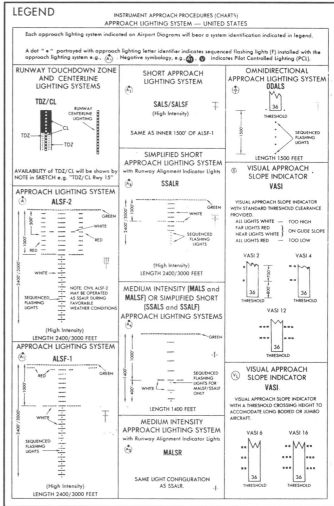

Fig. 10. NOS airport lighting legend.

similar to the error made by a woman who was having an affair with an airline pilot that lived down the street. When her boyfriend grew suspicious, he decided to confront her. He said, "Have you been messing around with that pilot down the street?" She replied, "Negative!" These are the types of errors that are very serious!

A young student pilot from Lyme
Whose negligence seemed just a crime
    Took off one fine day
    In the most careless way
Said, "I'm lost but I'm making good time."

Ellis S. Nelson

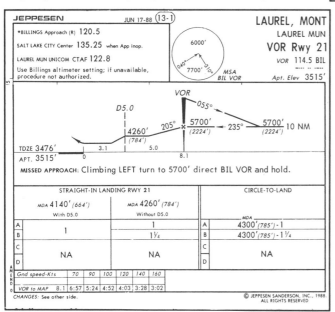

Fig. 11. On a nonprecision approach, pilots can create a visibility determination point to help them estimate inflight visibility.

*At 90 knots, the time required to cover one statute mile is 35 seconds. This is close enough to 40 seconds. Besides, the error is conservative and probably cancels itself out, in that it allows pilots a few seconds for their eyes to attain a slightly longer focal range, when shifting from the panel.

THE RUNWAY VISUAL REFERENCES

Up to this point, we have discussed how to determine the required inflight visibility for landing. But there is something else required for descent below the MDA or DA. FAR 91.175 C1(i) states that the pilot must have one of the visual references listed below, for the intended runway, in order to descend below the specified MDA or DA:

1. **The threshold;**
2. **The threshold markings;**
3. **The threshold lights;**
4. **The runway end identifier lights;**
5. **The VASI;**
6. **The touchdown zone or touchdown zone markings;**
7. **The touchdown zone lights;**
8. **The runway or runway markings;**
9. **The runway lights;**
10. **The approach lighting system, except that the pilot may not descend below 100 feet above the touchdown zone elevation, using the approach lights as a reference, unless the red terminating bars, or the red side row bars, are also distinctly visible and identifiable.**

Notice that the first nine items are on the landing side of the runway threshold. What happens if pilots can only see the approach lights, instead of one of the other nine visual references? Is it still legal to descend below the MDA or DA? Since the approach lighting system was intended as a transition towards the runway, the approach lights may be used for the initial descent below the MDA or DA. Approach lights are not on the landing side of the runway threshold, therefore, a limit exists as to how low pilots can go when using them as their only visual reference for the descent. The regulations specifically state that no descent below 100 feet above the touchdown zone elevation is approved, unless the red terminating bars, or the red side row bars, shown in figure 12, are identified. The ALSF I and II system are the only approach lights having these red bars. A visual identification of these red bars permits a continued descent below 100 feet above the touchdown zone elevation. The rational is that these red bars are close to the runway threshold and are easily seen, because of their color

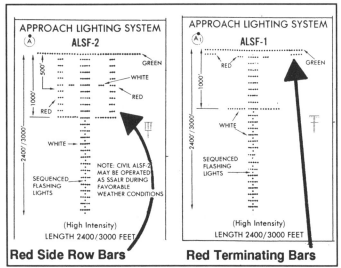

Fig. 12. ALSF-1 approach lighting system having red terminating bars, and ALSF-II approach lighting system having red side row bars.

contrast. In particular, the red terminating bars on the ALSF I system are butted up against the green threshold lights. If these bars are seen, then identification of the threshold is almost assured. It's assumed that as the airplane approaches the runway using these red bars, one of the other nine items previously listed will be identified.

What would happen if an approach were made to an airport with approach lighting other than the ALSF I or II type? Without the availability of red terminating bars or red side row bars, the pilot has automatically limited the descent to a minimum of 100 feet above the touchdown zone elevation, if the pilot cannot identify some reference on the landing side of the threshold. It's possible that a pilot, at 100 feet HAT, could not see a runway reference because the airport may be covered in snow, or enveloped in heavy rain. Under these circumstances, it may be difficult to pick out references on the landing side of the threshold, despite having the required flight visibility for the approach.

In the event a descent is made, using the approach lights as a reference, how would an altitude of 100 feet above the TDZE be determined? The simple answer is to add 100 feet on the TDZE altitude, shown in the profile. This is an important altitude reference for deciding to continue a descent. In a way, it's a second Decision Altitude. Pilots should determine what this altitude is ahead of time. When fishing for obstacles down below Decision Altitude, this is no time to be practicing basic arithmetic. Besides, it makes the passengers nervous when they watch the pilot's lips moving in precise choreography to this mental calculating. They know full well that he's not talking to anybody, and this quickly erodes their confidence in his skill. Perhaps this explains why one pilot always makes everybody wear oxygen masks when he's flying an approach. The masks don't provide any oxygen, they just muffle the screams from the passengers.

PROPERLY DONE

Credit where due

It was snowing heavily. The visibility 1/4 mile. We were cleared into position to hold. Turning to line up, my copilot saw a small twin, emerging from the clouds, on short final. Its pilot apparently saw us at the same time. He applied power, pulled up, passed overhead about fifty feet up and landed in front of us. I am sorry I cannot meet the pilot and compliment him on his alertness. He responded instantly to an emergency situation and averted, what could have been, a disastrous collision. I'll ride with him any day. **ASRS REPORT**

TOWERING IDEAS

On the approach, I forgot to give the signal to the flight attendants to take their seats in time for landing. Consequently, the FA's were enroute to their positions when touchdown was made. Fortunately, no one was hurt. It had been a long night, with many problems, delays and the season's first snowfall. The airport had just experienced frontal passage, an hour or so before our arrival. After several tricky approaches, a long night, the clear weather, and clearance for the visual with a warning to adhere to noise abatement procedures, the normal chain of events and procedures used all night was broken. Add to that unreported windshear, and you get the airline pilot's equivalent of target fixation. We had been lulled into the sense of "this was going to be easy," after what we had been through. When additional problems were laid on us on short final, we (or I) neglected normal routine procedures. The checklist caught the problem, but not in time. The last leg of a trip must be flown as is the first leg, or it may be the last leg of a career. **ASRS REPORT**

At Long Beach airport in Southern California, a relatively new CFI was about to have his first introduction into airport illusions. This instructor was soloing a very young and nervous student. He gave the student the familiar pep talk, with a request to do three full stops. As the student taxied toward the runway, he carefully navigated through the maze of six aircraft holding short and took off. The instructor thought, "How nice, the controllers are letting him go first because he's a solo." The first landing was an uneventful full stop. The student taxied back without looking at the instructor, navigated through the six airplanes that were holding short, and took off once more. The instructor thought, "Wow, this guy is lucky today, no waiting!" The student came around, landed and taxied through six airplanes once more. As it was rolling down the runway, it was being chased by two airport service vehicles and a police car. With lights flashing and sirens wailing, they were all flagging him to stop the takeoff roll. He took off over them and completed his last landing. While the instructor was thinking about how lucky his student was, the student was mesmerized to the point of oblivion. He didn't even think about requesting a takeoff clearance, much less hearing the tower's calls to stop.

In essence, things were much more complicated than they looked from the instructor's point of view. The same can be said for making decisions about landing minimums from the pilot's point of view. What appears to be the simple process of deciding to land is anything but simple. To effectively make decisions about landing minimums, pilots need to have a good understanding of approach light configuration, as well as IFR regulations and approach chart symbology. In a similar way, decisions about instrument departures are made with greater confidence when the pilot understands ATC expectations and IFR departure procedures.

17. INSTRUMENT DEPARTURES

An old fisherman sat on the riverbank with his pole in hand and line in the water. He patiently waited for a nibble, even through fishing season had not officially opened. A game warden observed him from a distance, then strolled up and quietly stood behind him for several minutes. "You the game warden?" the fisherman asked, glancing over his shoulder. "Yep," the warden replied. Cool as could be the old fisherman started to move his pole gently from side to side. After a couple of minutes, he lifted the line out of the water to reveal his bait, a small minnow wiggling on the hook. "Just teachin' him how to swim," the old fisherman explained.

Sometimes the law is unforgiving, even when a creative excuse is applied to a not-so-serious violation of that law. Unfortunately, a violation of Mother Nature's law is often just as unforgiving and is often met with serious consequences. Run an airplane into a solid wall of granite, and Mother Nature's law says someone is bound to get hurt. No amount of creativity, and no excuse, will make up for violating this law. Therefore, to avoid metal plating a mountain side, instrument rated pilots need to have more than a casual knowledge about IFR departures.

ATC's PURPOSE

The primary purpose of Air Traffic Control is to provide separation between IFR airplanes operating in controlled airspace. Yet, as unusual as it may seem, IFR aircraft can and do operate in uncontrolled (Class G) airspace. This often occurs during an instrument departure where the overlying controlled airspace (Class E) doesn't touch the ground. Airports having operating control towers usually have Class B, C or D airspace in existence. This airspace establishes controlled airspace at the airport's surface. Therefore, pilots departing tower controlled airports are usually given headings to fly or SIDs to follow. But, what happens when Class B, C or D (controlled) airspace isn't in effect? Inevitably, the IFR departure is forced to ascend through at least 700 feet or more of Class G (uncontrolled) airspace before reaching Class E (controlled airspace). This demands that IFR pilots understand their responsibility to avoid obstructions during this transition.

FLUTTER

I had just started the engine, received my IFR clearance, and was ready to taxi when I looked forward and slightly to the right of the aircraft because I saw an object moving very rapidly across the ramp toward me. It was a small object. As a matter of fact, it was going like @#$%. It was a small, gasoline-powered, radio-controlled, hobby model car! It barely missed the nosewheel of my aircraft, as it passed from right to left. The next thing I saw really scared the @#$% out of me! It was two young boys, about nine and eleven, running after it and directly toward my spinning prop! I did have time to shut the engine off before the boys reached what would have been a very hazardous position relative to my prop! The little model car continued across the ramp, under several other planes, before it struck the chain link fence. Looking further around the ramp, I saw a chartered small transport loading what appeared to be two families aboard for a trip to some vacation spot for their holidays. The laxity of the boys' parents, two mischievous boys, and the temptation to "try it out" on this wide open area nearly led to disaster!

ASRS REPORT

An IFR departure clearance into uncontrolled airspace will usually contain a few items with which pilots may not be familiar. The following is an ATC clearance similar to what a pilot should expect:

> "32B IS CLEARED TO BIGBOB AIRPORT. AFTER DEPARTURE, WHEN REACHING 700 FEET AGL, FLY HEADING 200 DEGREES TO INTERCEPT V-197, DIRECT BOBETTE VOR. CLIMB AND MAINTAIN 3,000 FEET, CONTACT DEPARTURE CONTROL ON 127.3 AND SQUAWK 1234. CLEARANCE VOID IF NOT OFF BY 12:00. IF NOT OFF THE GROUND BY 12:00, CONTACT BIGBOB FLIGHT SERVICE STATION NO LATER THAN 12:30

THE VOID TIME

Several items in this clearance are distinctly different from those given during tower controlled departures. Notice that a clearance void time is provided, as well as a request that ATC be notified if the flight didn't depart as planned. If the airplane's wheels didn't come off the ground by 12:00, then the window ATC has made for the departure has technically closed. Pilots shouldn't attempt a late IFR departure and hope the controller has kept the departure window open. Doing so is guaranteed to test the controller's pacemaker implant. ATC has most likely given that airspace over to another IFR pilot.

It's not unusual for controllers to give a pilot an immediate IFR departure window of two to three minutes duration. Accepting this clearance means that the airplane must depart within two to three minutes. This could present a problem if ground traffic is present, the runup hasn't been completed or extra time is needed for takeoff. Be reluctant about accepting immediate departure windows. If

SHOCKING ACTIONS

I needed a clearance to VFR on top. I was to climb to 4,000 feet; if not on top by 4.000 I was to maintain 4,000 and advise. I was on top at 4,000, but Departure was busy. Not thinking, I continued to climb to 4,800, prior to cancelling IFR. The clearance given correctly, copied correctly, read back correctly, but flown INCORRECTLY!

ASRS REPORT

necessary, ask for a longer departure window or a clearance release at some later time. This will provide enough time to prepare the aircraft for departure. I've seen pilots depart in such haste that they forget to untie one side of the airplane. They end up performing a new and non-approved commercial maneuver called, "turns around a tie down point." While this doesn't do much for a pilot's proficiency, it is a real crowd pleaser.

Pilots need to be willing to ask for what they want. After all, they are the pilot in command. They need only ask nicely. Once, while waiting in a restaurant, a gigantic, mean-looking waitress approached the table. She was very big and mean -- she was a waitrasaurous. I decided to ask for some ice tea, in a pleasant, non-demanding manner and use a sincere compliment to win her favor. I said, "Ma'am, I'd sure like an ice tea and, by the way, those are such beautiful earrings." Her head lowered as her eyes took aim at me. With a voice tone as low as a seismic wave, she said, "Those aren't earrings bud! They're transmitters that paleontologists use to keep track of my position." Well, I got my ice tea and managed to escape the restaurant without getting my head bitten off. The moral is: always ask nicely; don't demand; and request something as a favor. This is bound to win a greater advantage when working with others.

EXPERIENCING A
RUNAWAY HOBBS METER
DURING AN IFR DEPARTURE
IS TO EXPERIENCE THE
ULTIMATE FEAR KNOWN to MAN.

In addition to asking nicely, be willing to negotiate for the desired clearance. The controller may not want to extend a departure window because of traffic concerns. Assuming the weather in the departure area is VFR, there is something pilots can do to minimize the departure delay. I have found a good negotiating tool is offering to depart and climb with a VFR restriction, to an altitude that accommodates both the controller and the pilot. This prevents the controller from having to apply IFR separation standards between aircraft, thereby easing the departure window restrictions. Of course, pilots should not depart and climb VFR unless it is VFR. A good way to express this request is to state, "Sir, if it will help you, and possibly get us airborne sooner, we can climb with a VFR restriction to (feet)." This may prevent pilots from taking the delay on the ground and gets them airborne sooner.*

A pilot's obligation to ATC is not over if the flight didn't depart as planned. If the aircraft didn't depart prior to the void time, the pilot is still required to notify ATC by 12:30 of this cancellation. ATC has no way of knowing if the pilot departed successfully or experienced either lost communications or an inflight emergency after departure. Unless ATC is notified, some form of search and rescue will be undertaken.

HEADINGS BY CONTROLLERS

When controllers issue initial departure headings, they will apply only in controlled airspace. The clearance to Bigbob airport instructs the pilot to fly 200 degrees when reaching 700 feet above ground level.** This happens to be the floor of the overlying controlled airspace. The heading ATC gave should move the aircraft towards V-197. What is of the greatest importance for the pilot to understand is that this heading is not a radar vector! It's just a heading. ATC will not issue radar vectors until

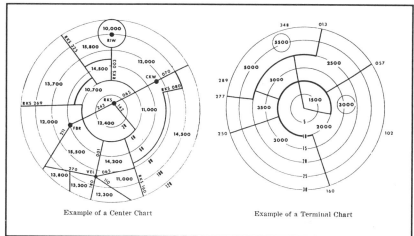

Example of a Center Chart

Example of a Terminal Chart

Fig. 1. Minimum vectoring altitude charts for Center and Approach control.

the airplane is at, or above, the Minimum Vectoring Altitude (MVA), as seen in figure 1. The only exception to this is when prominent obstructions have been marked on the controller's radar screen, and the aircraft is climbing to an altitude above these obstacles. The heading assigned in the clearance

*When ATC uses a vector to: prevent an IFR traffic separation problem, attain a Minimum Crossing Altitude, or reach the controller's Minimum Vectoring Altitude, pilots have the option of requesting a VFR restriction. This may allow them to continue along their route, while still on an IFR flight plan and minimize the delay. I have used a similar request when receiving a vector taking me beyond the gliding distance from shore. I don't like being out over water; especially since seeing the movie "Jaws."
**The clearance may also read, "When entering controlled airspace, fly heading 200 degrees..."

to Bigbob airport starts below the controller's MVA. In this instance, ATC can assign a heading that is not a radar vector, below the Minimum Vectoring Altitude, provided the route has been flight tested and shown to be free of obstructions.

Believing radar guidance is being provided when it is not is a very dangerous situation for aviators. After departure, the pilot may hear the words "RADAR CONTACT." Most pilots think that these words mean that the aircraft is now under radar guidance, and the pilot's chosen heading will be free

CAUGHT WITH WHEEL PANTS DOWN

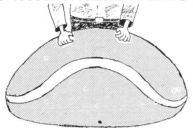

"...I said '075, the heading, right?' The First Officer looked at me quizzically and said...'Yeah, OK.' We continued to climb and were told to contact departure. They told us to turn immediately to 100, then asked 'What heading were you cleared to?' I said, 'tell them 075; that's what we read back, wasn't it?' The copilot did not answer me, so I looked at him and he again had that odd look. At no time were we aware of the serious problem with the other aircraft that, unbeknownst to us, had taken off on Runway 8. I believe it was solely due to poor cockpit communications. I thought 075 degrees was the correct departure heading, and to confirm it, I asked the copilot. But my question came at a time when we were very busy, and he thought I was asking his evaluation of a direction. Coincidentally, that, to him, was a good direction, and he answered in the affirmative. I took his answer as a concurrence of my question of proper takeoff heading." **ASRS REPORT**

from obstructions. Nothing could be further from the truth! This is quite similar to believing that giving a dog a can of "radiator stop leak" will keep it from wetting the carpet. Terrain and obstruction clearance is not provided by ATC until the controller begins to provide navigational guidance, i.e., radar vectors.

To be issued vectors, pilots must be at, or above, the Minimum Vectoring Altitude (MVA). Additionally, the aircraft must be identifiable on the radar screen. It's interesting to note that Minimum Vectoring Altitudes are established on the basis of obstruction clearance requirements only. These routes may not have been flight checked for radar coverage.* Aircraft may actually need to be higher than the MVA for the controller to establish radar identification. Without access to the controller's MVA charts, pilots can assume they are above

the MVA when they start receiving vectors. MVA's must provide at least 1,000 feet of obstacle clearance in non-mountainous terrain and 2,000 feet of obstacle clearance in mountainous terrain.

Additionally, the MVA must be established at least 300 feet above the base of controlled airspace.* In Class E airspace starting at 700 feet AGL (identified by a magenta border on sectional charts) this equates to 1,000 feet for the lowest usable MVA. If Class E (controlled) airspace starts at 1,200 feet AGL, the MVA will be at least 1,500 feet AGL (1,200' + 300'). Therefore, pilots shouldn't anticipate receiving vectors when less than 1,000 feet AGL. Considering the addition of obstacles and abundance of Class E airspace beginning at 1,200 feet AGL, the MVA is more likely to be 1,500 feet AGL or higher. In a designated mountainous area, pilots can expect the MVA to start at a minimum of 2,000 feet AGL. The pressing question is, "How can pilots be assured of avoiding obstructions when departing into

Class G (uncontrolled) airspace while operating below the controller's MVA? Keep in mind that departures into Class G airspace are most likely to occur from non-tower airports or airports where the tower is not in operation.

*Ref. 8260.19A. Note: "Minimum Vectoring Altitudes are established irrespective of the flight checked radar coverage. They are based on obstruction clearance requirements only. It is the responsibility of the controller to determine that a target return is adequate for radar control purposes."

3 METHODS OF AVOIDING TERRAIN

There are three ways of avoiding obstructions when departing a non-tower airport. First, a VFR departure may be made. With a reasonable amount of forward visibility and cloud clearance, pilots should be able to navigate safely to the enroute structure. Departing VFR is always a good idea when unfamiliar with the terrain and when obstructions surround the airport.

Second, a sectional chart could be used for deciding on a path free of obstructions during a solid IFR departure. This could easily make a pilot feel about as comfortable as a border patrol agent at a Cinco de Mayo festival. This is a risky proposition. I would recommend something less risky, like towing aerial gunnery targets for the military. The odds seem so much better. While it's not illegal for a Part 91 operator to takeoff with zero visibility and self-navigate around obstructions, this action is certainly not very smart. Pilots should always plan for the unlikely. What if an engine quits? Without forward visibility, there is no chance of selecting a safe landing site. Control over the landing is now a function of gravity, not pilot judgement. This is not good!

THE IFR DEPARTURE PROCEDURE

The last option is often the least understood. If the departure airport has an instrument approach, it may also have an IFR departure procedure.* Figure 2A shows the IFR departure procedure for Montague, California. This procedure is found on the bottom, left hand side of the first approach chart for the airport, or on the airport diagram chart. Users of NOS charts will find the IFR departure procedures located at the beginning of the chart booklet, as seen in figure 2B.

TAKE-OFF & IFR DEPARTURE PROCEDURE										FOR FILING AS ALTERNATE
Rwy 35			Rwy 17							
			CAT A & B AIRCRAFT			CAT C & D AIRCRAFT				
	With Mim climb of 300'/NM to 7000'		Other	With Mim climb of 350'/NM to 5500'		Other	With Mim climb of 350'/NM to 7400'		Other	
	Adequate Vis Ref	STD		Adequate Vis Ref	STD		Adequate Vis Ref	STD		
1 & 2 Eng	1/4	1	4000-2	1/4	1	2400-2	1/4	1	4100-2	A / B / C / D NA
3 & 4 Eng		1/2			1/2			1/2		
IFR DEPARTURE PROCEDURE: Rwy 17, climb direct MOG NDB. Continue climb to 10000'in MOG NDB holding pattern (North, right turns, 172° inbound). Rwy 35, climb to 7000' via runway heading and 352°						bearing from MOG NDB, then climbing right turn to 10000' direct MOG NDB. All aircraft depart MOG NDB at or above MEA for route of flight.				
CHANGES: See other side.						© JEPPESEN SANDERSON, INC., 1986, 1990. ALL RIGHTS RESERVED.				

Fig. 2A. The IFR departure procedure for Montague, CA.

These IFR departure procedures should not be confused with Standard Instrument Departures (SID's). SID's are prepackaged IFR clearances. They are developed for airports having a large amount of IFR traffic. They save controllers time by not having to read departure instructions to pilots. Controller lips can take only so much flapping in one day. Excessive flapping may require that controllers have their lips recapped.** For example, controllers simply tell the pilot to fly the "Vertigo One Departure," and the pilot just follows the written directions. This explains why pilots may have the controller read the directions off the SID when not in possession of the textual description.

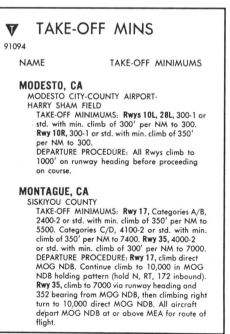

▼ TAKE-OFF MINS

91094

NAME   TAKE-OFF MINIMUMS

MODESTO, CA
MODESTO CITY-COUNTY AIRPORT-
HARRY SHAM FIELD
TAKE-OFF MINIMUMS: Rwys 10L, 28L, 300-1 or std. with min. climb of 300' per NM to 300. Rwy 10R, 300-1 or std. with min. climb of 350' per NM to 300.
DEPARTURE PROCEDURE: All Rwys climb to 1000' on runway heading before proceeding on course.

MONTAGUE, CA
SISKIYOU COUNTY
TAKE-OFF MINIMUMS: Rwy 17, Categories A/B, 2400-2 or std. with min. climb of 350' per NM to 5500. Categories C/D, 4100-2 or std. with min. climb of 350' per NM to 7400. Rwy 35, 4000-2 or std. with min. climb of 300' per NM to 7000. DEPARTURE PROCEDURE: Rwy 17, climb direct MOG NDB. Continue climb to 10,000 in MOG NDB holding pattern (hold N, RT, 172 inbound). Rwy 35, climb to 7000 via runway heading and 352 bearing from MOG NDB, then climbing right turn to 10,000 direct MOG NDB. All aircraft depart MOG NDB at or above MEA for route of flight.

Fig. 2B. NOS IFR departure procedure.

*There are a few airports, without instrument approaches, that have IFR departure procedures.
**I am not sure what the official medical procedure is, but I would suspect it's somewhat similar to that used on steel-belted radial tires.

IFR departure procedures can be used when ATC doesn't specifically inform the pilot about how to depart the airport. In other words, they are often used when a pilot departs into Class G (uncontrolled) airspace.* It's important to remember that even at busy airports, Class B, C, D & E controlled airspace may not be in operation on a 24 hour basis. When operating beyond the effective hours of this airspace, pilots will more than likely be departing into Class G airspace. Therefore, they have the option of using the IFR departure procedure, if available, to safely avoid obstructions after takeoff.

IFR departure procedures are provided when there are obstacles in the departure area. When obstacles penetrate a 152 foot per nautical mile climb plane, starting at approximately 35 feet above the end of the runway, an IFR departure procedure will be provided for that airport. This departure gradient is shown in figure 3. If obstacles do not penetrate this climb plane, a departure procedure will not be established. Obstacles penetrating this climb plane demand specific avoidance procedures. These will be specified as: headings, routes,

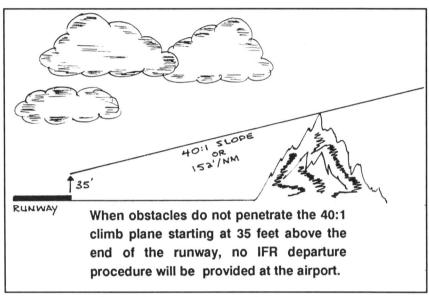

When obstacles do not penetrate the 40:1 climb plane starting at 35 feet above the end of the runway, no IFR departure procedure will be provided at the airport.

Fig. 3. IFR departure protected area.

climb gradients, ceilings or visibilities allowing visual avoidance of the obstacle. When specific climb gradients are not provided, it's assumed the pilot will maintain at least a 200 foot per nautical mile rate of climb to avoid obstacles. This guarantees a minimum obstacle clearance of 48 feet per nautical mile during the climb. This isn't a great deal of clearance. Most pilots look forward to this minimum clearance, as much as they do a Dean Martin-Jerry Lewis reunion. It's possible that a pilot departing an airport in a tired, old Cessna 150 freighter, will have some difficulty meeting this climb performance. Nevertheless, most aircraft are going to appreciably exceed this minimum climb rate.

KICK IN THE EMPENNAGE

I was lined up on the runway for takeoff in heavy fog (0/0, RVR 100 feet). I set the Directional Gyro to the magnetic compass heading for Runway 6. The tower cleared us for takeoff. I acknowledged and applied power. Rolling down the runway, the airspeed was almost to rotation speed when the tires made a strange sound on the pavement. I took my head out of the cockpit to see what happened. I looked back at the DG, and we were on a heading of 90 degrees! The next thing I knew, I had an airplane in front of me. By this time, the airspeed was good for rotating, and I did. To the best of my knowledge, I veered off the runway at the intersection and onto the taxiway. **ASRS REPORT**

IFR departure procedures may require a turn after departure. Figure 4 shows a left turn off Runway 8 at Santa Ynez, California. When a turn is required, it's assumed that a pilot will climb to a minimum of 400 feet above the airport elevation, before the turn is commenced. All climbs should be done at a minimum rate of 200 feet per nautical mile, unless otherwise noted on the chart. This rate of climb will put the airplane at a minimum of 400 feet AGL, within 2 miles of the departure threshold. This provides the pilot with a minimum altitude for obstruction clearance during the turning departure.

*Remember, if Class B, C, D or E airspace doesn't exist or is not in effect around an airport, then the pilot departs into Class G (uncontrolled) airspace before reaching the overlying controlled airspace.

It's the pilot's prerogative to use the IFR departure procedure when ATC has not told the pilot what to do immediately after departure. The clearance to Bigbob airport didn't provide instructions on how to depart the airport. Instructions were given to proceed to an airway when reaching 700 feet AGL. What should be done until reaching the controlled airspace at 700 feet AGL? Hopefully, the IFR departure procedure will be used. As far as ATC is concerned, they are hoping pilots will be doing something smart, like departing visually or using the IFR departure procedure.

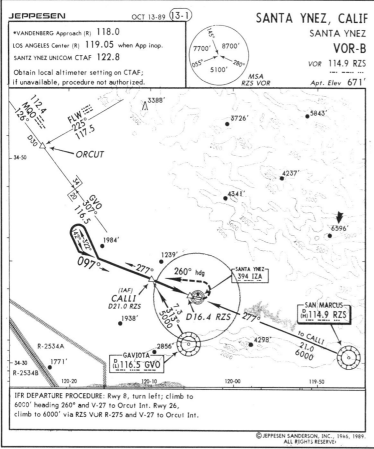

Fig. 4. The IFR departure procedure for Santa Ynez, CA.

If IFR departure procedures ensure an obstruction-free departure, why doesn't ATC assign them? The answer is, they do, when departing into Class B, C, D or E (controlled) airspace.* An IFR departure, made into Class G (uncontrolled) airspace is made at the pilot's own risk. ATC had no jurisdiction over this airspace. ATC may, however, assign an IFR departure procedure in Class G (uncontrolled) airspace when it's necessary to prevent a traffic separation problem. It's always a good idea to list in the remarks section of the flight plan that the IFR departure procedure will be used. This keeps controllers informed and makes them happy. Remember, departures into Class G (uncontrolled) airspace require pilots to make their own decisions about obstacle avoidance. The IFR departure procedure, if available, is always a wise choice in helping avoid these obstacles.

There is only one potential problem pilots may encounter when executing the IFR departure procedure. Sometimes, this procedure may temporarily head the aircraft in the opposite direction to be flown in the clearance. This is rarely a problem. But when it is, the controller may become confused about the pilot's intentions. Most of the time, IFR departure procedures take the aircraft to a fix, from which any direction of flight may be chosen. Pay attention to where the departure procedure ends. When the departure procedure heads the aircraft in a direction opposite that intended in the clearance, clarify this problem with ATC before flight. Additionally, if pilots are going to use the IFR departure procedure, they might want to file their route of flight starting from the fix or point where the departure procedure ends.

GROUNDED!

An IFR student tried to file an IFR flight plan from Albuquerque to Los Angeles. He put 4,000 feet as the initial IFR altitude. The FSS specialist gave him a number to call to file the flight plan. When the student asked about who the number belonged to, the FSS specialist said, "The bureau of land Management."

P.S. Albuquerque elevation is 5,352 feet

*At airports without control towers but within a Class E surface area, ATC will specify the takeoff\turn or initial heading to be flown after takeoff as is necessary. ATC will obtain or solicit the pilot's concurrence, before takeoff, that these items will allow compliance with traffic patterns, terrain or obstruction avoidance.

Pilots should learn to use what's available. It's like a fellow pilot who realized that it cost him $2.50 to have his shirt cleaned at the dry cleaners. He discovered there was another available resource he wasn't using. Now he donates them to the Salvation Army. They clean and press them, and he buys them back at 75 cents each. IFR departure procedures, like the Salvation Army, are wonderful resources. Use them when available!

MIND TWISTER

We were waiting for departure. The weather was indefinite zero, sky obscured, visibility 1/4, RVR at minimum. We were number one for departure, waiting for the arrival of a larger transport. The tower asked us to advise them when he went by the approach end of the runway, so we could take position. He landed, and we were cleared into position and instructed to hold. Also at this time, there was another larger transport on the approach. After about two minutes of waiting for the first aircraft to clear the runway, we were cleared for takeoff. After rolling about 200 feet, we were told to hold our position and cancel our takeoff clearance, due to the aircraft still on the approach. At this time, Tower advised that aircraft to go around, because we were still sitting on the runway. We never heard an acknowledgement from the aircraft. Still in position, the next thing we knew, he came right over the top of us and missed hitting us by -- it seemed like -- inches. His thrust rocked our aircraft. As he initiated a go-around, his aircraft came within five feet of touching down. After a minute or two we were cleared for takeoff.

ASRS REPORT

IFR departure procedures are not available at all airports. Nevertheless, safe IFR departures can be made if pilots talk to a few of the airport residents about airport geography and local departure procedures. Before departure, a determination should be made on what minimum visibility or ceiling requirement is necessary to avoid local obstructions. Professional recommendation has it that it's useful to take out a sectional chart and identify the highest obstacle in the departure path. This becomes the minimum ceiling height for departure. Using a minimum of one mile visibility for departures, until the aircraft is above or moving away from the referenced obstacle, provides an excellent safety advantage. The plain fact is that it's easier to avoid an obstacle that can be seen. Interestingly, FAA documents require that commercial operators (Part 121, 123, 129 and 135) must have a minimum of one mile visibility for departures, when a ceiling restriction is required. Of course, there are many circumstances that can raise or lower the ceiling and visibility weather requirements. Although not required for Part 91 operators, a minimum ceiling and/or visibility is often a pilot's best bet for avoiding obstacles.

While takeoff minimums and IFR departure procedures are not required for Part 91 operators, they are required for commercial operators. Consider that Part 91 was not necessarily written for passenger safety. It was written to provide the minimum common sense boundary between being legal and illegal in the eyes of the FAA. To find a block of regulations written for passenger safety, look at Part 135 or 121. These are regulations for air charter and air carrier operations. They were written to protect the passenger and are much more safety oriented.

Overheard in LAX Basin

"Riverside Flight Service Station, this is 2132B, I'd like to file an IFR flight plan, depending on where I am."

Figure 5 shows the Santa Ynez, California takeoff and IFR departure procedure minima box. A departure on Runway 26 would require either a 1/4 mile adequate visibility reference or 1/2 to 1 mile visibility, depending on how many engines are installed on the aircraft. An "adequate visibility reference" is defined as either the High Intensity Runway Lights (HIRL), Runway Centerline Lighting (RCL), Runway Centerline Markings (RCM) or, in unusual circumstances, where none of the above visual references is available, the runway is marked so that the pilot has visual reference to the line of forward motion at all times.

TAKE-OFF & IFR DEPARTURE PROCEDURE							FOR FILING AS ALTERNATE
Rwy 26		Rwy 8					
		CAT A & B AIRCRAFT		CAT C & D AIRCRAFT			
				With Mim climb of 280'/NM to 2000'		Other	
Adequate Vis Ref	STD	Adequate Vis Ref	STD	Adequate Vis Ref	STD		
1 & 2 Eng — 1/4	1	1/4	1	1/4	1	1100-2	A B C D — NA
3 & 4 Eng	1/2		1/2		1/2		

IFR DEPARTURE PROCEDURE: Rwy 8, turn left; climb to 6000' heading 260° and V-27 to Orcut Int. Rwy 26, climb to 6000' via RZS VOR R-275 and V-27 to Orcut Int.

CHANGES: Ramp, apt note.   © JEPPESEN SANDERSON, INC., 1986, 1989. ALL RIGHTS RESERVED

Fig. 5. Takeoff visibility requirements for commercial aircraft.

In the absence of an adequate visibility reference, standard takeoff minimums apply. The letters "STD" indicate the standard minimums for departure are: 1 mile (5,000 feet RVR) for 1 and 2 engine aircraft, or 1/2 mile (RVR of 2,400 feet) for 3 and 4 engine aircraft. If no climb gradient is shown, a standard rate of 200 feet per nautical mile applies. Although not required, Part 91 operators should use these minimums as their personal departure limitations. Keep in mind that these minimums are for professional pilots. It might be wise to increase them to accommodate a pilot's inexperience.

Runway 8 at Santa Ynez shows a different set of minima for departure. Category A and B aircraft essentially have the same minimums as a Runway 26 departure. Aircraft of the Category C and D type are required to have a minimum climb rate of 280 feet per nautical mile for departure, with the visibility being the same as for A and B categories. Category C and D aircraft, that cannot maintain this minimum rate of climb, would fall into the "Other" category listed for Runway 8, requiring a minimum of 1,100 foot ceiling and 2 miles visibility for departure.

Takeoff minima can provide a clue as to where terrain and obstructions lie around the airport. A quick glance at the takeoff procedure for Watsonville Airport, figure 6, provides valuable terrain insight. The runways with the lowest takeoff restrictions are Runways 8 and 19, requiring only the minimum rate of climb of 200 feet per nautical mile. A Runway 26 departure, on the other hand, requires a minimum of 230 feet per nautical mile to 600 feet. Commercial operators, unable to meet this climb gradient, must have a 400 foot ceiling and 1 mile

TAKE-OFF & IFR DEPARTURE PROCEDURE								FOR FILING AS ALTERNATE
Rwys 8, 19		Rwy 26			Rwy 1			
		With Mim climb of 230'/NM to 600'		Other	With Mim climb of 370'/NM to 2000'		Other	
Forward Vis Ref	STD	Forward Vis Ref	STD		Forward Vis Ref	STD		
1 & 2 Eng — 1/4	1	1/4	1	400-1	1/4	1	1800-2	A B C D — NA
3 & 4 Eng	1/2		1/2			1/2		

IFR DEPARTURE PROCEDURE: Rwys 1 & 8 turn right, Rwy 26 turn left. All aircraft proceed direct AY NDB and AY NDB bearing 196° to V-25. Northwest bound cross Mover Int at or above 4000'.

CHANGES: Caution note added.   © 1983 JEPPESEN SANDERSON, INC. ALL RIGHTS RESERVED

Fig. 6. Takeoff and departure procedure for Watsonville, CA.

visibility for departure. However, a runway 1 departure shows the highest takeoff minima of 370 feet per nautical mile to 2,000 feet, or an 1,800 foot ceiling and 2 miles visibility. Runway 1 is most likely obstructed with higher terrain or obstacles in the departure path.

A closer look at the sectional, figure 7, indicates that a departure on this runway takes the aircraft towards precipitous terrain. Reading just a little bit into the takeoff procedure information, as well as the IFR departure procedure, pilots can easily determine the preferential direction for an IFR departure.

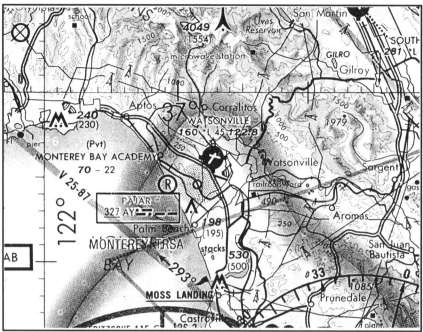

Fig. 7. Sectional chart showing Watsonville airport terrain.

In the early 1900's, New York City had transformer difficulty in their electrical station. No one knew how to solve the problem. Finally, one engineer said that he knew of a retired engineer who knew almost everything about the station. They gave him a call. He came down, took out a screw driver and went into an obscure corner of the building. After a few seconds, he tapped 3 times on a transformer relay. The lights came on and everything began working. He sent the New York station a bill for $1,000.02. They asked him why the odd amount. He said 2 cents was for tapping and $1,000 was for knowing where to tap.

Perhaps this is why professional pilots are paid the big bucks for flying the heavy metal. They get a few cents for the actual flying and thousands of dollars for knowing how to do it safely. Safety means knowing that IFR departure procedures and takeoff minimums are more than just legal dictates for commercial operators. They offer responsible guidelines for a pilot's decision making. The existence of a departure procedure implies a predetermined routing known to be free of obstructions. These routes should be used when available. Minimums for takeoff, while not required for Part 91 operators, offer instrument pilots a starting point for assessing their own, personal limitations, when contemplating an instrument departure.

There is one more chart with which instrument pilots need to develop knowledge -- the Low Altitude Enroute Chart. It's bursting with loads of useful information.

18. ENROUTE CHART SECRETS

Giving rides in a World War II vintage Stearman can be a hair-raising experience -- literally! This open cockpit, tandem-seat aircraft generated more adventure, and perhaps more embarrassment, than most people feel in a lifetime. I had a taste of both one morning. My first passenger of the day was a gentleman named Bob who brought along his new girlfriend to watch his first flight. I tucked him into the front seat, and we climbed out for a 1,500 foot tour of the Long Beach area.

Bob seemed to be enjoying his flight. His head swiveled right and left, absorbing the view. Then, I noticed something funny about his hair. It was starting to lift from the back of his head. Darndest' thing I've ever seen. I examined all the natural reasons for this occurrence and nothing made sense. Then it hit me. He was wearing a toupee -- an aerodynamically efficient one, at that! The air turbulence had dislodged his hair from its tiedown position, and it flapped on his head as a fresh fish on a boat deck. He couldn't even feel it with all the turbulence. Airflow over the upper cambered surface generated toupee lift. The turbulence grew worse, and this thing took on a life of its own. It was flapping as if it were a small animal trying to get free. I quickly calculated its stalling speed and tried to slow down. This had little effect. I tried pulling a few G's hoping the little critter would reattach itself to the top of his head. No such luck. The inevitable happened.

He slowly turned toward me. It happened in slow motion. His hair became airborne. He flipped his wig! It landed square on my face. I yelled out, "Ahhhhhhhhhhhhh!" and swatted it off. I could see it descending off to my left and was tempted to initiate pursuit. What could I do? I wasn't trained in airborne toupee tracking. I could only watch it swirl, spin and descend.

The poor fellow was so embarrassed. Somewhere in downtown Long Beach, what probably looked like Rocky, the Flying Squirrel, made an unauthorized landing on some busy street corner. We landed too, and Bob immediately engaged himself in Jeppesen-origami, otherwise known as Japanese chart folding. He grabbed one of my low altitude enroute charts and made a sailor's hat. I believe he told his girlfriend that it was considered quite normal to wear something associated with aviation after one's first flight. He was too embarrassed to let her see him as Mother Nature intended.

Low altitude enroute charts are tremendously valuable to the pilot. Not only can pilots wear them, as Bob found out, but they contain a wonderful amount of useful information. What most instrument pilots are not aware of, is that they often use only a small amount of the information available on the face of the chart. In much the same way that Bob was satisfied with what the chart did for him, instrument pilots are satisfied with what the chart has done for them. However, when pilots discover the information that has laid dormant, and how useful it can be to them, their appetite for more knowledge will be hard to satiate.

FACE IT

The face of Jeppesen's low altitude chart contains a plethora of useful information. Figure 1A shows panel coverage for the Jeppesen low altitude 3 and 4 chart. One subtlety that is immediately useful is the overlapping chart coverage area. Cities like Williams or Paso Robles are shown as reference points when they are on both sides of the chart. This helps to cue a change from one side of the chart to the other.

Figure 1A shows areas covered by shaded boxes located around major cities. These locations are further detailed by an area chart. There are 13 NOS area charts, while Jeppesen has 31. When navigating in a region covered by an area chart, be sure and use it for

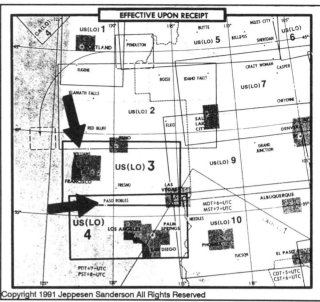

Fig. 1A. Jeppesen's low altitude, enroute chart front panel.

navigation! There are intersections shown on the area chart that are not shown on the enroute chart. Additionally, the scale is greater on the area chart, making the detailed symbols much easier to read. ATC once asked a friend of mine to report over "HEADD." This is an intersection, and it wasn't shown on the enroute chart. Without an area chart, it wasn't apparent that "HEADD" was an intersection. The controller's official request was, "32B, report over HEADD." My friend, somewhat confused, replied, "Sir, we're in the clouds right now, and we don't have time to look outside. Besides, we don't know where you're at!" The intersection name has since been changed, for obvious reasons. Figure 1B compares a section of Jeppesen's low altitude enroute chart with their area chart, figure 1C. West of LIMBO intersection on V-8 are two intersections: INISH and TANDY. These are not shown on the enroute chart. The most unusual clearance I've ever received was from LIMBO intersection to Paradise VOR. The clearance read, "32Bravo is cleared from LIMBO direct to Paradise." Most pilots only hear something like this once in a lifetime.

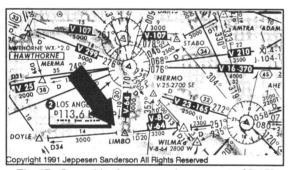

Fig. 1B. Low altitude enroute chart excerpt of LAX.

Fig. 1C. Area chart excerpt of LAX.

THE COMMUNICATIONS SECTION

The communications section on the Jeppesen charts is shown in figure 2. This section provides a tremendous amount of information on many airports covered by the chart. When overflying these airports on cross country flights it's easy to look at the communications section to acquire some useful information. Pilots often listen to ATIS information for local altimeter settings, as well as local weather information. On several occasions, I've even called an approach controller on the listed frequencies and inquired about local weather radar returns. One secret to successful instrument flying is knowing where to go to acquire information. The communications section is a good place to start.

PANEL INFORMATION

The communications section identifies Oakland airport with the letters "KSFO p1B," next to the airport name in figure 2. The KSFO means that Oakland is also shown on the San Francisco area chart. The "K" means that SFO is an airport of entry (customs). Any three or four letter sequence after the airport name means that the airport will be found on Jeppesen's area chart. The "p1B" means that the airport can be quickly found on panel 1, in quadrant B of the chart. To identify panels, look at the top of the communication section in figure 2. This is something peculiar only to Jeppesen charts. It is called the ZIGDEX or Zig Zag Index. To find panel 1, simply place a finger over the number "1" located to the left of the word "San Francisco," and unfold the chart. Panel 1 will be exposed. There are six panels on Jeppesen's low altitude chart -- three on one side of the chart and three on the other side. Each panel represents one third of the chart coverage area. On each panel there are four quadrants, identified by letters "A," "B," "C," and "D," dividing that panel, as seen in figure 3. Oakland will be found in the "B" quadrant, located in the upper right of the San Francisco panel.

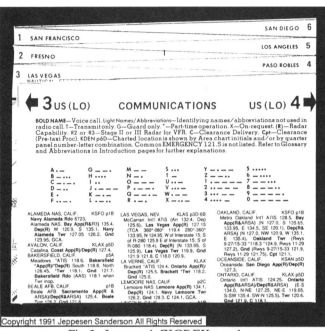

Fig. 2. Jeppesen's ZIGDEX panel.

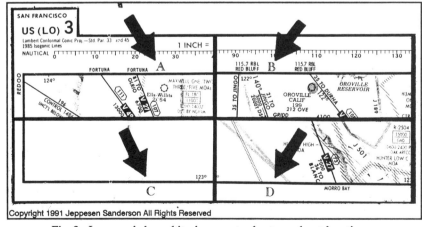

Fig. 3. Jeppesen's low altitude enroute chart quadrant locations.

Airports that are identified as being on an area chart are often not given quadrant locations on the communications section. La Verne, California, figure 2, is shown as being on the Los Angeles area chart without any specific quadrant information. When airports are located on area charts, they can be easily identified because of the smaller coverage area. Therefore, referring to the LAX area chart will reveal the location of La Verne.

THE FRONT SIDE OF THE CHART

◀ 4 US (LO)
1 INCH = 15 NM

JEPPESEN

US (LO) **3 ▶**
1 INCH = 15 NM

UNITED STATES
LOW ALTITUDE ENROUTE CHARTS
© JEPPESEN SANDERSON, INC., 1980, 1993. ALL RIGHTS RESERVED.

MEETS FAA REQUIREMENTS FOR AERONAUTICAL CHARTS

Within the continental U.S., the airways shown on these charts are effective up to but not including 18,000' MSL. At 14,500' MSL and above, all airspace is controlled Class E airspace. Shaded blue areas shown on the face of enroute charts designate airspace that is not controlled (Class G) below 14,500' MSL. The Jet Route structure is superimposed to show its relationship with the low altitude airways. For operational detail for Jet Routes at or above 18,000' MSL, use US(HI) charts.

REVISION DATA

CHART US(LO)3 31 DEC 93 Numerous CRPs redesig NCRPs. Alert Area A-252 revoked (NE of Sacramento, Calif VOR). Hummer MOA's revoked (NW of Squaw Valley, Calif VOR).

Fig. 4. Low altitude enroute chart for use up to, but not including, 18,000 feet.

Figure 4 shows the front of Jeppesen's low altitude enroute chart. This chart is for use up to but not including 18,000 feet MSL. At this altitude, the high altitude airway structure begins and high altitude charts should be used. Jeppesen superimposes high altitude jet routes on low altitude airways, as shown in figure 5. High altitude airways are depicted to allow an easy, more graceful transition between the high and low altitude structure. NOS charts do not depict high altitude airways on low altitude enroute charts. Besides, military pilots do so much low level work that I believe they get most of their navigational information from the latest issue of Field and Stream.

MILITARY TRAINING ROUTE DEPICTION

Since NOS charts are used by the military, these charts show military training routes (MTR's), as seen in figure 6. Jeppesen doesn't show MTR's on their charts. Figure 7 shows the face of the NOS low altitude enroute chart. Route identification and operating altitudes are depicted. This information isn't necessary for flight in the civilian IFR system. Air traffic controllers working military traffic provide IFR separation between military and civilian targets. Perhaps the only major difference between civilian and military is that military pilots fly IFR in formation a great deal. Well, at least they do it intentionally! I've often wondered if this is just because they get lonely much faster than civilian pilots. I suppose if I were strapped to a rocket, with thousands of gallons of explosive fuel and bombs under my body, I'd definitely want someone for company, too.

AIRPORTS WITH APPROACHES

Airports having instrument approaches are clearly identifiable on low altitude enroute charts. Jeppesen lists all airports with IFR approaches in capital letters. Figure 8 identifies several airports having IFR approaches. Merced, in the center of figure 8, has an instrument approach, while Chowchilla (this is not where they eat Chinchillas!), below and to the right, does not. NOS charts identify airports having an instrument approach in blue, while other airports are shown in brown. On Jeppesen and NOS charts, airports having an ILS show the feathered flag as can be seen at Merced, California. ILS feathered flags may not be shown if they clutter the picture.

ONLY THE SEASONED PROFESSIONAL, WITH YEARS OF EXPERIENCE, IS QUALIFIED TO SAY "WHO IS THE GREATEST PILOT, AND WHY AM I?"

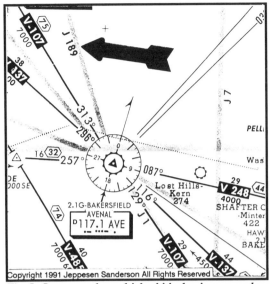

Fig. 5. Jeppesen shows high altitiude airways on low altitude enroute chart.

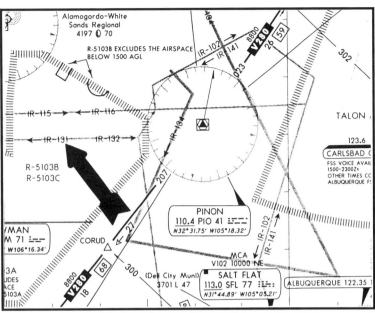

Fig. 6. NOS chart shows military training routes.

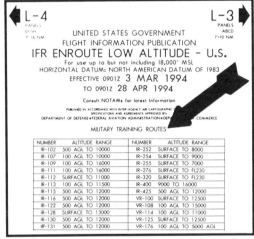

MILITARY TRAINING ROUTES

NUMBER	ALTITUDE RANGE	NUMBER	ALTITUDE RANGE
IR-102	500 AGL TO 10000	IR-252	SURFACE TO 8000
IR-107	100 AGL TO 10000	IR-254	SURFACE TO 9000
IR-109	100 AGL TO 16000	IR-255	SURFACE TO 7000
IR-111	100 AGL TO 16000	IR-276	SURFACE TO FL230
IR-112	SURFACE TO 11000	IR-320	SURFACE TO FL230
IR-113	100 AGL TO 11500	IR-400	9000 TO 16000
IR-115	500 AGL TO 12000	IR-425	500 AGL TO 12000
IR-116	500 AGL TO 12000	VR-100	SURFACE TO 12500
IR-122	500 AGL TO 12000	VR-108	100 AGL TO 15000
IR-128	SURFACE TO 13000	VR-114	100 AGL TO 11000
IR-130	500 AGL TO 12000	VR-125	SURFACE TO 12500
IR-131	500 AGL TO 12000	VR-176	100 AGL TO 5000 AGL

Fig. 7. Military training route altitudes are depicted on NOS enroute charts.

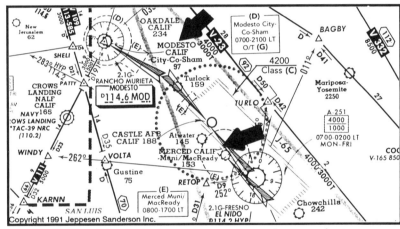

Fig. 8. Airports having instrument approaches on Jeppesen charts.

HOODWINKED

Lure of the bright lights

We finally got back down onto the glideslope and the localizer course about 3.5 to 4 miles out. About that time, the Flight Engineer asked if I saw the runway. I hadn't bothered looking because I wanted to get the ILS nailed down after the high, fast, overshooting intercept. When I looked up, I saw bright approach lights, runway centerline and runway edge lights. I went for the lights. The Captain asked why I was turning off course, and I noticed that there was another runway to the left of the brightly lighted runway which appeared, by contrast, to be barely lighted. I do not recall seeing the approach lights. Anyway, I turned slightly back toward the left and came in for an uneventful landing. The whole thing reminded me of the "moth to the flame" syndrome, and I never thought I would have done it. The crew concept paid off. I just wonder why the correct runway had to be so dimly lighted and the wrong runway so brightly.

ASRS REPORT

At Santa Maria airport there is a green box containing airport information as shown in figure 9A. Class D airspace exists at Santa Maria from 0600 to 2000 hours local time (LT). Underneath the local time reference are the letters "O/T (G)" meaning that Class G (uncontrolled) airspace exists at all "other times." Figure 9B shows

Fig. 9A. Jeppesen's depiction of Santa Maria's Class D airspace operating hours in local time.

Fig. 9B. NOS depiction of Santa Maria's Class D airspace operating hours in Zulu or UCT.

the NOS enroute chart excerpt for Santa Maria and the A/G (Air/Ground) communication panel from the side of the chart. A "D" in a box with an asterisk means that Class D airspace exists at that airport but is not depicted by green dashed lines as it is on Jeppesen charts. The asterisk indicates that the tower, and thus Class D airspace, is in operation part time. NOS users must go the the A/G panel on the side of the enroute chart to find the effective hours of the surface-based controlled airspace. Additionally, for NOS users, these effective times are in Zulu (UCT) and not local times.

Pilots should use caution when planning an IFR flight to an airport beyond the operating hours of its surface-based controlled airspace. It's not unusual for the approach minimums to increase when this airspace is not in effect. In fact, some approaches are not permitted unless the Class D or E surface-based airspace is in effect. Furthermore, some airports are

OGDEN, UTAH	OGD	(11-1) 18 FEB 94		JEPPESEN
-HINCKLEY		*ATIS 125.55		SALT LAKE CITY Departure (R)
N41 11.8 W112 00.7 099.3°/4.3 From OGD 115.7		*OGDEN Ground 121.7		121.1
Elev 4470' Var 14°E		*Tower CTAF 118.7		
		UNICOM 122.95		
		FOR FILING AS ALTERNATE		Authorized Only When Class D Airspace Effective or With Approved Weather Service Other
		Authorized Only When Twr Operating		
		ILS Rwy 3	LOC Rwy 3	
A				
B		600-2	800-2	800-2
C				
D		700-2		
ᵢCHANGES: Runway 16-34 lighting.		© JEPPESEN SANDERSON, INC., 1984, 1994. ALL RIGHTS RESERVED.		

Fig. 9C. Jeppesen chart showing requirements for operating tower or Class D airspace to list Hinckley field as an alternate.

not authorized for filing as alternates unless this airspace is in effect. Figure 9C shows Jeppesen's depicted limitations for listing Hinckley field in Ogden, Utah as an alternate on the IFR flight plan when the tower or Class D airspace isn't operating or effective. Users of NOS charts will find similar alternate limitations at the beginning of their chart booklet. The operating hours for Class D or Class E surface-based airspace are usually tied to the operating hours of the tower, FSS or other means of official weather observation. And, without an official means of weather observation, these airports cannot be listed on the flight plans as alternates.

VARIETIES OF AIRSPACE

Several types of special use airspace are shown on the low altitude enroute chart. Figure 10A shows the special use airspace around Navy China Lake, situated within closely spaced, hatched lines. This is restricted area R-2505 that extends from the ground to as high as aircraft fly. Military Operations Areas, or MOAs, are shown by wider spaced hatched lines, aligned in a direction opposite that of restricted areas. Surrounding the restricted area are several different MOAs. MOAs are usually used by fighter aircraft. The kid who used to race his Corvette up and down the street is now using this airspace to shock all land and air dwelling creatures into submission. And, he's probably waiting out there, for small aircraft, in a heavily-armed F-16. I have often thought MOA's, with more compelling names, would demand greater respect. Names like: UALLBECAREFUL-MOA, ITNOLOOKGOOD4U-MOA, UGOKABOOM-MOA, or the GETMEDOWN-MOA demand a pilot's attention. While flight through a MOA is not prohibited, extreme caution should be used because this is where military pilots go to practice their maneuvers. If they need practice, they may not be all that good at that particular maneuver. Personally, I don't like being around while they're still practicing. In fact, they don't call it a MOA for nothing. Go there once, get scared, and there will be no desire to go back "no-moa."

To the right of China Lake is an unusual symbol. Trona airport has a circle around it. Called an Aerodrome Traffic Zone, all airspace within this circle, less than 1,200 feet AGL, is not part of the MOA. Essentially, pilots within this circle, at less than 1,200 feet AGL, should be free of military traffic. Military pilots are not supposed to go in this area. However, if a G.A. pilot irked one or two of these jets, they could very well be waiting just outside this circle for the little guy to make a run for home.

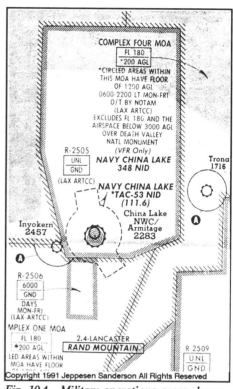

Fig. 10A. Military operations areas shown on Jeppesen's low altitude chart.

Underneath China Lake is a Remote Communication Outlet (RCO) labeled "Rand Mountain." Figure 10B shows the NOS version of the same RCO. Communication with the Riverside FSS can be made on frequency 122.4. An isolated (remote) transmitter and receiver communicates directly with Riverside via a ground line. Pilots should address Riverside FSS by using something similar to the following phraseology: "Riverside Radio, this is Cessna 32B, listening Rand, 122.4, over." The FSS will know immediately on which remote outlet the pilot is communicating. Flight Service Specialists may be responsible for several outlets and not know exactly which one the pilot is using. This saves the specialist a great deal of time trying each transmitter out, saying, "Hello?, click, Hello?, click, Hello?"

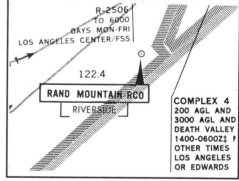

Fig. 10B. Limited remote communications outlet shown on NOS charts.

MENTAL TWISTER

Loaded

On takeoff the aircraft demonstrated the performance of a lead sled. The Captain's concern prompted a check and double check of fuel, cargo, and passenger weights. It took a bit of doing to determine that most of the passengers were attending a coin collectors' convention and had carry-on bags which weighed 60 to 75 pounds. Collectively, the collectors' collections caused considerable cockpit crew consternation.

ASRS REPORT

ATC BOUNDARIES

Boundaries of the nearest Air Traffic Control Center are depicted by dotted lines for the Jeppesen charts, or serrated lines for the NOS charts, as shown in figures 11A and 11B. Sector discrete frequencies are shown in the ARTCC box, figure 11C. The name of the center is shown in larger letters. To contact the Oakland center, use frequency 128.7 MHz or 126.9 MHz. Don't refer to the controller as the, "Priest controller" for two reasons: one, they might like it; and two, they will know that

the pilot just received his instrument rating. Priest is the sector name. Address the controller as, "Oakland Center." This is the frequency on which to make a request for a pop-up IFR clearance, or to activate the IFR portion of a composite flight plan. I always make it a point to listen in on Center frequency when I'm VFR and not receiving traffic advisories. Sometimes, little clues about atmospheric turbulence, winds and other weather observations can be heard during ATC communications with other IFR and VFR aircraft.

NAVIGATIONAL STATIONS

VOR's come in several shapes and sizes. Otto VOR and Anton Chico VOR (Note: all VORTAC's are referred to as VOR's) are seen on the Jeppesen chart, figure 12A, and the NOS chart, figure 12B. Jeppesen depicts any navigation stations having DME capability with a small, circular, spoked center.

KICK IN THE EMPENNAGE

A "compass" rose by any other name...

It was a VFR takeoff and climb. A map check indicated the flight would bypass a restricted area to the north. Over the fix, I set the LORAN and proceeded on the course. I then asked my wife (student pilot) to watch the altitude, course and traffic while I prepared a speech. I glanced up from time to time, and we seemed to be on course and at the proper altitude. I had the autopilot engaged. My wife inquired about an air field almost directly below us. I checked the chart and identified the field as being just inside the north edge of the restricted area. But the directional gyro had moved almost 20 degrees off course towards the south. This had caused the autopilot to gradually steer the aircraft right of our intended course. There is no question that my attention to flying would have prevented this possible intrusion into restricted airspace. My wife has many hours in the right seat, both VMC and IMC, but she didn't notice the increasing irregularity between the DG (autopilot) and magnetic compass.

ASRS REPORT

Anton Chico VOR, figure 12A, has DME capability, while Otto VOR does not. Additionally, Jeppesen shows a small "D" in the frequency box when DME is available on that navaid. NOS charts identify the availability of DME when a UHF TACAN identifier and its two or three number channel follows the navaid's VHF frequency. Figure 12B shows that Anton Chico VOR has DME (ACH 125), while the Otto VOR doesn't. Additionally, DME is indicated by three black, filled in "dog ears" on the VOR symbol at Anton Chico.

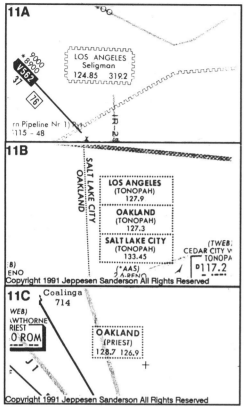

Fig.11A,B,C. Sector boundaries shown on Jeppesen's chart 11A, and the NOS chart 11B, and sector discrete frequencies shown in the ARTCC box 11C.

FOG BOGGLERS

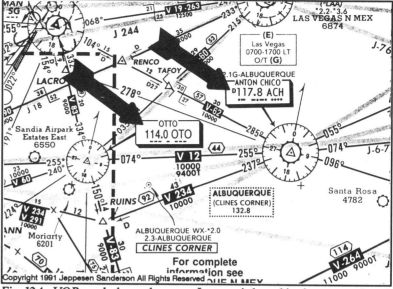

Fig. 12A. VOR symbols, as shown on Jeppesen's low altitude enroute chart.

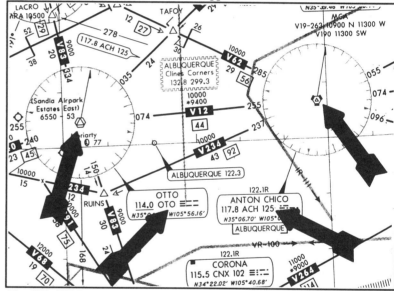

Fig. 12B. VOR symbols, as shown on the NOS low altitude enroute chart.

I rented a small aircraft at the airport for the purposes of flying to the coast to practice some maneuvers. Flying over the town after takeoff, I had a whim to find my old baseball field that I had played on for so many years as a youth. In doing so, I inadvertently went below the minimum altitude (1,000') in an area considered to be congested. Upon finding the field, after approximately five minutes, I made a pass over it at about 3 to 400'. After passing, I climbed out to 2,500' enroute to the coast, which turned out to be fogged in; so, I then returned to the airport. After landing, I was made well aware of my mistake by the airport manager. Apparently, several complaints were phoned in of a low-flying plane in the area. This is a totally ignorant mistake on my part. I never really stopped to think about what I was doing. I've learned a valuable lesson and am very sorry. I wanted to make aviation my career. This is a very humiliating experience and never again will I "not think" before acting. Such an unnecessary, idiotic mistake!

ASRS REPORT

Sometimes an airport will have TACAN (UHF azimuth and DME) capability, without any VOR azimuth information. Figure 13A shows a TACAN station at Vandenberg AFB on the Jeppesen chart. Notice, there is no compass rose; however, there is a spoked circle and the VHF frequency for receiving DME information. Figure 13B shows the NOS version of DME depiction. The paired VHF DME frequency isn't depicted on NOS charts, despite its availability. Pilots with NOS charts, desiring to use the DME at Vandenberg, would have to know that the paired frequency on Channel 59 is 112.25. This information is available from NOS in a separate booklet called the, "IFR Supplement."

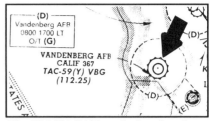

Fig. 13A TACAN symbol on Jep chart.

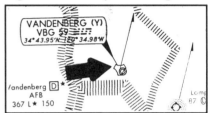

Fig. 13B. TACAN symbol on NOS chart.

CHART OVERLAP

Figure 14 shows thin faded blue lines with numbers 9 and 10 embedded in the fade. These numbers identify low altitude charts that overlap this particular section of the chart. This makes it a great deal easier to find the next chart to use, when flying toward the border of the chart. If anything, it impresses the passengers when the pilot doesn't have to keep turning the map over, trying to ascertain the plane's location. The disadvantage is that the passengers are deprived of the cooling, fan-like, qualities from the rotating paper.

Outside the chart border, on figure 14, there are words where the airways exit the frame line. The names on the outside of the border represent the next navaid to which the total airway mileage is given. Daggett, Goffs and Hector also represent the next VOR making up the airway. The frequency and identifier of an off-chart navaid

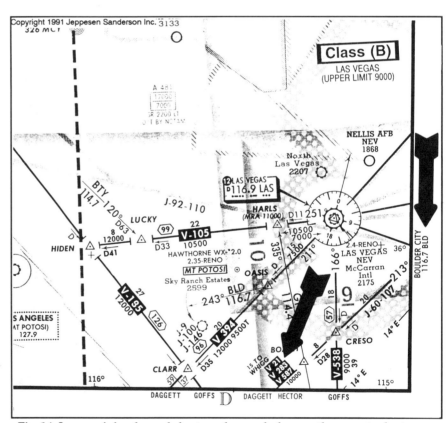

Fig. 14. Jeppesen's border and chart overlap symbology on the enroute chart.

are shown when the navaid designates an "on-chart" reporting point, changeover point or course change. In the case of V-21, V-283 and V-587, these airways are established by the Boulder City VOR 213 degree radial, coming from the right hand corner of the page.

Names inside the border represent the first reporting point, outside the chart coverage, to which the mileage and MEA are shown. Figure 15 shows 41 miles to VICCO intersection, which is the next intersection on the overlapping chart. Also note that Gila Bend VOR and Buckeye VOR are the next navaids to which V16-94 connects when they split into separate airways at VICCO intersection.

INTERSECTION IDENTIFICATION

Intersection identification is made easy by using the little arrows positioned next to every intersection. REDDE intersection on V-248, shown on the Jeppesen chart in figure 16A, can be identified two ways. Little arrows, bordering the intersection, are from the facility designating that intersection. Paso Robles and Priest VOR are the facilities used to identify REDDE intersection. Avenal VOR shouldn't be used to identify REDDE intersection, even though it is the same distance from the intersection as is Paso Robles VOR. The arrows are very explicit in identifying which navaid should be used. The small "D," next to the arrow from Paso Robles VOR, indicates that DME can also be used to identify this intersection. Notice, there is no "D" next to the arrow coming from Priest VOR. This is because Priest VOR doesn't have DME capability. Figure 16B shows the NOS version of this same chart. The only difference is that a hollow-tipped arrow is used to identify when DME is capable of being used for intersection identification.

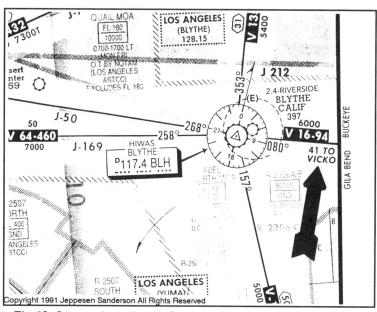

Fig. 15. Jeppesen's symbology for intersections beyond chart border.

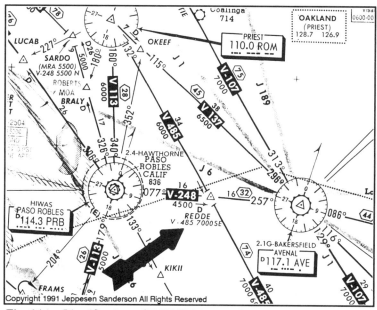

Fig. 16A. Identification of REDDE intersection on Jeppesen's enroute

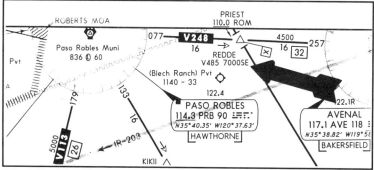

Fig. 16B. Identification of REDDE intersection on NOS enroute chart.

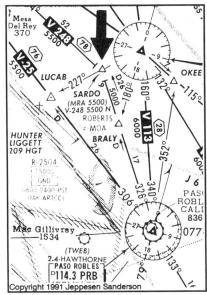

Fig. 17. DME distance tally for SARDO on Jeppesen enroute chart.

Sometimes DME distances are tallied for ease of identification. SARDO intersection, figure 17, off the 326 degree radial of Paso Robles, is 26 miles from the VOR. BRALY intersection is 17 miles from Paso Robles. When no DME tally is shown next to an intersection, this is probably the first intersection past the navaid. The route segment distance should be used in identifying the intersection.

When an intersection is to be identified by cross radials, the MEA along the route being flown may not be adequate for reception of the off-course VOR. Therefore, a Minimum Reception Altitude (MRA) will be established. Figure 18A shows an MRA of 9,000 feet next to OHIGH intersection on the Jeppesen chart. Figure 18B shows the NOS version of the same intersection. OHIGH is identified, either by cross radial identification from the Ventura and Fillmore VOR or radial and DME information from the Ventura or Fillmore VOR. Aircraft flying westbound on V-386, at the MEA of 8,000 feet, would be too low to identify V-485 which makes up the cross radial identifying OHIGH. Notice that the MEA on V-485, northbound past HENER, is 9,000 feet. This is the minimum altitude needed to identify the Ventura VOR 311 degree radial making up V-485. Therefore, pilots desiring to identify any intersection by cross radials, in lieu of DME, need to be at, or above the MRA.

AIRWAY MILEAGE AND CHANGEOVER POINTS

Jeppesen depicts total airway mileage between navaids with a six-sided polygon near the route. This represents the summation of the distance between intersections from one VOR to the next. Figure 19A shows a total airway distance of 42 miles on V-23 between Shafter VOR and Gorman VOR. V-165 has a distance of 56 miles between Shafter VOR and its ending point at Lake Hughes VOR, as is indicated by the dogleg near AMONT intersection. The NOS chart version of this same area is shown in figure 19B. NOS charts use a square figure to enclose total airway distance.

Airway changeover points are indicated by what appears to be a half swastika (ϟ). GRAPE intersection, figure 19A, is the changeover point on V-23. When no changeover point is indicated, it's assumed that the changeover is at the midpoint of the airway. Changeover points are not only established for the purpose of avoiding loss of a navigation signal. A changeover point can also be established to avoid signal interference from another navaid.

It's worthwhile to note that the outbound airway direction from the Gorman VOR on V-23 is 328 degrees up to GRAPE intersection. After GRAPE, the inbound direction changes to 330 degrees (the reciprocal of 150 degrees). Low altitude airways may look straight, but may change as much as 2 degrees in direction at the changeover point. This may be due to an actual directional change, or a change in the magnetic variation. When the airway changes direction 3 degrees or more at the changeover point, and no intersection designates this spot, a mileage breakdown fix, identified by a small "x", is marked on the airway. Just right of LOPES intersection, on V-197, in figure 19A, is a mileage breakdown fix. At this point, the new airway direction would be set in the course selector.

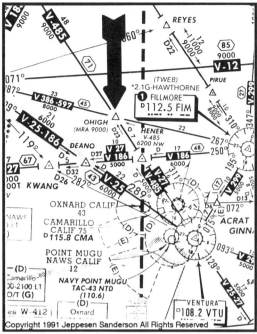

Fig. 18A. Minimum reception altitude (MRA) established at OHIGH intersection on Jeppesen enroute chart.

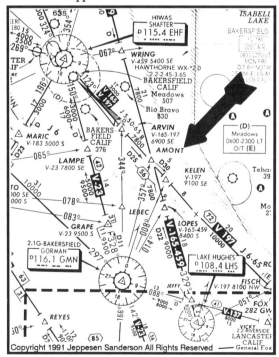

Fig. 19A. Symbology for airway distance, changeover point and mileage breakdown fix on Jeppesen's enroute chart.

THE BOTTOM LINE

There's nothing like being in truly stormy weather conditions to remind you that, if you don't fly for a living every day, be prepared to see your skills deteriorate quickly!

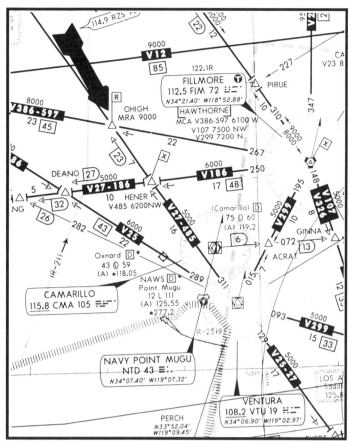

Fig. 18B. Minimum reception altitude established at OHIGH intersection on NOS enroute chart.

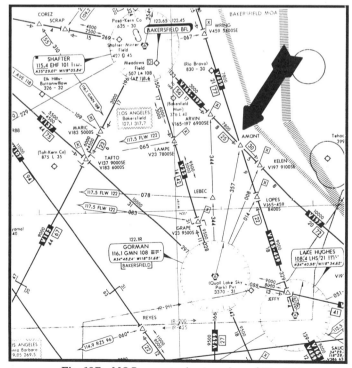

Fig. 19B. NOS enroute chart version of Fig. 19A.

MEA's, MOCA's AND MCA's

Minimum Enroute Altitudes are established along airways to ensure obstruction clearance and navigation station reception, as well as communications. Figure 20 shows V-113 from Panoche VOR to Priest VOR, with 7,000 feet listed under the airway designator. This is the Minimum Enroute Altitude for this section of the airway. The MEA guarantees 1,000 foot obstruction clearance in non-mountainous terrain and 2,000 foot obstruction clearance in mountainous terrain. Certain routes through mountainous regions, may actually have less than 2,000 feet obstruction clearance. When FAA flight inspectors consider lowering the obstruction clearance altitudes, they give a great deal of thought to the type of terrain that exists in the local area. Sometimes obstructions are located on precipitous terrain which could cause an aberration in altimeter readings during strong wind conditions. This is known as the Bernoulli or Venturi effect.* Where the Bernoulli effect isn't likely, airway builders may actually lower MEA's or MOCA's.

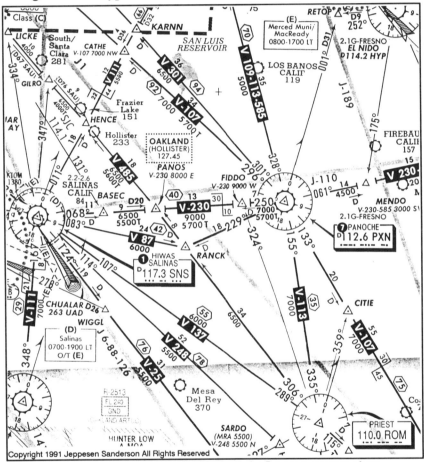

Fig. 20. MEA's, MOCA's and MCA's on the Jeppesen enroute chart.

There are times when the MEA must be substantially increased because of problems with navigation station reception, or because of precipitous terrain along a portion of the airway. When this happens, it is convenient to offer an altitude lower than the MEA that can be flown when close to the VOR. This lower altitude is called the Minimum Obstruction Clearance Altitude, or MOCA. It is indicated by an altitude with a "T" next to it on the Jeppesen charts or an (*) on the NOS charts. It is usually found underneath the MEA. Figure 20 shows an altitude of 5,500T on V-230 between Salinas VOR and PANOS intersection. The MEA for this section is 6,500 feet, and the MOCA is 5,500 feet. The MOCA provides both obstruction clearance and adequate reception within 22 nautical miles of the VOR. Beyond 22 nautical miles, the MOCA guarantees only obstacle clearance.

When a MOCA is created for a particular route, the airway designers first ask what minimum altitude is necessary along the route to provide only the required obstruction clearance of 1,000 or 2,000 feet. After this is determined, the route is flight checked to determine what additional increase in altitude, if any, is necessary to receive navigation transmissions along the first 22 nautical miles of the route.

*When wind flows over hilly terrain, it can cause a lowering of pressure at the top of the mountain. Think of this as wind flowing over a wing. An alteration of pressure on top of the wing makes the aircraft fly. This could alter the altimeter's reading. Precipitous terrain is likely to cause this phenomenon.

This minimum altitude then becomes the MOCA. MEA's are created by the same process, except the minimum altitude is increased so as to receive navigation and communication signals along the entire route.

What value is there in having a MOCA beyond 22 NM's when it can't be used for navigation? If an airplane was having engine trouble, what would the pilot be interested in most? Talking? Navigating? Most pilots I'm familiar with would be interested in their height above the terrain. The MOCA provides immediate altitude protection of 1,000 or 2,000 feet above obstructions for the entire length of the route.

MEA CHANGES

Notice how the airways depictions are interrupted at PANOS intersection, shown in figure 20. V-485 has an airway line that stops and continues on the other side of PANOS. V-230 has perpendicular " ⊣ ▷⊢ " barriers where the airway breaks. The " ⊣◁ ⊢ " barriers indicate an MEA change, at this point along the airway. From HENCE intersection to Priest VOR, the MEA is 6,500 feet. There is no MEA change at HENCE although the MOCA of 5,600T is only good between HENCE and PANOS intersections on V-485. There is an MEA change at PANOS intersection on V-230 from 6,500 to 9,000 feet eastbound.

The " ⊣ ▷⊢ " barriers become very important during lost communications. These barriers alert the pilot to expect a change in the MEA. On V-230, figure 20, there is no MEA change at BASEC intersection. However, there is an MEA change at PANOS and FIDDO intersection. The FAR's state that in the event of lost communications, pilots should maintain their last assigned altitude, the altitude ATC said to expect in a further clearance or the MEA, whichever is higher. In the absence of being assigned a higher altitude, a pilot would start a climb to the next MEA at the " ⊣ ▷⊢" barrier. Assume that a pilot had lost communications at Salinas VOR and was enroute to Panoche VOR at an assigned altitude of 7,000 feet. An MCA or Minimum Crossing Altitude is shown under PANOS intersection. V-230 8000 E, means that 8,000 feet is the Minimum Crossing Altitude for V-230, eastbound at PANOS. Because of the MCA, pilots should start their climb early, so as to be at 8,000 feet by PANOS, then continue the climb to the next highest MEA, which is 9,000 feet. When the MEA changes at an intersection, and no MCA is present, pilots should start their climb or descent to the next MEA, when reaching that intersection.

MINIMUM CLIMB RATES

With every MEA, or MCA change for a particular intersection, a minimum rate of climb is expected, so as to remain clear of obstacles. Assume that a flight is eastbound on V-230 from Salinas VOR. The MCA at PANOS intersection is 8,000 feet eastbound on V-230. The minimum rate of climb, beyond the MEA, or MCA, is determined by the altitude at which the aircraft crosses the intersection. If the minimum crossing altitude at an intersection is 5,000 feet or less, a 150 foot per nautical mile minimum rate of climb is required to the next MEA. If the minimum crossing altitude is greater than 5,000 feet MSL, up to 10,000 feet MSL, the minimum rate of climb is 120 feet per nautical mile. If the minimum crossing altitude is greater than 10,000 MSL, the minimum rate of climb is 100 feet per nautical mile. Since PANOS intersection has an MCA of 8,000 feet MSL, the aircraft should be able to climb at 120 feet per nautical mile, or 240 feet per minute, at 120 knots ground speed (2nm/min) to the next highest MEA of 9,000 feet. This rate of climb would allow the pilot to maintain the required obstacle clearance.

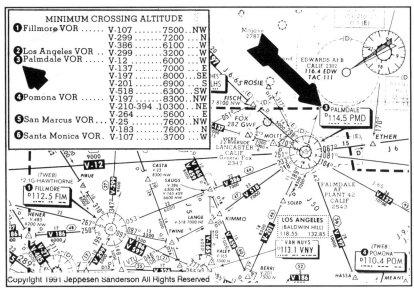

Fig. 21. Jeppesen chart showing minimum crossing altitudes at VOR's.

This rate of climb might not be that easy to achieve with an aged Cherokee 140 with only 3 out of 4 cylinders working. Couple this with a massive tailwind at altitude, and it might be easy to end up with less than the desired clearance above obstacles. So, don't be stingy with altitude gain. Be conservative, and start the climb well in advance of the intersection when an MCA is present.

If Minimum Crossing Altitudes exist at specific intersections, they will be shown underneath the intersection name. At VOR's, where many airways converge, Jeppesen will tally MCA's in a separate box, located nearby on the chart. Figure 21 shows the Palmdale VOR with a "ball flag" located in the frequency box. Figure 21 additionally shows the Minimum Crossing Altitude box, with information on MCA's, at Palmdale. On NOS charts, the presence of an MCA is indicated by an "X" located within a flag, as seen in figure 22. Directly over the Palmdale VOR is a flag, signaling the presence of an MCA. Under the VOR compass rose are all the MCA's for the Palmdale VOR.

As a young instrument student, hardly a night passed without my mind swirling with instrument charts. Even when I wasn't flying, a great deal of time was spent sitting in front of my Jeps, lost in fantasy, dreaming about far-off approaches. My charts took me there. They symbolized the essence of instrument flying. There was a neatness, a perfection that enamored me. They gave me a sense of power. I understood the cryptic symbology and non-pilots couldn't. And, in a peculiar way, I found great comfort in this. Many pilots find similar satisfaction in the study of

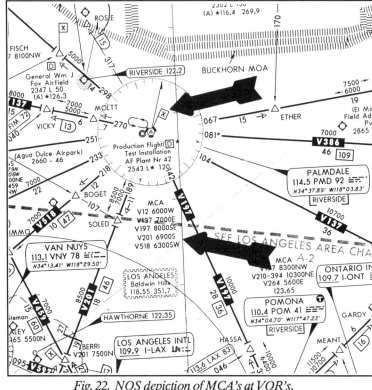

Fig. 22. NOS depiction of MCA's at VOR's.

IFR charts. They make it their purpose to know them -- to become intimate with them. This is time well spent. Maps are the pilot's umbilical to earth. They serve their purpose in getting pilots down, yet seldom have they ever let them down.

EDITOR
Kathy Carey

Kathy is a commercial and instrument rated pilot. She graduated with honors from California State University at Los Angeles in 1971 with a Bachelor of Arts Degree in American Studies and Journalism. Her experience as a professional writer has many dimensions. In a varied career with several large corporations, over the last twenty years, Kathy has written about everything from dog food to automobiles. She's written, published and sold press releases, service, editorial and feature articles and scripts for electronic and motion picture productions. Kathy has taught courses at the university level in Journalism including: "Creative Writing;" "Writing For Results;" "Corporate Communications;" and "Conducting a Successful Public Relations Campaign."

TECHNICAL EDITORS

Diane Titterington

Diane is a commercial and instrument rated pilot and has been flying since 1973. Her love of aviation was sparked as a child, when her father, a wind tunnel engineer at Wright Patterson Air Force Base, would bring home stories of different aircraft in Flight Test. Diane's flying has included air racing, flying fire patrol, and ferrying new Cessnas from the factory. As a member of the Ninety-Nines International Group of Women Pilots, she has held various chapter offices, including chairman, and has organized many aviation safety seminars and flying events. Formerly a radar qualified air traffic controller at Houston Center, Diane presently is the owner of The Aviation Speakers Bureau.

Dave Gwinn

Dave is an airline pilot for a major air carrier. He is an aviation journalist and educator having seventeen ratings and over 12,000 hours of flight time. Dave was formerly a corporate pilot and was assigned for 11 years to the pilot training center of his airline for the B707, B727, B767, L1011, and DC-80 programs. The weather radar seminars he teaches are in great demand and Dave travels nationally and internationally to share his expertise on this subject. He was invited to join respected windshear scientists in a national windshear symposium that was filmed and distributed to 500 companies. His testimony as an expert witness has been requested in numerous aviation court cases. Dave can be seen on *Wonderful World of Flying* and heard on *Pilot's Audio Update*.

THE AVIATION SPEAKERS BUREAU

THE AVIATION SPEAKERS BUREAU FEATURES <u>SPEAKERS</u> FOR YOUR CONVENTION, BANQUET, CONFERENCE, TRADE SHOW EDUCATIONAL SEMINAR, KEYNOTE, FORUM, CORPORATE EVENT, AIRSHOW, SAFETY PROGRAM OR ASSOCIATION MEETING.

TOPICS

SAFETY ˜ WEATHER ˜ INSTRUMENT FLYING ˜ INSPIRATIONAL
COCKPIT RESOURCE MANAGEMENT ˜ AVIATION HUMOR
UNDERSTANDING AIRSPACE ˜ TEST PILOTS ˜ TEAMWORK
STRESS ˜ FIGHTER PILOTS AND ACES ˜ WEATHER RADAR
INFLIGHT EMERGENCIES ˜ MULTI ENGINE PROCEDURES
CELEBRITIES ˜ VIETNAM PILOTS ˜ AVIATION MANAGEMENT
APPROACH AND IFR CHARTS ˜ COMEDY ˜ AIR RACERS
POLICIES AND POLITICS OF AVIATION ˜ MOTIVATIONAL
INDUSTRY SPECIFIC TRAINING ˜ MANEUVERS
SUCCESS ˜ PATRIOTIC ˜ AND MUCH MORE

We guarantee a perfect match for your needs and objectives.
We recommend only the very best in speakers.
Our professionals shine and make YOU look good every time!

Please Call
(714) 498-2498
(800) AIR - 121.5

P.O. Box 6030
San Clemente, CA 92674-6030

"We will help you find the perfect speaker for your budget and there is never a charge for our services." DIANE TITTERINGTON

VIDEOS BY ROD MACHADO

DEFENSIVE FLYING
The Video

Watch with over 300 pilots in this live, entertaining and educational video presentation as Rod Machado discusses how pilots can learn to fly defensively. While laughing along with the audience, this presentation will help you take a new look at flying safely. Learn several new ways of thinking to enhance your development of Defensive Flying habits. Learn about acknowledging your own limitations, natural pilot enemies and never underestimating the enemy. Listen to an actual inflight emergency as two professional pilots exercise one of the most important skills in Defensive Flying. This presentation contains stories and humor not previously heard on Rod's audio tapes. Time 1:45 - $29.95

AVIATION HUMOR
The video - Part one

Watch along with 2,000 pilots as Rod Machado entertains his audience with some of the best of his aviation stories. As a professional humorist, Rod has always been known for his ability to move people off the edge of their seats and onto the floor with his fast paced, humorous presentations. After so many requests for a video version of his very popular audio tapes, this video is sure to be a popular addition to your library. Time 1 hour - $29.95

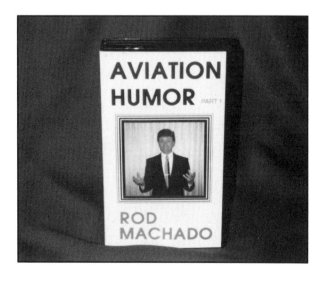

ORDERING INFORMATION ON NEXT PAGE

LAUGH AND LEARN CASSETTE CONTENTS

WHAT PEOPLE ARE SAYING

"Mary Poppins once sang, 'A spoon full of sugar helps the medicine go down.' Rod Machado goes one step further by sugar coating invaluable aeronautical wisdom with entertaining wit and humor."
Barry Schiff
TWA Captain/Noted Author

"Rod has a wonderful sense of humor that will keep you in stitches and when you're done laughing, you'll be amazed at how much you've learned."
John & Martha King
King Video

"Rod Machado brings a new perspective to aviation education... he blends facts, personal experiences and practical education that will leave you smiling - and smarter! You will actually enjoy learning with these tapes."
Richard Taylor
Author of *Instrument Flying*

"Machado is energy. He's a degreed Psychologist, an educator and an entertainer. He is a verbal gymnast, and any one (or all four) of his professional identities may rebound at any one time. He's addictive - you will wear out the tapes!"
Dave Gwinn
TWA Pilot and Professional Writer

Volume One:
All Live Presentations

Tape 1 - Thinking Like The Pros (50/50)*
Tape 2 - Secrets Of The Test Pilots (40/60)*
Tape 3 - Understanding Weather (30/70)*
Tape 4 - Handling Inflight Emergencies 1 (10/90)*
Tape 5 - Handling Inflight Emergencies 2 (10/90)*
Tape 6 - Handling Inflight Emergencies 3 (10/90)*

*(%Humor content / %Information content)
**(%Humor & %Information varies with topic)

Volume Two:
All Live Presentations

Tape 1 - A/Laugh Your Empennage Off (100/0)*
B/Samurai Airmanship (30/70)*
Tape 2 - Reducing Cockpit Stress Between
The Sexes (60/40)*
Tape 3 - A/ Cockpit Management (40/60)*
B/An Aviation Sense Of Humor (95/5)*
Tape 4 - A/Pilots & Their Tribes (99/1)*
B/The Adventure Of Flight (99/1)*
Tape 5 - A/Decision Making Psychology (10/90)*
B/Advanced Aviation Topics **
Tape 6 - Creative Solutions To The Aviator's
Most Common Problems (40/60)*

*(%Humor content / %Information content)
**(%Humor & %Information varies with topic)

Credit card orders may call:
1-800-437-7080 or
FAX (714) 498-2344
Thank You!

CUT & MAIL COMPLETED FORM TO: AVIATION SPEAKER'S BUREAU, P.O. BOX 6030 SAN CLEMENTE, CA 92674-6030

Order & Registration Form

Title		Quantity	X	=	Total
Defensive Flying Video			$29.95		
Aviation Humor Video			$29.95		
What They Didn't Teach You	Vol 1		$49.95		
In Flight School (Audio Tapes)	Vol 2		$49.95		
Instrument Pilot's Survival Manual			$29.95		
IFR Flying Tips & Techniques Video			$29.95		
			Product Subtotal		
Sales Tax - CA Residents only		Product Subtotal x .0775			
Product shipping & handling (US)		——	——	$3.00	
International shipping $10/Canada $6 (PAL videos available upon request)					
			Total		

Name _____

Address _____

City _____ State ____

Zip _____

Phone (____) _____

Check # _____ or:
We accept checks, MasterCard, VISA
American Express and Discover.

Credit Card # _____

_____

Expiration Date: _____

Authorized Signature _____

PROGRAMS BY ROD MACHADO

THE POWER OF PERSUASIVE SPEAKING

Psychology Today magazine once printed that public speaking produces a fear greater than the fear of death. Individuals who effectively persuade an audience are held in high esteem by their peers. Learning the art of persuasive public speaking will enhance your self-esteem and credibility. Let Rod Machado, a recognized platform professional, show you the shortcut method for accelerating your development as a persuasive speaker. This 1 to 3 hour seminar presents a unique, one of a kind, approach to understanding the elements of persuasive presentations. Learn how to develop a presentation, overcome stage fright and employ a four step speaking model used by the world's most powerful speakers. Benefit from recently developed techniques in persuasion, practiced in Politics and Marketing and learn entertainment skills to communicate more effectively with your audience. This seminar can be tailored to specific client needs.

THE LOST ART OF THINKING

Professor Mortimer J. Adler once said that 3% of the people think, 3% of the people think they think and 94% of the people would rather die than think. Thinking is a learnable, cognitive behavior that is seldom mastered and yet it is one of the most important skills we can develop to ensure our personal growth and survival. If we don't learn to think critically, reason, exercise good judgement, see through persuasive smoke screens, understand and control the process by which we make decisions, then we are doomed to have someone else do our thinking for us. This 1 to 2 hour presentation focuses on the competent thinking strategies used by masters of productive thought and how to replicate these specific behaviors. This program is an excellent selection for a humorous dinner or banquet speech.

ZEN & THE ART OF GETTING ALONG WITH THE DIFFICULT PERSON

Everyone has had an experience with a difficult person in their life. These individuals often leave you feeling angry, helpless, and frustrated. This program deals with identifying the most troublesome personality types and how to responsibly direct their behavior to a favorable outcome. Applying the sublime, yet powerful mental strategy of AIKIDO, a martial art that renders the attack of an opponent ineffectual, you'll learn a four step technique to reduce the threat and change the behavior of the difficult person in your life. You'll learn how to handle: the aggressive and frightening "Mack Truck" type personality that can leave you feeling like you've just been pummeled, the undercover "Sharp Shooters" who's aggressiveness is often camouflaged, the "Detonator" who's explosive personality leaves a wake of fear and helplessness in their path, the "Complainers", the "Negativist", the "Know-It-Alls" and several more. This 2 to 3 hour presentation is of immense value to individuals in management and service industries.

USING HUMOR FOR A CHANGE

The application of humor as a management and motivational tool has long been regarded as a lofty if not mystical skill often difficult to acquire. Modern psychology teaches us otherwise. The use of humor isn't just telling jokes, it's sound communication theory using cognitive skills that are easily mastered. Rod practices what he preaches in this presentation as he energizes his audience with laughter and guides them towards an understanding and application of humor. This 1 to 3 hour seminar is a must for management and is sure to be a real crowd pleaser for your next convention, banquet or dinner speech.

MAN, MACHINE & ENVIRONMENT - DEVELOPING THE SAFETY REFLEX

Modern commercial aviation has achieved an unprecedented level of safety in the melding of man with his machine and the environment. The heightening of an individual's awareness and an understanding of the factors causing complacency, inattention and distraction are the key elements for aviation's ever increasing safety record. Rod Machado's research in awareness and safety psychology is now available to the nonaviation industry in this dynamic program. This engaging 1 to 3 hour seminar will help your company prevent loss of life, limb and property by providing attendees with specific mental strategies for obtaining this heightened awareness in what has become known as the "Safety Reflex."

HANDLING INFLIGHT EMERGENCIES

Designed for aviation audiences of all experience levels, this program helps pilots deal with a variety of inflight emergencies and has received an outstanding response. Program topics include: handling inflight fires, autopilot failure, flight control failure, propeller failure, gear malfunction, enroute engine failure, engine failure on takeoff, electrical system loss, emergency landings, bird strikes, avoiding structural failure, using fire extinguishers and much more. Actual video footage and radio conversations of inflight emergencies "Successfully" handled by pilots accompanies this program. (2 - 6 hours)

WHAT THEY DIDN'T TEACH YOU ABOUT INSTRUMENT CHARTS

IFR charts, frequently perceived as a bland topic, are presented in a different manner with lots of humor and great stories to ensure learning is a fun experience. This seminar is intended for instrument rated pilots of all experience levels. Program topics include a detailed presentation on Jeppesen and NOS: enroute charts, approach charts, SID's and STAR's. Many advanced instrument approach procedures are included in this presentation. (2 - 3 hours)

COCKPIT WEATHER

This highly popular presentation teaches pilots how to make better weather decisions. Not just another dry weather lesson! Rod combines a unique blend of application and theory based on his twenty years of aviation experience. The seminar covers weather topics of concern to all aviators. Program content includes: microbursts, wind shear, low level jet stream, thunderstorms, icing, weather services, and meteorological decision making. (2 - 3 hours)

THE INSTRUMENT REFRESHER COURSE

This presentation is designed for instrument pilots wanting to upgrade their understanding of instrument flying. This fast paced, popular seminar, enjoyed by the newly rated to the seasoned ATP, will give pilots more confidence and better prepare them for their next instrument flight. Program topics include: advanced instrument scanning techniques, IFR regulations, IFR departure procedures, flight planning, ATC radar procedures, cockpit management, hazardous inflight weather, approach procedures and other aspects of IFR flying. (2 - 6 hours)

DEFENSIVE FLYING

This presentation will help pilots take a new look at flying safely. Pilots will learn several new ways of thinking to enhance their development of defensive flying habits. Listeners will learn about acknowledging their own limitations, natural pilot enemies, and never underestimating the enemy. Examples are used of pilots that exercise the most important skills in flying defensively and how those skills have been life saving. (2 - 3 hours)

THINKING LIKE THE PROS

Years of aviation exposure leads to subtle, yet measurable changes in how pilots think. These changes increase a pilot's probability of fending off the insidious dangers of flight, giving them a quality known as the "Survival Advantage." This program demonstrates how pilots can acquire these new thinking behaviors and modify their thought patterns. Participants are guaranteed to laugh and learn as they gain many new and valuable cockpit skills. (1 - 2 hours)

AVIATION HUMOR

A hilarious keynote speech of some of the very best stories you will love to hear. After listening to Rod's rapid fire delivery of humor and aviation wit, you will realize how he earned the byline of "Mach 2 with Machado." This is aviation humor at its best. (45 minutes - 2 hours)

I hope you have enjoyed this book! Please feel free to contact me at the address below. Your comments are appreciated.

Rod Machado
P.O. Box 6030
San Clemente, CA
92674-6030

P.S. Thanks for not using this book for navigation

SUGGESTED READING

Butcher, Ralph. *Instrument Flying Manual and Simulator Training Guide.* California. 1983.
This is one of the most fascinating books I have come across for its unique approach to teaching the basics of instrument flying. This book is a must for every flight instructor and instrument student. It can be ordered from Butcher Enterprises at 2703 E. Grove Ave., Orange, CA 92267

Newton, Dennis. *Severe Weather Flying.* New York, McGraw-Hill. 1983.
One of the most interesting books I have read on determining thunderstorm and icing potential.

Taylor, Richard. *Instrument Flying.* New York, Macmillan. 1972.
This book did a lot for me when I was first learning to fly instruments. It's a classic and should be read by all IFR pilots. Taylor has several other books available. Grab them and read them. This gentleman knows what he's talking about.

Yeager, Chuck. *Yeager, an Autobiography.* New York, Bantam. 1985.
Any person that can survive as long as this man has something to teach!

Bach, Richard. *Illusions.* New York, Dell. 1972
If the reader hasn't read this book, they probably shouldn't be flying!

Murchie, Guy. *Song of the Sky.* New York, Ziff-Davis. 1954.
A perspective on weather that makes this book a classic.

Anything by Barry Schiff.

Anything by Dave Gwinn.

Anything by Richard Collins.

Buck, Robert. *Weather Flying.* Macmillan. 1972.
One of the best introductions to weather I have ever seen.

Thom, Trevor. *The Pilot's Manual/Instrument Flying.* New York, Center for Aviation Theory. 1990.
What an amazing resource of material! This book is a keeper for your library. It can be ordered though the AOPA.

A

Airspeed indicator:
  and pitot static system, 13
  errors, 21
  in climb, 15
  in descent, 15
  use in instrument flying, 15, 16

Alternatives in flight, 3

Altimeters, 15

Alternate static source, 14

Altitude violations, 17

Anticipating change, 37

Approach chart information:
  additional equipment for the approach, 138
  airport reference circle on plan view, 154
  approach segments, 181
  chart amendment number, 127
  chart effective date, 126
  chart navigation restrictions, 136
  chart structure, 126
  communications data, 130
  DME source identification on plan view, 156, 157
  heading data, 135
  height above airport (HAA), 163
  height above touchdown (HAT), 163
  intersection identification on plan view, 154, 155
  Jeppesen filing system, 128
  maltese cross on profile view, 164
  max, min and mandatory altitudes on plan view, 158
  plan view, 149
  plan view orientation, 158
  profile view, 159
  step down fixes, 165, 166, 167
  terrain depiction on plan view, 151, 152
  threshold crossing height, 168
  touch down zone elevation, 205
  VFR and IFR airports on plan view, 150

Approach gate, 83

Approach procedure track, 142, 144

Assertiveness, 5

ATC as a copilot, 39

ATIS, 4, 77

Attitude indicator:
  errors, 12, 13, 21
  features, 12
  in climb, 10
  in descent, 10
  in straight and level flight, 10, 15
  in turns, 10
  power source, 12, 13
  use in instrument flying, 10, 11, 12

Automatic direction finder:
  course intercepts, 47
  manually rotated ADF card, 46
  orientation, 44
  principles, 43
  tracking, 47
  two important rules, 45
  use in emergency, 13
  wind correction, 48

C

Center, air traffic control, 64

Chart organization, 40

Charted visual flight procedures, 140

Circling approaches, 139

Circling descent gradients, 139

Clearances:
  approach clearance, 84, 86, 132
  departure windows, 208
  void times, 209

Cockpit management, 35

Constant airspeed climbs, 15, 16

Controlled airspace:
  control areas, 210
  control zones, 207
  for IFR flight, 63

D

Dead reckoning terminal routes, 146

D.B. Cooper, 77

Defensive thinking, 6, 7

Defensive flying, 40

Descent management, 80, 86

DME arcs, 146

Dysnumeria, 27

E

Elvis, 77

Enroute chart information:
  aerodrome traffic zone, 222
  area chart coverage, 218
  ATC boundaries, 224
  changeover points, 228
  communications section, 218
  front side of Jeppesen chart, 218
  identifying airports with IFR approaches, 220

identifying VOR's/VORTAC's/TACAN/DME stations, 224
Jeppesen enroute chart panel information, 219
military training route depiction, 220
MOA depiction, 222

Equipment knowledge, 41

Experience, flight, 38

F

Final approach fix/point/segment, 164, 189, 190

Flight director, 89

Flight plan:
alternate airports, 67
composite flight plans, 74, 75
cancellation requirements, 70, 73
data strips, 70
non-tower departures, 70
pop-up IFR flight plans, 74, 78
remarks section, 72
tower enroute control (TEC) routes, 65

G

Get-home-itis, 4

Glideslope:
false glideslope, 88, 160, 161
glideslope out procedure, 165
intercept, 88
sensitivity, 89
techniques, 89

H

Heading indicator:
in straight and level flight, 15
power source, 12

Holding patterns:
four step procedure, 55
heading indicator overlay method, 61
inbound leg, 54
modified heading indicator overlay method, 62
NASA survey, 51
plastic overlay method, 59
split pattern method, 60

I

Icing:
area forecast, 117
avoidance, 115
constant pressure chart, 118, 119
effect on aircraft, 112
freezing level chart, 118
how it forms, 113
radar summary chart, 122
significant weather prognostic chart, 122
stability chart, 121
two types of icing, 112
weather depiction chart, 117
where it forms, 114

Identifying navaids, 81

IFR departure procedures:
adequate visibility reference, 215
aircraft categories, 215
availability at airports, 214
ceiling restrictions, 214
location on Jeppesen/NOS charts, 211
minimum climb rate, 212, 230
protected area, 212
requiring turns, 212
terrain avoidance, 211
when ATC assigns it, 213
when is it required, 214
when to use it, 212, 213

Inflight visibility assessment, 196, 202, 204

Initial approach fix/segment, 182, 183, 184

Instrument landing system (ILS):
approach lighting system, 197
structure, 196
scan technique, 18
using VSI, 22, 89

Instrument scan:
climbing/descending turns, 15, 18
constant airspeed climbs and descents, 15
ILS approaches, 18
level turns, 15
monitor scan, 18
peripheral vision and instrument scanning, 20
radial scanning non-control items, 20
setting power, 14
step one of the instrument scan, 10
step two of the instrument scan, 15
step three of the instrument scan, 18
straight and level, 15, 17
techniques, 10
three steps, 10
trimming, 15

Intermediate fix/segment, 185-188

L

Lighting, approach:
decision bar, 198, 199
length, 197, 200, 201
lighting on airport diagram, 201
ALSF 1 & 2, 199, 204
LDIN, 200
MALS, 199
MALSF, 200
ODALS, 200
RAIL, 200
REIL, 200
SSALF, 200
SSALR, 200

Localizer:
identification, 81
minimum altitudes, 160

M

Marker beacons:
  inner marker, 162
  middle marker, 162
  outer marker, 162
  principles, 162
  sensitivity switch, 162

Memory, 28

Minimum crossing altitude (MCA), 230

Minimum descent altitude (MDA):
  on flight tests, 91
  operation below MDA, 195, 199

Minimum enroute altitude:
  MEA changes, 231
  MEA minimum climb rate, 231
  obstacle clearance, 230

Minimum obstruction clearance altitude (MOCA), 230, 232

Minimum sector altitude (MSA), 131-133

Minimum vectoring altitude (MVA), 84, 209, 210

Missed approach:
  from holding fix, 137
  holding patterns, 174
  information on chart, 168
  point determination, 91
  segments, 192
  technique, 92, 192, 193

N

NDB identification, 82

Non-radar IFR operations, 72

NOTAMS:
  class 2 notams, 127
  FDC notams, 127

P

Pilot in command authority, 4

Pop-up IFR flight plan, 74, 77

Position awareness, 83

Power indicator for straight and level flight, 15

Practical test standards, 91

Preferred IFR routes, 66-68

Primary instruments, 15

Priorities, 35, 87

Procedure turns:
  45/180 procedure turn, 170
  aircraft turning radius, 173
  airports without procedure turns, 170
  distance limitations, 176
  holding pattern in lieu of, 170, 177, 178, 179, 180
  minimum altitudes, 174
  obstacle protection, 172
  teardrop turns, 168
  techniques, 172
  when it is not legal, 171
  when it is required, 171, 175

R

Radar:
  air route surveillance radar (ARSR), 131
  airport surveillance radar (ASR), 131
  communication phraseology, 210
  coverage at MVA, 210
  separation, 65
  weather information, from ARTCC radar, 106, 107

S

Self talk:
  avoiding numerical problems, 27
  awareness, 29
  big picture awareness, 24
  controlling panic, 23
  emergency self talk, 31
  FAF self talk, 34
  holding pattern self talk, 55
  six T's, 33, 90

Short term memory, 28

Skepticism, 5

Standard instrument departures (SID), 207, 211

Standard rate turns, 10, 173

T

Taking command, 4

Terminal routes, 86, 141, 144

Terminal routes required on procedure, 136

Thinking, 1, 2

Thinking ahead, 2

Thunderstorms:
  air mass, 94
  area forecast, 96
  composite moisture stability chart, 98
  convective outlook, 97
  height and intensity, 95
  k-index, 99-101
  lifted index, 99
  mesoscale convective complex, 94
  PIREPS, 105

radar summary chart, 102
severe weather outlook chart, 96
significant weather prognostic chart, 98
steady state, 94
three types, 94
weather depiction chart, 101
winds aloft forecast, 104, 105

Tower enroute control (TEC), 65

Transponder, 79

Triangle of agreement:
for pitch, 13
for turns, 12

Turn radius, 173

Turn rate, 173

Turn coordinator:
in turns, 15
power source, 12

Tzu, Sun, The Art of War, 7, 112

U

Uncontrolled airspace, 207

V

Vectors for the approach, 79, 81, 82, 84, 152

Vectors to the final approach course, 82

Vertical speed indicator (VSI):
and the pitot static system, 13
breaking glass, 13, 14
effect of static line blockage, 13
in climb, 16
in descent, 16
use as a trend indicator, 22
use on instrument approaches, 18
use in trimming, 18

Visual illusions, 153

Visual descent point (VDP), 191

VOR orientation, 26

W

Weather minimums:
landing, 195, 196, 202, 204
takeoff, 214, 215